MOORE'S HISTORICAL GUIDE TO
The Wilmington Campaign
and the
Battles for Fort Fisher

USS Brooklyn - RATE: Second; TONNAGE: 2,070; CLASS: Screw Steamer; CREW: 367; GUNS: 26; COMMANDER: Capt. James Alden   *Harper's Pictorial History of the Great Rebellion in the United States*

The *Brooklyn* was positioned in the North Atlantic Blockading Squadron's Line No. 2 during the first bombardment of Fort Fisher (December 24-25, 1864), and in Line No. 1 during the second bombardment (January 13-15, 1865). See maps on pages 20 and 40.

SAVAS PUBLISHING COMPANY
202 First Street SE. Suite 103A
Mason City. Iowa
(515) 421-7135

MARK A. MOORE

Manufactured in the United States of America

All rights reserved. No part of this book may be reproduced or transmitted in any form or by any means electronic or technical, including photocopying, recording, or by any information storage and retrieval system, without written permission from the publisher.

Moore's Historical Guide to the Wilmington Campaign and the Battles for Fort Fisher by Mark A. Moore

10 9 8 7 6 5 4 3 2 1 (First Edition)

ISBN 1-882810-19-8

© 1999 Mark A. Moore
© 1999 of maps, modern photographs, blockade runner, and cannon drawings Mark A. Moore

Includes bibliographical references and index

SAVAS PUBLISHING COMPANY
202 First Street SE, Suite 103A
Mason City, Iowa 50401

Distribution:
Stackpole Books (800) 732-3669

This book is printed on 50-lb. Glatfelter acid-free paper.

The paper in this book meets or exceeds the guidelines for performance and durability of the Committee on Reproduction Guidelines for Book Longevity of the Council on Library Resources.

Printed and bound by McNaughton & Gunn, Saline, Michigan.

Book design and production by the author.
Cover design by the author.

All modern photographs by the author.

Cover image: "The Assault and Capture of Fort Fisher, January 15, 1865."
Harper's Weekly, February 4, 1865.

For tourist information contact:
Cape Fear Coast Convention and Visitors Bureau
24 N. Third St.
Wilmington, N.C. 28401
(800) 222-4757

Fort Fisher State Historic Site
P.O. Box 169
Kure Beach, N.C. 28449
(910) 458-5538

Brunswick Town/Fort Anderson State Historic Site
8884 St. Philips Rd. SE
Winnabow, N.C. 28479
(910) 383-3806

Dedicated to the loving memory of

Robin Moore Yellin

(January 18, 1958—October 25, 1997)

Army Nurse (Maj.),
Gulf War Veteran,
Third Year Law Student

her husband,
Dr. Lawrence Brett Yellin

infant son,
Nathan Wesley Yellin

and sister-in-law,
Nancy Sara Yellin

Loved Ones Gone Too Soon . . .

MOTHERS AGAINST DRUNK DRIVING

Gold Coast Chapter
18 South J. Street
Lake Worth, Florida 33416
Phone: (561) 533-1021
Fax: (561) 533-1025

All that could never be said,
All that could never be done,
Wait for us at last,
Somewhere back of the sun . . .
—Sara Teasdale

Table of Contents

— MAPS and PLANS —

— PHOTOS and ILLUSTRATIONS —

Foreword

"We had some very important naval victories during the war, but none so important as Fort Fisher," boasted former Union Rear Adm. David D. Porter in his Civil War memoirs. In his autobiography, Lt. Gen. U. S. Grant echoed Porter's assessment of Fort Fisher, calling its capture "one of the most important successes of the war." On the other side, Confederate Vice President Alexander Stephens recalled that "the fall of this fort was one of the greatest disasters which had befallen our Cause from the beginning of the war." Stephens likened Fisher's loss to that of Vicksburg and Atlanta.

Fort Fisher was indeed an important place. Recognized as the most powerful seacoast fortification in the Confederacy, it was the main guardian of Wilmington, North Carolina—the South's last major port along the Atlantic seaboard open to trade with the outside world. For more than three years blockade-running ships smuggled much-needed supplies into the Confederacy through the Tarheel seaport. Military cargo was transported up the Wilmington & Weldon Railroad to Southern forces in Virginia. By the summer of 1864, that artery was the principal supply route for the Army of Northern Virginia, prompting Gen. Robert E. Lee to caution that if Wilmington fell, he could not maintain his army. Another gray-clad officer observed that by late in the war Wilmington was the most important city in the Confederacy, with the exception of the capital of Richmond.

The U.S. Navy tried for years to close Wilmington to overseas trade by naval blockade. When that strategy ultimately failed, the Federals launched the largest combined army-navy operations of the war against Fort Fisher. The U.S. Navy's bombardments of the mighty sand bastion at Christmas 1864 and a renewed attack three weeks later were unprecedented in their intensity and severity in modern warfare up to that time. When Federal forces finally captured Fort Fisher in mid-January 1865, they turned their sights on Wilmington itself. After a five-week campaign, Wilmington was abandoned by Confederate forces and Union troops marched triumphantly into the city. Forty-five days later the war was over, just as Robert E. Lee had predicted if Wilmington fell.

Despite the significance of Fort Fisher and Wilmington to the Confederacy's downfall, the public soon lost interest as several more important events occurred in rapid succession: Gen. William T. Sherman's successful and highly publicized Carolinas Campaign, Robert E. Lee's surrender at Appomattox Courthouse, and the assassination of President Abraham Lincoln. Front-page stories of Fort Fisher's and Wilmington's capture in the nation's leading newspapers quickly gave way to more stirring stories of the Confederacy's collapse and the loss of the martyred president.

Confederate and Union survivors of the Wilmington Campaign kept the story alive in their memoirs, unit histories, and at reunions, but failed in their efforts to persuade Congress to designate Fort Fisher a national historic site. As the line of veterans grew thin and then disappeared altogether, local antiquarians and chroniclers retold the Fort Fisher and Wilmington story. Yet their works received scant publicity.

In 1988, James M. McPherson gave considerable coverage to Wilmington's wartime significance in *Battle Cry of Freedom* (Oxford University Press), which won the Pulitzer Prize for history. Three years later HarperCollins published Rod Gragg's *Confederate Goliath*, the first full-length treatment on the battles for Fort Fisher. Gragg's award-winning monograph revived national interest in the Fort Fisher story after 126 years. In 1997, Savas Publishing released my own study of the important role Wilmington played during the war. *Last Rays of Departing Hope: The Wilmington Campaign* detailed both engagements at Fort Fisher, and the campaign for possession of Wilmington that followed.

Much of the success of *Last Rays* was due to the phenomenal thirty-one maps that complement the study. To the delight of his authors, publisher Ted Savas insists that good maps (and a goodly number of them) are essential to understanding battles and campaigns. Consequently, he enlisted cartographer Mark A. Moore to provide each of his publications with the very best maps. Mark Moore proved to be an incomparable mapmaker. So striking and accurate are his maps and charts that Edwin C. Bearss—who is one of the most renowned Civil War historians and today's leading battlefield guide—has dubbed Moore the "Jedediah Hotchkiss (Stonewall Jackson's mapmaker) of the twentieth century."

More than a cartographer, however, Mark Moore is a first-rate historian in his own right. He proves it in *Moore's Historical Guide to the Wilmington Campaign and the Battles for Fort Fisher*. Moore has drawn upon *Last Rays of Departing Hope* and other sources to weave his tight-knit narrative, the whole sprinkled with a healthy dose of dramatic quotes from soldiers and period photographs and engravings. He also improved on the maps that first appeared in *Last Rays* and has provided many additional maps.

Moore's study is also replete with a comparative analysis of the fall of Fort Fisher and the Russian fortress of Sebastopol during the Crimean War. Moore's text and appendices are chock-full of charts detailing Fort Fisher's armament, casualties of the battles, orders of battle, a list and brief history of Civil War shipwrecks along the Cape Fear coastline, citation sketches of Medal of Honor recipients in the battles of Fort Fisher and Wilmington, a glossary of military jargon, and an extensive bibliography.

In short, Moore has produced a campaign study and compendium rolled into one. But as the title suggests, this book is first and foremost a guide to the Lower Cape Fear's Civil War sites. There is a comprehensive driving tour, and Moore provides user-friendly maps for historians and buffs alike to visit the forts, batteries, battlefields, historic markers, and other points of interest in the area.

I first met Mark Moore at Jerry Russell's Congress of Civil War Round Tables, which held its annual symposium in Wilmington in October 1993. That was a fateful weekend. It was then that I was also introduced to Mark L. Bradley— who, along with Mark Moore, was then working on a study of the Battle of Bentonville—Bradley's soon-to-be wife Nancy, and Ted Savas, who had just started a publishing firm. Ted, as the two Marks and I learned that weekend, was interested in publishing studies of lesser-known Civil War campaigns and battles.

Savas Publishing Company first released Mark Bradley's *Last Stand in the Carolinas: The Battle of Bentonville* (with maps researched and drawn by Moore), followed soon thereafter by *Last Rays of Departing Hope: The Wilmington Campaign* and *Moore's Historical Guide to the Battle of Bentonville*. With his talents for mapmaking and writing good history, Mark Moore has carved his own niche in Civil War studies. *Moore's Historical Guide to the Wilmington Campaign and the Battles for Fort Fisher* is the best book of its kind to ever come along. Read it, use it, and enjoy it!

Chris E. Fonvielle, Jr.
University of North Carolina at Wilmington
August 20, 1999

Introduction

In the closing months of the American Civil War, the Federal government of the United States hatched a grand scheme to close the important Southern port of Wilmington, North Carolina. Though torn asunder by the necessary evil of blockade running, this once-quiet riverside town enjoyed a successful contraband shipping trade longer than any other major port in the Confederacy. By late 1864, despite a vigilant Union blockade, the city had become the last hub for shipment of goods and munitions of war to Robert E. Lee's Confederate army in Virginia. As the South's principal eastern military force struggled to sustain itself against U. S. Grant's powerful Union "army group," Lee depended upon a continued flow of supplies via rail from Wilmington—the "lifeline of the Confederacy."

The plan for an expedition against Wilmington was championed by Gideon Welles, President Abraham Lincoln's outspoken Secretary of the Navy. Welles, weary of the Northern war effort's tardiness in focusing attention on Wilmington, pestered the Lincoln administration to endorse a combined campaign to capture the troublesome port. It would not be an easy operation. The largest and most powerful earthen fort in the Confederacy anchored an elaborate defensive network of riverside batteries and fortifications that guarded the approaches to the city. Any hope of a successful expedition, the secretary reasoned, would depend upon the combined forces of the Federal army and navy.

While Secretary Welles lobbied openly to close the port of Wilmington, Maj. Gen. W. H. C. Whiting was equally emphatic about keeping it open. Having overseen most of the design and planning of Cape Fear's strong defenses, this talented engineer warned the Confederate War Department repeatedly of an impending Federal attack on Wilmington. Laboring under a tarnished reputation, the energetic Whiting fought an uphill battle to convince his superiors to provide adequate manpower to defend the harbor at Cape Fear.

Finally, the attack occurred as Whiting had predicted. A first attempt on Wilmington in late December 1864 ended in frustration for Union forces. But the attack was renewed with vigor in mid-January 1865, and after an amphibious landing the determined Federals captured Fort Fisher and waged a successful land campaign against Wilmington. This fascinating military expedition illustrated for both sides the overwhelming power of interservice cooperation between army and naval forces. The two phenomenal bombardments of Fort Fisher by Rear Adm. David D. Porter's armada were unlike any the world had seen up to that time, and the campaign would remain the largest combined operation in U.S. military history until World War II.

It was a small operation, geographically. The ground over which the Wilmington Campaign was fought can be covered in an easily-traveled 40-mile loop along both banks of the Cape Fear River, primarily between the port city and present-day ferry crossing below Fort Fisher. This study examines the origins of the campaign, its military history, and various points of interest along the loop—including two major state historic sites—and provides visual comparisons between historic and modern areas.

If the battlefield of Bentonville* is a prime case study in the construction of Civil War fieldworks, the remains of the Cape Fear defenses offer ample evidence of heavy seacoast fortifications. The massive, beautifully preserved earthen remains of Fort Fisher and Fort Anderson provide a fascinating insight into mid-nineteenth-century military architecture.

In addition to the state historic sites mentioned above, this guidebook provides orientation to the less-publicized attractions of the area. These include the Forks Road battlefield, the area of the Sugar Loaf defenses, Battery Buchanan, Fort Johnston (Pender) at Southport, Orton Plantation, and the battlefield at Town Creek.

A series of appendices at the end of the book includes a detailed driving tour, Union and Confederate orders of battle, information on war-related shipwrecks of the Cape Fear, an in-depth analysis and comparison of Fort Fisher and Crimean War fortifications, and points of interest within the town of Wilmington.

A tour of the Cape Fear region provides an opportunity to view the ground where a major Civil War campaign was waged—a campaign that had a direct impact on the course of the war, and thus transcends the boundaries of North Carolina. For those who may never see this area in person, I have attempted to provide enough description, comparisons, maps, photos, and illustrations to give readers a vivid picture of an absorbing and thought provoking event in our nation's military history.

—**Mark A. Moore**
Raleigh, N.C., June 1999

* The Battle of Bentonville, fought March 19-21, 1865, was the culminating event of the Carolinas Campaign—waged by William T. Sherman and Joseph E. Johnston during the winter and spring of 1865. For an in-depth look at this North Carolina battlefield, see *Moore's Historical Guide to the Battle of Bentonville* (Savas 1997).

Acknowledgments

My thanks to the following people for their friendly assistance during my work on this project: Richard Lawrence, of the North Carolina Historic Preservation Office's Underwater Archaeology Unit at Fort Fisher. Richard provided assistance with shipwreck locations in the Cape Fear vicinity; site manager Barbara Hoppe, Leland Smith, and Tammy Bangert of Fort Fisher State Historic Site. I spent the summer of 1991 working with Barbara, Leland, and now-retired site manager Gehrig Spencer, and it was here that my interest in the Fort Fisher-Wilmington expeditions began to take off.

Thanks also to Jimmy Bartley and Bert Felton of Brunswick Town/Fort Anderson State Historic Site, Dr. Rick Knapp and Charles Wadelington, of the North Carolina Division of Archives and History's Historic Sites Section; and Donna Kelly of the division's Historical Publications Section.

My friend Dr. Chris E. Fonvielle, Jr.—who knows the campaign like no one else—provided the foreword herein, and Chris and his family shared their home and hospitality during my work on this project. On a hot August day in 1997, Chris and I drove the "Wilmington loop," toured the less public areas along the route, and discussed the campaign at length. Chris' vast knowledge of Cape Fear Civil War history is amazing, and results from a lifetime of study. For evidence, catch *Last Rays of Departing Hope*, his ground-breaking study on Wilmington.

My appreciation also goes out to my friend Cliff Tyndall, of the Historic Sites Section, for the hospitality in Wrightsville Beach during the summer of 1997, and to Larry Misenheimer and other staff members at Archives and History Administration, for putting up with my strange schedule and time off during my work on this book.

I am greatly indebted to historians Edwin C. Bearss, of Arlington, Virginia (who also proofed my Bentonville study), and Steven E. Woodworth, of Texas Christian University—both of whom gave the manuscript a careful reading and offered many valuable suggestions. I've enjoyed walking the fields of Bentonville with Ed in the past, and look forward to many similar tours for the Wilmington Campaign. Steve Woodworth's books on the Western campaigns of the Civil War (along with those of William C. Davis and others) are doing much to increase our understanding of this once-neglected theater where the outcome of the war was decided. Like Bentonville, the Fort Fisher-Wilmington Campaign was born of an interesting amalgam of elements from *both* of the war's main theaters.

I owe a deep debt of gratitude to historian Andrew D. Lambert, of the Department of War Studies, King's College, London, who reviewed my cross-war comparative analysis of the fall of Fort Fisher and the siege of Sebastopol during the Crimean War. Dr. Lambert offered several key suggestions and clarifications, and provided context with a brief introduction to this important section of the book (which offers a fresh look at the reasons for Fort Fisher's demise). His participation has made this a better study.

Michael Hargreave Mawson, of the Crimean War Research Society, also contributed with certain bibliographical references.

As always, I am grateful for the continued encouragement of my parents, Dorothy A. Moore and Robert P. Moore, and my sister, Terry Sechler. It has been an eventful and difficult two years (for all of us) since the release of my last publication, and my family has always been there for support.

Lastly, I owe a large debt of thanks to my wife, Nancy Carter Moore, who has been supportive, patient, and understanding during the many long hours it took to write, illustrate, and produce this project. •

"I will give you a piece of information, which is confidential . . . *. General Grant is ready with his men and we will attack* Wilmington *in 5 days from now . . . . Keep your eyes open for newspaper accounts, and I wish you would keep every paper . . . . I am anxious to keep full account of this fight, which will be the grandest naval fight of the world either in ancient or modern history. If I come out all right I shall feel proud to say I participated in the splendid engagement."*
—Ensign John Grattan, U.S. Navy, to "Pa and Ma," December 1, 1864.

"Prepare to get underway . . ."

Decline of a Thriving Port City

Gleason's Pictorial Drawing-Room Companion

"Wilmington, the chief town of North Carolina, is situated at the confluence of two principal branches of the Cape Fear River . . . . Brunswick was the principal town and seaport of North Carolina, until the settlement of Wilmington, which first, from its superior location, became [Brunswick's] rival, and then its gravedigger.

"There is nothing attractive to the tourist in traveling through the State of North Carolina; its sandy soil and monotonous scenery affording but a tiresome prospect, and any change being welcome which relieves the interminable pine forests. Of the western section [of the state] we cannot speak with so much accuracy; but on a recent trip from Weldon, on the northern boundary of the State, to Wilmington . . . we were struck with the *unchangeableness* of the scene.

"There was little to relieve the monotony of the interminable pine forests and cypress swamps, except an occasional log cabin, with its rude inmates, or an occasional collection of huts with a water-tank, collectively dignified with the high-sounding name of Washington, Warsaw, or some other euphonious title. This immense tract, however, furnishes the staple commodities of the State, viz., tar, pitch, turpentine, and lumber.

"Wilmington, although it presents nothing to attract the attention of the visitor, is a growing and healthy place. Its numerous turpentine distilleries have served to keep off the epidemics which might otherwise have been looked for from its near location to swampy lands, and for consumptives no atmosphere could be more beneficial.

"The harbor at Wilmington has a dangerous shoal at its entrance, but will admit vessels of two hundred tons. There are two islands, enclosed by different channels of the river, opposite town, on which are some of the finest rice fields of the south. Wilmington is at the terminus of the great series of southern railroads extending from New York, and branching in various directions from the main route."

—View of antebellum North Carolina and Wilmington by staff members of *Gleason's Pictorial*, a Northern newspaper out of Boston, Massachusetts, July 16, 1853.

The view at left of 1853 Wilmington faces southeast across the Cape Fear River from the sawmills at Point Peter. In addition to the ships in the river, a timber raft and flatboat carrying bales of rice straw can be seen.

The tall structure of St. James Episcopal Church is visible against the sky in the background.

Navigation improvements in the river, coupled with the construction of railroads and North Carolina's adoption of the plank road system, facilitated Wilmington's growth in the years before the Civil War. Commerce grew rapidly, and the town became a market for naval stores.

"The epidemic of yellow fever in Wilmington was in the fall of 1862. A vessel [the blockade runner *Kate*] from Nassau loaded with bacon and other supplies . . . came up the Cape Fear River, entered the port at Wilmington and anchored at the foot of Market and Water streets.

"The quarantine laws were overlooked in our zeal and gratitude in obtaining the food and other supplies that were so much needed for our soldiers on the battlefield. This was the first week in September 1862. After a few days had elapsed, our physician . . . reported several cases of fever, with symptoms of yellow fever, and upon investigation it was found there had been cases of yellow fever aboard the vessel from Nassau, and then it developed that some of the sailors from that vessel had been for water on the premises where we lived.

"The disease spread rapidly . . . I made my way over to the window one day about the middle of October [and] as I looked out I saw all windows closed with no sign of life save the 'Little Sisters of Mercy' darting across the streets—flitting from door to door, entering to administer to the sick and dying. Then as I gazed on, I saw a shabby old hearse coming across the corner, drawn by a lean horse, looking as if he had the fever and a young colored man leaning over, too sick to hold the reins, and before the setting of another sun he was laid by the side of many of his fellow men, white and colored in a deep trench that had been provided for the dead in Oakdale Cemetery . . . . [I]n the short space of about two months there were from 1000 to 1100 of the dead." —**Mrs. Charles Pattison Bolles**, Wilmington resident and yellow fever survivor. Of 1,500 reported cases, there were 654 recorded deaths. Though unknown to doctors of the time, the *Aedes* mosquito was the culprit, and a sudden snowstorm on November 6, 1862, checked the spread of the disease.

"Went over the river to Wilmington in the afternoon. The city is rather a pretty place and wears more of a Southern look than any city I have yet seen. There were some very fine buildings, but I was more attracted by the pretty appearance of the dooryards, and garden flowers were blooming, some of them new to me and most beautiful. I could not help but contrast it with the climate in Ohio, where my friends write me that the sleighing is fine. Snow has not fallen here this winter. As we came up to this place the frogs were croaking in the swamps. As we waded through them, I saw both snakes and lizards, and at night the mosquitoes were singing around our ears. Wilmington [at this stage in the war] is apparently mostly composed of colored people . . . at least they are very abundant and white people are scarce."—**Maj. Thomas C. Thoburn**, 50th Ohio Infantry, during the Federal occupation of Wilmington, February 27, 1865

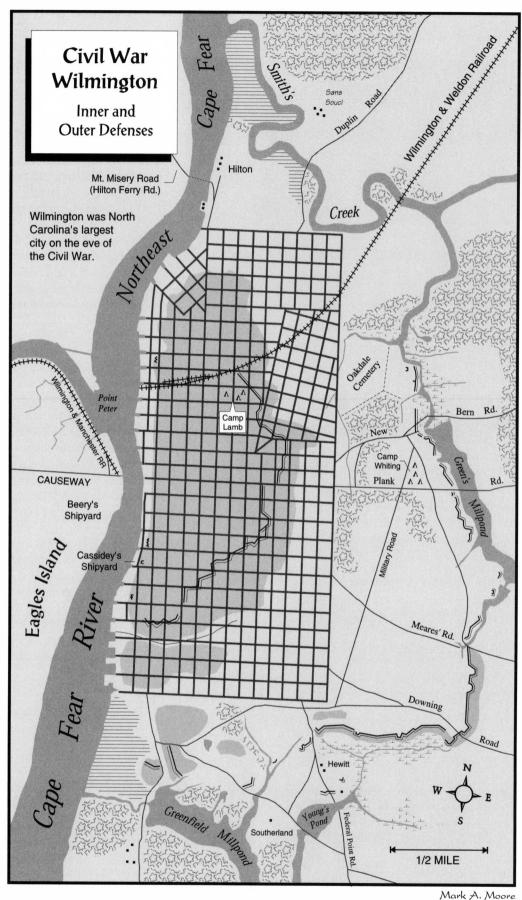

Civil War Wilmington

Inner and Outer Defenses

Wilmington was North Carolina's largest city on the eve of the Civil War.

Mark A. Moore

"This [Cape Fear] river was quite full of blockade-runners . . . all handsome leaden-coloured vessels, which ply their trade with the greatest regularity . . . . I cannot suppose that in ordinary times there would be anything like such a trade as this, at a little place like Wilmington, which shows the absurdity of calling the blockade an efficient one." —**Lt. Col. Arthur J. L. Fremantle**, British observer in the Confederacy, 1863

"After the Capital of the Confederacy there was not in the South a more important place than the little town of Wilmington, North Carolina."
— **John Johns**, Confederate officer stationed in Civil War Wilmington

With a population of roughly 10,000, Wilmington weighed in as North Carolina's largest city on the eve of the American Civil War. It was still a small town by comparison, and Wilmington did not enjoy the success or reputation of larger port cities of the era, such as Savannah, Georgia; Charleston, South Carolina; or New Orleans, Louisiana. Nevertheless, antebellum Wilmington flourished as an active seaport, engaging in the export of tar, pitch, turpentine, and lumber.

During the first years of the war, the Federal government focused its attention on the larger and more active Southern seaports, and aside from a coastwise blockade proclaimed by President Abraham Lincoln in April 1861, Wilmington thrived in virtual anonymity. Bolstering its maritime commerce were two commercial shipyards, a sword and button factory, an ironworks, several banks, and perhaps most importantly, three major railroads. The most notable of the latter was the Wilmington & Weldon Railroad, which ran directly north from Wilmington into Virginia—the very heart of the war's Eastern Theater. With its busy mercantile trade between New York, Philadelphia, and the Caribbean islands, Wilmington soon emerged as one of the most important cities in the Confederacy.

The town rapidly became a haven for various profit minded entrepreneurs who made a living by running the Federal blockade in order to supply the isolated South with needed military provisions, everyday necessities, and even items of luxury. It was a rewarding trade. All through the war the Federal navy's thinly stretched blockading force struggled vainly to squelch the influx of foreign goods into the Confederacy, and the export of "white gold" cotton. As blockade running soared, Wilmington declined from a quaint and beautiful port city, "gay and social" in its dealings, to a bustling maritime center teeming with the dregs of society.

"Here resorted the speculators from all parts of the South, to attend the weekly auctions of imported cargoes," noted blockade runner John Wilkinson, *"and the town was infested with rogues and desperadoes, who made a livelihood by robbery and murder. It was unsafe to venture into the suburbs at night, and even in daylight there were frequent conflicts in the public streets, between the crews of the steamers in port and the [Confederate] soldiers stationed in the town, in which knives and pistols would be freely used; and not unfrequently [sic] a dead body would rise to the surface of the water in one of the docks with marks of violence upon it . . . . The civil authorities were powerless to prevent crime."*

As the social climate deteriorated many of Wilmington's permanent citizens left their houses and fled for the countryside. Those who remained were more inclined toward seclusion, as the city streets "swarmed with foreigners, Jews and Gentiles." Beggars lined the docks as the newly-arrived steamers unloaded their wares, and Wilmington's garrison troops struggled to keep order in a town turned upside down.

Times were hard, and despite the decline of Wilmington's social order, precious goods arriving at the docks were welcome indeed. As the war progressed, everyday necessities—and certainly luxury items—became increasingly hard to obtain. Soon the arrival of a heavily laden blockade runner was looked to with great anticipation, as a needy population "looked the other way," glad to have an opportunity for obtaining items not otherwise available.

In November 1862, Maj. Gen. W. H. C. Whiting—brusque in manner and known for his abrasiveness—was assigned to command of the District of the Cape Fear. Whiting was transferred to Wilmington when Robert E. Lee restructured the Army of Northern Virginia at the request of Confederate president Jefferson Davis. Outspoken and candid, Whiting had criticized Davis' handling of military affairs in Virginia, and Lee also found Whiting's alarmist tendencies bothersome. The general was hurt by the transfer, but was well suited for his new post. He was a talented engineer, and the increasingly important city of Wilmington needed a strong defense system to repel any attempt by the Federal army or navy to close the port, and thereby deprive the Confederate cause of the sinews for waging war.

General Whiting enjoyed the confidence of the troops under his command, and *"though there were constant rumors of expeditions against [Wilmington],"* observed John Johns, *"we scarcely believed they were coming [but] . . . it seemed singular to us that the United States should so long neglect to close the only port . . . of the Confederacy into which every 'dark of the moon' there ran half a dozen or so swift blockade runners, freighted with cannon, muskets, and every munition of war."* As supplies of all sorts continued to pour into Wilmington, the military provisions were funneled straight up to Lee's army in Virginia via the Wilmington & Weldon Railroad—the "lifeline of the Confederacy."

"The defenses of the City [of Wilmington] consisted of a chain or system of ponds, dams and earthworks extending in a crescent half around the north eastern side of the City, then from North East [Cape Fear] River to Smith's Creek and across a sand ridge . . . and a mile from the City all around. There were dams with water gauges at each of these ponds, and it is said to have been a very skillful piece of engineering. In the City were two batteries of ten inch Columbiad Cannons with Magazines of Ammunition. One battery was on a bluff at the upper side of the City, and the other on a bluff near the southern suburbs. These batteries and chains of dams along with several Government sheds on the side of the river in front of the City, were the principal points to protect the 10th Battalion. These sheds at times were filled with immense quantities of goods and Government supplies landed there by the numerous fleets of blockade runners then coming into port; just as eager to get our cotton, as we were to get the necessary goods brought for exchange . . . . Many foreigners and strangers were in the City at all times coming on the blockade runners."
— **Charles S. Powell**, 10th North Carolina Regiment

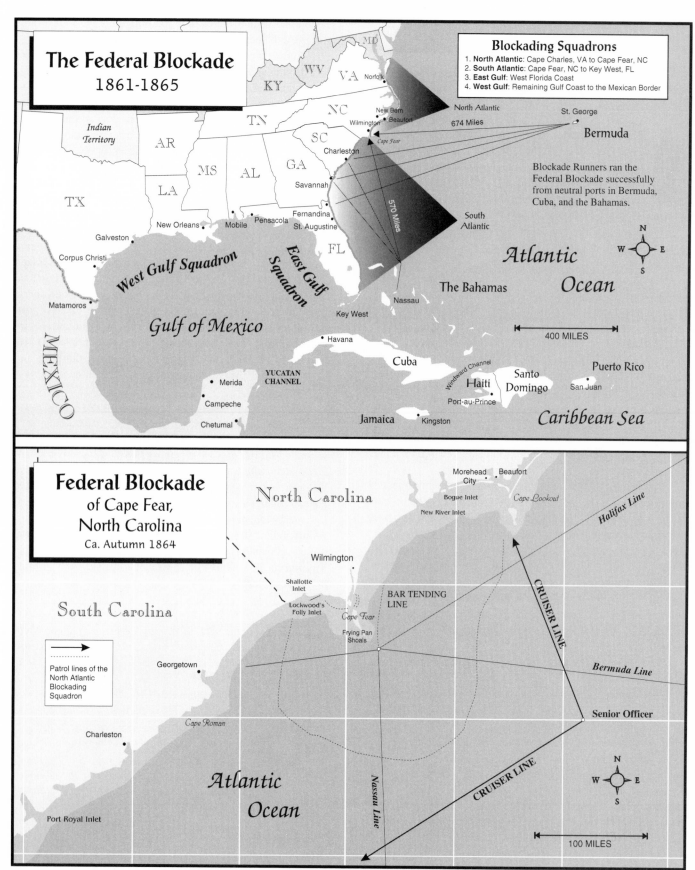

The Federal Blockade
1861–1865

Blockading Squadrons
1. **North Atlantic:** Cape Charles, VA to Cape Fear, NC
2. **South Atlantic:** Cape Fear, NC to Key West, FL
3. **East Gulf:** West Florida Coast
4. **West Gulf:** Remaining Gulf Coast to the Mexican Border

MD

WV

VA

Norfolk

KY

NC

TN

New Bern

SC

Wilmington   Beaufort

North Atlantic

674 Miles

St. George

Cape Fear

Bermuda

Indian Territory

AR

Charleston

570 Miles

Blockade Runners ran the Federal Blockade successfully from neutral ports in Bermuda, Cuba, and the Bahamas.

MS

AL

GA

Savannah

TX

LA

Fernandina

St. Augustine

South Atlantic

New Orleans   Mobile   Pensacola

Galveston

FL

Atlantic Ocean

N
W   E
S

Corpus Christi

West Gulf Squadron

East Gulf Squadron

The Bahamas

Matamoros

Gulf of Mexico

Nassau

Key West

400 MILES

MEXICO

Havana

YUCATAN CHANNEL

Cuba

Windward Channel

Santo Domingo

Puerto Rico

San Juan

Merida

Haiti

Port-au-Prince

Campeche

Chetumal

Jamaica   Kingston

Caribbean Sea

Federal Blockade
of Cape Fear, North Carolina
Ca. Autumn 1864

Morehead City   Beaufort

North Carolina

Bogue Inlet   *Cape Lookout*

New River Inlet

Halifax Line

Wilmington

South Carolina

Shallotte Inlet

Lockwood's Folly Inlet

Cape Fear

BAR TENDING LINE

CRUISER LINE

→
·········▶
Patrol lines of the North Atlantic Blockading Squadron

Georgetown

Frying Pan Shoals

Bermuda Line

Senior Officer

Charleston

Cape Roman

N
W   E
S

Nassau Line

CRUISER LINE

Atlantic Ocean

Port Royal Inlet

100 MILES

Mark A. Moore

"Wilmington is at present the most important point of entry in the South, and the custom-house receipts . . . far exceed anything they had ever been during a similar period before the war. There were about a dozen blockade-running steamers lying at the wharves . . . . One great treat we had here was to find English newspapers in abundance, and of dates little more than a month old . . . . but the great sight is when they come up to the wharves. They all dress up with flags as if for a victory . . . . The cheering, too, is vociferous, and all those who have any interest in the vessel must, no doubt, feel extremely comfortable, as every successful trip brings an enormous profit." —**FitzGerald Ross**, English cavalry officer, serving with the Austrian Hussars, on a tour through the Confederacy, 1863

Running the Blockade

"I am satisfied that no vessel should escape out of Wilmington after the blockade is perfected if the orders I have instituted are strictly carried out."
— **Rear Adm. David Dixon Porter**, United States Navy, Commanding North Atlantic Blockading Squadron

Situated on the eastern bank of the Cape Fear River, some 25 miles north of its confluence with the Atlantic, North Carolina's principal seaport could not have been better suited for running the blockade. The town was safely out of range of any Federal bombardment from the ocean, and its close proximity to the major transshipment points for incoming European goods was ideal. Nassau in the Bahamas was only 570 miles away, while Bermuda was 674 miles nearly due east of Wilmington. Transatlantic merchantmen ferried goods earmarked for the Confederacy to these and other neutral ports. Here the materials were off-loaded onto sleek, shallow draft steamers for the last leg of the journey: the dash through the Federal blockade lines and into the Cape Fear River, under protection of its formidable defensive works. Having safely delivered their cargoes the runners then returned through the blockade to the transshipment points, usually bearing Southern export items such as cotton, naval stores, or lumber.

The Federal dragnet consisted of three main blockade lines. Farthest out to sea was the cruiser line, whose ships patrolled the ocean with a sharp lookout for incoming vessels headed for Cape Fear. Further in was a middle line, followed by a line of "bar tenders" just off the shoal waters of Cape Fear. The navy's lighter vessels ventured in as close to the river inlets as they dared, especially at night. Blockaders that closed within range of Confederate shore batteries were sure to draw hostile fire.

As the war progressed the blockade became more and more effective, but the navy could not meet the challenge of stopping *all* shipping trade helpful to the Confederate cause. As a result, the officers and men of the North Atlantic Blockading Squadron were operating under strict orders from Adm. David D. Porter. Blockaders engaging a suspicious vessel had to give proper signals as to the direction of the chase, in order to ensure the vessel's capture. For example, if a runner eluded the bar tending line of blockaders, the middle line was to be notified so that it could either stop the runner, or notify the cruiser line of the runner's approach.

Failure to adhere to the rules brought the wrath and disdain of Admiral Porter. In November 1864, the English steamer *Annie*—laden with cotton, tobacco, and spirits of turpentine—was captured by the *Wilderness* and *Niphon* while attempting to run the blockade from New Inlet. The runner surrendered after a brief chase of ten minutes, during which 13 shots were fired from the Federal gunboats. As the crew of the *Annie* was being transferred to the *Niphon*, the guns of Fort Fisher joined the action, and a shell entered the *Wilderness*, causing some damage. During this affair, the captors made no signal to other Federal vessels in the area, and were thus promptly accused of trying to claim the prize for themselves. Porter was furious, maintaining that the *Annie*'s capture was jeopardized by the failure to warn the adjacent vessels of her approach. The officers of the *Wilderness* and *Niphon* were reprimanded. *"This war is not being conducted for the benefit of officers or to enrich them by the capture of prizes,"* Porter declared, *"and every commander is deficient in the high moral character which has always been inherent in the Navy who for a moment consults his private interests in preference to the public good, hesitates to destroy what is the property of the enemy, or attempts to benefit himself at the expense of others."*

This incident illustrates the danger of tackling blockade runners under the guns of Fort Fisher. This giant installation, the largest earthen fort in the Confederacy, was the key to the river defense system below Wilmington.

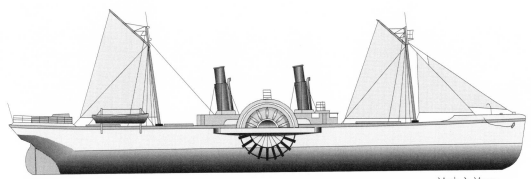

LENGTH: 200 feet; WIDTH: 22 feet; DRAFT: 10 feet
ENGINES: 250 H.P.

Mark A. Moore

Blockade Runner

Typical style of vessel used to run the blockade.

This shallow draft paddle-wheel steamer might reach a speed of 15-16 knots, while carrying some 400 tons of cargo.

Short spars and low superstructures gave these ships a reduced silhouette, and with their sails furled they were difficult to spot from a distance.

"A blockade-runner was almost as invisible at night as Harlequin in the pantomime. Nothing showed above the deck but two short masts . . . and the lead-colored hull could scarcely be seen at a distance of one hundred yards. Even on a clear day they were not easily discovered."
— **John B. Tabb**, clerk serving with Capt. John Wilkinson

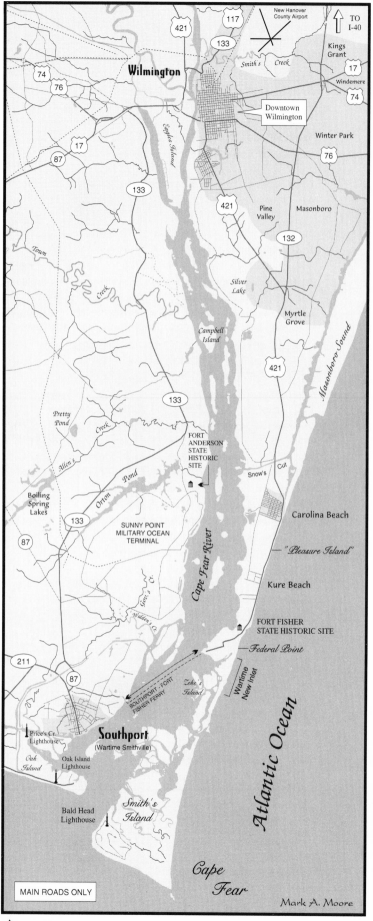

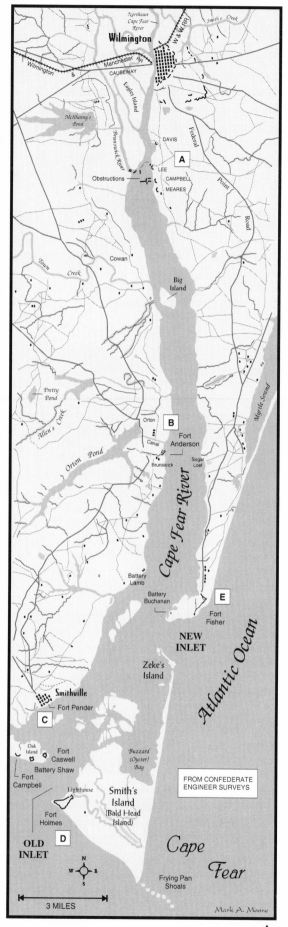

▲ Modern Area   -----The Cape Fear Estuary and Approaches to Wilmington-----   Wartime Area ▲

The River Defenses

"That Wilmington has not hitherto been attacked is owing to the fact that to overcome her natural and artificial defense would require the withdrawal of too large a force from operations against points which [Northern policy makers] deem more important to us. If that cause should ever cease to exist we may expect [the enemy] fleets and armies at the mouth of the Cape Fear."
— **Jefferson Davis**, Confederate president, December 15, 1864

The Cape Fear River's formidable defensive works were the crowning addition to the ideal geographical location Wilmington enjoyed as a haven for blockade runners. The fall of Norfolk, Virginia in May 1862, rendered Wilmington the closest active seaport to the Eastern Theater battlefront, and as the town's importance grew so did its network of defenses. The efforts of Confederate soldiers, together with forced labor from Indians and numerous slaves impressed from neighboring plantations, produced a vast array of earthen forts and batteries to protect the South's most important seaport. After Charleston, South Carolina, it was the most heavily fortified city on the Atlantic seaboard.[1]

In addition to the inner and outer defenses of the town itself,[2] four large river batteries dominated a bluff known as Mt. Tirza about three miles below Wilmington. From north to south, these were Forts Davis, Lee, Campbell, and Meares {A}. The Mt. Tirza batteries commanded the river approach to Wilmington, while sunken cheveaux-de-frise and other obstructions blocked the narrow channel below Eagles Island. Blockade runner pilots were given instructions on how to safely navigate these dangerous obstacles.

Guarding the western land approaches 15 miles south of Wilmington was Fort Anderson {B}. Originally named Fort St. Philip, this massive collection of earthen batteries was erected by Confederate engineers in 1862, amid the decaying ruins of a colonial settlement known as Brunswick Town. In the days before the American Revolution, Brunswick had served as Great Britain's main port of entry into North Carolina, and it was the British who burned the little town in 1776. Fort Anderson's largest batteries, mounting nine heavy cannon, dominated the low bluffs on the west bank of the Cape Fear, where the navigation channel would bring approaching enemy vessels directly under its guns. A series of aquatic mines known as "torpedoes" further obstructed the river channel here, while a low sand curtain stretched westward from the main batteries for nearly a mile to Orton Pond. Though Fort Anderson weighed in as the largest interior structure in the Cape Fear defensive network, its weaknesses would be quickly exploited by invading Union troops in February 1865.

Several miles below Fort Anderson, at the mouth of the Cape Fear, stood the small and rustic village of Smithville (present-day Southport). Having neither railroads nor major highways, Smithville lacked the necessary infrastructure to sustain itself as a viable port town. It was, however, an important stop for out-bound blockade runners. At anchor in the harbor at Smithville, the heavily laden steamers could easily view the Federal blockading forces guarding both Old Inlet and New Inlet. They used this vantage point to assess the chances of a successful breakthrough, and to choose an inlet from which to run the gauntlet. Protecting the harbor at Smithville was Fort Pender {C}, a small four-gun earthwork which the Confederates had erected over the existing structure of colonial Fort Johnston.

Guardians of the Estuary

That there were two entrances into the Cape Fear River was a source of major frustration for the Federal blockaders. Stemming the flow of contraband shipping was a difficult task made worse by an uncertainty as to which inlet would be chosen at any given time by a blockade runner. The overwhelming success of running the blockade at Cape Fear was due in no small part to two shallow inlets heavily fortified against the threat of naval or amphibious assault.

Old Inlet, the main river entrance and known as the Western Bar, was well guarded from both east and west {D}. The defenses at Oak Island were anchored by Fort Caswell and Fort Campbell, with the tiny, single-gun Battery Shaw located midway between the two. Fort Caswell was an old masonry structure built between 1826 and 1838 by U.S. army engineers. Forts Caswell and Johnston were seized from Federal authorities at the outbreak of the war. As they had with Fort Johnston, Confederate troops strengthened Fort Caswell and brought in more heavy seacoast artillery pieces.

Situated at the tip of Bald Head Point on Smith's Island, Fort Holmes dominated Old Inlet from the east. This large earthwork fortification was begun in September 1863, and remained a work in progress for the remainder of its brief existence. Conforming to the southern and western shores of the island, its combination of sand curtains and gun emplacements stretched for one and one-half miles.

East of the Cape Fear River, on a narrow peninsula known as Federal Point, lay the key to Wilmington's defense—the behemoth Fort Fisher, which protected New Inlet {E}. Fisher was constructed much like the other large forts in the system, but on a much grander scale. At the tip of Federal Point was Battery Buchanan, which commanded both the inlet and the river behind Fort Fisher.

This elaborate system of protective installations drew praise from all who viewed it, and Confederate authorities were banking on the impregnability of Fort Fisher to sustain Wilmington in its vital role as "lifeline" to the Confederate war effort. Indeed, the works were strong; but would there be enough manpower to hold them during an enemy attack?

---

[1] Wilmington's city and river defenses were begun under Confederate District of the Cape Fear commander Joseph R. Anderson, and his successor, Samuel G. French. William H. C. Whiting assumed command of the district on November 8, 1862.

[2] For a map of the city's earthwork system, refer to p. 2.

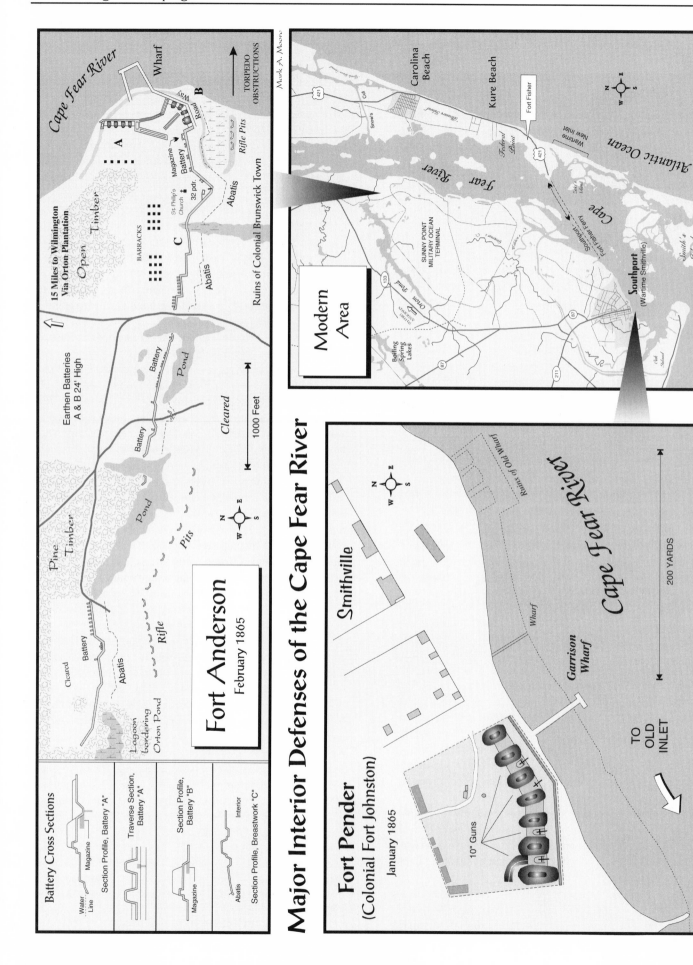

Major Interior Defenses of the Cape Fear River

Fort Anderson
February 1865

Cape Fear River

Wharf

B

A

Magazine
Battery
32 pdr.

St. Philip's Church

BARRACKS

C

Abatis

Abatis

Rifle Pits

TORPEDO OBSTRUCTIONS

Ruins of Colonial Brunswick Town

15 Miles to Wilmington Via Orton Plantation

Open Timber

Earthen Batteries A & B 24' High

Pine Timber

Battery

Battery

Pond

Pond

Cleared

Rifle Pits

Battery

Abatis

Lagoon bordering Orton Pond

Cleared

1000 Feet

Battery Cross Sections

Water Line

Magazine

Section Profile, Battery "A"

Traverse Section, Battery "A"

Magazine

Section Profile, Battery "B"

Abatis

Interior

Section Profile, Breastwork "C"

Modern Area

Carolina Beach

Kure Beach

Fort Fisher

Federal Point

Wartime New Inlet

Atlantic Ocean

Cape Fear River

Snow's Cut

Masonboro Island

Sunny Point Military Ocean Terminal

Orton Pond

Boiling Spring Lakes

Southport (Wartime Smithville)

Southport / Fort Fisher Ferry

Cape Fear

Battery Island

Smith's Island

Wartime Old Inlet

133

421

421

87

87

211

Fort Pender
(Colonial Fort Johnston)
January 1865

Smithville

Ruins of Old Wharf

Garrison Wharf

Wharf

Cape Fear River

10" Guns

TO OLD INLET

200 YARDS

Mark A. Moore

Ruins of St. Philip's Church at Fort Anderson

Fort Anderson

"A beautiful and substantial structure of turf."
— **James R. Randall**, Secretary to William F. Lynch, commander of the Confederate States Navy at Wilmington

When Confederate engineers surveyed the area in March 1862, the ruins of Old Brunswick had long been consumed by a wild vegetation of pine and cedar trees. Nevertheless, Brig. Gen. Samuel G. French, having assumed command of the District of the Cape Fear on March 15, 1862, assigned Lt. Thomas W. Rowland the task of erecting a defensive work at Brunswick Town. The new earthwork fortification would guard the land and river approaches on the west side of the Cape Fear River.

The initial segment of the fort abutted the river, with two large batteries commanding the river's navigation channel. The channel at this point was several hundred yards wide, and it brought any vessels that were headed upriver close under the guns at Old Brunswick. A low and crooked breastwork stretched westward from the batteries, snaking between the foundation ruins of the old court house and several private dwellings. The works dipped sharply to the south for a short distance, yielding to the ancient shell of St. Philip's Church, before resuming a more westerly course. Two more segments of sand curtain would eventually stretch the length of the fort to nearly one mile, blocking the routes northward between the river and Orton Pond.

After arriving in Wilmington in October 1861, and serving on the staff of Brig. Gen. Joseph R. Anderson, Maj. William Lamb of Virginia assumed command of the new fortification. On May 11, 1862, in a nod to the *"struggle of our fathers for liberty and independence,"* the young commandant christened the structure Fort St. Philip, after the ancient church *"whose venerable walls, by the grace of God, will witness our successful maintenance of that same liberty and independence."* Three days later Lamb was elected colonel of the 36th North Carolina Regiment (Second Artillery). He had studied law at William and Mary College in Williamsburg, Virginia, and he displayed an enthusiastic interest in military engineering. Lamb's abilities and intellect did not go unnoticed by his superiors. Interestingly enough, it was on Independence Day 1862, that he *"received a most unexpected order to proceed to Fort Fisher, and take command."*

On July 1, 1863, the structure was renamed Fort Anderson in honor of Brig. Gen. George B. Anderson, a North Carolinian who was mortally wounded at the Battle of Antietam (Sharpsburg) in September 1862. Work on strengthening the fort continued for the next three years.

As Wilmington continued to thrive on the neglect of Northern policy makers, life at Fort Anderson was routine, if not dull. Nevertheless, the garrison was kept busy, *"being drilled and carefully exercised in the artillery manual,"* noted T. A. McNeill of the 9th North Carolina Battalion. A day would soon arrive when such skills would be needed. Across the river on Federal Point, Colonel Lamb diligently went about strengthening the disjointed network of earthworks and batteries that comprised Fort Fisher in 1862. He was destined to lead the Confederacy's greatest bastion in its most dire hour of need.

After its occupation, a young Federal soldier observed Fort Anderson and its surroundings on a mist-shrouded morning in February 1865: *"The brick walls of a church [St. Philip's] are still in a good state of preservation. The lintels are cedar and are still sound. It is a large structure and would do honor to modern times . . . . Cedar and pine trees are growing out of the top of the wall. Large trees have grown up from the ground inside the wall, but had recently been cut down for fire wood . . . . There are quite a number of tomb-stones near the church. Some of them had been there 100 years and out in the forest there are ancient tomb-stones with old trees growing over them. The roots had penetrated between the bricks and as they grew larger they burst the wall.*

The day was foggy, the trees with their evergreen foliage and the long gray moss which hung from the limbs, and the scream of the blue jay, all conspired to make it seem an appropriate place for a burying ground. As I walked among the trees I noticed that the ground was rough and irregular, and on a closer inspection I discovered that the depression was what was formerly the cellar of the houses [of colonial Brunswick Town] and the brick cellar walls were still there in a good state of preservation."
— **Maj. Thomas C. Thoburn**, 50th Ohio Infantry[*]

---

[*] Major Thoburn arrived at Cape Fear with Maj. Gen. Darius N. Couch's two divisions, XXIII Army Corps, on February 22, 1865. By March, Couch's troops would be en route overland to Kinston, N.C.

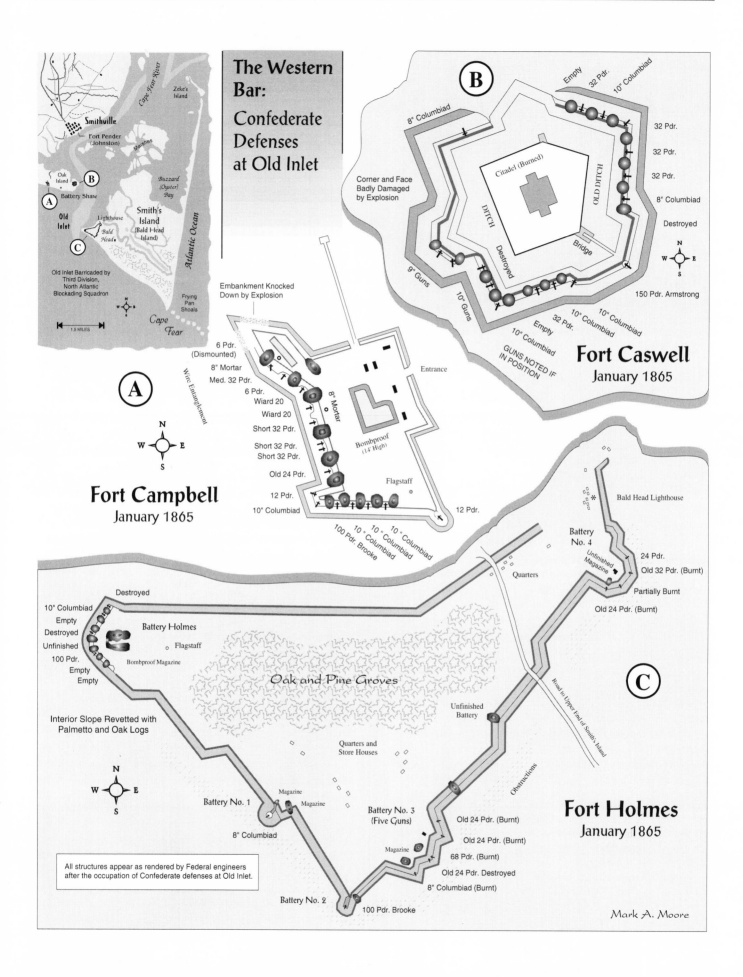

The Western Bar: Confederate Defenses at Old Inlet

Fort Campbell January 1865

Fort Caswell January 1865

Fort Holmes January 1865

Mark A. Moore

All structures appear as rendered by Federal engineers after the occupation of Confederate defenses at Old Inlet.

Harper's Weekly

Federal Blockaders in Position at Old Inlet: To the left of this view is Oak Island and Forts Campbell and Caswell. To the right is Smith's Island and Fort Holmes. The Bald Head lighthouse is visible on the far right of the drawing.

Action at Old Inlet

"The [blockade runner] Ella *is hulled and full of water. She is lost."*
— **Brig. Gen. Louis Hébert**, in command at Bald Head, to Maj. Gen. W. H. C. Whiting, December 3, 1864

Life in the isolated island outposts at Old Inlet was anything but easy for Confederate troops stationed in the area. They suffered for lack of adequate food and shelter, and disease was rampant. The summer weather was oppressive, *"absolutely hot,"* according to a soldier at Fort Caswell on Oak Island in 1862, *"and when night comes instead of getting cooler it positively gets warmer, and the mosquitoes come in swarms."* Things were no better in the remote, jungle-like wastes of Smith's Island. Among swamps and groves of live oak and palmetto trees, the soldiers here shared an existence with alligators and other native creatures. But as work continued on Fort Holmes, the men drilled, pulled guard duty, and kept a sharp watch for Federal blockaders. When the enemy ventured too close to shore, the guns of Fort Holmes were quick to greet their arrival.

In December 1863, the 40th North Carolina Regiment was organized at Bald Head from companies that had been stationed at various points along the Cape Fear defensive network. Their new commander was Col. John J. Hedrick, who had commanded the fledgling Fort Fisher until the summer of 1862. The industrious colonel soon had his men at work clearing roads through the forest to the east side of the island. Hedrick reasoned that these avenues could be used, when necessary, to bring the garrison's Whitworth guns to bear upon Federal warships south of New Inlet. On March 6, 1864, the USS *Peterhoff* fell victim to the scheme. After only six shots from the Confederates, she sank in the shallows east of Smith's Island and eventually broke apart *"in a heavy northeast wind and sea."*[1]

Later that year, at dusk on December 2, a blockade running steamer inbound from Nassau slipped into the shoal waters south of Smith's Island. In close pursuit was the USS *Pequot*, which had followed her along the coast from South Carolina. Eager to catch the contraband vessel, Lt. Cmdr. D. L. Braine quickly launched a barrage of rockets and "burned the night signal" to gain the attention of neighboring blockaders. At 5:30 a.m. on the 3rd, the USS *Emma* caught sight of the prey and closed for the kill. The fugitive was *"a very long, low, side-wheel steamer,"* noted Lt. Thomas C. Dunn of the *Emma*, and was *"schooner-rigged, with two smokestacks."* In attempting evasive action, the runner promptly ran aground on one of the shoals below the island. Colonel Hedrick was concerned about the accident, noting that *"if she can be lightened before day the ship can be saved."* The crew abandoned the stricken vessel, and at first light Confederate shore batteries began shelling the fleet. The incident quickly escalated, attracting the attention of a veritable flock of Federal blockaders eager to take part in the action.

George W. Young of the USS *Maratanza*, senior officer of the attacking flotilla, ordered the gunboats *Britannia, Aries,* and *Tristram Shandy* to begin a long range bombardment of the grounded blockade runner. The blockaders *Chippewa* and *Huron* soon arrived and added their eleven-inch guns to the fray, while the *Pequot* exploded the ship's boilers after only a few shots. Young estimated that the runner *"was struck some 40 times,"* and Lt. Cmdr. Thomas O. Selfridge boasted that the *Huron "had the satisfaction of putting some shots through her."* That night a plan to board the vessel and set her ablaze was postponed due to poor visibility.

At dawn the next morning, *"as soon as we were visible from the shore,* reported *Tristram Shandy*'s Edward F. Devens, *"Fort Holmes . . . opened on us, their shots striking the water close to and many going over us."* The Federal warships were quick to answer, and on-shore Gen. Louis Hébert notified W. H. C. Whiting: *"We keep the enemy off, but their shots reach the ship."* By 7:00 a.m., remembered Lt. Cmdr. Young, the runner had *"bilged and gone down by the head."*

The damaged steamer lay foundering on the shoal as night fell on December 4. Dunn, *"deeming the opportunity a favorable one for attempting her destruction,"* made plans that night to send a boarding party to set the ship on fire. Finally, at 1:00 a.m. Ensign Isaac S. Sampson of the *Emma*, with one officer and six men, was dispatched on a risky mission which would bring them directly under the guns of Fort Holmes. Stealing through the waters with muffled oars the tiny crew, armed with cutlasses and pistols, drew alongside the stranded vessel. They were only about 250 yards from the beach, and could clearly hear *"the [Confederate] sentries passing the word on shore."* Leaving behind a few men to guard the boat and keep watch, Sampson and the others quietly tip-toed aboard. The hold was half full of water. Guided by a "dark lantern," the party spread turpentine throughout the ship's rooms and on the fuel well, and placed several 24-pound artillery shells with cut fuses near the engines. When all was ready, *"I deemed it prudent to light my fires and make good my retreat,"* reported Sampson. Soon the sky *"was well illuminated by the flames,"* and the guns of Fort Holmes roared into action. One-half hour into the blaze, the ship's machinery exploded, and by 4:30 a.m. the little boarding party had safely returned to the fleet.

The blockade runner *Ella*, bound for Wilmington with munitions of war, had been destroyed.[2] Nevertheless, the garrison at Smith's Island enjoyed a bountiful harvest of liquor and other goods that washed ashore from the wreck: *"[T]he Yankees fired into [the Ella] and we have been a whole week wrecking,"* wrote Cabe L. Ray. *"[W]e got hats and calico and a good many other things off of it."*

As the month of December wore on, rumors were rife that an all out Federal invasion of Cape Fear was close at hand. *"We are still working on breastworks,"* noted Ray, for the Confederate troops at Old Inlet might be called upon to repel a landing by the enemy on the beaches of the Western Bar.

---

[1] For location of the wreck of the *Peterhoff*, see Appendix C, p. 167. This vessel's remains have been well studied by the N.C. Division of Archives & History's Underwater Archaeology Unit, and many artifacts have been raised and preserved. The historic 32-pdr. tube on display in Shepherd's Battery at Fort Fisher State Historic Site, and an identical piece in front of the Fort Fisher visitor center were originally aboard the *Peterhoff*.

[2] For location of the wreck of the *Ella*, see Appendix C, p. 167.

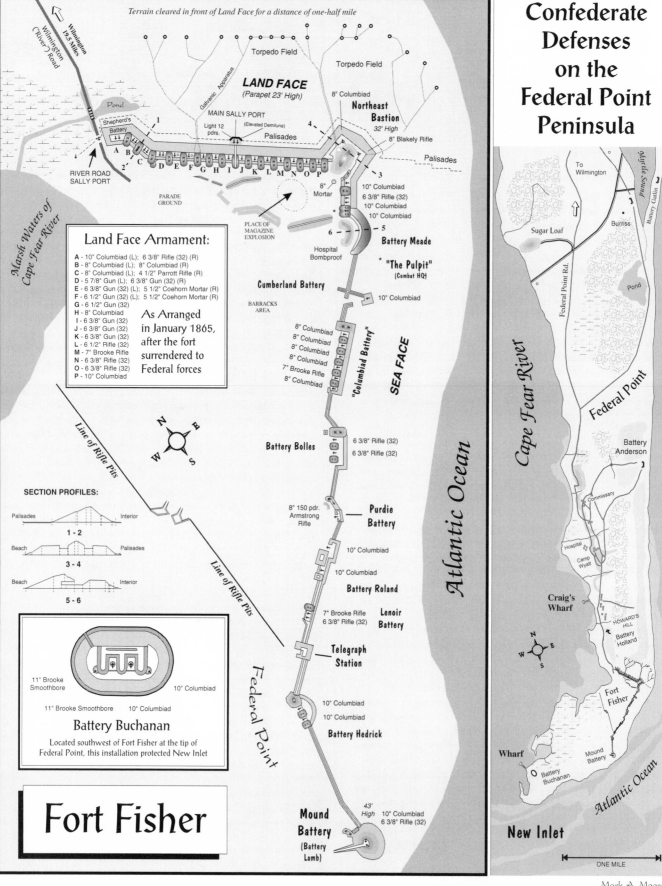

Confederate
Defenses
on the
Federal Point
Peninsula

Land Face Armament:

A - 10" Columbiad (L); 6 3/8" Rifle (32) (R)
B - 8" Columbiad (L); 8" Columbiad (R)
C - 8" Columbiad (L); 4 1/2" Parrott Rifle (R)
D - 5 7/8" Gun (L); 6 3/8" Gun (32) (R)
E - 6 3/8" Gun (32) (L); 5 1/2" Coehorn Mortar (R)
F - 6 1/2" Gun (32) (L); 5 1/2" Coehorn Mortar (R)
G - 6 1/2" Gun (32)
H - 8" Columbiad
I - 6 3/8" Gun (32)
J - 6 3/8" Gun (32)
K - 6 3/8" Gun (32)
L - 6 1/2" Rifle (32)
M - 7" Brooke Rifle
N - 6 3/8" Rifle (32)
O - 6 3/8" Rifle (32)
P - 10" Columbiad

As Arranged in January 1865, after the fort surrendered to Federal forces

Fort Fisher

"I was down [at Fort Fisher] one night . . . [and] had to rough it in a casemate till morning. As luck would have it, we discovered a blockade-running steamer, the *Hansa*, under our guns at dawn, and at the same time the Yankee blockaders also became aware of her presence . . . . To get within range they had to expose themselves to the metal of the fort, which soon drove them off . . . . Fort Fisher is one of the strongest coast defences I have seen, not excepting any of those at Charleston, that have hitherto held an entire iron-clad fleet at bay." —**Frank Vizetelly**, artist and war correspondent, *Illustrated London News*, 1864

Fort Fisher

"I determined at once to build a work of such magnitude that it could withstand the heaviest fire of any guns in the American navy."
— **Col. William Lamb**, Commander of Fort Fisher

Construction of defensive works on Federal Point commenced in the spring of 1861. In April, Maj. Charles Pattison Bolles was the first to begin work on a series of batteries about a mile north of New Inlet. His plans were approved by Brig. Gen. Theophilus H. Holmes, organizer of the Southern Department of Coastal Defenses, and by W. H. C. Whiting. At this early date Whiting, Bolles' brother-in-law, held the rank of major and was the inspector general of the defenses of North Carolina. When Bolles was transferred to Oak Island, Capt. William Lord DeRosset took his place on May 7, 1861. DeRosset arrived with the Wilmington Light Infantry, which was the first company to see garrison duty at the fledgling post. His stay was brief, but Captain DeRosset oversaw the strengthening of Battery Bolles, so named in honor of his predecessor, which became the first armed redoubt in what was to become Fort Fisher.

During the first 16 months of the war, a succession of commanders came and went on Federal Point. The best qualified officers were quickly assigned other duties, and both Holmes and Whiting were transferred to the fighting front in Virginia. In the meantime a training post known as Camp Wyatt was established one and one-half miles north of Battery Bolles in the summer of 1861, and by the end of August the area had a new commander.

Seawell L. Fremont, colonel of the 1st Corps of North Carolina Volunteer Artillery and Engineers, was put in charge of the state's coastal defense, and he focused attention on guarding the river inlets, especially New Inlet. Soon, with the aid of engineers John C. Winder and Richard K. Meade, several new batteries appeared on Federal Point. Battery Meade was established north of Battery Bolles and a short-lived two-gun installation was placed on Zeke's Island south of the inlet. Two oceanfront batteries were also constructed several miles up the peninsula: Battery Anderson was north of Camp Wyatt and Battery Gatlin, the farthest north, was located on a narrow sand spit between Myrtle Sound and the Atlantic. In September Fremont christened the new post "Fort Fisher," in honor of Col. Charles F. Fisher of the 6th North Carolina Infantry, who had been killed at the Battle of Bull Run (Manassas) in Virginia the previous July.

That fall a new artillery company from Mississippi was brought down to Camp Wyatt for training. The desolate terrain of Federal Point seemed forbidding to the new arrivals, and Lt. Patrick C. Hoy described "*a country which has a scrubby growth of timber but few settlements. It looked as if we [were] going to nowhere . . . . The few settlers here appeared to be very poor, a small garden or patch of open ground their only source of support.*" The newcomers gazed with curiosity at the long ladders which were occasionally seen stretching to the highest reaches of the tall pines. They were told by locals that the ladders were used by river pilots, who would scan the ocean with a "spy glass" for incoming blockade runners. Having received the proper signal, the pilot would hurry down to his small boat and "*hasten to the vessel and convey it to the mouth of the river and on up to Wilmington.*"

As work continued at Fort Fisher, Lt. Samuel A. Ashe oversaw the improvement of its armament via rifling machinery that was imported from Charleston. The longer range afforded by rifled guns enabled the fort's garrison to work more freely and without the risk of being fired upon by Federal blockaders lying close off the bar. The Federal warships were forced to keep their distance. "*There are two steamers in sight [off Fort Fisher] this morning,*" wrote G. H. Beatty in 1861, as he boasted to his mother that "*there is no danger of a battle, I think.*" Garrison life on the point was for the most part monotonous and uncomfortable, and when his company was left behind when the 18th North Carolina departed for points more interesting, young Beatty and many of his comrades were disappointed.

That September, Seawell Fremont was replaced by Brig. Gen. Joseph R. Anderson, who was soon the first officer placed by Confederate authorities as commander of the District of the Cape Fear. Fremont returned to his pre-war post as superintendent of the all important Wilmington & Weldon Railroad, and Anderson appointed Col. John J. Hedrick in January 1862 to oversee the continuation of earthwork fortifications at Fort Fisher. Under Anderson, and his successor Brig. Gen. Samuel G. French, Hedrick labored to strengthen the growing installation. But by the summer of 1862, the fort was still a patchwork of disconnected batteries and bits of sand curtain.

Finally, in July, the fort received its final commander. Before dusk on the day that Col. William Lamb arrived he had "*thoroughly inspected the works.*" The sharp young colonel was less than pleased with what he found, noting that there were only 17 guns "*of respectable calibre*" and that "*as a defence [sic] of New Inlet against a Federal fleet, our works amounted to nothing.*" Soon the garrison, and perhaps as many as 500 slaves, were hard at work on conforming the works at Fort Fisher to Colonel Lamb's own design. He incorporated the existing structures whenever possible and added many new ones. Before long a massive line of earthen batteries stretched from Shepherd's Battery on the Cape Fear River all the way to the ocean, forming the fort's Land Face. Eventually the Sea Face would extend the distance of nearly a mile. The terminus of the Sea Face was the colossal Battery Lamb, more commonly known as the Mound Battery. This 43-foot-high structure was built in the spring of 1863, using a steam engine on an inclined railway to haul sand to the top of a scaffold. Hundreds of laborers were employed in dumping the sand from the top of the scaffold to form the giant mound. This battery would become Fort Fisher's most notable landmark, and was probably the most impressive engineering feat accomplished during its construction. Because of its high visibility, Lamb installed signal lights on the Mound to communicate with incoming blockade runners.

The improvement in the structure was something to behold. "*Powerful batteries, traverses, palisades, covered ways and gun chambers were erected,*" remembered T. A. McNeill, "*many of these latter mounting rifled guns of English pattern, and of great calibre.*" In November 1863, Confederate president Jefferson Davis paid a visit while on hand to inspect the defenses of Wilmington. Davis arrived by boat at the tip of Federal Point and rode on horseback to the Mound Battery. He was accompanied by W. H. C. Whiting, who had returned as district commander in November 1862. From the top of the towering battery, Davis took in the impressive view of the fort as it sprawled northward along the beach. "*As soon as he reached the top,*" wrote Lamb, "*the sea-face guns being manned for the purpose, gave him the Presidential salute of twenty-one guns. We doubt whether many of the forts in the South could claim the distinction of having fired such a salute.*"

Further guarding the inlet to the south was Battery Buchanan, a large four-gun structure completed in October 1864 and designed by engineer Reddin Pittman. Buchanan completed the defenses on Federal Point, which was aptly dubbed "Confederate Point" by its new inhabitants. "*During 1864,*" remembered Lamb, "*the ten companies of the Thirty-sixth North Carolina had been collected at Fort Fisher, and the works had assumed formidable proportions.*" But could the "Confederate Goliath" withstand an enemy bombardment from the sea, or an all-out assault by Federal infantry upon its land defenses?

A Conjoint Attack Upon Wilmington

"The importance of closing Wilmington and cutting off Rebel communication is paramount to all other questions—more important, practically, than the capture of Richmond [Va.]"
— **Gideon Welles**, United States Secretary of the Navy, September 15, 1864

Whatever merit lay in the strength of the Cape Fear River defenses, the continued success of Wilmington and its contraband shipping trade was due largely to neglect afforded by Northern attention being focused elsewhere—a fact well understood by President Jefferson Davis and the Confederate War Department. By the summer of 1864, however, North Carolina's thriving little port had taken on new political significance in the eyes of policy makers in Washington.

On August 5, 1864, Adm. David D. Farragut entered Mobile Bay with a squadron of warships, and within a few weeks served a crushing blow to Confederate commerce by closing the port of Mobile, Alabama. The loss of Mobile, the sole remaining major port of entry in the Gulf of Mexico, left Wilmington the last major Southern seaport open to the outside world. Gideon Welles, the U.S. Secretary of the Navy in Washington, had for months been extolling the virtues of an expedition against Wilmington, even when others—particularly the army—showed no interest in the scheme. Welles used the Mobile Bay affair as leverage in expressing his idea for a *"conjoint attack upon Wilmington."*

"Something must be done to close the entrance to the Cape Fear River," Welles noted in his diary on August 30. *"[T]here seems some defect in the blockade which makes Wilmington appear an almost open port . . . . Could we seize the forts at the entrance of the Cape Fear and close the illicit traffic, it would be almost as important as the capture of Richmond on the fate of the Rebels, and an important step in that direction."*

Abraham Lincoln agreed with Welles. The U.S. president was under pressure from Northern merchants to combat the bothersome commerce-raiding ships that were operating out of Wilmington. These successful privateers were attacking United States vessels in Northern waters, and were yet another embarrassing problem to deal with in addition to enforcing the blockade. It was also an election year, and in November Lincoln would be asking Northern voters for a second term in office. Political pressure was mounting, and another major Union victory like that at Mobile Bay would not hurt the president's chances at the polls. Nevertheless, Lincoln stopped short of giving his approval for Welles' plan to attack Wilmington, deferring instead to the judgment of the nation's general-in-chief, Ulysses S. Grant.

Consequently, on the night of September 1, U.S. Secretary of War Edwin M. Stanton wired Grant, whose Army of the Potomac was embroiled in the bitter siege of Petersburg, Virginia: *"The Navy Department appears very anxious that the army should take Wilmington . . . . General [Quincy A.] Gillmore has been directed to accompany [Assistant Secretary of the Navy Gustavus] Fox to see you on the subject. Whether any operations there be possible [or] expedient to be undertaken now, is left wholly to your judgment by the President."* Major Gen. Henry W. Halleck, the U.S. Army chief of staff, was quick to warn Grant that the plan *"originates in the Navy, not in the War Department. I think we have more irons [in the fire] now than we can keep from burning."*

Gillmore, a veteran of previous combined operations in South Carolina and Georgia, and Assistant Secretary Fox journeyed to Grant's headquarters at City Point, Virginia, the following day. The general-in-chief listened with little enthusiasm to their proposal for a full-scale army-navy attack to close Wilmington. Grant's attention was understandably focused on Robert E. Lee's Army of Northern Virginia, and he worried over dispatching troops to North Carolina before he could receive replacements for them. But at the same time Grant understood Lincoln's political dilemma, and agreed to consider the appeal from the president's emissaries.

That same day, September 2, 1864, the Northern war effort received an astounding boost when Maj. Gen. William T. Sherman's enormous "army group" captured the important Rebel city of Atlanta, Georgia. Washington was soon abuzz with the news. Abraham Lincoln tendered to Sherman *"the applause and thanks of the nation,"* and Grant heartily congratulated his old friend on having *"accomplished the most gigantic undertaking given to any general in this war, and with a skill and ability that will be acknowledged in history as unsurpassed."* This major event in the war, as the balance further tipped in favor of the Union, virtually assured Lincoln's reelection in November. Thus the political expediency of capturing Wilmington quickly fell by the wayside.

Nevertheless, the seed had been planted in Grant's mind. On September 12, still unsure of the operation, he wrote to Sherman seeking the general's views on future military plans, and explaining that *"I want to send a force of from six to ten thousand men against Wilmington . . . . This will give us the same control of the harbor of Wilmington that we now have of the harbor of Mobile."* Grant further said that it would be early October *"before any of the plans here indicated will be executed."*

From Atlanta, Sherman replied on September 20: *"The utter destruction of Wilmington, North Carolina, is of importance only in connection with the necessity of cutting off all foreign trade to our enemy."* But he also suggested that his army's further penetration into Georgia would be ill advised *"without an objective beyond,"* and that the capture of Wilmington coupled with his own occupation of Savannah, Georgia, would open the door for Sherman to strike northward into the Carolinas. Sherman was beginning to form explicit strategic plans toward ending the war, and Grant would soon accept them. But for now, Sherman quipped to Grant that *"If you can whip Lee and I can march to the Atlantic, I think Uncle Abe will give us a twenty days' leave of absence to see the young folks."* The two generals shared a high confidence in one another that would become increasingly important during the war's final months.

The fall of Atlanta notwithstanding, the Navy Department in Washington upheld its zeal for a campaign against Wilmington. Secretary Welles set about planning the invasion in consultation with Quincy A. Gillmore, who outlined two detailed options for the attack. The first option involved a landing at Old Inlet and the capture of Smith's Island by a force of 6,000 men. The second called for a 12,000-man expedition against Fort Fisher on Federal Point. Both Grant and Welles were in agreement that the second plan was the most favorable. A landing on Federal Point would place the attackers closer to Wilmington, and afford them better maneuverability should they have to besiege Fort Fisher.

As the plot took shape, Welles fretted over choosing the right commander for the naval half of the operation. "*It has been impossible to get the War Department and military authorities to enter into the spirit of this work,*" Welles complained in his diary. "*They did not appreciate it. But they and Grant have now engaged in it, and Grant is persistent. Just at this crisis [Rear Adm. David G.] Farragut unfortunately fails.*" The long-awaited approval had come, and the hero of Mobile Bay was not interested in leading the new expedition. Citing reasons of health Farragut, leader of the West Gulf Squadron, graciously declined the offer of command. After carefully considering a handful of candidates the Navy Secretary focused on Farragut's foster brother, Adm. David Dixon Porter, who was then commanding the Mississippi Squadron. Welles was not without reservations. "*Porter is young,*" he worried, "*and his rapid promotion has placed him in rank beyond those who were his seniors. But . . . personal considerations must yield to the public necessities. I think Porter must perform this duty.*" Though the admiral enjoyed a reputation for conceit and arrogance, Porter was an energetic and competent commander. He spent the autumn of 1864 preparing for the expedition against Wilmington, assembling a large fleet of some 150 vessels at Hampton Roads, Virginia.

It was now up to Ulysses S. Grant to choose a commander for the campaign's army ground forces. The experienced Gillmore wanted the job, and was endorsed by Secretary of War Stanton, but Grant rejected the general with complaints that Gillmore was too timid for command of such an important operation. Passing over several higher profile officers, Grant selected Maj. Gen. Godfrey Weitzel, the little-known chief engineer of the Army of the James. The operation at Cape Fear would place Weitzel under the jurisdiction of Maj. Gen. Benjamin F. Butler, who commanded the U.S. military's Department of Virginia and North Carolina. In preparation for the expedition Weitzel traveled to Cape Fear in late September, and from a vantage point off New Inlet inspected the Confederate defenses on Federal Point. Soon after Weitzel returned to Virginia, in mid-October, the expedition against Wilmington was promptly postponed. Grant had learned that news of the invasion had been leaked to the public, and feared that the enemy had become wise to the plan. Indeed, the South would make use of the delay in sending Federal troops to attack Fort Fisher.

Confederate Preparations

From the time he assumed command at Cape Fear in November 1862, Maj. Gen. W. H. C. Whiting had deluged the Confederate War Department in Richmond with dire predictions of an imminent Federal attack upon Wilmington. He understood that it was merely a matter of time before an assault was made, especially since the forts guarding the entrances to Mobile Bay had fallen to the enemy. But Whiting's vituperative pleas were all too commonplace, and President Davis and various Whiting detractors grew weary of the familiar refrains. The general also labored under a far-reaching reputation for drunkenness, which tarnished his credibility even more than his constant pestering of Confederate authorities. Indeed, North Carolina governor Zebulon Vance, who appreciated Whiting's engineering abilities, would not overlook the allegations of alcoholism. Whiting was undaunted. He was certain that the next Southern port to be attacked would be Wilmington.

By September 1864, intelligence sources and Northern newspaper reports indicated that either Charleston or Wilmington might soon be attacked. Confederate Secretary of War James A. Seddon conceded the threat and informed General Whiting, adding sarcastically that "*I need scarcely add any reason to stimulate your habitual vigilance to discover and guard against the approach of the enemy.*" The Cape Fear District commander promptly ordered the further strengthening of the river defenses below Wilmington. The most noticeable problem facing Whiting's command, however, was lack of manpower.

The Cape Fear District accounted for some 100 miles of shoreline, but by the summer of 1864 it could count only about 2,400 troops for its defense. Moreover, the garrison forces had seen little or no combat to date, aside from occasional duels with Federal blockaders. Thus Whiting's entreaties to Richmond continued, requesting a reinforcement of veteran infantry for the area. He most feared an attack from the port of New Bern, about 90 miles north of Wilmington, which had been under Federal control since March 1862. Barring that, he concluded that the enemy would land at either Smith's Island or Federal Point. "*The warning of Mobile is before us,*" Whiting cautioned Seddon, and in the event of an enemy landing "*great disaster may occur.*"

For his part Gen. Robert E. Lee never doubted the importance of preserving Wilmington and his army's "lifeline" via the Wilmington & Weldon Railroad. But he worried over where to find additional troops to send to Cape Fear. The Army of Northern Virginia was bogged down against Grant and Maj. Gen. Philip H. Sheridan in Virginia, and Lee was loath to dispatch a force to North Carolina under the circumstances. For now, reinforcements for the Cape Fear defenses would have to come from North Carolina. Though he preferred to have veterans, Governor Vance agreed to send local militia units to help safeguard Wilmington. Whiting also asked Confederate naval authorities to place more obstructions in the Cape Fear River, and ordered Capt. Francis Hawks of the Engineer Corps to construct a line of breastworks across the Federal Point peninsula between Sugar Loaf and Myrtle Sound. This new position would give the Rebels a strong defensive line from which to contest an amphibious landing by the enemy.

By mid-October 1864 it finally became clear to authorities in Richmond that Wilmington would probably be the target of a Federal assault. Whiting had been correct in his prediction, but instead of any acknowledgment from Richmond he was promptly relieved of his command. Two years of thoughtful and zealous preparation, a thorough knowledge of the Cape Fear defensive network, and Whiting's personal interest in the area went for naught. The Confederate high command simply had no confidence in the general who had so often pleaded for their assistance. General Lee thought Whiting was "*a man of unquestionable knowledge suited to his position, but whether he would be able at the required time to apply these qualifications and to maintain the confidence of his command is with me questionable.*" Lee wanted Gen. Pierre G. T. Beauregard to command the defense of Wilmington. President Jefferson Davis, however, put matters to rest with his own choice for the job, and thus appointed Gen. Braxton Bragg as the new commander of the District of the Cape Fear.

The controversial Bragg, a favorite of Davis, possessed a personality both dour and combative. Saddled with a stormy history of field command in the western Army of Tennessee, his career had been marked by failure and intrigue. By this stage in the war Bragg's reputation preceded him, and the general's arrival at Wilmington on October 22 was bemoaned by many a loyal Confederate.

Bragg immediately fell in with the administration's view of Whiting: "*I found General Whiting much worried and disconcerted,*" he wrote to Davis on the 25th, "*and, believing that his abilities and experience could be made valuable, [I] deem it prudent to shape my order assuming command as to wound his pride as little as possible . . . . His appearance does not indicate recent dissipation. He is very industrious . . . and deeply interested in the success of his labors here. [He] attaches too much importance, probably, to reports and rumors not well grounded, and is too apt to allow his excitement to lead to indiscreet advice to the people [but] With such means as can be drawn from the resources of my command we shall make the best defense possible, should [Wilmington] be the point assailed.*"

That same day Bragg reported his assessment of the Cape Fear defenses to General Lee: "*[I]t gives me pleasure to report favorably of their strength and condition. They are now prepared to oppose a powerful resistance to any naval attack, and will hold any considerable land force in check for a considerable time, if the garrisons will do their duty.*" But with a seeming lack of understanding of the task at hand, Bragg added that "*Whether the importance of the harbor is such as to justify the withdrawal of [troops] from other points, also endangered . . . your own judgment can best decide.*"

Bragg's assessment notwithstanding, General Whiting and Governor Vance renewed their pleas for reinforcements. On November 15, 1864, after a visit to the area, Vance pointedly reminded Jefferson Davis of the manpower shortage at Cape Fear: "*I deem it my duty to address you in regard to the situa-*

tion of Wilmington," he wrote. "*So far as I am able to judge there seems to be nothing wanting but troops. If attacked in strong force I humbly conceive that its capture is inevitable, unless strengthened by at least two brigades of veteran troops. The militia assembled . . . I fancy will be totally inadequate to resist a land attack in the rear of Fort Fisher, which seems to be the point of real danger . . . . I respectfully suggest that General Lee should spare a few veterans as a nucleus for the raw troops defending Wilmington, notwithstanding the great pressure on his lines. Except for the moral effect involved in losing our capital, I cannot see that Richmond itself is of any greater importance to us now than Wilmington.*"

Davis forwarded Vance's suggestion to Robert E. Lee, who was still reticent about sending a portion of his beleaguered army to North Carolina, and weary of the requests. "*In my opinion troops are as much required [in Virginia] as at Wilmington,*" he responded. "*The difference between the two places at present is, that Richmond is besieged by an army three times as large as that defending it. There is no enemy as yet on the shores of Wilmington. To attack it, troops must be drawn from elsewhere, when I trust re-enforcements can be sent from the point from which the pressure [on my lines] is relieved. In the meantime, the North Carolina troops, as brave as any in the Confederacy . . . . are capable of protecting it.*" Lee was telling the War Department that when Grant pulled a force from the Richmond-Petersburg lines to attack Wilmington, Lee would send a corresponding force to protect it.

These were dire times for the Confederacy. By mid-November 1864, Gen. William T. Sherman's army in Georgia had begun its infamous "March to the Sea." Having struck out from Atlanta on the 16th, Sherman was cutting a wide swath of destruction eastward toward the port city of Savannah. To help resist Sherman's advance, President Davis told Bragg on November 22 to proceed to Georgia in order to bolster Confederate forces under Lt. Gen. William J. Hardee, who were falling back before the Union juggernaut. Just as authorities in North Carolina were screaming for reinforcements at Cape Fear, they were about to lose troops instead of gain them. As scant reinforcements trickled into the region from points across North Carolina, Bragg depleted the estuary's principal forts by more than 2,000 men and hurried them off to Georgia at Davis' request.

The timing was not good. In Virginia, Federal inertia regarding the Wilmington expedition was finally on the wane. Ulysses S. Grant was becoming impatient. He had learned of the depletion of Confederate forces at Cape Fear from Georgia newspapers, and reasoned that the time for attack was at hand. There would, however, be one more small delay. The imaginative Gen. Benjamin F. Butler, in whose military department the expedition would take place, was taking excessive pains to assure that all was ready. He was fiddling with a grand scheme to reduce Fort Fisher in one fell swoop.

The issue of Confederate manpower shortage, and its relevance to the defense of Cape Fear, is discussed in Appendix A, page 137.

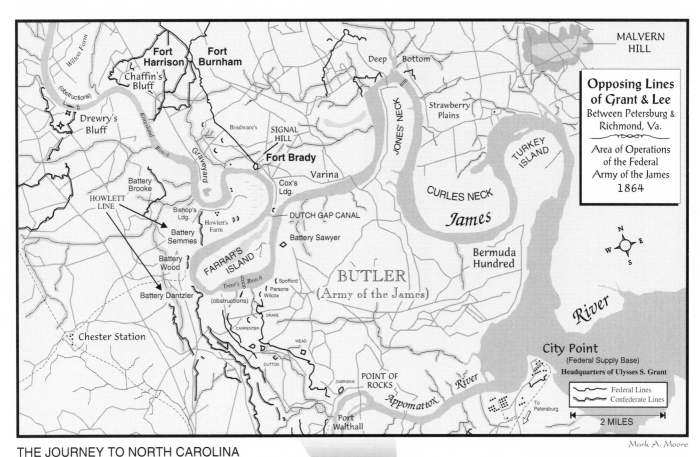

Opposing Lines of Grant & Lee
Between Petersburg & Richmond, Va.

Area of Operations of the Federal Army of the James 1864

Mark A. Moore

THE JOURNEY TO NORTH CAROLINA

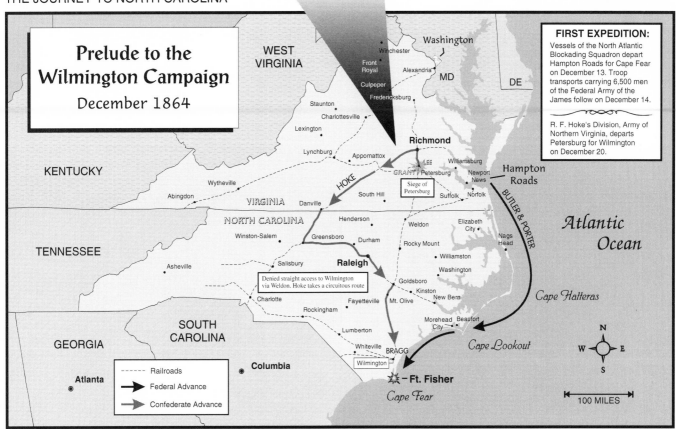

Prelude to the Wilmington Campaign
December 1864

FIRST EXPEDITION: Vessels of the North Atlantic Blockading Squadron depart Hampton Roads for Cape Fear on December 13. Troop transports carrying 6,500 men of the Federal Army of the James follow on December 14.

R. F. Hoke's Division, Army of Northern Virginia, departs Petersburg for Wilmington on December 20.

Denied straight access to Wilmington via Weldon, Hoke takes a circuitous route

Railroads
Federal Advance
Confederate Advance

Mark A. Moore

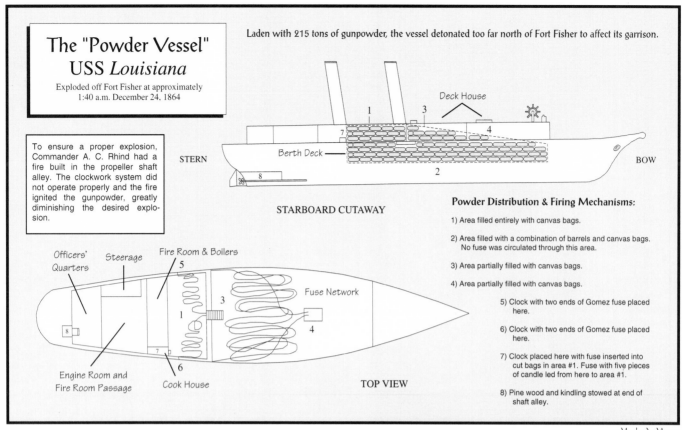

The "Powder Vessel" USS *Louisiana*

Exploded off Fort Fisher at approximately 1:40 a.m. December 24, 1864

Laden with 215 tons of gunpowder, the vessel detonated too far north of Fort Fisher to affect its garrison.

Deck House

STERN

BOW

Berth Deck

STARBOARD CUTAWAY

To ensure a proper explosion, Commander A. C. Rhind had a fire built in the propeller shaft alley. The clockwork system did not operate properly and the fire ignited the gunpowder, greatly diminishing the desired explosion.

Officers' Quarters

Steerage

Fire Room & Boilers

Fuse Network

Engine Room and Fire Room Passage

Cook House

TOP VIEW

Powder Distribution & Firing Mechanisms:

1) Area filled entirely with canvas bags.

2) Area filled with a combination of barrels and canvas bags. No fuse was circulated through this area.

3) Area partially filled with canvas bags.

4) Area partially filled with canvas bags.

5) Clock with two ends of Gomez fuse placed here.

6) Clock with two ends of Gomez fuse placed here.

7) Clock placed here with fuse inserted into cut bags in area #1. Fuse with five pieces of candle led from here to area #1.

8) Pine wood and kindling stowed at end of shaft alley.

Mark A. Moore

Harper's Weekly

USS *Louisiana*

RATE: Fourth; TONNAGE: 295; CLASS: Screw Steamer; CREW: 85; GUNS: 5

During her career the *Louisiana* had captured three blockade runners, and participated in the Federal conquests of Elizabeth City and New Bern, North Carolina. Stripped and laden with gunpowder, the sacrificial vessel was disguised as a blockade runner in order to escape suspicion as it approached Fort Fisher.

Maj. Gen. Benjamin F. Butler

Like Braxton Bragg, Ben Butler had a reputation that preceded him. His powerful political connections in Washington were often a source of anger and resentment among his peers in the army, and his career had been marked by controversy. Though a failure at field command, the eccentric Butler was a man of ideas, a lofty visionary who was enthralled by new technology.

A Mere Puff of Smoke

"I had no confidence in the success of the scheme, and so expressed myself."
— **Ulysses S. Grant**, General-in-Chief, United States Army

By late October 1864, the U.S. Navy's massive armada of warships and transports had been assembled at Hampton Roads, Virginia. Adm. David D. Porter was ready to begin the expedition against Fort Fisher. Ulysses S. Grant, however, had yet to furnish the army ground forces necessary for the operation's success. After visiting with Grant, Porter came away feeling that the general was stalling for lack of interest, and felt that Grant simply wanted to end the war in Virginia—without the help of the navy. The admiral complained to the Navy Department in Washington.

Secretary of the Navy Gideon Welles sought to hurry matters by again reminding Abraham Lincoln of the importance of the army's participation. On October 28 he wrote the president: *"You are aware that owing to the shoal water at the mouth of the Cape Fear River a purely naval attack can not be undertaken against Wilmington . . . but until recently there never seems to have been a period when [the War] Department was in a condition to entertain the subject."* Welles further explained that Porter's immense flotilla was *"lying idle, awaiting the movements of the army . . . . [Braxton] Bragg has been sent from Richmond to Wilmington to prepare for the attack, and the autumn weather so favorable for such an expedition is fast passing away. The public expect this attack and the country will be distressed if it be not made; to procrastinate much longer will be to peril its success."*

Yielding to political pressure, Grant once more agreed to detach an infantry force to accompany the expedition. But by early November Maj. Gen. Benjamin F. Butler, commander of the Department of Virginia and North Carolina, had concocted an ambitious scheme to blow down the walls of Fort Fisher and stun its garrison into submission by means of a giant floating bomb. Though Lincoln showed little interest, Assistant Navy Secretary Gustavus Fox loved the idea, and ordered the navy's Bureau of Ordnance to assess its feasibility. Not without skepticism, they concluded that a "powder boat," well placed and properly fitted, just might succeed in reducing the fort. Before long Admiral Porter decided that the scheme was worth a try, much to the chagrin of General Grant and Secretary Welles. The admiral decided to sacrifice the USS *Louisiana* for the grand experiment, and by the end of November she lay at Gosport Navy Yard, where she was stripped and disguised to look like a blockade runner.

As the Federal dragnet off Cape Fear tightened in late 1864, the number of captured blockade runners increased. Though quick to berate his subordinates for perceived greediness, Porter lined his pockets with large sums afforded by the 1798 Prize Law of the Navy, which gave the captors of illicit cargo a hefty reward. But with early December came Grant's turn to become impatient about the delay in embarking for North Carolina. He had recently learned of Bragg's departure from Cape Fear with reinforcements to oppose Sherman's advance in Georgia. In his opinion, now was the time to act. On the 4th he wrote to Butler: *"I feel great anxiety to see the Wilmington expedition off . . . . Sherman may be expected to strike the sea coast [at Savannah] any day, leaving Bragg free to return. I think it advisable to notify Admiral Porter and get off without any delay with or without your powder boat."* Grant hounded Butler repeatedly until mid-December, when the flotilla finally got under way.

The transports carrying 6,500 men of the Federal Army of the James arrived off Cape Fear on December 15. Porter arrived on the 18th with 64 warships, having stopped at Beaufort, N.C., to take on fuel and ammunition for his unwieldy ironclad monitors, and to finish fitting the *Louisiana* with a huge complement of gunpowder.

On Monday, December 19, the favorable weather at Cape Fear deteriorated. A violent gale blew in, disrupting the fleet, and forcing the army transports to return to Beaufort for four days. The warships remained off Cape Fear. Onshore the Confederates made good use of the bad weather, which gave them more time to prepare for the coming assault. Colonel William Lamb removed his slave laborers from the area, and evacuated his wife and children to Orton Plantation on the west side of the Cape Fear. By December 17, Bragg had returned to Wilmington.

The long awaited Federal invasion was at hand. With great reluctance, Robert E. Lee finally dispatched a force of veteran infantry to oppose the impending attack on Wilmington. On December 20, Maj. Gen. Robert F. Hoke's Division set out on a miserable journey by rail to North Carolina.

By December 23, the Federals were preparing to launch the powder boat against Fort Fisher. With the fleet stationed 12 miles out, Cmdr. A. C. Rhind steered the *Louisiana*, burdened with 215 tons of powder, toward the shore. Under cover of darkness, the USS *Wilderness* towed her into the shallows. After setting an elaborate fuse and clockwork system and building a fire in the shaft alley, Rhind dropped anchor, abandoned the doomed ship, and was pulled in a launch to the *Wilderness*. By the sound of the crashing waves he estimated the powder vessel was about 300 yards from the Northeast Bastion of Fort Fisher. It was 12:20 a.m. Unbeknownst to Rhind, an undertow and offshore breeze had pulled the *Louisiana* off course.

The Federals waited impatiently for the grand finale. Finally, at 1:40 a.m. on Christmas Eve, the floating bomb erupted in bright flames and a shock wave rolled across the ocean, gently rattling the spars and rigging of the vessels. But Fort Fisher remained intact, for the *Louisiana* had detonated too far from the structure to cause any damage. "Butler's Folly" had proven a complete failure, and when word reached Washington Secretary Welles lamented in his diary that the whole affair had ended in *"a mere puff of smoke."*

"It was a much too clear and starlight night for such a purpose . . . the parapets and embrasures of the fort loomed up almost as distinctly as in the day time . . . . It took some twelve or fifteen minutes for [Commander Rhind] to start the clocks, and adjust the fuzes, which being done he gave the signal, and we pulled him alongside [in a launch]. The rebels now discovered us and challenged us from the beach, but we cut the hawser by which we were moored and the little Wilderness *dashed forward to seaward as if she too knew the value of every moment of time till we were out of range of the guns of the fort and clear of the powder ship . . . . [T]he* Louisiana *blew with a terrific explosion. An immense column of flame rose towards the sky, and four distinct reports like that of sharp heavy thunder were heard and a dense mass of smoke enveloped everything."*
— **Lt. Roswell H. Lamson**, USS *Gettysburg*, in command of the *Wilderness* for the grand experiment

"I watched the burning vessel for half an hour . . . . Returning to my quarters, I laid down on my lounge to get a rest before the anticipated engagement next day [when] I felt a gentle rocking of the small brick house . . . which I would have attributed to imagination or vertigo, but it was instantly followed by an explosion, sounding very little louder than the report of a ten-inch Columbiad . . . . The vessel was doubtless afloat when the explosion occurred [as opposed to grounded], or the result might have been very serious."
— **Col. William Lamb**, Commander of Fort Fisher

"On the 24th, I took my position in the line . . . with a kedge upon my port quarter, acting as a spring, letting go my port anchor, with 25 fathoms of chain, which brought my starboard broadsides to bear upon the forts. I immediately opened a vigorous fire upon the batteries, paying special attention to Fort Fisher [Northeast Bastion] with my XI-inch gun, and to the Mound with my two 100-pounder Parrotts, and with my IX-inch guns to the batteries more immediately abreast of us . . . I got underway, continuing the action, and stood into 4½ fathoms water, from which every shot told with great effect . . . At 3:10 p.m. the end of our spanker gaff was shot away, and our flag came down with it . . . about the same time the rebel flag [on the Northeast Bastion] was shot away and was not raised again during the action. At 3:45 p.m. the flagstaff on the Mound was shot away, which shot is claimed by our pivot rifle.

"On the 25th . . . at 2:10 p.m. we opened fire, which was replied to by the batteries abreast of us more vigorously than the day before . . . At 3:30 p.m. a port main shroud was shot away [and] soon after we were struck three times in pretty rapid succession. One shot struck us under No. 3 port, 3 feet above the water line, passing through into a store room, and depositing itself in a mattress; it is a solid VIII-inch shot. Two shot struck under No. 2 port, 20 inches below the water line, one remaining in the side and the other going through and lodging in a beam on the orlop deck, causing the ship to leak badly. A glancing shot struck the stern of the ship, but did no material injury, and some of our running rigging was shot away . . . . [I]t appears to me utterly impossible that any works could withstand such a fire [as ours] and not be terribly damaged." —**Commodore James Findlay Schenck**, commander, USS *Powhatan*, Line No. 2, Christmas 1864 bombardment of Fort Fisher

"On the [morning] of the 25th instant at 9:10 the fleet was again in motion and bearing down to the scene of the previous day's conflict. Their relative position was the same, with the difference that the larger number took position so as to fire on the land face of the fort . . . the [*New*] *Ironsides* leading. The position of a double-turreted monitor [*Monadnock*] immediately off the redan [Northeast Bastion] enabled us to bring a 10-inch columbiad, No. 27, and an 8-inch columbiad, No. 25, on her, but we could not be said to have affected her fire in any way. During this day's fight the guns of the fort were fired with even greater deliberation than the day previous . . . but the effect of the enemy's fire upon the armament of the fort was more severe." —**Maj. William J. Saunders**, Col. William Lamb's Chief of Artillery during the Christmas 1864 bombardment of Fort Fisher

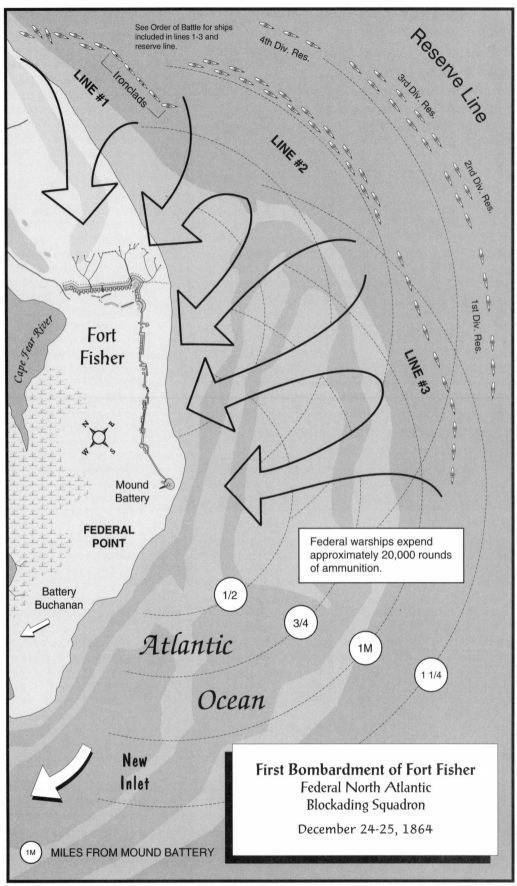

See Order of Battle for ships included in lines 1-3 and reserve line.

Reserve Line

4th Div. Res.

3rd Div. Res.

2nd Div. Res.

1st Div. Res.

LINE #1

Ironclads

LINE #2

LINE #3

Cape Fear River

Fort Fisher

Mound Battery

FEDERAL POINT

Battery Buchanan

Federal warships expend approximately 20,000 rounds of ammunition.

1/2

3/4

1M

1 1/4

Atlantic

Ocean

New Inlet

First Bombardment of Fort Fisher
Federal North Atlantic Blockading Squadron

December 24-25, 1864

1M MILES FROM MOUND BATTERY

Mark A. Moore

The Christmas Battle

"The first shot fired by the enemy was from the [USS New] Ironsides. . . . Soon after the bombardment commenced in earnest, shot and shell, shrapnel, &c., flying thick as hail, but perhaps a little hotter."
— **Capt. Samuel B. Hunter**, Company F, 36th North Carolina Regiment

From Wilmington, on the eve of the first bombardment of Fort Fisher, Maj. Gen. W. H. C. Whiting was still complaining to Confederate authorities about the shortage of manpower at Cape Fear. *"We seem in the midst of disasters all round,"* he worried. *"Our position here is very precarious, and as the enemy's fleet are off New Inlet in heavy force, in our present depleted condition it may be carried at any moment unless the enemy delay until Hoke [arrives]."* Though Robert F. Hoke's Division had departed the Army of Northern Virginia on December 20, it had not yet reached Wilmington, let alone points south. As the menacing Federal fleet drew in close to the shallows off Federal Point on Christmas Eve morning, Whiting waited with "great anxiety" for the arrival of his reinforcements.

December 24, 1864, dawned with a thick fog shrouding the ocean, as the grand armada began moving westward toward its assigned battle position. As the morning wore on, the mist burned off and the imposing array of 64 warships was plainly visible to the Confederates onshore: *"A grander sight than the approach of Porter's formidable Armada towards the fort was never witnessed on our coast,"* observed Col. William Lamb. *"With the rising sun out of old ocean there came upon the horizon one after another, the vessels of the fleet, the grand frigates leading the van, followed by the iron-clads."* The Federal navy's five largest frigates were on hand for the occasion: the *Susquehanna*, *Wabash*, *Colorado*, *Powhatan*, and *Minnesota*. Colonel Lamb correctly noted that some of these "floating fortresses" alone had nearly as many or more guns than all of Fort Fisher could train upon the enemy. By this time the fort had 47 heavy guns and mortars placed for battle, exclusive of its light artillery. The USS *Colorado* alone weighed in with 52 guns. These vessels, combined with the remaining warships of various classes, afforded the North Atlantic Blockading Squadron an astounding 630 cannons.

"On the vessels came," remembered Lamb, *"growing larger and more imposing as the distance lessened between them and the resolute men who had rallied to defend their homes."* At 12:40 p.m., as she approached her battle station, the USS *New Ironsides* opened the contest by hurling a massive 11-inch shell toward the fort. With a few range-finding shots the Federals found their mark, and enemy iron began to rain upon Fort Fisher. As the other warships came into position they faced their starboard sides to the shore and joined the action, stretching in a large arc just off the shoal waters of Cape Fear. Onshore the Confederates answered with a round from a 10-inch columbiad in the Pulpit Battery. The spherical shot glanced off the surface of the ocean and punched a hole through the smokestack of the *Susquehanna*. The remaining guns of the garrison opened on the fleet, the exchange escalating to a deafening thunder as the two sides commenced a naval bombardment of proportions unimagined until this point in the war.

The clamor and concussion of heavy weapons soon took their toll on both ships and gunners, and the *"ocean fairly trembled"* under the din of battle. Aboard several vessels the concussion from continual firing tore loose or damaged some of the ships' cutters and other fittings. The begrimed sailors toiled with powder-blackened faces, burning eyes, and clothes dusted with saltpeter. A few bled from the nose as their bodies absorbed the shock. It was not much better for Confederate gunners onshore. The tight space of the gun emplacements, which were surrounded on three sides by traverses and parapet, worsened the effects of concussion. Private George W. Benson and his battery mates stood on their tiptoes and held their mouths wide open with each shot: *"If you didn't, it would knock you silly and jar your teeth out."*

The day was bright, with little or no breeze to disperse the cloying gunpowder smoke which soon enshrouded everything. On some of the ships, spotters were sent high up into the rigging to better assess the damage being inflicted upon the fort. Many of the projectiles overshot their mark and splashed harmlessly into the Cape Fear River. These errant rounds kept the Confederate gunboat *Chickamauga*, which had come down the river to lend her support, at a safe distance. Between palls of smoke the sailors could see occasional geysers of sand as their shots told upon the battlements. By mid-afternoon the little brick building of Lamb's headquarters had been knocked to pieces. Flames from the burning barracks onshore were visible from the fleet, and clouds of thick black smoke billowed into the air. It looked bad, and Admiral Porter was sure that Fort Fisher was being destroyed.

For their part, the Confederates were conservative with return fire, each gun averaging a shot once every half-hour. The smoke made it difficult to assess any damage done to the fleet. Fort Fisher contained about 3,600 rounds when the fight began, and Colonel Lamb wanted to be sure he had plenty to expend should the enemy attempt to cross the bar and enter New Inlet. Nevertheless, the Federal warships began to feel the sting of Confederate fire, with damage ranging from light to severe. Five vessels had 100-pounder Parrott rifles burst from the strain of heavy use, and these accidents inflicted more Union casualties than were received from enemy fire.

Despite the noisy pyrotechnic display Fort Fisher weathered the storm well, suffering few casualties and the loss of several guns. Structural damage to the earthen batteries was light, and nothing that could not be repaired. *"Never since the invention of gunpowder,"* boasted Lamb, *"was there so much of it harmlessly expended as in the first day's attack on Fort Fisher."* At dusk, after having engaged the fort for more than five hours, the fleet hauled off and returned to positions further out to sea. General Whiting, however, knew the contest was far from over, and he expected an enemy landing party on Federal Point at any time. As expected, the fleet returned on Christmas morning to once again pummel the Confederate shore installations, including Battery Gatlin and Battery Anderson north of the fort. The Federals shelled these areas incessantly to soften resistance prior to sending a ground force ashore to attack Fort Fisher.

"It has not been my lot to witness any operation comparable in force or in effect to the bombardment of Fort Fisher by the fleet, and I feel satisfied that any attempt to keep out of their bombproofs or to work their guns would have been attended with great loss of life to the rebels, and would have proven a fruitless attempt."
— **Cmdr. Daniel Ammen**, USS *Mohican*

"During this [Christmas] day's bombardment the enemy must have fired at least 15,000 shells, and never since the foundation of the world was there such a fire. The whole interior of the fort, which consists of sand, merlons, etc., was as one XI-inch shell bursting. You can now inspect the whole works and walk on nothing but iron."
— **Lt. Richard F. Armstrong**, Confederate States Navy, engaged on the Sea Face of Fort Fisher

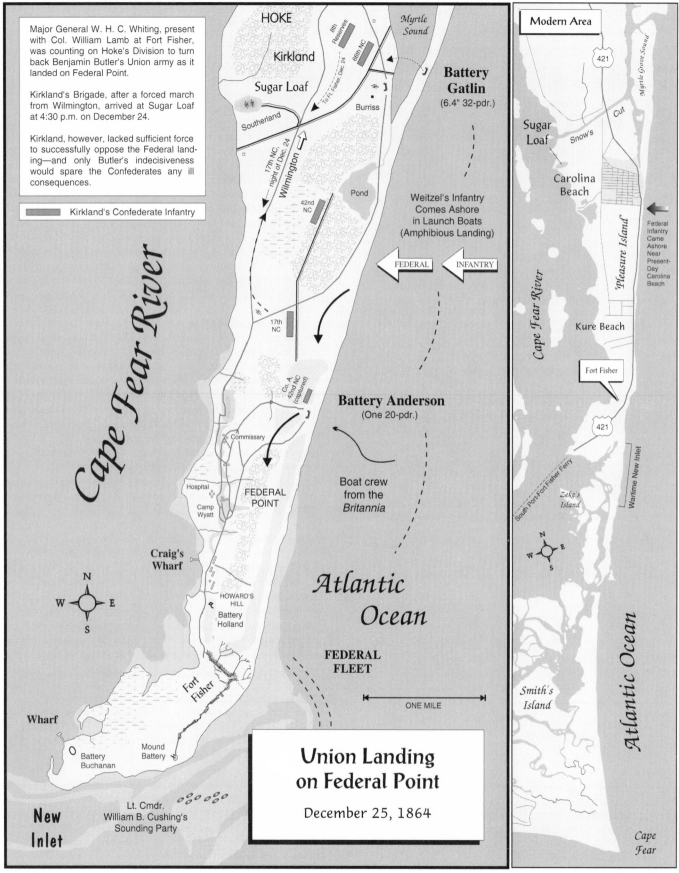

Major General W. H. C. Whiting, present with Col. William Lamb at Fort Fisher, was counting on Hoke's Division to turn back Benjamin Butler's Union army as it landed on Federal Point.

Kirkland's Brigade, after a forced march from Wilmington, arrived at Sugar Loaf at 4:30 p.m. on December 24.

Kirkland, however, lacked sufficient force to successfully oppose the Federal landing—and only Butler's indecisiveness would spare the Confederates any ill consequences.

Kirkland's Confederate Infantry

HOKE

Kirkland

Sugar Loaf

Southerland

8th Reserves

66th NC

Myrtle Sound

Battery Gatlin
(6.4" 32-pdr.)

To Ft Fisher, Dec. 24

Burriss

17th NC, night of Dec. 24

Wilmington

42nd NC

Pond

Weitzel's Infantry Comes Ashore in Launch Boats (Amphibious Landing)

FEDERAL INFANTRY

17th NC

Co. A, 42nd NC (captured)

Battery Anderson
(One 20-pdr.)

Commissary

Hospital

Camp Wyatt

FEDERAL POINT

Boat crew from the *Britannia*

Cape Fear River

Craig's Wharf

HOWARD'S HILL

Battery Holland

Atlantic Ocean

FEDERAL FLEET

ONE MILE

N W E S

Wharf

Fort Fisher

Battery Buchanan

Mound Battery

New Inlet

Lt. Cmdr. William B. Cushing's Sounding Party

Union Landing on Federal Point

December 25, 1864

Modern Area

421

Sugar Loaf

Snow's Cut

Myrtle Grove Sound

Carolina Beach

"Pleasure Island"

Federal Infantry Came Ashore Near Present-Day Carolina Beach

Cape Fear River

Kure Beach

Fort Fisher

421

Wartime New Inlet

South Port-Fort Fisher Ferry

Zeke's Island

Atlantic Ocean

N W E S

Smith's Island

Cape Fear

Mark A. Moore

"[Our advance] pressed close upon and drove their skirmish line back upon their main body, which was covered by the guns of at least thirty men of war lying broadside to the beach. It would have been madness to have advanced farther."
— **Brig. Gen. William W. Kirkland**, commanding brigade, Hoke's Division

Major Gen. W. H. C. Whiting entered Fort Fisher late on the afternoon of December 24, 1864, just as the Federal naval bombardment began to diminish in intensity. Though the fort had thus far withstood a terrific pounding from the fleet, Whiting knew a Federal ground attack was imminent. He was banking on the arrival of Hoke's Division to repel the enemy landing on Federal Point.

The lead elements of Hoke's force had finally pulled into Wilmington around midnight on December 23, after a long and harried rail journey from Virginia. Soon after sunrise on the 24th Brig. Gen. William W. Kirkland set his brigade in motion for Federal Point. Kirkland reached Sugar Loaf at 1:00 p.m. and his command of 1,300 men arrived by 4:30, about the same time Whiting reached Fort Fisher. At Sugar Loaf Kirkland found a small collection of local militia units, including about 800 boys from the 4th, 7th, and 8th Battalions of North Carolina Junior Reserves, and 400 men of the 8th North Carolina Senior Reserves. Also present was a detachment of the 2nd South Carolina Cavalry, an artillery battery commanded by Lt. Col. John P. W. Read, and Capt. Thomas J. Southerland's company of the 10th North Carolina Regiment (1st Artillery). Local ordnance included two Whitworth guns from Southerland's and Capt. Andrew Paris' batteries. General Kirkland assumed command of the local units and deployed his troops along the Sugar Loaf line, whose breastworks spanned the peninsula for the distance of one mile between Sugar Loaf Hill and Myrtle Sound. It would be up to Kirkland to turn back an enemy ground force attempting to land on Federal Point.

On Christmas morning about 20 Union warships moved into position off Federal Point, several miles north of Fort Fisher. They began shelling the beach and surrounding woods to soften resistance prior to putting an infantry force ashore. General Kirkland's regiments took cover as best they could while the warships, led by the USS *Brooklyn*, shelled Battery Gatlin and Battery Anderson to assure a safe landing zone for Federal troops.

Shortly before 2:00 p.m. Confederates troops observed the steam transports lowering their gigs and launches, which soon formed a long line as the infantry of Brig. Gen. Adelbert Ames' division was ferried ashore. At 2:10 p.m. Bvt. Brig. Gen. N. Martin Curtis was the first Federal soldier to hit the beach, followed closely by Gen. Godfrey Weitzel and 500 men of Curtis' brigade. Ulysses S. Grant had chosen Weitzel alone to command the expedition against Fort Fisher, but to Grant's displeasure Benjamin Butler managed to take the reins from Weitzel. The controversial Butler was already at odds with Adm. David D. Porter over the conduct of the campaign, and the interservice rivalry did not bode well for success of the expedition.

As the launches hit the beach the Federal infantry poured ashore, sparring with Kirkland's skirmishers all the while. General Curtis planted a naval standard on a nearby sand dune to mark the landing zone, and quickly formed a party to reconnoiter Fort Fisher. As Ames' remaining brigades landed, Curtis struck southward with 450 men of the 142nd New York and 50 men of the 112th New York regiments. As they neared Battery Anderson, Company A of the 42nd North Carolina began waving a flag of surrender. This company held the isolated extreme right flank of Kirkland's thinly-stretched line, and

the fast approaching enemy would overrun it before the nearest supporting troops could arrive. The white flag attracted the attention of sharp-eyed sailors aboard the nearby warships, and several of them hastily lowered gigs to row ashore and capture the Confederates at Battery Anderson before Curtis' infantry could get there. A boat crew from the *Britannia* won the race, and the honor of having bagged the first Rebel prisoners of the campaign.

General Kirkland pushed southward with the 17th North Carolina, but after briefly engaging the enemy found he was out numbered. He was also too far from his main line at Sugar Loaf, and if the growing number of Union troops on the beach should suddenly turn northward, there would be only the Reserves and 100 men of the 66th North Carolina to stop them. If the line broke, the road to Wilmington would be wide open. Under cover of a strong picket force, Kirkland wisely decided to withdraw his command to Sugar Loaf to await further reinforcements from Hoke's Division.

As Weitzel's infantry came ashore, the Federal fleet continued its unmerciful bombardment of Fort Fisher, upon the Sea Face in particular. Admiral Porter wanted to silence the Mound Battery and others nearest New Inlet before trying to get his light-draft gunboats into the Cape Fear River. At 2:00 p.m., in order to assure his ships a safe course across the bar, Porter dispatched a party of small boats under Lt. Cmdr. William B. Cushing to find the channel and take soundings. This foray was soon cut short by a furious fire from the Mound Battery and Battery Buchanan at the inlet. Their accurate fire shattered one of Cushing's boats and drove the rest back toward their ships. The impatient Porter steamed in aboard his flagship *Malvern* for a closer look at the channel, and the ship promptly received an iron bolt through its boiler from Fisher's 150-pounder Armstrong gun. Despite two days of grueling bombardment it was apparent that the Confederate guns had not been silenced, and Porter was satisfied that the inlet was too dangerous to cross without being properly marked.

Several miles up the peninsula, N. Martin Curtis was advancing his reconnaissance-in-force toward Fort Fisher. Having missed much of the war, due to injuries received in Virginia during the Peninsula Campaign of 1862 and subsequent departmental duty, General Curtis was anxious to engage the Confederates in battle.

"[T]he ironclads and their consorts thundered away at Fort Fisher with such stunning violence that the ocean fairly trembled. I can imagine nothing like the bellowing of our fifteen inch guns . . . . The din was deafening. Above the fort the countless flash[es] and puffs of smoke from bursting shells spoke for the accuracy of our guns [and] columns of sand heaved high in the air suggested that possibly the casements were not so safe and cozy after all . . . . We watched [the landing of Curtis' brigade] anxiously. Before they touched shore, the men were over the sides of the boats waist deep in water and were actually deploying . . . skirmishing and advancing at a double quick ere they had reached dry land. A rousing cheer—a stentorian Christmas cheer—went up from the whole fleet." —**Edward King Wightman**, 3rd New York, Curtis' brigade, from a vantage point aboard the transport *Weybosset*

"It was pitiful to see some of those gray-haired patriots [of the Senior Reserves] dead in the woods, killed by shells from the fleet. Among those who carried a musket there was Mr. William Pettigrew, brother of the heroic General [J. Johnston Pettigrew] . . . . [I] saw the ships extending as far as I could see down the beach [and] rode down through the woods and found a large [Federal] force on the beach and more coming, while the woods around us were filled with shrieking shells." —**Capt. Charles G. Elliott**, Assistant Adjutant-General, Kirkland's Brigade, on Federal Point during the Union landing

"**A** tongue of land runs down from the main, having the Atlantic on one side and the Cape Fear River on the other, called Federal Point . . . . About two miles north of [New Inlet] was the land face of Fort Fisher, its immense traverses looking from [our] ship's deck like a row of mounds in a grave yard . . . . It was a beautiful sight to see the boats as they started together for the shore, [and] it was the general opinion of the officers and men on the spot, that the Fort could have been taken at that time by vigorous assault." —**William L. Hyde**, Chaplain, 112th New York, Curtis' brigade

"**T**he curtain [of Fort Fisher's Land Face] does not extend all the way to the Cape Fear River. I think that troops could march into the work through this interval. I saw Fort Wagner [on Morris Island, South Carolina]; I would rather assault Fort Fisher from what I saw. I think that the One hundred and forty-second New York Volunteers could have marched in and taken the work. From all that I saw the rebels seemed to be very much demoralized. There were no rebels on guard up to the time that General Curtis and his staff moved with the flag off the fort; from that time out a slight fire was continued . . . . I was sanguine that the work could be taken." —**Lt. George W. Ross**, aide-de-camp on the staff of Gen. N. Martin Curtis, present during the reconnaissance of Fort Fisher, December 25, 1864. Lieutenant Ross correctly assessed the fort's Achilles' heel.

"**O**ur regiment reached Wilmington during the night of the 24th, and on the morning of the 25th, Christmas day, took up its weary march along the sandy road below Wilmington in the direction of Sugar Loaf Hill. As it went along and drew nearer and nearer to Fort Fisher, the sound of the shelling from the gunboats assembled there could be more and more distinctly heard, and as we reached a point just below Sugar Loaf Hill . . . the shelling from the gunboats became terrific . . . . [W]e were very soon engaged in quite a strong skirmish with those of the enemy who had landed and were about to land and they were soon driven back. Immediately after this first shelling was over, the division commenced to build a line of breastworks from the top of Sugar Loaf Hill diagonally across the strip of land between it and the ocean and in the direction of a battery which was located on the beach. Here we remained for some days, throwing up the fortifications which we made strong and, to us, seemed impregnable for any land attack that could be made by land forces; but we were not long allowed to remain . . . [We] were ordered back to Wilmington . . . for the purpose of holding a grand review." —**George M. Rose**, Adjutant, 66th North Carolina, Kirkland's Brigade

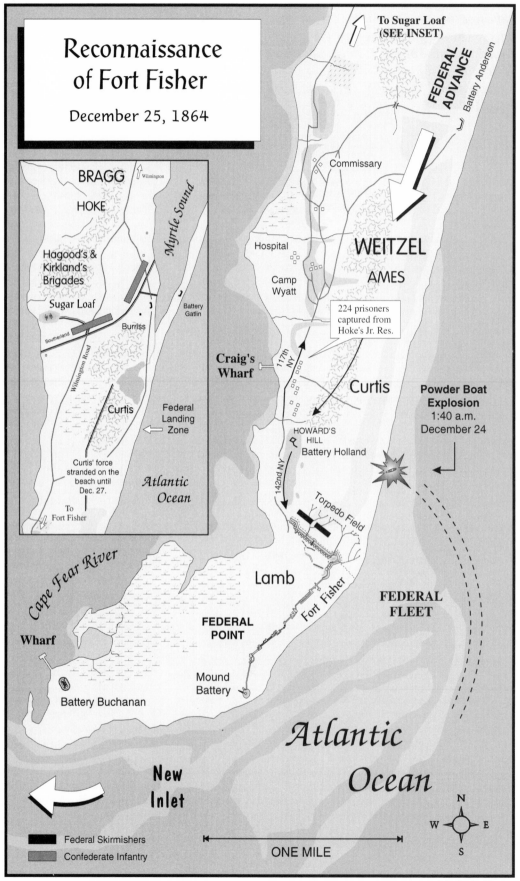

Reconnaissance of Fort Fisher

December 25, 1864

Mark A. Moore

"I saw plainly that [Fort Fisher] had not been materially injured by the heavy and very accurate shell fire of the navy . . . and having a distinct and vivid recollection of the two unsuccessful assaults on Fort Wagner [S.C.], both of which were made under four times more favorable circumstances than those under which we were placed, I returned [to Gen. Benjamin F. Butler aboard the gunboat Chamberlain] *and frankly reported to him that it would be butchery to order an assault on that work under the circumstances."*
— **Maj. Gen. Godfrey Weitzel**, commanding XXV Army Corps

Around 3:00 p.m. on Christmas afternoon Gen. Godfrey Weitzel and Bvt. Brig. Gen. N. Martin Curtis, with about 250 men of the 142nd New York, advanced to within one and one-half miles of the Land Face of Fort Fisher. Weitzel peered through his field glass across the open plain below, which had been cleared of foliage to give the Confederates a clear field of fire. From his vantage point on a small ridge the general could see no evidence of damage to the massive fort, and he counted at least 17 heavy guns still in position between the high traverses. Weitzel had never before seen so large a defensive structure, and he was mindful of previous disasters suffered when attacking installations far less formidable than Fort Fisher. His overall assessment for a successful ground campaign was bleak, and Weitzel wanted to discuss the matter with Gen. Benjamin Butler. Before heading back up the beach Weitzel gave General Curtis permission to get a closer look at the Confederate bastion, but instructed him not to bring on a general engagement until Weitzel had conferred with Butler.

By the time Curtis neared Fort Fisher, he had only a small skirmish line. The rest of the force had been deposited as flankers along the route southward, *"thus leaving every twenty or thirty paces a soldier to warn the line of any approach of the enemy from the forest,"* remembered Curtis, *"which was some thirty or forty rods to the west of us toward the Cape Fear River."* When the reconnaissance force reached Howard's Hill and the abandoned Battery Holland, Curtis viewed the imposing bastion, noting the conspicuous absence of enemy troops on the battlements. Emboldened by having received no challenge thus far from the fort's defenders, Curtis pushed his men to within 75 yards of Shepherd's Battery at the fort's western salient. The Federals were about as far as they could safely advance, and the continuing naval bombardment caused a few friendly casualties among Curtis' skirmishers.

As incoming rounds from the fleet crashed along the northern front of the fort, several of Curtis' men decided to move in for a closer look. Around 3:20 p.m. Lt. William H. Walling scampered through a shot-induced hole in the fort's palisade fence and hauled off a flag—a *"large garrison flag,"* boasted Curtis—that had been blown down from Shepherd's Battery by naval gunfire. From his hiding place along the River Road near the sally port, Pvt. Henry Blair shot and killed Confederate Pvt. Amos H. Jones, a young mounted courier outbound with a dispatch asking for light artillery reinforcements for the fort.

But the most interesting foray by one of General Curtis' men was made by Lt. George Simpson, an aide-de-camp on the general's staff. After having freed an unfortunate mule from its dead harnessmate near the sally port, Private Simpson rode the beast back to the Federal skirmish line. Soon thereafter he spied the telegraph wire running northward from the fort. Simpson shinned up the telegraph

pole and severed the line with a hatchet. The view of Fort Fisher from Simpson's perch on the telegraph pole was an enlightening one. He could see that the work consisted of only two sides which converged near the ocean. Based on previous assessments, General Weitzel and others still believed the fort to be a four-sided structure. Simpson could now see that the rear of Fort Fisher was completely open. The news excited Curtis, and similar testimony from several other skirmishers strengthened his own conviction that the bastion could be captured by an infantry assault. Curtis sent word to his reserves to hurry toward the front.

Benjamin Butler, however, agreed with Weitzel's assessment that it was too risky to attempt a ground assault. The hour was growing late, he reasoned, and Federal troops might not be safe on the beach after dark, owing to the presence of Confederate infantry at Sugar Loaf. Butler called a halt to the expedition.

Dark clouds gathered at dusk over Federal Point, and the wind picked up considerably. Curtis, too, worried over the safety of his men, but felt it would be a mistake to retreat when the fort was ripe for the taking. Chief Engineer Cyrus Comstock and Gen. Adelbert Ames reached Battery Holland at nightfall, and Ames encouraged Curtis to make an attack. Comstock agreed, and in the gathering gloom the Federal skirmish line, composed of elements of the 3rd, 117th and 142nd New York regiments, advanced on Fort Fisher.

At dark the incessant naval bombardment abruptly ceased. Like General Whiting, William Lamb felt this signaled a ground attack, and the wily colonel hurried many of his troops from their bombproofs on both faces of the work to man the northern battlements. The fort's reluctant Junior Reserves and other soldiers poured through the main sally port and manned the slight depression behind the palisades. Colonel Lamb stood on the parapet as the oncoming Federals shot blindly in the dark. He then gave the order to fire and his troops and artillery at the sally ports opened upon the attackers.

The heavy return fire startled General Ames and Colonel Comstock. The fort had suddenly produced a large force of defenders where there seemed to be none only a short time earlier. The bombardment had not greatly affected the garrison after all. After briefly squabbling over continuing the attack, Comstock and Ames heeded Butler's orders and returned to the landing zone. Curtis remained until one of Ames' staff officers arrived to tell the disappointed general that most of the main body of Federal troops had returned to the transports offshore. Curtis and his men were virtually alone on the windswept peninsula. He reluctantly gave in and marched the troops back to the landing zone, but the deteriorating weather had whipped the ocean into a frenzy, leaving the general and more than 600 of his command stranded on the beach for two days.

"[A] large shell from one of the monitors struck the ground near us, ploughing a trench so deep that some of our men took refuge therein, the shell ricochetting [sic] into the river beyond. Another shot cut down the Confederate flag from the fort . . . . I had gone but a few steps when one of the great monitor shells passed in front of me and exploded before reaching the river. I confess I was frightened, and for an instant halted involuntarily, stunned by the fearful crash . . . . [A] shell had cut a hole in the palisade . . . . I entered, passed along toward the river, gained the parapet, secured the flag and returned, uninjured as I had gone, to the picket line."
—**Lt. William H. Walling**, 142nd New York, Curtis' brigade

"In the evening, about sundown, I saw the enemy advancing under cover of the houses in front of the fort. I opened on them with grape and canister . . . . I did not capture any of the enemy, but am confident that I killed some."
—**Lt. Irvin Fulford**, Company K, 10th North Carolina Regiment

▲ Brig. Gen. Adelbert Ames

Adelbert Ames graduated fifth in the West Point class of May 6, 1861. After varied and distinguished service, including a stint as commander of the 20th Maine Infantry, the first expedition against Fort Fisher found Ames in command of the Second Division, XXIV Army Corps, Army of the James.

On Christmas Day 1864, the general went ashore with his Second Brigade, after N. Martin Curtis' force had already landed. The skirmish fire was brisk, and Ames quickly informed General Butler that Kirkland's Brigade had arrived from Virginia. "It was dusk when I reached the front," Ames reported. "At this time I did not know that it had been decided not to attack the fort, and that the troops were to re-embark. Upon the report of Brevet Brigadier-General Curtis that he could take the fort I sent his brigade forward to make the attempt. By the time he reached his position it was dark, and the navy had almost entirely ceased its fire. The [Confederate] troops, which during the day had to seek shelter, now boldly manned their guns. Had the attack been made it would have failed."

Godfrey Weitzel graduated second in the West Point class of 1855. Throughout the war this talented engineer was closely associated with Benjamin Butler, having served with him during the New Orleans campaign of 1862 and later as chief engineer of Butler's Army of the James.

Weitzel was Ulysses S. Grant's first and only choice to command the expedition against Fort Fisher. The general-in-chief was furious when Butler returned to Virginia: "[I]t was never contemplated that General Butler should accompany the expedition," Grant complained to Secretary of War Edwin M. Stanton. "Weitzel was especially named as commander . . . I am inclined to ascribe the delay [in launching the expedition], which has cost us so dearly, to an experiment—I refer to the explosion of gunpowder in the open air [USS *Louisiana*]. [Butler] states that he returned after having effected a landing [but my] instructions contemplated no withdrawal, or no failure after a landing."

Maj. Gen. Godfrey Weitzel ▲

Harper's Pictorial History of the Great Rebellion in the United States

(From a photograph)

◄ Admiral David Dixon Porter

A midshipman in the U.S. Navy by the age of 15, David Dixon Porter rose to prominence in the Civil War while serving on the Mississippi River during the campaigns against New Orleans and Vicksburg. Though an excellent officer and capable commander, Porter's bombastic and boastful personality often brought conflict with his peers. The admiral and Gen. Benjamin Butler did not get along. There was an interservice rivalry between the navy and Butler's army, and Porter was openly critical of the failure of the first Wilmington expedition.

"I was in hopes I should have been able to present to the nation Fort Fisher as a Christmas offering," Porter told Secretary of the Navy Gideon Welles on December 26, "but I am sorry to say it has not been taken yet . . . . I don't pretend to put my opinion in opposition to General Weitzel, who is a thorough soldier and able engineer, and whose business it is to know more of assaulting than I do, but I can't help thinking that it was worth while [sic] to make the attempt after coming so far."

In response to Butler's explanation for calling off the ground attack, Porter could not help chiding the general about the decision. "I wish some more of your gallant fellows had followed the officer [Lt. William H. Walling] who took the flag from the parapet, and the brave fellow who brought the horse out from the fort," the admiral wrote to Butler on the 26th. "I think they would have found it an easier conquest than is supposed."

Porter further explained to the Navy Department: "I shall go on and hammer away at the forts [on Federal Point], hoping that in time the people in them will get tired and hand them over to us. It is a one-sided business altogether, and in the course of time we must dismount their guns, if, as General Weitzel says, we can not '*injure [Fort Fisher] as a defensive work*.'" Porter would be satisfied with nothing less than a total reduction of the Confederate stronghold. "The Government may also think it of sufficient importance," he predicted, "to undertake more serious operations against these works."

"Thus ended this extraordinary movement—extraordinary in the magnitude of the preparation, the formidable character of the fleet, the severity of the fire, and the feebleness of the enemy's effort on land."
— **Maj. Gen. W. H. C. Whiting**, Confederate observer, adviser and combatant at Fort Fisher

Wasting little time after the decision was made to end the expedition, Gen. Benjamin Butler departed for Hampton Roads, Virginia, on December 26. Curtis' force—stranded on Federal Point with several hundred Confederate junior reserves captured by the 117th New York—waited impatiently to return to the Federal transports. General Braxton Bragg reached Sugar Loaf just before noon on the 26th, and Maj. Gen. Robert F. Hoke arrived with Johnson Hagood's brigade and the rest of Kirkland's men later that afternoon. But instead of overwhelming Curtis' vulnerable troops Bragg was content to let them escape, and on December 27 the Federals were finally rescued. As the Union fleet sailed away from the shores of Cape Fear, Col. William Lamb had his gunners fire a defiant parting volley toward the "beaten" enemy.

Lamb and General Whiting were irritated that Bragg had not captured Curtis' troops, but Whiting was relieved that the ordeal was over. In the wake of the largest naval bombardment in history, the pragmatic engineer counted Confederate blessings and was grateful for Union inertia. *"That great and irreparable disaster did not overtake us we owe to God,"* reported Whiting. *"Whatever the power of resistance of the fort, and it is great, no doubt the delay due to the heavy weather [on December 21 and 22] after the arrival of the fleet was its salvation, the small number of artillerymen then present being totally inadequate to so extensive a line . . . . The appearance of a garrison after such a bombardment, intact and ready to repel an assault, no doubt intimidated them, while the advance of Hoke's Division completed their discomfiture; but we cannot always hope for such aid from the weather or the blunder of the enemy manifest here from his not landing and occupying [Fort Fisher] . . . and I trust the lesson will not be lost."*

As news of the failed expedition reached Washington, Navy Secretary Gideon Welles was not surprised. *"It is to be regretted that Butler went with the expedition,"* he lamented. *"He did not land [with sufficient force to attack Fort Fisher]. General Weitzel is totally under his influence and the two did nothing."* Welles went to the president with the news and *"asked what was now to be done,"* but the chief executive would only say that *"I must refer you to General Grant."*

Indeed, Abraham Lincoln had already been in contact with his general-in-chief. At 5:30 p.m. on December 28 he wired Grant for information: *"If there be no objection, please tell me what you now understand of the Wilmington expedition, present and prospective."*

An exasperated Grant replied to the president that same day: *"The Wilmington expedition has proven a gross and culpable failure. Many of the troops are now back here. Delays and free talk of the object of the expedition enabled the enemy to move troops to Wilmington to defeat it. After the expedition sailed from Fort Monroe [Va.] three days of fine weather were squandered, during which the enemy was without a force to protect himself. Who is to blame I hope will be known."*

Fort Fisher—with its garrison—was still intact, and the port of Wilmington remained open to the outside world. Before the Federal fleet was out of sight at Cape Fear the steamer *Wild Rover* ran the blockade at New Inlet on the night of December 27, followed early the next morning by the *Banshee*.

Brig. Gen. William W. Kirkland ▲

▼ **Maj. Gen. William H. C. Whiting**

Images from the *Official Records of the Union and Confederate Navies in the War of the Rebellion*

◀ USS Colorado

"A Few Days' Work Will Repair All Damage"

The Federal Navy's five largest frigates were inviting targets for Confederate gunners at Fort Fisher, and each of the five was struck by enemy fire during the Christmas 1864 bombardment. The *Colorado,* flagship of the North Atlantic Blockading Squadron's First Division, seems to have attracted the most attention.

The ship was pummeled with a combination of solid shot, bolts and shells. On December 24, she received no less than four direct hits in the vicinity of her gangway, bow, and cutwater. The stern kedge was lost, and the stream hawser was shot away, resulting in the loss of the ship's anchor.

On the 25th, the fleet stood in closer to shore, allowing Federal gun crews to fire with greater accuracy. The closer range also aided the Confederates, and the *Colorado* again felt the sting of enemy iron. As U. S. Army ground forces approached Fort Fisher that evening, the ship ceased firing for nearly 30 minutes. She quickly opened again "after we had been hulled several times by a vicious gun which appeared to be fired from the N. E. angle of Fort Fisher," reported the ship's captain. At 4:15 p.m. it was recorded in the ship's log that "shells from Fort Fisher [are] falling around us fast." Fifteen minutes later a massive 10-inch solid shot struck gun No. 4 on the main deck, killing one sailor and wounding five others. The round then passed over and carried away the axle and starboard truck of gun No. 5 on the port side of the vessel. The "Enemy are hulling us," the crew frantically signalled to the USS *Minnesota* nearby. "[F]ire for your own protection."

During two days of action, in addition to direct hits, the *Colorado* suffered heavy damage to its rigging, braces, stays, guys, bowlines, and other fittings—particularly on her starboard side.

RATE: *First*; TONNAGE: *3,425*; CLASS: *Screw Steamer*; CREW: *626*; GUNS: *52*; COMMANDER: *Commo. Henry K. Thatcher* - Rounds Expended in the Christmas Battle: *2,795*; CASUALTIES: *1 killed & 6 wounded*

Federal Warships Officially Reported as Hit or Damaged by Confederate Fire During the First Attack on Fort Fisher:

Alabama, Canonicus, Colorado, Emma, Iosco, Juniata, Mackinaw, Mahopac, Malvern, Minnesota, Osceola, Pawtuxet, Pontoosuc, Powhatan, Quaker City, Santiago de Cuba, Shenandoah, Susquehanna, Ticonderoga, Wabash

100-Pounder Parrott Rifle Accidents:
Juniata, Mackinaw, Quaker City, Ticonderoga, Yantic

LARGE WARSHIPS OF THE UNITED STATES NAVY

Casualties sustained aboard the *Wabash* during the Christmas Battle: 9 wounded

USS Wabash ▶

This illustration shows the *Wabash* from her starboard side, with a good view of the battery that bombarded Fort Fisher. On December 24, she stood inshore with the fleet, anchored in five fathoms of water. When the attack began her gunners were using 10-second fuses on their shells, and the rounds were falling short of the fort. The crew compensated by using longer-burning fuses, increasing gun elevation, and firing "on the roll to port" for maximum range. The engagement on Christmas Day found enemy gunners "making severe practice on the ship," and the crew answered with *Wabash*'s entire starboard battery.

RATE: *First*; TONNAGE: *3,274*; CLASS: *Screw Steamer*; CREW: *550*; GUNS: *46*; COMMANDER: *Capt. Melancton Smith* - Rounds Expended in the Christmas Battle: *2,468*

THE IRON-CLAD MONITOR MONADNOCK.

Harper's Pictorial History of the Great Rebellion in the United States

◀ USS Monadnock

RATE: *Third*
TONNAGE: *1,564*
CLASS: *Ironclad Steamer*
CREW: *146*
GUNS: *4*
COMMANDER: *Enoch G. Parrott*

Admiral David D. Porter's enormous fleet of 64 warships contained five armored vessels. The largest was the USS *New Ironsides*, a cumbersome, lumbering vessel covered with thick strips of iron plating. The *New Ironsides* was considered the most powerful ship in the United States Navy. She was difficult to maneuver but mounted 20 heavy cannon, including 14 eleven-inch Dahlgren guns. The other four ironclads were the monitor class gunboats *Canonicus*, *Mahopac*, *Saugus*, and *Monadnock*.

The largest of the monitors was the double-turreted *Monadnock*, which mounted four heavy guns (two per turret). Assistant Navy Secretary Gustavus Fox was critical of *Monadnock*'s design features, noting that placement of the ship's boats obstructed her field of fire. If the boats were stowed below deck, he argued, "her guns will fire in all directions excepting at each other's turret."

Despite Fox's reservations, Admiral Porter was proud of the *Monadnock*, and sang its praises openly. "From all accounts this is the best monitor afloat," he boasted, noting that she could "safely and expeditiously go anywhere, and in any weather." Porter declared that the gunboat "could ride out a gale at anchor in the Atlantic Ocean. She is certainly a most perfect success, so far as the hull and machinery are concerned . . . . The *Monadnock* is capable of crossing the ocean alone (when her compasses are once adjusted properly), and could destroy any vessel in the French or British navy, lay their towns under contribution, and return . . . without fear of being followed." "I have only to remark," Porter concluded, "that the principle [of monitor class gunboats] is a good one, if the vessels are all built like the *Monadnock*."

During the Christmas Battle Porter's ironclads were arrayed in a single line northeast of Fort Fisher, with their starboard sides toward the shore. It would be these vessels that would do most of the damage to the fort's Land Face.

"We engaged at 1,100 or 1,200 yards' distance," reported *Monadnock*'s commander E. G. Parrott. "The fire of the fort was very soon controlled by that of our ships, and during both attacks [December 24 and 25] was quite feeble, especially on the second day. I noticed long intervals of silence on the part of the rebels. Most of their guns were abandoned, and the few fired from time to time were only loaded after repeated efforts. Their men were often driven away as many as five times before completing the loading.

"The projectiles from our vessels rained upon the fort, and did, I think, whatever damage shot and shell are capable of doing to sand fortifications.

"There could have been, in my opinion, no troops in or near Fort Fisher not protected by casemates, bombproofs, or other close shelter, which were kept immediately available when a few men ventured out to load a gun. I think their number, compared with that of our land forces, must necessarily have been small [and] with great deference to the opinions of others, mine is that an [infantry] assault would have been successful . . . . Our fire [from *Monadnock*], was, I think, accurate and effective."

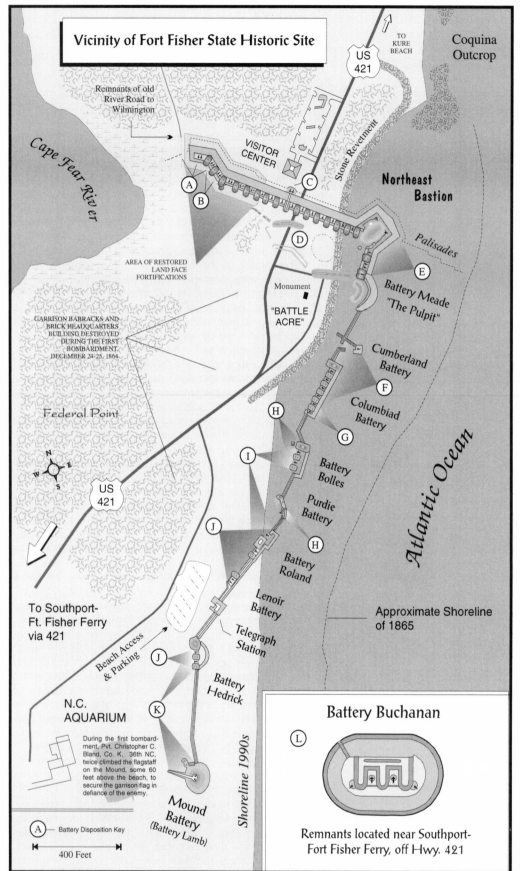

Vicinity of Fort Fisher State Historic Site

TO KURE BEACH

US 421

Coquina Outcrop

Remnants of old River Road to Wilmington

Cape Fear River

VISITOR CENTER

Stone Revetment

Northeast Bastion

A

B

C

D

AREA OF RESTORED LAND FACE FORTIFICATIONS

Palisades

Battery Meade "The Pulpit"

E

Monument

"BATTLE ACRE"

Cumberland Battery

F

GARRISON BARRACKS AND BRICK HEADQUARTERS BUILDING DESTROYED DURING THE FIRST BOMBARDMENT, DECEMBER 24-25, 1864.

Columbiad Battery

G

Federal Point

H

W N E S

US 421

I

Atlantic Ocean

Battery Bolles

Purdie Battery

H

Battery Roland

J

Approximate Shoreline of 1865

To Southport-Ft. Fisher Ferry via 421

Lenoir Battery

Telegraph Station

Beach Access & Parking

J

N.C. AQUARIUM

During the first bombardment, Pvt. Christopher C. Bland, Co. K, 36th NC, twice climbed the flagstaff on the Mound, some 60 feet above the beach, to secure the garrison flag in defiance of the enemy.

Battery Hedrick

K

Shoreline 1990s

Mound Battery (Battery Lamb)

Battery Buchanan

L

Remnants located near Southport-Fort Fisher Ferry, off Hwy. 421

A — Battery Disposition Key

400 Feet

Match battery disposition key with *Guns of Fort Fisher* section, pp. 31-32.

Mark A. Moore

Fort Fisher State Historic Site

Location:
Kure Beach, 20 miles south of Wilmington on U.S. Highway 421.

Address:
P. O. Box 169
Kure Beach, NC 28449

Tel: (910) 458-5538
Fax: (910) 458-0477

Hours:
April - October
Mon.-Sat.: 9:00 a.m.-5:00 p.m.
Sun.: 1:00 p.m.-5:00 p.m.

November - March
Tues.-Sat.: 10:00 a.m.-4:00 p.m.
Sun.: 1:00 p.m.-4:00 p.m.
Closed Monday
Closed most major holidays.

The map at left illustrates the wartime structure of Fort Fisher in relation to the modern shoreline and restored Land Face fortifications.

Erosion has taken away much of the Sea Face, and few visible traces remain of the southern seaside batteries.

A new stone revetment has been installed to help slow the effects of erosion in the vicinity of the fort's restored Land Face.

Other Points of Interest

North Carolina Aquarium at Fort Fisher
2201 Ft. Fisher Blvd. South
Kure Beach, NC 28449

Tel: (910) 458-8257
Program Information:
(910) 458-7468

Southport-Fort Fisher Ferry
P.O. Box 10028
Southport, NC 28461

Tel: 1-800-368-8969
North Carolina Ferry Information:
1-800-BY-FERRY

The Guns of Fort Fisher: December 24-25, 1864

LAND FACE
Maj. James Reilly
10th North Carolina Regiment, commanding

River Road Sally Port
(A) - Capt. John M. Sutton (December 25)
Company C, 3rd North Carolina Battalion
Ordnance
6-pounder Napoleon (light artillery)

Shepherd's Battery
(A) - Capt. John M. Sutton (December 25)
Company C, 3rd North Carolina Battalion
Ordnance
First Battery: *One 32-pounder (banded rifle):* Lt. Edward L. Faison, 36th North Carolina Regiment, commanding; *One 10-inch columbiad:* left trunion knocked off and upright and cheek of carriage broken; gun and carriage disabled
Second Battery: Lt. John G. Frame, commanding; *One 8-inch columbiad:* piece knocked off right cheek of barbette carriage; still serviceable; *One 8-inch columbiad:* struck, dented, and cracked; barbette carriage and chassis dented

(B) - Lt. George D. Parker
36th North Carolina Regiment
Ordnance
(December 24) **Second Battery:** two 8-inch columbiads
(December 25) **Third Battery:** one 8-inch columbiad and one Parrott rifle

Main Sally Port
(December 25)
(C) - Capt. Zachariah T. Adams
13th North Carolina Battalion
Ordnance
Two 12-pounder Napoleons (light artillery)

Other Land Face Batteries
(D) - Lt. Irvin Fulford
Company K, 10th North Carolina Regiment
Ordnance: five 32-pounders (smoothbore)

(D) - Lt. Thomas Arendell
Company F, 10th North Carolina Regiment
Ordnance: four 32-pounders

(D) - Capt. Daniel Patterson
Company H, 36th North Carolina Regiment
Ordnance: one 10-inch columbiad, two single-banded rifles, one double-banded rifle, and 32-pounder (smoothbore)

Ordnance Damage
32-pounder (smoothbore): rim knocked off wheel of barbette carriage and one spoke split; nuts knocked off bolts of upright; still serviceable
32-pounder (double-banded rifle): carriage struck on left trunion plate and somewhat mashed; still serviceable
32-pounder (smoothbore): right cheek of barbette carriage split and

piece knocked off lower end; still serviceable
32-pounder (smoothbore): right cheek and rear transom of carriage broken and tongue of chassis cut in two; both carriage and chassis disabled
32-pounder (smoothbore): muzzle of gun knocked off and carriage broken at trunion plate; gun and carriage disabled

NORTHEAST BASTION (The "Redan Battery") and adjoining works
(D) - Company F, 10th North Carolina Regiment
Ordnance (December 24)
One 32-pounder rifle
One 8-inch columbiad (dismounted by recoil)

(E) - Capt. Samuel B. Hunter
Company F, 36th North Carolina Regiment
Ordnance (December 24)
One 8-inch Blakely gun, and three 10-inch columbiads
Ordnance (December 25)
One 8-inch Blakely rifle, one 10-inch mortar, one 8-inch columbiad, and one 10-inch columbiad

8-inch Blakely rifle: muzzle slightly broken by shell fragment; rear transom of chassis struck; still serviceable
10-inch columbiad: left cheek and carriage broken by shot; replaced
10-inch columbiad: dismounted by premature discharge; pintle broken (**Pulpit Battery**)

SEA FACE
(F) - Lt. Daniel R. Perry
Company B, 36th North Carolina Regiment
Ordnance (December 24)
One 10-inch columbiad and four 8-inch columbiads
Ordnance (December 25)
One 10-inch columbiad and three 8-inch columbiads

Cumberland Battery
10-inch columbiad: left rail and left upright of carriage broken by shot; carriage still serviceable

Columbiad Battery
8-inch columbiad: carriage disabled December 24
8-inch columbiad: carriage disabled December 25

Columbiad Battery
(G) - Lt. Frances M. Roby, C. S. Navy
(Detachment of 29 men from Battery Buchanan)
Ordnance (December 24 and 25)
Two 7-inch Brooke rifles: both guns burst and carriages disabled on December 25

Battery Bolles
(H) - Capt. Zachariah T. Adams (December 24)
13th North Carolina Battalion
Lt. Samuel H. Forbes in immediate command
Ordnance
One 32-pounder (single-banded rifle)
One 32-pounder (double-banded rifle)

FIRST EXPEDITION

(I) - Capt. James L. McCormic (December 25)
1st North Carolina Battalion
Lt. John T. Rankin in immediate command
Ordnance
One 32-pounder (single-banded rifle)
One 32-pounder (double-banded rifle)

Purdie (Armstrong) Battery
(H) - Capt. Zachariah T. Adams
13th North Carolina Battalion
Lt. Charles Latham in immediate command
(December 24 and 25)
Ordnance
150-pounder Armstrong Gun
(Center transom split and gangway down; repaired)

Battery Roland
(J) - Capt. Oliver H. Powell (December 24)
Company E, 36th North Carolina Regiment
Ordnance
Two 10-inch columbiads

(I) - Capt. James L. McCormic (December 25)
1st North Carolina Battalion
(Engaged on the Land Face night of 25th)
Ordnance
Two 10-inch columbiads

Lenoir Battery
(J) - Capt. Oliver H. Powell (December 24 and 25)
Company E, 36th North Carolina Regiment
Ordnance
Two 7-inch rifles

Battery Hedrick
(K) - Capt. William F. Brooks (December 24)
Company K, 36th North Carolina Regiment
Ordnance
Two 10-inch columbiads

(J) - Capt. Oliver H. Powell (December 25)
Company E, 36th North Carolina Regiment
Ordnance
Two 10-inch columbiads

Mound Battery
(K) - Capt. William F. Brooks (December 24 and 25)
Company K, 36th North Carolina Regiment
Ordnance
One 10-inch columbiad (truck axle broken at nut; repaired)
One 6.4-inch Brooke rifle

Battery Buchanan
(L) - Lt. Robert T. Chapman, C. S. Navy, commanding
(December 24 and 25)
Ordnance
Two 11-inch Brooke guns (smoothbore)
Two 10-inch columbiads

THE COLONEL'S LADY

Sarah Anne Chafee Lamb ("Daisy") *College of William and Mary*

As her husband, William, planned and oversaw the construction of Fort Fisher, young Daisy Lamb—after an earlier stay in Wilmington—relocated to Federal Point from her family home in Providence, Rhode Island. She came south to be with her husband after the untimely death of the couple's third child. Leaving her infant son in the care of her parents, Daisy arrived at Federal Point with her two oldest children, Maria and Richard, in 1863. She had been forced to obtain permission from Federal authorities to cross the Potomac River to rejoin her husband, for the colonel's lady was a Yankee. William Lamb, happy for the reunion, employed the post carpenters in erecting a small wooden cottage for his family at Craig's Landing, overlooking the Cape Fear River.

When Admiral Porter's fleet appeared off Cape Fear in December 1864, Daisy packed up the children and took refuge west of the river at spacious Orton Plantation. On Christmas Eve, with a pair of powerful field glasses, she watched with dread as enemy shells began bursting over Fort Fisher. "I kept up bravely, (*for you know I am brave, and would, if I thought I could,* whip Porter and Butler myself)," an indignant Daisy wrote to her parents. "I was overcome at last and laid my head on the fence and cried for the first and last time during it all." As the battle raged below them, "in the midst of the roaring and awful thundering," young Dick Lamb approached his mother: "Mamma," he said, "I want to pray to God for my papa." The child knelt down and "said his little earnest prayer," and feeling the better for it, exclaimed "Oh, sister, I'm so glad! I'm so glad! [N]ow *God* will keep care of my papa!"

On December 25, Daisy left for Wilmington aboard a steamer filled with sick and wounded soldiers, and waited there "for a few days in great suspense." After enduring dire rumors of her husband's personal misfortune, a much relieved Mrs. Lamb returned to Orton when she learned that all was right, and that the Federals had been driven from the shores of Cape Fear. Then "Will came over for me and took me to the fort," she wrote.

Daisy toured the shot-torn post with Colonel Lamb: "I rode all over on horseback," she boasted. "The fort was strewn with missiles of all kinds. [I]t seemed a perfect miracle how any escaped, the immense works were literally skinned of their turf, but not injured in the slightest; not a bomb-proof or a magazine—*and there are more than one*—touched . . . . [T]he men had very comfortable quarters in the fort—pretty little whitewashed houses—but the shells soon set fire to them, making a large fire and dense smoke, but the works are good for dozens of sieges . . . . We expect the Armada again."

Casualties and Other Numbers
December 24-25, 1864

FORT FISHER GARRISON

Forces Engaged:

Command	Effectives
Garrison	Approx. 425
Reinforcements December 21:	
C. S. Navy Detachment	28
Reinforcements December 23:	
40th North Carolina Regiment	110
2 companies 10th NC Regiment	110
1 company 13th NC Battalion	115
North Carolina Junior Reserves	140
Additional Reinforcements:	
4th, 7th, & 8th Battalions NCJR, December 25	443
Total:	Approx. **1,371**

Casualties:

Personnel	December 24		December 25	
	Killed	Wnd.	Killed	Wnd.
Commissioned Officers	-----	2	-----	3
Non-Comm. Officers	-----	3	-----	6
Privates	-----	16	3	17
Seamen	-----	2	-----	8
Marines	-----	-----	-----	1
Total	-----	23	3	35
Aggregate:				**61**

Rounds Expended:

Magazine	December 24	December 25[1]
No. 1	40	35
No. 2	34	62
No. 3	55	60
No. 4 (Armstrong Gun)	---------	4
No. 5	105	19
No. 6	106	18
No. 7	112	70
No. 8	25	84
No. 9	59	114
No. 10	6	70
No. 11	---------	60
No. 14	130	122
Total	**672**	**718**
Aggregate:		**1,390**

[1]Approximately 118 rounds expended on the 25th were grape, canister, and shell fired at Federal boats and ground forces. Fort Fisher contained some 3,600 rounds when the engagement began.

HOKE'S DIVISION

Forces Engaged:

Command	Effectives
Kirkland's Brigade	1,300
17th, 42nd, & 66th NC Regiments	
Local units subject to Kirkland's orders:[2]	
4th, 7th, & 8th Battalions NC Junior Res.	Approx. 800
8th NC Senior Reserves	400
Total:	Approx. **2,500**

[2]Force also includes 2nd Co. I, 10th North Carolina Regiment (Southerland's Battery), the Staunton Hill Artillery (Paris' Battery), and a detachment from the 2nd South Carolina Cavalry. On December 26, after the arrival of a portion of Hagood's Brigade and the remainder of Kirkland's, the arms-bearing force at Sugar Loaf was reported as follows: *Connally's Brigade*, 600; *2nd South Carolina Cavalry*, 350; *Paris' Battery*, approx. 125; *Southerland's Battery*, approx. 125; *Hagood's Brigade*, 720. Total: approximately 3,398.

Casualties:

Unit	Killed	Wounded	Missing	Total
17th NC	3	11	1	15
42nd NC	1	2	82[3]	85
66th NC	1	1	-----	2
Reserves	-----	-----	224[4]	224
Artillery	-----	2	-----	2
Aggregate:	5	16	307	**328**

[3]Soldiers of Company A, 42nd North Carolina, captured at Battery Anderson south of Sugar Loaf.
[4]Captured by the 117th New York Infantry.

UNITED STATES ARMY

Forces Engaged:

Command	Number
Army of the James	6,500 present[5]

[5]Approximately 2,300 troops from three brigades of the Second Division, XXIV Army Corps (Brig. Gen. Adelbert Ames), were landed on Federal Point December 25, 1864. A small detachment of N. Martin Curtis' brigade saw action as skirmishers in front of Fort Fisher.

Casualties:

Unit	Killed[6]	Wounded	Captured	Total
142nd NY	-----	11	1	**12**

[6]One man drowned in the surf upon reembarkation. General Benjamin F. Butler reported an additional two men killed.

UNITED STATES NAVY

Forces Engaged:

Number of Warships:	**64**

Casualties:

Killed	Wounded	Total
20	63	**83**

Rounds Expended:

Projectiles	Weight
20,271	1,275,299 pounds

Fort Fisher State Historic Site

Tour Trail and Points of Interest
With Direction of Advance of the Federal Infantry Reconnaissance, December 25, 1864

Bvt. Brig. Gen. N. MARTIN CURTIS
(First Brigade, Second Division)
XXIV Army Corps

Detachments from the 142nd, 3rd, & 117th New York Infantry

Federal Skirmishers

Remnants of Old River Road to Wilmington

Marsh

Bridge

(D)

Shepherd's Battery

8 (A) (B)

7 (C)

RIVER ROAD SALLY PORT

River Marsh

Restoration of Shepherd's Battery

River Marsh

Underwater Archaeology Unit at Fort Fisher:
An agency of the State Historic Preservation Office, North Carolina Division of Archives & History

Boat Storage

Lab

No Public Access

Dive Shop

Main Offices

Outdoor Exhibit Shelter

Pavilion

Exhibit *Hidden Beneath the Waves* Open to the Public

NO PUBLIC ACCESS

Maintenance Complex

Airstrip (World War II Era)

TO KURE BEACH & CAROLINA BEACH

PUBLIC PARKING

PUBLIC PARKING

VISITOR CENTER

U.S. 421

5 *Tour Trail*

1

2

4 *Reconstructed Palisades* 3

Detachment of garrison troops and NC Junior Reserves manned the palisade fence during the evening of December 25.

6

PRESERVED EARTHWORKS OF FORT FISHER'S LAND FACE

Fence Barrier

9 Capture! 10 Stairs

LAND FACE

Visible, Unpreserved Remnants of Fort Fisher's

TO NC AQUARIUM, SOUTHPORT-FORT FISHER FERRY, & REMNANTS OF BATTERY BUCHANAN

Airstrip (World War II Era)

Grove of Live Oaks

*Reconstructed cannon exhibits feature historic 32-pounder tubes from the USS *Peterhoff*

CAPE FEAR RIVER

ATLANTIC OCEAN

Wayside Exhibits:

1. Tour Trail Begins Here
2. Blockade Running
3. History Trail
4. Growth of Fort Fisher, 1861 - 1862
5. Lamb Expands the Fort, 1862 - 1865
6. River Road Sally Port
7. Shepherd's Bombproof
8. Shepherd's Battery
9. Union Fiasco: The First Battle
10. Fort Fisher Since 1865

(A) **First Battery:** Capt. John M. Sutton, Co. C, 3rd NC Battalion, commanding. 10" columbiad, left; 32-pounder (banded rifle), right—December 25.

(B) **Second Battery:** Capt. John M. Sutton, Co. C, 3rd NC Battalion, commanding. Two 8" columbiads—December 25.

(C) **Third Battery:** Lt. George D. Parker, 36th NC (adjutant on the staff of Col. William Lamb), commanding. 8" columbiad, left; 4.5" Parrott rifle, right—December 25.

(D) **Lt. William H. Walling,** commanding Co. G, 142nd New York, passed through a shot-induced hole in the palisade fence and scaled the outer wall of Shepherd's Battery, capturing a garrison flag (still attached to a 12-foot section of flagstaff) which had been knocked down by Union naval gunfire—3:20 p.m. December 25. The defenders of Shepherd's Battery were sheltered in their bombproofs when the flag was lost.

Mark A. Moore

The Fall of Fort Fisher

"The country will not forgive us for another failure at Wilmington."
— **Gustavus V. Fox**, Assistant Secretary of the Navy, Washington

Following the Federal departure from Cape Fear in late December 1864, Col. William Lamb immediately set about repairing damage to Fort Fisher caused by the massive naval bombardment. Efforts were made to restore gun carriages, tubes, and damaged parapet to proper working condition. Displaced earth was restored to the shot torn mounds, and work parties struggled to clear the hundreds of spent rounds and shell fragments that littered the beach and open plain behind the fort. Colonel Lamb had the post's broken telegraph line restored for communication with Confederate forces at Sugar Loaf, and had another "submarine" line laid westward across the Cape Fear River to Battery Lamb. Both the colonel and Gen. W. H. C. Whiting were astonished that the Federals had given up so easily after staging such an elaborate effort to conquer the great bastion. They were grateful for the temporary success, but each knew that it was only a matter of time before the Federal fleet would again darken the horizon off Fort Fisher.

As all of Wilmington rejoiced that the enemy had been driven from the shores of Cape Fear, Gen. Braxton Bragg proclaimed a great victory, and recalled the men of Hoke's Division from Sugar Loaf to Camp Whiting east of town. The Confederate district commander felt little concern for a renewed attack upon Wilmington, and the removal of Hoke's troops would cost him dearly.

The Second Expedition

In Washington, the Navy Department was impatient to renew the campaign against Wilmington. Tempers flared and accusations flew over Gen. Benjamin Butler's bungling of the first expedition, and Butler, despite favorable press from the *New York Tribune*, was caught in a firestorm of controversy. As Adm. David D. Porter vociferously blamed the army for the failed attempt to capture Fort Fisher, Navy Secretary Gideon Welles and Assistant Secretary Gustavus Fox fretted over the prospect of a timely renewal of the campaign. At issue was whether they could afford to let Porter keep the huge armada that had been assembled for the first attempt on Wilmington. *"We shall undoubtedly get the place,"* Welles predicted anxiously, *"but I hardly know when. In the meantime [Porter] holds a large part of our naval force locked up."* President Abraham Lincoln simply told Welles and Fox that he hoped the navy then had enough vessels to blockade the remaining Southern ports, and again referred the Navy Department to the army's general-in-chief. The timetable was once again in the hands of Gen. Ulysses S. Grant.

But things would be different this time. Grant was himself eager for the return of army ground forces to Cape Fear, and for his part they would play a more prominent role than in the previous campaign. On this expedition, beyond the capture of Fort Fisher, the town of Wilmington itself was to be taken and occupied for Federal use. Indeed, the Carolina port had taken on new strategic significance as the year 1864 drew to a close. Grant's friend and trusted subordinate, Gen. William T. Sherman, was about to strike from Savannah, Georgia, into the very heart of the Confederacy with 60,000 men—on a march northward through the Carolinas.

Having accepted Sherman's aggressive scheme to join him in Virginia by means of a land campaign through the Carolinas, Grant realized the immediate importance of capturing Wilmington. He meant to assure the success of Sherman's forthcoming maneuver, and a friendly base on the coast of North Carolina—through which supplies and reinforcements could be funneled to Sherman—would be a large step in that direction. Wilmington had the necessary infrastructure to support Sherman's campaign. The Cape Fear River was navigable for 100 miles inland to Fayetteville, and its three major railroads could bring in supplies from points across the South.

By the end of December Grant's decision had been made. The effort to capture Wilmington would be renewed as soon as possible. *"I assured [Admiral Porter] that I fully sympathized with his disappointment,"* Grant recalled, *"and that I would send the same troops back [to Cape Fear] with a different commander."* There would be no failure this time, Grant asserted, and Benjamin Butler would not be a part of the operation. Acting on a tip from his aide-de-camp, the general-in-chief called a meeting with the capable and easy going commander of the XXIV Corps, Army of the James. Alfred H. Terry, though little known, had by this time gained a solid reputation for competence among superiors and subordinates alike. Having been favorably impressed, and eager to get the expedition underway, *"I selected A. H. Terry to command,"* wrote Grant.

Based in part on Butler's involvement in the first expedition, and the dismal result, the Navy Department was wary of the new appointment *"Grant has not discriminating powers as regards men,"* worried Secretary Welles, *"and fails in measuring their true character and adaptability to particular service."* General Terry, however, would prove equal to the task, and soon win the favor of even the caustic Adm. David D. Porter.

On December 30, Grant notified Secretary of War Edwin M. Stanton of his intentions, mindful of the costly information leak that had jeopardized the first expedition: *"Not a person here knows the object of this [operation] but myself, chief of staff, and cipher operator.... It will not be known by another. When all is ready I will send the troops and commander selected to Fortress Monroe and out to sea with sealed instructions.... You will understand why I would say no more. I am in hopes by secrecy the enemy may be lulled into such security as to induce him to send his Wilmington forces against Sherman, or bring them back here [to Virginia] by the time we are ready to start. There will be no delay on the part of [our] troops."*

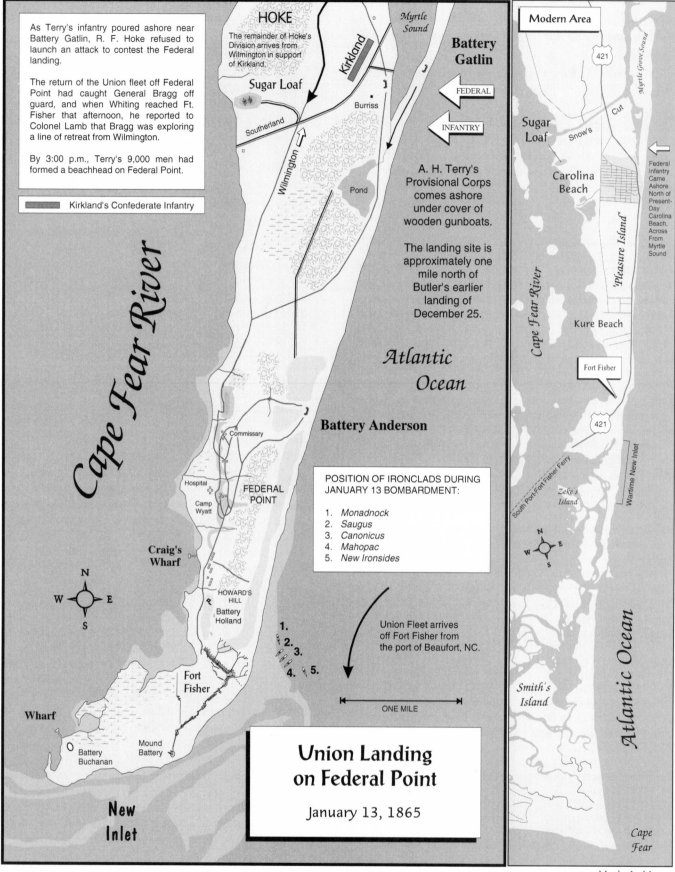

As Terry's infantry poured ashore near Battery Gatlin, R. F. Hoke refused to launch an attack to contest the Federal landing.

The return of the Union fleet off Federal Point had caught General Bragg off guard, and when Whiting reached Ft. Fisher that afternoon, he reported to Colonel Lamb that Bragg was exploring a line of retreat from Wilmington.

By 3:00 p.m., Terry's 9,000 men had formed a beachhead on Federal Point.

Kirkland's Confederate Infantry

HOKE

The remainder of Hoke's Division arrives from Wilmington in support of Kirkland.

Kirkland

Sugar Loaf

Southerland

Wilmington

Burriss

Myrtle Sound

Battery Gatlin

FEDERAL

INFANTRY

A. H. Terry's Provisional Corps comes ashore under cover of wooden gunboats.

The landing site is approximately one mile north of Butler's earlier landing of December 25.

Pond

Cape Fear River

Commissary

Hospital

Camp Wyatt

FEDERAL POINT

Atlantic Ocean

Battery Anderson

POSITION OF IRONCLADS DURING JANUARY 13 BOMBARDMENT:

1. Monadnock
2. Saugus
3. Canonicus
4. Mahopac
5. New Ironsides

Craig's Wharf

HOWARD'S HILL

Battery Holland

1.
2. 3.
4. 5.

Union Fleet arrives off Fort Fisher from the port of Beaufort, NC.

ONE MILE

Wharf

Fort Fisher

Battery Buchanan

Mound Battery

New Inlet

Union Landing on Federal Point

January 13, 1865

Modern Area

421

Sugar Loaf

Snow's Cut

Myrtle Grove Sound

Carolina Beach

Cape Fear River

"Pleasure Island"

Kure Beach

Fort Fisher

421

Federal Infantry Came Ashore North of Present-Day Carolina Beach, Across From Myrtle Sound

Wartime New Inlet

Zeke's Island

South Port-Fort Fisher Ferry

Smith's Island

Atlantic Ocean

Cape Fear

Mark A. Moore

"I hope that on any renewal of an attempt to land, the enemy will not be allowed to do so without opposition." — **Maj. Gen. W. H. C. Whiting**, to Braxton Bragg, January 8, 1865

As he had done so many times during his tenure at Cape Fear, Gen. W. H. C. Whiting could only plead his case and hope for the best. On January 8, 1865, he began to press Braxton Bragg for the return of Robert F. Hoke's 6,424-man division to Sugar Loaf: *"I think it not at all unlikely that a renewal of the attack on Wilmington will be made very soon. It is hardly possible that the enemy will put up with such a failure as the last. I should keep one good brigade and a battery at Sugar Loaf.... Information received from Morehead City indicates so far that another attack is imminent, and therefore these suggestions are respectfully offered."*

On the evening of January 12, peering into the darkness toward the Atlantic, Col. William Lamb observed the arrival: *"I saw from the ramparts of the fort the lights of the great armada, as one after another appeared above the horizon."* Lamb was furious, for the fort *"was not even advised of the approach of the fleet,"* he complained, but instead *"its arrival was reported from Fort Fisher to [Bragg's] headquarters in Wilmington."* The army transports carrying nearly 10,000 Federal troops had departed Hampton Roads, Virginia, for Cape Fear in the small hours of January 6, 1865. After a weather-induced delay at Beaufort, North Carolina, Admiral Porter's 58 warships and the transports sailed for Fort Fisher on January 12. By 10:00 o'clock that night, most of the vessels had rendezvoused off New Inlet. Lamb *"commenced at once to prepare for action."* He needed reinforcements, for the garrison at Fisher then numbered only 800 artillerymen of the 36th North Carolina, and at least 100 of that number were physically unfit for duty. The colonel asked Gen. Louis Hébert at Smithville to provide extra manpower for the fort, and for the second time made arrangements for his wife and family to be ferried to a safe location west of the Cape Fear River.

Having received word of the fleet's arrival, Bragg ordered Hoke's Division to move immediately to Sugar Loaf, approximately 15 miles south of Wilmington. Kirkland's Brigade was hustled into steamers at Wilmington for a trip by water to the sand dune defenses, and by 1:00 a.m. on the 13th the remainder of Hoke's men were moving out by land on the Federal Point Road. As the Confederate infantry headed southward, Col. Archer Anderson of Bragg's staff reminded R. F. Hoke that *"The commanding general expects you to make every effort to prevent a landing of the enemy [on Federal Point]."*

"The fleet is off Masonborough; be on your guard," General Whiting warned Lamb, assuring the colonel that *"I will be with you, either inside or out."*

At 7:20 a.m. on January 13, a division of gunboats broke off from the fleet and began shelling Federal Point four miles north of Fort Fisher, at the site chosen for putting A. H. Terry's Federal infantry ashore. To the south Admiral Porter's warships began moving into position to bombard the fort itself. At 8:00 a.m., using hundreds of gigs and launches, the army began disembarking from the transports, and soon the soldiers were rowing ashore in the choppy surf. The landing zone was a narrow sand spit above the head of Myrtle Sound, about a mile north of the site of the December 1864 landing.

As the army came ashore, a Federal reconnaissance party confirmed the presence of Confederate infantry at the sand dune defenses west of Myrtle Sound. Kirkland's Brigade and a detachment of the 2nd South Carolina Cavalry had reached Sugar Loaf in time to witness the landing. Hoke himself arrived as the first Federal troops hit the beach, and soon the advance of Hoke's remaining brigades marched into view from the north. Hoke entrenched the bulk of his force on the Sugar Loaf line, and watched as thousands of Federal soldiers poured ashore. Despite having been warned to repel an enemy landing, Hoke had no intention of launching an all-out assault. The general reasoned that the sound posed too great an obstacle to a Confederate attack, and that the Union beachhead was too well protected by *"the heavy metal of the fleet."* Hoke worried that the enemy might turn and move on Wilmington. He was content to sit and guard the main land approach to the port city while the enemy built a large presence between himself and Fort Fisher.

To the south Porter's ironclad division was embroiled in *"quite a spirited engagement"* with the guns of Fort Fisher. The incessant naval gunfire quickly severed the fort's telegraph wires, and the heavy battle smoke prevented Confederate signal flags from being seen at Battery Lamb across the river. The signal corps operators were forced to move to Smithville for the all-important communication by telegraph with Wilmington and Sugar Loaf. During the bombardment Colonel Lamb received a welcome 700-man reinforcement of artillerymen and marines, who landed at Battery Buchanan and made their way through the bursting shells to the fort. This force brought the garrison total to approximately 1,500 officers and men.

The indefatigable General Whiting also came ashore at Buchanan, and together with his staff headed to Fort Fisher to meet with Colonel Lamb, who was growing more and more alarmed as he watched the enemy masses come ashore virtually unopposed. Lamb quickly offered command of the fort to Whiting, who declined as he had the previous December. *"Lamb, my boy, I've come to share your fate,"* the general remarked. *"You and your garrison are to be sacrificed."* The colonel was stunned. Where was Hoke's Division? The cynical Whiting's blood was up, and on this day he fired off the first of many direct challenges to Braxton Bragg to pitch into the Federals and come to the relief of Fort Fisher: *"The enemy have landed in large force. [Fort Fisher's] garrison [is] too weak to resist assault and prevent their advance. You must attack them at once."*

"It is seldom, even in war, that a grander sight presents, than was afforded [off Federal Point] that morning. The greater armed portion of that majestic fleet was flashing, and raining its fiery judgments on the fort and garrison, while the bellowing of ponderous artillery, filled the entire space, bound by the visible horizon.... The [USS] Brooklyn, like an enraged lioness, went up and down parallel with the beach, covering the debarking troops. From her wide mouthed guns, now and then, streams of fire leapt out over the waters, with a deafening explosion, then the huge shell, taking up the sound, went tearing and screeching throught the air, when back came the faint report of its distant explosion... Dozens of little boats were plying to and fro and about great transport ships, reminding one of a country lake scene, where downy web footed infantry, glide confidingly in the shadow of their graceful paternity. After a few of these buoyant little messengers had made a trip to the beach, a collection of our boys in blue presented a pleasant contrast to the white sandy background." — **J. A. Mowris**, Surgeon, 117th New York, Curtis' brigade

"Every foot of ground between our line and [Fort Fisher] was in easy range of the guns of the enemy's fleet. No line of battle could have existed under the enfilading fire of the fleet and exposed to a heavy infantry fire in front, if the attempt should have been made to assault the enemy's line. Hence an assault being impractical, the force at Sugar Loaf could do nothing more than prepare to meet the enemy, should he attempt to move towards Wilmington. Accordingly, we worked night and day, until our line presented a strong appearance." — **H. T. J. Ludwig**, Drummer, Company H, 8th North Carolina, Clingman's Brigade

SECOND EXPEDITION

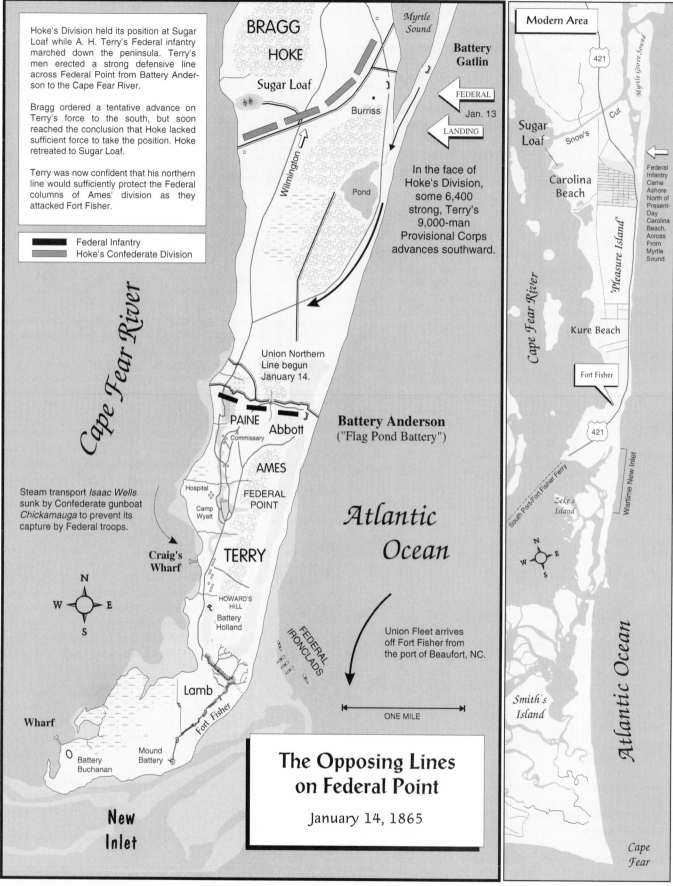

Hoke's Division held its position at Sugar Loaf while A. H. Terry's Federal infantry marched down the peninsula. Terry's men erected a strong defensive line across Federal Point from Battery Anderson to the Cape Fear River.

Bragg ordered a tentative advance on Terry's force to the south, but soon reached the conclusion that Hoke lacked sufficient force to take the position. Hoke retreated to Sugar Loaf.

Terry was now confident that his northern line would sufficiently protect the Federal columns of Ames' division as they attacked Fort Fisher.

Federal Infantry
Hoke's Confederate Division

BRAGG
HOKE
Sugar Loaf
Myrtle Sound
Battery Gatlin
FEDERAL Jan. 13
LANDING
Wilmington
Burriss
Pond

In the face of Hoke's Division, some 6,400 strong, Terry's 9,000-man Provisional Corps advances southward.

Cape Fear River

Union Northern Line begun January 14.

Battery Anderson ("Flag Pond Battery")

PAINE Abbott
Commissary
AMES
Hospital
FEDERAL POINT
Camp Wyatt

Steam transport Isaac Wells sunk by Confederate gunboat Chickamauga to prevent its capture by Federal troops.

Craig's Wharf
TERRY
HOWARD'S HILL
Battery Holland

Atlantic Ocean

FEDERAL IRONCLADS

Union Fleet arrives off Fort Fisher from the port of Beaufort, NC.

ONE MILE

Wharf
Lamb
Fort Fisher
Battery Buchanan
Mound Battery

New Inlet

The Opposing Lines on Federal Point

January 14, 1865

Modern Area
421
Sugar Loaf
Snow's Cut
Myrtle Grove Sound
Carolina Beach
"Pleasure Island"
Cape Fear River
Kure Beach
Fort Fisher
421
South Port-Fort Fisher Ferry
Zeke's Island
Wartime New Inlet
Smith's Island
Atlantic Ocean
Cape Fear

Federal Infantry Came Ashore North of Present-Day Carolina Beach, Across From Myrtle Sound

Mark A. Moore

"The first object which I had in view after landing was to throw a strong defensive line across the peninsula, from the Cape Fear River to the sea, facing Wilmington, so as to protect our rear from attack while we should be engaged in operating against Fort Fisher."
— **Bvt. Maj. Gen. Alfred H. Terry**, commander, Fort Fisher Expeditionary Force

As A. H. Terry's Federal infantry established a beachhead at Myrtle Sound on January 13, 1865, Braxton Bragg sought to reassure Robert E. Lee in Virginia that matters were well in hand: *"[The] enemy has effected a landing on the narrow sand spit east of Masonborough Sound,"* he admitted.° *"With the sound intervening, we could not possibly prevent this."* Amazingly, the district commander went so far as to tell Lee that the landing gave the enemy *"no advantage."*

With his 9,600 men massed on the beaches of Federal Point, General Terry made preparations to secure a position from which to attack Fort Fisher. Around 5:00 p.m. he struck southward with two brigades of United States Colored Troops from Gen. Charles Paine's division, and two brigades from Gen. Adelbert Ames' division commanded by Galusha Pennypacker and Louis Bell. Finding the terrain near the landing zone too swampy to support breastworks, the Federals were forced to push further south in search of higher ground.

At Fort Fisher, Colonel Lamb and General Whiting watched the enemy build-up with growing dismay, and by 8:00 p.m. Whiting was exasperated: *"[The] enemy are on the beach, where they have been all day,"* he complained to Bragg. *"Why are they not attacked?"*

General Terry finally chose the area west of Battery Anderson to establish his defensive position, and by 2:00 a.m. on January 14 his soldiers were busy digging a line of entrenchments that would span the entire width of the peninsula. Employing 800 shovels, the men toiled through the night, and by 8:00 a.m. on the 14th had constructed a formidable line of breastworks. The Federal commander was now feeling confident, astutely observing that *"from this time [on] our foothold on the peninsula was secured."* If all went well the Union northern line would hold in check the Confederate infantry at Sugar Loaf, while the three brigades of Ames' division attacked Fort Fisher.

Braxton Bragg, having arrived at Sugar Loaf on the 13th, was also feeling confident—though he had no intention of attacking the Federals. Bragg feared that a push toward Terry's position might allow the enemy to get in behind him, and gain a clear road to Wilmington. He was content to keep a strong force at Sugar Loaf, and hoped that the swamps and heavy timber on Federal Point would prevent Terry's force from establishing a formidable position in the dark. Bragg also hoped unrealistically that Terry's men would maneuver in such a way as to lose their protection from the Federal fleet. But as long as Terry occupied Federal Point the guns of the fleet would always be in range for fire support. The uncontested Federal landing, which allowed the enemy a massed presence on the peninsula, was an irreversible setback for the Confederates.

A reconnaissance on the morning of January 14 by both Bragg and General Hoke brought the unwelcome news of Terry's fortified line at Battery Anderson. The realization jolted the complacent Bragg, who ordered Hoke to dislodge the enemy, if *"at all practicable."* Hoke, however, quickly determined that his force was outnumbered, and that Terry's position was too strong to break under these circumstances. Bragg accepted Hoke's assessment, and determined to reinforce the garrison at Fort Fisher. *"I did not feel the slightest apprehension for the fort,"* Bragg would soon write. *"I felt perfect confidence that the enemy had assumed a most precarious position, from which he would*

escape with great difficulty."

At low tide, shortly before noon, General Whiting reasoned that Porter's gunboats could not cross the bar at New Inlet until the tide rose later that evening. *"[The] sooner you attack the enemy the better,"* he prodded Bragg. At 1:30 p.m. Whiting impatiently laid his cards on the table: *"The game of the enemy is very plain to me . . . . I have received dispatches from you stating that the enemy had extended to the river-bank. This they never should have been allowed to do; and if they are permitted to remain there the reduction of Fort Fisher is but a question of time. This has been notified frequently both to yourself and to the Department. I will hold this place to the last extremities; but unless you drive that land force from its position I cannot answer for the security of this harbor."*

That evening Bragg informed Whiting that the fort would be reinforced with a contingent from Hoke's Division. The Confederate commander then boldly asserted to Whiting that these reinforcements, together with the earlier lot sent from General Hébert's force at Smithville, *"will render you impregnable against assault,"* and promised, *"if opportunity occurs,"* to attack the enemy if it advanced on Fort Fisher. Under the circumstances, both Whiting and Colonel Lamb felt no confidence in the word of Braxton Bragg.

As the Confederate gunboat *Chickamauga* shelled Federal Point from the Cape Fear River, yet another Confederate setback occurred when the steamer *Isaac Wells*, bound from Wilmington with supplies for the garrison at Fort Fisher, docked at Craig's Landing instead of continuing southward to the safety of the wharf at Battery Buchanan. The boat promptly fell into the hands of Brig. Gen. N. Martin Curtis' Federal brigade, depriving the fort of much needed ammunition and cornmeal. To prevent the Federals from using the boat, the *Chickamauga* sunk the *Isaac Wells* with a well placed shot through her hull.

General A. H. Terry and the expedition's chief engineer, Col. Cyrus Comstock, arrived at the abandoned Battery Holland late that afternoon, and proposed to get a closer look at the imposing Confederate bastion. As he had during the December 1864 expedition, N. Martin Curtis led a reconnaissance force toward Fort Fisher. Terry advanced to within 400 yards of Shepherd's Battery, and was encouraged by what he saw. The naval gunfire from Porter's monitors had destroyed much of the fort's palisade fence, and appeared to have disabled most of the guns on the northern battlements. Conditions looked favorable for an infantry assault. Terry pointedly asked Curtis if he thought the fort could be carried by assault without greatly depleting the northern defensive position recently established. Curtis replied that the three brigades of Ames' division could handle the job, *"if the dispositions were properly made, and the navy should support the troops from start to finish."* That was good enough for Terry. *"It has already been decided,"* the Federal commander told Curtis, *"that in case an assault is ordered you will make it."*

General Terry then departed with Comstock to confer with Admiral Porter aboard the flagship *Malvern*. Eager for a successful campaign, Porter embraced Terry's plan for an infantry attack the following day, but determined to put ashore *"1,600 sailors and 400 marines to accompany the troops in the assault—the sailors to board the sea face, while the [army] assaulted the land side."*

"[The] successful accomplishment [of the Union northern line] was not considered as placing the fort in much danger, if boldly defended by a vigilant garrison, as our communication with [Fisher] by water at night could not be interrupted unless the fleet forced a passage into the river."
—**Gen. Braxton Bragg**, commander, District of the Cape Fear

° Myrtle Sound formed the extreme southern end of Masonboro Sound.

SECOND EXPEDITION

"Imagine a cold, bright day in the middle of January; a low sandy coastline, with a dull surf combing up on the beach; a tremendous fort of the most elaborate construction, with ramparts in some places 30 feet high; huge bastions every little way; deep-throated embrasures from which frowned the muzzles of seven, eight and 10-inch Armstrong and Brooke rifled cannon and Columbiads; and the doomed flag of the gallant Confederacy floating defiantly from its tall staff!

"Look, then, seaward, and see 60 steam men-of-war formed in a great arc of a circle, all steaming slowly to their anchors and rolling great volumes of smoke from their funnels. Inside of this outer arc are [four] of those low, black, sullen monitors 'in line abreast,' as the sailors called it, slowly and steadily creeping toward the fort, no visible sign of life about them, except now and then you could see an officer's head come up over the breastwork or barbet [sic] on top of the turret.

"I cannot describe the discharges of those 13 and 15-inch Rodman guns of the monitors, or the explosion of their great shells in the air over the fort or among its traverses. To me it seemed like firing meteors out of volcanoes . . . . I would watch the turrets of the monitors through my glass. They would turn their iron backs on the enemy to load, and I could distinctly see the big rammer staves come out of the ports. Then they would wheel round on a line with the fort, there would be two puffs of blue smoke about the size of a thunder cloud in June, and then I could see the big shell make a black streak through the air with a tail of white smoke behind it—and then would come over the water, not the quick bark of a field gun, but a slow, quivering, overpowering roar like an earthquake, and then, away among the Rebel traverses, there would be another huge ball of mingled smoke and flame as big as a meeting house." —**Augustus Buell**, observing the bombardment from a troop transport off Federal Point

"A tremendous fire was kept up from the entire fleet . . . directed at different portions of the work, which was kept up at intervals of ten and twenty minutes. Its effect was terrible, the works being torn to pieces and every gun on the land face (except one 8-inch columbiad) dismounted. Our mortars, with this gun, however, kept up a steady fire upon the enemy's line of infantry, whilst our sea-face batteries replied with steadiness and coolness to the fire of the fleet . . . . The exhausted condition of our men, now greatly decimated by fifty-six hours of hard fighting . . . rendered it necessary to fire at the fleet seldom and at long intervals." —**Maj. William J. Saunders**, Col. William Lamb's Chief of Artillery, Second Battle of Fort Fisher

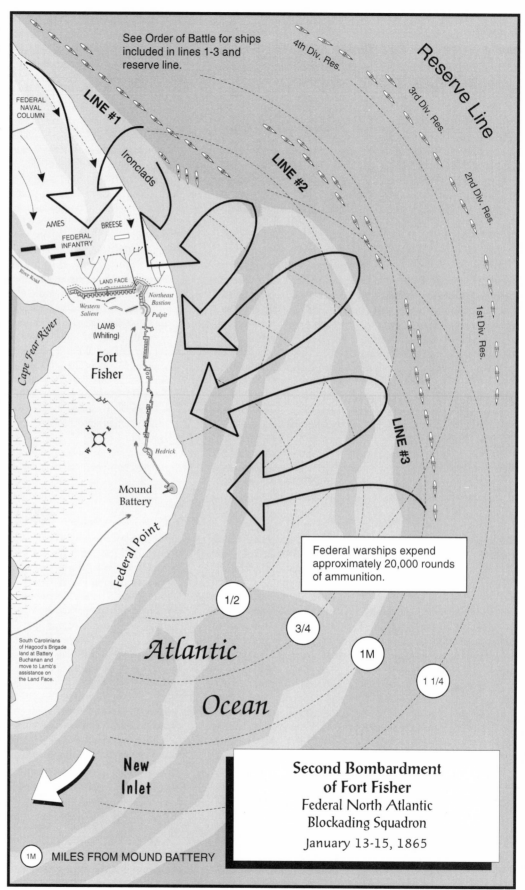

See Order of Battle for ships included in lines 1-3 and reserve line.

Reserve Line

4th Div. Res.

3rd Div. Res.

2nd Div. Res.

1st Div. Res.

LINE #1

LINE #2

LINE #3

FEDERAL NAVAL COLUMN

Ironclads

AMES   BREESE

FEDERAL INFANTRY

River Road

LAND FACE

Western Salient   Northeast Bastion   Pulpit

LAMB (Whiting)

Fort Fisher

Cape Fear River

Hedrick

Mound Battery

Federal Point

South Carolinians of Hagood's Brigade land at Battery Buchanan and move to Lamb's assistance on the Land Face.

Federal warships expend approximately 20,000 rounds of ammunition.

1/2

3/4

1M

1 1/4

Atlantic

Ocean

New Inlet

1M   MILES FROM MOUND BATTERY

Second Bombardment of Fort Fisher
Federal North Atlantic Blockading Squadron
January 13-15, 1865

Mark A. Moore

"All felt the importance of this bombardment, and . . . such a storm of shell was poured into Fort Fisher, that forenoon, as I believe had never been seen before in any naval engagement."
— **Lt. Cmdr. Thomas O. Selfridge**, USS *Huron*

As the sun went down on January 14, most of the guns and carriages along the northern battlements of Fort Fisher were in shambles. Commander Daniel Ammen of the USS *Mohican* remembered that *"certainly the fort had a sorry appearance,"* and nightfall brought no relief from the incessant naval gunfire. Colonel Lamb found that repair work on Fisher's battered land front was impossible, as the Union monitors *"bowled their eleven and fifteen-inch shells along its parapet, scattering shrapnel in the darkness."* In the small hours of the 15th the first reinforcements from Johnson Hagood's brigade (the 21st South Carolina) arrived at Battery Buchanan, having embarked on the steamer *Sampson* from Gander Hall Landing on the Cape Fear River.

The Final Day

"We are trustfully looking to your operations; may Divine favor crown your efforts."
— Confederate president Jefferson Davis to Gen. Braxton Bragg, January 15, 1865

On the cold, clear morning of January 15, the remainder of the Federal fleet once again stood in to join the ironclads in pounding the beleaguered bastion. The sea was calm, and the naval rounds told upon the fort with a practiced and concentrated accuracy. By midday the fleet had so punished the land front that only two guns remained operative: two 8-inch columbiads survived on opposite ends of the work, one at the Northeast Bastion and another on the western salient. Confederate casualties were mounting.

The *Sampson* reappeared at the wharf at Battery Buchanan during the height of the Federal naval bombardment, and succeeded in unloading only a portion of Hagood's 11th and 25th South Carolina regiments before being driven away by the heavy naval ordnance. A long and dangerous mile-and-three-quarters lay between the South Carolina reinforcements and their destination at the land front of Fort Fisher. As the newcomers picked their way northward, incoming enemy shells were bursting over the works and open sand plain *"like the roar of heavy peals of thunder,"* and at the astounding rate of about two per second.

As the Confederate garrison braced itself for the impending ground attack, William Lamb directed his men from combat headquarters in the Pulpit, which gave the colonel *"the best view of the works and their approaches by sea and land."* General Whiting was with him, and "Little Billy" continued to hound Braxton Bragg unmercifully with dispatches pleading for assistance. *"Is Fisher to be besieged, or you to attack? [I] should like to know,"* jabbed Whiting.

While Federal infantry skirmishers of Adelbert Ames' division pushed ever closer to the fort, Admiral Porter's contingent of 2,261 sailors and marines poured ashore about one and one-half miles to the north. The tars and leathernecks, under command of Fleet Capt. Kidder Randolph Breese, hailed from 35 different warships, forming a diverse combat group that had never before operated as a cohesive unit. They came ashore eagerly, glad to be temporarily free from the physical confines of life at sea.

As the naval contingent hit the beach, Fleet Capt. Breese sent Flag Lt. Samuel Preston with a party of sailors to prepare a defensive position for the marines, who would provide fire support for the attacking naval column. Preston, working under sporadic fire from the fort, and supported by 50 marines under Lt. Louis Fagan, oversaw construction of three successive lines of breastworks. The southernmost line was dug within about 200 yards of Fort Fisher's ruined palisades, and connected with Gen. N. Martin Curtis' infantry skirmishers to the west. The marine division, led by Capt. Lucien Dawson, moved down to Preston's position, and soon the three-division naval column began advancing southward along the beach toward Fort Fisher and its place in history.

With shells bursting fiercely over the battlements, William Lamb hurried along behind the works and through the fort's internal galleries, issuing final instructions for the fort's defense. While the 8-inch columbiad in the Northeast Bastion occasionally harassed the approaching Federals, Lamb ordered his light artillery—two Napoleons at the main sally port and one at the gate on the river road—to rake the approaching columns with grape and canister. The gun crews *"fearlessly obeyed,"* lamented the colonel, *"but at a sad sacrifice in killed and wounded."* Lamb knew that the naval bombardment would cease on the land front as the enemy ground forces attacked, and he quickly instructed that sharpshooters be deployed in the gun chambers, in an effort to pick off Federal officers as the assaulting columns approached. The remaining battery crews were ordered to rush immediately to man the parapet when the enemy fusillade subsided. Lamb was counting on an ace in the hole with his line of buried torpedoes arrayed in front of the fort. With the enemy massed in his front, he planned to engage the galvanic apparatus and blow the first attacking wave to smithereens. Perhaps this would demoralize the enemy, and give Fisher's garrison a better chance to fend off the aggressors.

Around 2:30 p.m. Hagood's reinforcements finally reached the fort's Land Face. The South Carolinians, breathless and frightened, were herded by the colonel into a commissary bombproof to rest and await deployment. Of the 1,000 troops Bragg had sent to the relief of Fort Fisher, only a pathetic 350 had ultimately arrived to help. Though he cursed Bragg for not sending more, Lamb welcomed the new arrivals, who swelled the garrison to about 1,900 men.

As the young commander was making his way back to the Pulpit a shout rang out, as *"one of my lookouts called to me. Colonel, the enemy are about to charge."* Whiting lost no time in dispatching a final, desperate plea to the district commander at Sugar Loaf: *"Enemy [is] on the beach in front of us in very heavy force,"* he wired Bragg frantically. *"Attack! Attack! It is all I can say, and all you can do."*

SECOND EXPEDITION

Second Fort Fisher
The Union Ground Assault:
Advance of the Naval Storming Party

January 15, 1865

Federal Infantry

Federal Naval Column

3rd DIVISION

4th DIVISION
Dawson (Marines)

Selfridge

2nd DIVISION

Atlantic Ocean

Parker

1st DIVISION

Naval Attack Commences
at Approximately 3:30 p.m.

Cushman

Canister Fire

AMES' DIVISION
Moves into
Position

Galvanic Apparatus Disabled

Sand
Knolls

C

BREESE

Wilmington Road

LAND FACE

Slough

Northeast
Bastion

BRIDGE

Shepherd's
Battery

Palisades

Demilune

Main Sally Port

Palisades

River Road
Sally Port

4

B

A

Palisades

Reilly
250 Defenders

5

8-inch
Mortar

5

LAMB
500 Defenders

"The Pulpit"

Combat HQ

Western Salient

Hospital
Bombproof

**Battery
Meade**

*Marsh Waters of
Cape Fear River*

Lamb orders 350 reinforcements
from Hagood's Brigade to support
Reilly's force on the Western Salient

(WHITING)

BARRACKS
AREA

**Cumberland
Battery**

Operable Confederate Artillery:

① Two 12-pdr. Napoleons
at the Main Sally Port

② One 12-pdr. Napoleon behind
sandbagged wall, blocking the
River Road Sally Port

③ One 3.2-inch Parrott rifle
posted in the river marsh

④ One 8-inch columbiad in the
Northeast Bastion

⑤ Two 24-pdr. Coehorn mortars
mounted in 5th and 6th gun
chambers, and one 8-inch
mortar mounted behind the
works

Columbiad Battery

SEA FACE

Fort Fisher

**All Other Land Face
Heavy Artillery Disabled**

A Compare these positions
B with positions on sketch
   map drawn by Lt. Cmdr.
C James Parker, p. 44

**Battery
Bolles**

Line of Rifle Pits

☐ Federal Sailors
◣ Federal Marines
▰ Confederate Defenders
   on the Parapet

**Purdie
(Armstrong)
Battery**

Right panel

BRAGG
HOKE

Battery
Gatlin

Sugar Loaf

Burriss

Site of
Federal
Infantry
Landing

Cape Fear River

Atlantic Ocean

Union Northern
Line begun
January 14.

PAINE Abbott

Naval
Storming
Party Comes
Ashore About
Midday,
January 15

Commissary

AMES

Hospital

FEDERAL
POINT

Camp
Wyatt

Craig's Wharf

TERRY

HOWARD'S
HILL

FEDERAL
IRONCLADS

Battery
Holland

Lamb

Wharf

Mound
Battery

Fort Fisher

Battery
Buchanan

ONE MILE

New Inlet

**Federal Infantry
and Naval
Columns Advance
Toward Fort Fisher**

Fleet Captain Kidder Randolph Breese

Battles and Leaders

Mark A. Moore

"Such a hell of noise I never expect to hear again. Hundreds of shell[s] were in the air at once . . . all shrieking in a grand martial course that was a fitting accompaniment to the death dance of the hundreds about to fall."

— **Lt. Cmdr. William B. Cushing**, USS *Monticello,* on the moments prior to the attack of the Federal naval column at Fort Fisher, January 15, 1865

The Union Ground Assault

The two-thousand-man naval contingent advanced grandly down the beach, hugging the edge of the surf as it moved southward into position. Heading the first division was Lt. Cmdr. Charles H. Cushman of the USS *Wabash.* The second division was led by the *Minnesota's* Lt. Cmdr. James Parker, and the third by Lt. Cmdr. Thomas O. Selfridge of the *Huron.* Selfridge remembered that the seamen were enthusiastic, viewing the adventure "*in the light of a lark, and few thought the sun would set with the loss of one-fifth of their number.*" The long blue column's numerous battle flags snapped in the ocean breeze as the sailors pulled to within 600 yards of the *"frowning fort."* Here the men lay down for cover along the beach slope and awaited the signal to commence their attack. The sun shone brightly upon the stark white sand, and William B. Cushing noted that the bluejackets stood out in sharp contrast, "*the officers all in uniform, bright with gold lace and every man dressed as for inspection.*" Feebly armed with cutlasses and Remington and Whitney revolvers, the Federal sailors were determined to plant their flags upon the ramparts of Fort Fisher.

Shortly after 3:00 p.m., as he waited for Alfred Terry's Federal infantry to move into attacking position to the west, Fleet Capt. K. R. Breese ordered Lucien Dawson's marines to move from their entrenchments to the beach shelf for cover. This maneuver, as the marines crowded onto the narrow sand strip, would prove costly for Breese's command. The various units of sailors and marines became inextricably mingled as they vied for shelter along the slope. At the same time, they were subjected to hostile rounds from Fort Fisher's remaining eight-inch columbiad, from the Mound Battery, and from the two 12-pounder Napoleons stationed at the fort's main sally port. To make matters worse, incoming friendly rounds from the fleet were occasionally falling short and bursting among the Federal troops. Some of the earlier enthusiasm waned under the circumstances, and the men grew impatient for action.

The army was finally ready to begin the assault by 3:20 p.m., and General Terry's signal corpsmen flagged Admiral Porter to cease firing upon Fisher's land front. At 3:25 p.m., following the lead of the flagship *Malvern,* the vessels of the Federal fleet sounded an ear-splitting, unison blast from their great steam whistles—hailing the commencement of the ground attack. Inside Fort Fisher, Col. William Lamb was returning to the Pulpit when the soaring blare rolled up from the ocean: "*a soul-stirring signal both to the beseigers [sic] and the beseiged.*"

As the relentless bombardment subsided along the northern battlements, Lamb's exhausted Confederates emerged by the hundreds from the bowels of the great sand bastion. The soldiers clambered atop the parapet, where they were formed into two separate forces. Major James Reilly deployed 250 defenders along the western salient, while Lamb arrayed an additional 500 men along the Northeast Bastion and adjoining batteries. Reilly's force would confront the army ground forces of Adelbert Ames' division while Lamb's contingent faced off against Breese's tars and leathernecks. The 350 South Carolina reinforcements from Hagood's Brigade, still sheltered in the commissary bombproof, were under orders to support Reilly's North Carolinians on the left. The artillery crews on the Sea Face continued to answer the naval bombardment as best they could. Having withstood for 56 hours the rain of nearly 20,000 Federal naval rounds, the Confederate defenders steeled themselves for the final act in the drama. The majority would defend their fort, not as artillerymen, but as infantrymen armed with rifled muskets.

On the beach to the north, as the naval bombardment was redirected to the fort's lower Sea Face, Fleet Capt. Breese lost no time in commencing the attack. Though under orders to guide his movements on the advance of the army's infantry, Breese waved his men forward without waiting: "*Charge! Charge!*" The men sprang to their feet, cheering wildly, and raced along the beach toward the Northeast Bastion of Fort Fisher. Breese and the other officers, their swords aloft, struggled to keep up with the surging mass, Lt. Cmdr. James Parker's long greatcoat flapping madly behind him. As the rush began Captain Dawson became alarmed, for his 400 marines were out of position along the beach. Instead of remaining at the breastworks as ordered to provide fire support for the attacking sailors, most of the marine force was swept up in the excitement of the advance. The leathernecks charged along with the column, shouting as they raced for the fort. The bluejackets stormed into the battle without the fire support Breese was expecting from Dawson's command.

As the storming party closed the distance to the fort, the ranks were raked by canister fire from the sally port, and Lamb's sharpshooters began to find their marks. Federal bluejackets and marines began to scream and fall. A round splintered one of the naval flagstaffs, wrenching it from the hands of Seaman Auzella Savage, who gathered the shortened pole and ran on with his flag held high. Within 300 yards of the fort the withering canister fire brought the main column to a sudden halt. The men in front hugged the ground for cover, impeding the progress of those bunched up behind them. The column's unit organization deteriorated rapidly in the confusion, while many of the Federals continued to rush unchecked toward the great walls of Fort Fisher.

William Lamb watched intently as the attack unfolded, withholding a concentrated fire until the Federals were close under the battlements. Nearby, Chase Whiting stood defiantly atop the parapet, glaring at the onrushing enemy. The years of planning for this very moment, the repeated warnings, the vitu-

Continued on page 45

Lieutenant Commander James Parker's Diagram of the Naval Ground Assault on the Northeast Bastion of Fort Fisher

When Admiral Porter selected Kidder Randolph Breese to lead the naval contingent onshore, James Parker waived his seniority and commanded the second division as Breese's subordinate.

(A) Initial Contact with the Palisade Fence

It was here, as the advance of the column was decimated by an overwhelming fire of musketry, that the officers and men became bunched and crowded along the fence. Parker reported that the men were punished severely without being able to return the fire.

(B) The Advance to the First Angle

Rather than surging around the end of the palisades, the attackers veered to the right along the fence and advanced to the first angle. Here, through a narrow opening torn by exploding naval rounds, Parker observed the enemy jeering at the attackers, challenging them to "board" the fort. Some "*were seemingly unarmed,*" he wrote, "*waving their hats to us, and beckoning us forward.*"

With Breese moving along the column trying to rally the wavering mass of Federals, Parker took charge at the head of the column. Shouting the command "*Forward,*" he stepped through the gap, followed by a number of officers and men.

The renewed attack was short lived, and the survivors scampered back to the north side of the fence. When Parker entered the breach, he turned to see if the rest of the men were following, but by then the rout had begun. To his "*intense surprise and mortification,*" Parker observed the remainder of the column "*ingloriously flying along the beach away from the fort.*"

(C) The Sand Knolls

With a party of about 60 survivors, division leaders Charles Cushman, Thomas Selfridge, Lucien Dawson, and Parker took cover as best they could along the north side of the fence and hillocks at point "B."

Breese struggled vainly to stop the stampeding sailors and marines, running after the men and screaming for them to return. Having failed to rally the column, Breese returned "*under a shower of bullets*" to point "C."

Those who stayed at the front remained under cover until after dark. Many of the tars and leathernecks who would later receive the Medal of Honor employed themselves in pulling their wounded comrades to safety in the rear.

Compare Points A, B, and C on Parker's sketch to the same points on the naval assault map, p. 42.

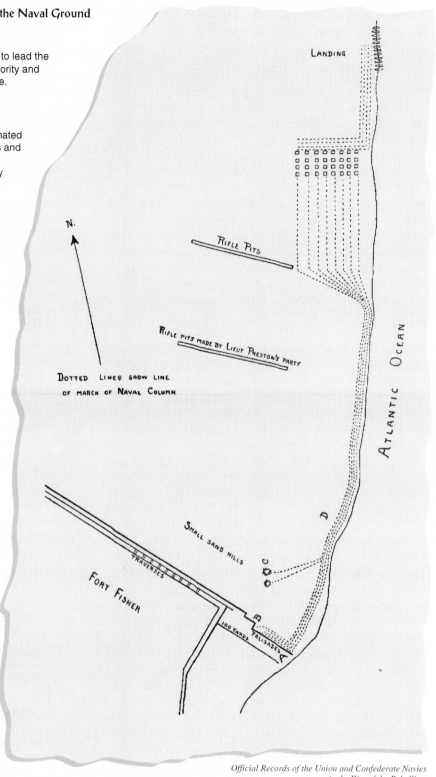

Official Records of the Union and Confederate Navies in the War of the Rebellion.
Ser. 1, Vol. 11

While most of the marine sharpshooters were out of position when the naval attack began, a small contingent performed the task assigned them:

"*The advanced position that was to be occupied was extremely dangerous owing to the nearness of the enemy and the continuous rain of shot and shell that swept over it . . . Volunteers were not plentiful; indeed for a time not a single one offered his services for the undertaking. Then Lieutenant [Charles] Williams volunteered the whole guard of which I was sergeant . . . . We crawled the entire distance to our posts [and] were compelled to stay from 1 o'clock until dark amid the bursting shells and the whizzing hail of bullets . . . . to show your hat above cover meant almost instantly to have it knocked off by a bullet.*" —**Sgt. Richard Binder**, United States Marine Corps, USS *Ticonderoga*. Medal of Honor recipient at Fort Fisher.

perative pleas for assistance, had all gone for naught. The fort's garrison was vastly outnumbered (the naval column alone outnumbered the Confederates), and it was all too apparent that there would be no assistance from Braxton Bragg. Whiting could do nothing now but shout encouragement to the gray-clad defenders whose rifles bristled from the ramparts.

In a moment the attackers—including all of the column's executive officers—arrived in a headlong rush at the palisades below the Northeast Bastion. Colonel Lamb shouted for his men to open fire, and a devastating volley erupted from the parapet. The *"murderous fire greeted them and swept them down,"* the young colonel boasted. From his vantage point some 50 yards away and below the enemy, Fleet Capt. Breese noted that the parapet *"was lined with one dense mass of musketeers, who played sad havoc with our men."* The sailors and marines were dropping quickly. While a handful of men surged around the end of the palisade, the main body turned to the right and filed along the fence to the first angle in the stockade. Though original plans had included bypassing the palisades to assault the upper Sea Face, the detour along the fence provided the Federals better protection from the sustained enemy rifle fire.

The dense blue mass of humanity below the Northeast Bastion was at near point blank range, and the Confederates could not miss. James Parker reported that *"almost every shot from the enemy carried its message of wound or death to some one of our number."* High above the attackers the animated Whiting was barking orders, cursing, and challenging his men to kill the enemy. The Confederate riflemen in turn taunted the bluejackets, screaming obscenities at the assailants. *"We were now so close that we could hear the voices of the rebels,"* Ensign Robely Evans of the *Powhatan* later recorded, *"and what they said need not be written here."*

As the advance of the column crowded along the palisade fence, K. R. Breese, under a hail of gunfire, went back to urge units in the rear to come to the aid of those in front. Breese called out over the din of battle: *"Rise, men, and charge!"* But few were eager to push forward. *"Oh, such a fire as [we] were under,"* wrote Lt. John Bartlett of the *Susquehanna*. *"Sailors and officers were dropping all around me [but] I got a rifle from a marine and settled a few rebels."* *"Come on,"* shouted Thomas O. Selfridge as he made his way to where Parker and Charles Cushman stood at a narrow, shot-induced opening at the angle of the fence. The crisis of the engagement was at hand for Breese's command. The men were exhausted from the long charge down the beach, and the column began to waver. *"The situation was a very grave one,"* remembered Selfridge. *"The rush of the sailors was over; they were packed like sheep in a pen, while the enemy were crowding the ramparts not forty yards away, and shooting into them as fast as they could fire."* In an effort to renew the attack, Parker stepped through the breach in the stockade and urged the men forward.

A handful of courageous Federals pushed through the gap. Others had passed through similar openings with little success: Robely Evans was shot down as he clambered up the fort's outer wall, and as he struggled to continue was struck again. Incapacitated with severe wounds in both legs, Evans lay bleed-

ing as a Confederate marksman tried to finish the young ensign for good. One of Evans' toes was shot off before he succeeded in rolling over and squeezing off a succession of pistol rounds at the determined Confederate rifleman. Evans won the feverish duel, as one of the shots struck his antagonist in the neck. The Confederate soldier tumbled from the parapet and lay dead beside Evans on the sandy slope of the fort's outer wall. Another taunting Confederate was leveled by a marine from the USS *Fort Jackson*, while quarter gunner James Tallentine of the *Tacony* marked the zenith of the naval assault. Tallentine, an Englishman who received a Medal of Honor for heroism during the capture of Plymouth, N.C., two months earlier, was shot and killed on the parapet. Tallentine apparently toppled over into the ranks of the enemy.

Pushing past Parker and Cushman and through the shot-torn palisades, Acting Ens. George Wood of the *Chippewa* noted that at least five of his comrades were ahead of him, *"but it was too hot. The parapet of the fort seemed to be lined with men, and one rebel officer stood up there clapping his hands, singing out to his men, to kill the Yankee [sons of bitches]."* As the survivors made their way back to the north side of the fence the panicked words, *"They are retreating,"* began to make their rounds among the Federals. The mob quickly became demoralized, unable to match the overwhelming Confederate fire. Selfridge lamented that *"flesh and blood could not long endure being killed in this slaughter-pen."* Finally, the marines and sailors in the rear of the column, witnessing the plight of their comrades in front, broke and fled northward up the beach. *"Soon the order of retreat rang from mouth to mouth,"* reported the *Mackinaw*'s Abraham Louch, *"and the whole party were in a disorganized retreat."*

Breese, mortified by the inglorious flight, tried vainly to persuade the mob to return to the front, but the rout was complete. Giving up the chase, the fleet captain returned to where the naval division leaders, including Captain Dawson and a few marines, were cowering with about 60 men who remained close under the battlements. The party sought cover along the palisades and sand knolls as best it could.

As the tars and leathernecks were driven from the beach in a perfect rout, a resounding shout of defiance rose up from the Confederate defenders atop the earthen mounds of Fort Fisher. *"The enemy began to cheer,"* wrote James Parker, and as if to punctuate their success, they fired on the remaining party of Federals with renewed vigor. *"In an instant . . . four officers fell at my side,"* continued Parker, among them the first division's Charles Cushman. This small detachment would be forced to hold its position until darkness allowed them to escape to the north.

The dead and wounded lay scattered by the hundreds. William B. Cushing passed unmolested toward the rear in an effort to rally his men, and later remembered that *"That retreat was a fearful sight. The dead lay thick[ly] strewn along the beach, and the wounded falling constantly, called for help to their comrades, and prayed to God that they might not be left behind. I saw the wounded stagger to their feet all weak and bloody, only to receive other and more fatal wounds and fall to rise no more."* That evening, continued Cushing, the tide rolled in *"and drowned many of our number who fell upon the beach; and swept off into the remorseless ocean the hero clay of many a gallant sailor. How few realize at what cost our Nation's unity has been purchased!"*

Caught up in the excitement of the moment, Lamb and Whiting were elated at the outcome of the attack, and Fisher's defenders cheered wildly. With *"small loss to ourselves,"* observed William Lamb, *"we witnessed what had never been seen before, a disorderly rout of American sailors and marines."* But the young commander of the South's largest fort would soon lament that *"it was a Pyrrhus victory."* * Shouts of elation were still ringing along the battlements when Lamb and Whiting looked suddenly to their left, stunned to see several large flags of United States infantry units waving above the western salient of Fort Fisher.

Vessels of the Naval Storming Party:

Brooklyn, Chippewa, Colorado, Fort Jackson, Gettysburg, Huron, Iosco, Juniata, Kansas, Mackinaw, Malvern, Maratanza, Minnesota, Mohican, Montgomery, Monticello, Nereus, Osceola, Pawtuxet, Pequot, Pontoosuc, Powhatan, Rhode Island, Santiago de Cuba, Sassacus, Seneca, Shenandoah, Susquehanna, Tacony, Ticonderoga, Tristram Shandy, Tuscarora, Vanderbilt, Wabash, Yantic

---

* This reference to Pyrrhus reflects a well-educated William Lamb's familiarity with ancient military history. Pyrrhus (319-272 B.C.E.) was king of a district in ancient Greece known as Epirus. Having assumed the throne as a boy, Pyrrhus was deposed, but rose again to reclaim his reign over Epirus with the aid of Egypt's king Ptolemy I. King Pyrrhus then launched a massive military conquest of neighboring territories. He conquered much of the kingdom of Macedonia and all of Thessaly, only to be driven out in defeat in 283.

When Roman legions began threatening their Mediterranean neighbors, the despotic military adventurer allied himself with Tarentum, a Greek colony in what is now southern Italy. As champion of the Italiote Greeks, Pyrrhus arrived with a military force of nearly 30,000 men in 280 B.C.E. At Heraclea, he engaged in a bloody battle and defeated the Romans, who were terrorized by the strange beasts (elephants) that Pyrrhus unleashed upon them.

Pyrrhus clashed with the Romans a second time in 279, in the collosal Battle of Asculum in the province of Apulia. In this engagement he faced a better-prepared Roman army. Pyrrhus again employed his elephants, but the forty-thousand-man Roman force fought fiercely. Pyrrhus managed to emerge victorious, but at enormous cost to his army. Casualties were staggering—perhaps 10,000-12,000 on both sides—and Pyrrhus lost the best elements of his force. There are several translations for Pyrrhus' remark on this dearly won triumph, but it can be paraphrased as *"One more such victory and we are undone."*

Thus through history, a victory achieved at great cost (or whose cost outweighs its benefits) has been termed a "Pyrrhic victory." The repulse of the Union naval column at Fort Fisher was a Pyrrhic victory for the Confederates. It brought no great loss of manpower, but it diverted and held the attention of a sizeable portion of the garrison while U.S. ground forces breached the fort at the western salient.

Though eventually toppled by the Romans at Beneventum in 275, Pyrrhus was considered in antiquity as one of the great generals of Hellenistic times. But his military conquests were temporary—as brief in the grand scheme of things as Colonel Lamb's perceived triumph over the sailors and marines along the Northeast Bastion of Fort Fisher.

Flag Lt. Samuel W. Preston   *Harper's Weekly*

Samuel Preston and Benjamin Porter were the best of friends. They had studied in the same class at the United States Naval Academy, and subsequently spent much of the war together. After being captured during a night attack on Fort Sumter in 1863, the two young officers served time together in a South Carolina prison. The pair were paroled in time to accompany the expeditions against Fort Fisher, and by all accounts they were among the navy's most promising officers—the *"brightest ornaments"* on the personal staff of Adm. David Dixon Porter.

Porter (no relation to the admiral) was just 19 years old, and commanded the flagship *Malvern*. The 23-year-old Preston was the fleet's flag lieutenant, and would serve as an aide to K. R. Breese in the forthcoming ground attack.

On the bloody Sunday of January 15, 1865, the two friends raced together toward their destiny before the great sand bastion of Fort Fisher. Porter, holding the admiral's standard aloft, fell dead with a bullet through his chest about 100 yards from the fort's palisades. Preston was at the head of the attacking column when an enemy shot ploughed through his left thigh, severing the femoral artery.

Lieutenant Roswell H. Lamson, a fellow Annapolis classmate, saw a sailor stoop down to assist Preston, only to fall upon the stricken officer with a wound of his own. Someone pulled the man away as Preston, bleeding profusely, *"turned over on his back and soon expired."* Lamson lay bleeding nearby. *"It made my heart sick to see [Preston] stetched out on the sand,"* he wrote, *"and I mourned him."*

During the retreat Lt. John Bartlett stopped under fire to check on Porter. *"I ran to him and dropped beside him,"* he explained. Bartlett hastily gathered a few of Porter's personal belongings, and then *"Oh! How I did run for a little way."*

Lt. Benjamin H. Porter   *Harper's Weekly*

Official Records of the Union and Confederate Navies

ABOVE: Admiral David Porter's flagship USS *Malvern*, commanded by Lt. Benjamin H. Porter. Before embarking for Federal Point on the morning of January 15, 1865, Lt. Samuel Preston left a note in his cabin requesting that he be buried on the grounds of the U.S. Naval Academy, in the event of his death at Fort Fisher. At ten past midnight on January 16, almost 14 hours after going ashore to participate in the naval ground attack, the bodies of Samuel Preston and Benjamin Porter were returned to the *Malvern* "*and properly cared for.*" Later that morning, with the ship's flag at half-mast, Ensign John Gratton viewed his friends for the last time: "*A calm, peaceful smile played around [Porter's] mouth,*" he noted, "*but Preston wore a look of agony as his suffering must have been terrible.*" At 2:30 that afternoon, in a cold, drizzling rain, the fallen officers were transferred aboard the *Santiago de Cuba* for the journey northward via Hampton Roads, Virginia.

LEFT: Federal troops come ashore on Federal Point, January 13, 1865. In the right background, shells are bursting above Fort Fisher.

SECOND EXPEDITION

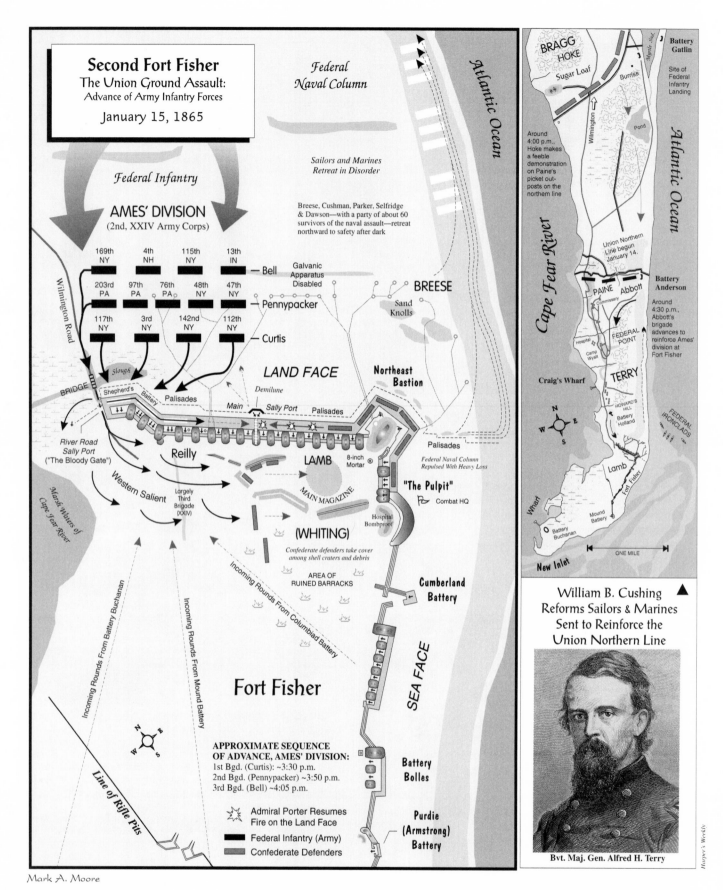

Second Fort Fisher
The Union Ground Assault:
Advance of Army Infantry Forces
January 15, 1865

Federal Naval Column

Atlantic Ocean

Federal Infantry

AMES' DIVISION
(2nd, XXIV Army Corps)

Sailors and Marines Retreat in Disorder

Breese, Cushman, Parker, Selfridge & Dawson—with a party of about 60 survivors of the naval assault—retreat northward to safety after dark

169th NY	4th NH	115th NY	13th IN	— Bell
203rd PA	97th PA	76th PA	48th NY	47th NY	— Pennypacker
117th NY	3rd NY	142nd NY	112th NY	— Curtis

Galvanic Apparatus Disabled

BREESE

Sand Knolls

Wilmington Road

Slough

BRIDGE

Shepherd's Battery

LAND FACE

Palisades

Demilune

Main Sally Port Palisades

Northeast Bastion

River Road Sally Port ("The Bloody Gate")

Reilly

Western Salient

Largely Third Brigade (XXIV)

LAMB

8-inch Mortar

MAIN MAGAZINE

"The Pulpit"

⚑ Combat HQ

Palisades

Federal Naval Column Repulsed With Heavy Loss

Marsh Waters of Cape Fear River

(WHITING)

Hospital Bombproof

Confederate defenders take cover among shell craters and debris

AREA OF RUINED BARRACKS

Cumberland Battery

Incoming Rounds From Battery Buchanan

Incoming Rounds From Mound Battery

Incoming Rounds From Columbiad Battery

Fort Fisher

SEA FACE

APPROXIMATE SEQUENCE OF ADVANCE, AMES' DIVISION:
1st Bgd. (Curtis): ~3:30 p.m.
2nd Bgd. (Pennypacker) ~3:50 p.m.
3rd Bgd. (Bell) ~4:05 p.m.

✺ Admiral Porter Resumes Fire on the Land Face
█ Federal Infantry (Army)
█ Confederate Defenders

Battery Bolles

Purdie (Armstrong) Battery

Line of Rifle Pits

Mark A. Moore

BRAGG
HOKE

Sugar Loaf

Burriss

Myrtle Snd.

Battery Gatlin

Site of Federal Infantry Landing

Cape Fear River

Atlantic Ocean

Around 4:00 p.m., Hoke makes a feeble demonstration on Paine's picket outposts on the northern line

Wilmington

Pond

Union Northern Line begun January 14.

PAINE Abbott

Commissary

Hospital

Camp Wyatt

Craig's Wharf

FEDERAL POINT

TERRY

HOWARD'S HILL

Battery Holland

Battery Anderson

Around 4:30 p.m., Abbott's brigade advances to reinforce Ames' division at Fort Fisher

FEDERAL IRONCLADS

Lamb

Wharf

Mound Battery

Battery Buchanan

Fort Fisher

ONE MILE

New Inlet

N W E S

William B. Cushing ▲
Reforms Sailors & Marines Sent to Reinforce the Union Northern Line

Harper's Weekly

Bvt. Maj. Gen. Alfred H. Terry

"All the land face [of Fort Fisher] now looked as if wrapped in smoke and flame—the screaming, exploding shells tearing the earthwork, making holes in the traverses, and in all the history of war it is doubtful if a more infernal fire ever fell upon a fort." — **Sgt. T. A. McNeill**, 1st North Carolina Heavy Artillery, garrison of Fort Fisher, on the naval bombardment just before the Federal ground assault.

"Not far in advance towered the frowning Fortress . . . and, though none saw, all knew, that above, in imperial majesty, sat the Angel of Death."
— **Surgeon J. A. Mowris**, 117th New York, Curtis' brigade

Alfred Terry's Federal infantry forces spent the hours leading up to the ground assault in vigorous preparation for the advance. Lieutenant Col. Cyrus Comstock, Terry's chief engineer, oversaw the strengthening of the Union northern line against a possible Confederate attack from Sugar Loaf. This strong defensive post was held by Brig. Gen. Charles J. Paine's 3,300-man division of United States Colored Troops, and Col. Joseph C. Abbott's brigade, for a total of approximately 4,700 men.

By noontime the brigades of Galusha Pennypacker and Louis Bell (of Adelbert Ames' division) had advanced southward as far as Craig's Landing, while N. Martin Curtis' brigade occupied its position of the previous night in the vicinity of Battery Holland. General Terry established his combat headquarters at this outwork approximately 500 yards north of Fort Fisher.

As the men of Ames' division (approximately 4,200 strong) prepared for the attack, tensions between Curtis and the temperamental Ames threatened to undermine the operation. As a result, Curtis was receiving orders directly from Terry, leaving a seething Ames to oversee his remaining two brigades. Despite the personality conflict (a common occurrence on Civil War battlefields) Del Ames was a competent officer. He was 29 years old, and had received his first taste of division command in the summer of 1863. Having turned over the 20th Maine Infantry to a young colonel named Joshua Lawrence Chamberlain, Ames was then commanding a brigade in the Army of the Potomac's XI Corps. When his division commander, Francis Barlow, was wounded, Ames assumed temporary command and led the division through the successful defense of Cemetery Hill at Gettysburg on July 2.[1] Prior to the Fort Fisher expeditions, he commanded a division during the siege of Petersburg, Virginia.

At 2:00 p.m. on January 15, 1865, General Terry began final preparations for the assault on Fort Fisher. Ames was ordered to deploy a detachment of sharpshooters from the 13th Indiana Infantry—a unit armed with Spencer repeating rifles—to provide fire support for the men of Curtis' advance line of skirmishers, which lay within 175 yards of the fort's western salient. The main body of Curtis' brigade moved from Howard's Hill to within 300 yards of Shepherd's Battery. General Ames then supervised the deployment of his remaining two brigades, advancing Pennypacker's brigade to Curtis' former position, and Bell's brigade to within 200 yards behind Pennypacker. In this manner, the Federal infantry eased to within attacking distance.

"The whole division was covered from the fire of the enemy, as far as possible, by the inequalities of the ground and slight pits formed by throwing up the sand." —**Brig. Gen. Adelbert Ames**

THE FEDERAL INFANTRY ATTACK

"The one weak point in the 'Malakoff' was the gate."
— Lt. Martin Van Buren Richardson, 4th New Hampshire, Bell's brigade

Unlike the naval ground attack, which was commenced in a long and narrow column, the initial Federal infantry advance would be made in regular line of battle. This was Curtis' plan, and it was approved by Cyrus Comstock and Alfred Terry.

As the Union naval bombardment subsided along the northern front of Fort Fisher, Maj. James Reilly's Confederate riflemen appeared atop the battlements and began finding their marks among the ranks of Curtis' brigade—despite the fire support provided by the 13th Indiana. The Federals lay down, hugging the sandy plain and digging shallow trenches to protect themselves as best they could while waiting for the order to advance. *"The final rush will be made,"* Curtis had told Terry, *"when you see me rise in the middle of my line and hear me call aloud."* The assured Federal commander replied to Curtis: *"With your brigade on the parapet I shall feel certain of success."*

The Attack of Curtis' Brigade

Arrayed in a battle line that stretched eastward from the Wilmington Road to a point opposite the fort's main sally port, the men waited impatiently for Curtis to launch the assault. *"It was an awful moment,"* noted an observer, and *"with compressed lips our troops were breathing a silent petition for home and country."* Captain A. G. Lawrence, of General Ames' staff, approached Curtis and received permission to accompany the advance. Though sent to the front by Ames, Lawrence understood that the First Brigade commander was acting independently of the division commander's supervision. The staff officer took a position within the ranks of the 117th New York Infantry, and waited for the order to charge.

That order would be *"simply the loosing of a yell,"* for Curtis feared that the usual series of commands for maneuver would take too long, allowing Reilly's Confederates an opportunity to cut down the Federal advance before a charge could be mounted. Every officer and man was instructed that the line of advance would oblique toward the right, and that the initial point of attack would be the "gate" and the area between the first and second traverses of the fort. Finally, at 3:25 p.m. the signal to advance was given by General Terry, and the shrill steam whistles of the Federal fleet announced the decision to both attackers and defenders. As the head of Fleet Capt. Breese's naval column raced toward its slaughter before the Northeast Bastion of Fort Fisher, N. Martin Curtis rose and called aloud: *"Forward."*

In an instant the men sprang up and rushed forward. There were a few shouts of excitement, but Curtis had warned the troops to refrain from cheering. The men were running *"at the top of their speed,"* and would need all their remaining energy to force an entry at the western salient. Reilly's Confederates immediately unleashed a concentrated fire upon the onrushing

Federals, while the light artillery in the sally ports opened upon the flanks of the enemy battle line.

With many of the attackers falling rapidly, the right of Curtis' battle line swarmed into the deep slough in front of Shepherd's Battery, and around the causeway leading to the sally port. The two light fieldpieces guarding the gate and its approaches opened upon the Northerners as they floundered in the mire. Many of the men became stuck fast in the unforgiving bog, and were shot down easily by Confederate riflemen who blazed away from atop the western salient and through loopholes in the palisades near the gate. The garrison had pulled the planking from the wooden bridge, leaving only the narrow stringers—which would have rendered a crossing difficult under any circumstances. While the lone Napoleon at the gate discharged its rounds directly up the road, the Parrott rifle near the river raked the bridge with a terrible enfilade fire. Some of the men took shelter beneath the bridge as best they could, while others scurried to gain the base of the fort's outer wall. Confederate small arms from atop the battlements and artillery fire from the center sally port also told severely upon the left of Curtis' line, which had a longer distance to travel in its oblique movement to the right. The 112th New York lost its commander almost immediately, as Col. John F. Smith fell mortally wounded at the head of his regiment.

Splashing through the mire, the men began crowding in front of the fort's palisades. Though the fence had been severely damaged by naval gunfire, it was more intact in front of the western salient than it was further to the east. Consequently, the openings in front of Shepherd's Battery were fairly narrow. Of Curtis' 1,000 men, roughly 100 were armed with heavy axes, and under a hail of gunfire these "pioneers" began feverishly chopping the fence to widen the gaps so the infantry could pass through more easily.[2]

A thin complement of Rebel gunners struggled to maintain the fire of the riverside fieldpieces. The guns thundered up the River Road, rendering the bridge and its approaches momentarily uninhabitable. The men of the 117th and 3rd New York regiments began crowding to their left to escape the line of fire. On the left of the Federal line the troops of the 112th and 142nd New York, desperate for cover, hugged the ground and began gathering sand and sod around them. Soon *the whole line was invisible*," remembered Chaplain William Hyde of the 112th, "*the men having, like worms, worked themselves into the sand.*" Confederate bullets rained upon the bluecoats, striking flesh and piercing and clanging off of their accouterments. It was a *a terrific storm of death*," but with every lull in the firing the survivors on the left of the line would scurry toward the right to await their opportunity to enter the fort. With all order lost, the attackers became bunched in a teeming mob before the western salient.

As the gaps in the fence began to widen, however, Curtis' infantry poured through and raced toward the base of the fort's mammoth wall—and by this time they were cheering and screaming wildly. Among the first to breach the stockade was Captain Lawrence, of General Ames' staff, but the volunteer combatant was soon dismembered by fragments from an exploding shell. The 142nd New York's William Walling—flag-stealing hero of the December 1864 reconnaissance of the fort, and newly-promoted captain of Company C—was determined to lead his men to glory on this day at Fort Fisher. But the excited youngster, overcome with anxiety, suffered a panic attack and had to fairly crawl to the slope of the outer wall at Shepherd's Battery, where he collapsed in exhaustion. The Federals surged through and began massing at the base of the exterior slope, along a ditch formed by the excavation of earth for the fort's construction. In this depression, close under the battlements, the men enjoyed a measure of welcome safety from the deadly Confederate fire.

The enemy had finally reached the fort, and at this moment of crisis Major Reilly's defenders suffered a critical lapse of judgment. Instead of climbing out to man the crest of the parapet, where they could shoot directly down into the attackers (as the contingent under Whiting and Lamb were doing at the Northeast Bastion), the defenders inexplicably kept their stations on the floors of the gun chambers. "*If there was any error in the command of the Confederates,*" General Curtis would later note, "*it was in not driving out their command and fighting us at the ditch, before we ascended the parapet.*" Thus the woefully out-manned garrison at the western salient lost the one small advantage it might have employed to slow the Federal advance.[3]

The lead elements of Curtis' force, regimental flags and guidons in hand, mounted the exterior slope and began their determined rush toward the summit of the wall, some 23 feet above. The Confederates at Shepherd's Battery, under Capt. Kinchen Braddy, braced themselves to meet the inevitable. The enemy standards soon bobbed into view, and when the attackers began clambering for a foothold on the parapet, Braddy's Rebels unleashed an awful volley. Scores of Federals were cut down, and the color bearer of the 3rd New York was knocked off the wall, tumbling back down the slope into his oncoming comrades. Driven by shear weight of numbers, however, the bluecoats poured over the crest, and the discharge of weapons became fast and furious. The distance had been closed, and the fight became a desperate close-quarters brawl, with combatants falling rapidly on both sides. The men, shouting and cursing, clubbed each other with their weapons, and jabbed and slashed with their bayonets and swords. It was the beginning of one of the worst hand-to-hand fights of the American Civil War.

The first Union standard to be planted on the enemy bastion belonged to the 117th New York Infantry. Sergeant Fred Boden thrust a flagstaff into the sod, only to have it shot in half by a rifle ball. He planted the flag a second time, and again it was knocked down by rifle fire. The persistent sergeant, digging in the sand in an effort to protect himself, managed to plant the flag for a third and final time. By day's end its fabric would be riddled with bullet holes.

Conspicuous among the surging host of Federals was the indefatigable N. Martin Curtis, who was one of the first to reach the summit of the wall. The First Brigade commander lumbered upon a Rebel gunner who was reportedly trying to discharge one of the battered seacoast pieces in the second gun chamber. When the artilleryman ignored a demand for his surrender while continuing to fit the weapon with a friction primer, *"a sharp blow from my saber on his outstretched hand,"* boasted Curtis, put an end to the matter.

Slowly, the Federals began to wrench the first two gun chambers from their overwhelmed defenders. Many Confederates were made prisoners, and others were forced eastward onto the parade ground and into the adjacent batteries. Curtis urged his men forward, pulling them aboard the fort, and pushing them forward up the high traverses. By this time, however, the men were exhausted—and they began to lose some of their momentum.

Pennypacker's Advance

Alfred Terry watched the action unfold from his command post at Battery Holland, and within ten minutes of the advance of Curtis' brigade he hurried Col. Galusha Pennypacker's command forward. After a few personal words of encouragement from General Terry, the young colonel—just 20 years old—led his troops to the front. *"We had not long to remain [lying down] under the withering shower of iron,"* remembered an officer in the 97th Pennsylvania, *"and [we] moved forward with a bound."* Adelbert Ames and his staff, who had *"watched with anxious eyes the charge of the First Brigade,"* accompanied the advance toward the fort.

The units of Pennypacker's Second Brigade were no strangers to attacking heavy seacoast fortifications. Four of the brigade's five regiments had participated in the siege of Battery Wagner—on Morris Island, South Carolina—during the latter half of 1863. Two of these regiments (the 48th New York and 76th Pennsylvania, as part of George C. Strong's brigade) had participated in the unsuccessful direct assaults upon Wagner, and had suffered greatly for it. The 76th Pennsylvania took part in both the July 11 and July 18 (1863) attacks, suffering more than 100 casualties. The 48th New York briefly held the slope of Battery Wagner on July 18, but it paid dearly for the endeavor, and came away with a loss of 242 men. The 97th Pennsylvania and 47th New York took part only in the siege of Wagner, and thus suffered fewer casualties. The fifth regiment in Pennypacker's brigade, however, was the newest. Having been organized at Philadelphia in September 1864, the 203rd Pennsylvania Infantry was barely four months old. It had participated briefly in operations against Richmond, Virginia, before arriving at Cape Fear to help capture Fort Fisher. By the end of the day on January 15, 1865, the 203rd would count the highest casualty rate of any Federal unit in the attack on Fisher, with three changes of command and a loss of 187 men.

Major Reilly's Confederates, despite the foothold gained by Curtis' men, continued to rake the plain below with a killing fire. Pennypacker's men *"came on like an avalanche,"* and as the troops approached the fort they began to feel the sting of enemy bullets. One of the Napoleons at the center sally port thundered upon their left flank, just as it had done to Curtis' line, and the 47th New York lost its entire color guard to a single canister blast. Lieutenant Col. William B. Coan and Col. John S. Littell, commanders of the 48th New York and 76th Pennsylvania respectively, had survived unscathed the carnage

at Battery Wagner. Both men would fall this day upon the sands of Federal Point, without ever reaching Fort Fisher. Coan was severely wounded while forming his regiment for the advance, and Littell was shot down while crossing the slight rise of ground in front of the bog at the western salient.

The men of the Second Brigade, *"in neat fighting trim,"* rushed up behind the rear elements of Curtis' command and joined them in clambering up the walls of Shepherd's Battery. The newcomers also overlapped the crowded base of the outer slope, and a portion of the 203rd Pennsylvania Infantry surged ahead to force a passage at the riverside gate.

The thin garrison of Fort Fisher had all it could handle in struggling with the attackers atop the parapet. Moreover, many of the fort's "defenders" were cowering within its bombproofs and internal passages, refusing to help repel the enemy. The "gate" at the River Road sally port was not really a gate at all, but rather an open entrance guarded by a low sandbagged wall and a single piece of artillery. The Confederates failed to muster enough men to defend the fort at its most vulnerable point, and the Federals quickly exploited the deficiency. The few Confederates on hand to defend the gate consisted of half of 2nd Company C, 36th North Carolina Regiment—a pitiful 30 to 35 men. Worse, the gunners of Company D, 13th Battalion North Carolina Light Artillery (under Lt. Charles Latham, and to whom the two cannons belonged) were among those who refused to come out and fight. This left the men of Captain Braddy's company to serve the fieldpieces, in addition to using their small arms through the loopholes in the palisades.

The Parrott rifle near the river marsh soon fell silent, allowing Federal sharpshooters to creep around the end of the fence and begin picking off the gunners manning the Napoleon at the gate. Captain James McCormic (commanding Company D, First Battalion North Carolina Heavy Artillery), arrived with about 40 Confederates collected from nearby bombproofs, but they weighed little against the powerful tide of the enemy. The situation began to deteriorate rapidly for the Confederates. Captain Braddy rushed off to collect reinforcements for the gate area, but when he rounded the angle of the salient on the parade ground, he and his entourage were mistakenly fired upon by a group of Hagood's South Carolinians near the center sally port. There were no reinforcements to be had.

The gun chambers of Shepherd's Battery were now teeming with Federal soldiers, many of whom turned their weapons upon the defenders of the gate below. The range was close and deadly. As the Rebel gunners fell, the few remaining would step up to take their places. The rounds from the Napoleon thundered up the causeway leading to the gate, directly into the faces of the 203rd Pennsylvania Infantry and elements of the 97th, who were floundering in the mire around the bridge.

The tide, however, was turning in favor of the attackers, and the Federals soon began knocking down the sandbag wall at the sally port. *"I looked around and saw the stars and stripes floating from the top of the parapet,"* remembered Pvt. Zack Fulmore, *"with what seemed to me to be a thousand bluecoats around it."* Private Fulmore attempted to spike the Napoleon at the gate, but he and his comrades were soon overrun by members of the 117th New York, who swarmed down from

Shepherd's Battery and captured them. Confederate POWs were soon en route toward the Federal rear echelon near Battery Holland. If defending *"the most defenseless spot in all Fort Fisher against Curtis' brigade,"* Fulmore would remark years later, *"and only surrendering after being completely surrounded by another brigade, isn't pretty good evidence of true soldiery, I would be glad to see a specimen of it."*

To complete the chaos and desperation that marked the fight at the River Road sally port, incoming Confederate rounds from the heavy seacoast guns at Battery Buchanan—located at the base of the peninsula—began to rain upon the western salient. This long-range fire was intended to blunt the Federal assault, but it brought death and destruction to friend and foe alike. The 142nd New York's Lt. George Simpson remembered that *"Rivulets of blood ran from the gateway."*

Scaling the outer wall of Shepherd's Battery at the head of his command, Galusha Pennypacker mounted the parapet brandishing the regimental standard of the 97th Pennsylvania Infantry. The regiment's color bearer, Cpl. William McCarty, had been shot on the outer slope, and Pennypacker swept up the colors and carried them to the summit. Nearby was Col. John W. Moore, commanding the 203rd Pennsylvania. Boasting of the regiment he had once commanded, young Pennypacker waved the banner of the 97th and called out to his subordinate: *"Moore, I want you to take notice that this is the flag of my old regiment."*

The Confederate resistance was stiff and the terreplein, gun chambers, and parapet itself were crowded with the dead and wounded of both sides. The firing was face to face across the sandy mounds, and there seemed to be no escaping the hail of bullets. *"A comrade next to me on the traverse was shot in his brains and killed,"* lamented Cpl. Henry McQueen of the 1st North Carolina Battalion. *"His brains splattered in my face."* McQueen himself soon fell victim to a Federal bullet.

Colonel Pennypacker pushed boldly onto the fort's third traverse *"amid a shower of bullets,"* and jabbed the flagstaff of the 97th's colors firmly into the sod. At that moment, however, the earnest youngster was knocked off his feet when a Rebel bullet crashed into his right hip and exited his lower back. Thus Pennypacker became the first of three Union brigade commanders to fall in the assault on Fort Fisher, and he was borne from the works with what appeared to be a mortal wound. All eight of the 97th Pennsylvania's officers were cut down on the parapet, together with many of the leading officers from the other Federal regiments.

Nearby on the second traverse Colonel Moore, at the head of his 203rd Pennsylvania, pushed ahead with the regiment's flag in hand. Moore was *"waving his colors and commanding his men to follow,"* remembered a fellow officer, when he was felled by a bullet in the torso. Gasping with a mortal wound, Colonel Moore—not much older than Pennypacker at age 25—struggled to urge his men forward: *"No, boys, I am not killed . . . keep on and give them hell."*

As the men of Pennypacker's brigade poured through the riverside gate, General Ames and his staff entered Fort Fisher for the first time. Passing to the rear of the western salient, where many of the attackers were engaged in clearing the angle's

internal galleries, Ames examined the terrain and disposition of the enemy. The open ground to the east was a vast wreck of ruined barracks and shell craters, and many of the defenders (some of whom had been driven from Shepherd's Battery) were collecting among the debris for protection; and perhaps for a final resistance of the Federal onslaught. Moreover, the Federal advance seemed to be stalling in the vicinity of the fourth traverse, and the division commander determined to call forward the Third Brigade. Ames proposed to deploy the men in line of battle facing eastward on the open plain, and to *"charge into the angle formed by the land and sea faces [of the fort]."*

Bell's Advance

Louis Bell had been despondent over the failure of the first expedition against Fort Fisher—the *"Great Wilmington Fizzle,"* as he termed it—and the 27-year-old colonel was eager to take part in the action. The son of one-time New Hampshire governor Samuel Bell, the young brigade commander had been a lawyer in his native New Hampshire before the war.

Bell had recently written his wife a heartfelt and wistful reassurance that everything would be okay if he did not make it home. He had seemed outwardly cheerful the day before the assault, and Sgt. John Hutchinson noted that the colonel's *"habitual smile"* was in evidence. As the brigade commander *"stepped upon the sandy beach,"* wrote Hutchinson, *"his eye, always on the alert for natural curiosities, espied a beautiful piece of white coral."* Bell reached down, grasped the little object, and slid it into his pocket. *"This will do for my little daughter,"* he told a staff officer.

Having moved his troops into position near Battery Holland, *"with a ramrod in his hand as a walking stick,"* Louis Bell waited anxiously for orders to move forward. When the request finally came from General Ames, Alfred Terry lost no time in sending the Third Brigade to the front. *"Forward! Double-quick,"* shouted Bell, and within 15 minutes of Pennypacker's advance, the men were trotting toward Fort Fisher. The same storm that had greeted the Second Brigade's advance—*"a terrible fire from the sharpshooters who lined the parapets of the fort"*—now fell upon Bell's brigade as it drew near. The colonel and his aides took pains to keep the ranks in parade-like order, despite the hail of bullets. In the ranks of the 169th New York, however, one company commander struggled to keep up with the advance. Lieutenant E. R. Mosher had been contused by a spent ball on January 13, but insisted upon joining the assault. Mosher *"went into action . . . being obliged to use a cane,"* reported Col. James A. Colvin of the 169th, and *"he hopped into the fight, leading his men."* Bell called to a staff officer: *"How well the brigade are coming on under so severe a fire!"*

The able young brigade commander, the pride of those who served under him, never made it into the fort. As the men rushed toward the riverside gate, a bullet slammed into Bell's chest and exited from his lower back. He was knocked to the ground just before crossing the bridge, and as the attackers herded past their fallen leader, Bell was borne to the rear a bloody mess. Colonel Alonzo Alden assumed command as Bell was taken away.

Fortunately, some resourceful members of Pennypacker's brigade had replaced the planking that had been torn from the bridge, and Bell's men were able to cross more easily than the earlier attackers. Most of the Third Brigade swarmed in behind the western salient, while some joined their comrades on the walls and parapet of Fort Fisher. In a quest for a share in the glory, the standard bearers of Bell's brigade rushed to plant their colors on the ramparts. Sergeant Peter Keck was one of the first to reach the summit, where he planted the flag of the 115th New York on the first traverse. A standard belonging to the 13th Indiana followed close behind, as did the flags of the 4th New Hampshire and 169th New York. On the plain below, as a heated return fire began to develop from among the ruins south of the land front, the Federals turned the captured Napoleon upon its former owners and opened fire.

By this time the mounds and gun chambers of Shepherd's Battery were overly crowded, as men from three different brigades struggled for room to maneuver among the living, the wounded, and the dead. The 115th New York was divided into two wings, one of which advanced on the open plain below, and the other of which picked its way across the gun chambers and traverses. Of the latter Lt. Col. Nathan Johnson, commanding the 115th, reported that "the officers and men in the advance, with officers and men of the other brigades [were] all vying with each other in the noble emulation of who should be the first in the grand achievements of that memorable day."

Barely 30 minutes had passed since the initial advance of Curtis' brigade, and more than 4,000 Federal infantrymen were crowding the base, slopes, and walls of the western salient, and pushing onto the parade ground to the south. The Federal advance, however, was cautious, for incoming rounds from Battery Buchanan were still bursting along the angle.

Confederate Resistance

On the Northeast Bastion of Fort Fisher, Col. William Lamb had been observing the rout of the Union naval column when his attention was finally diverted toward Shepherd's Battery: "I turned to look at our left and saw, to my astonishment, several Federal battle-flags upon our ramparts." Major William J. Saunders, Fisher's chief of artillery, had been overseeing the fire of the redan's remaining 8-inch columbiad. "I immediately ordered the officer in charge (Lieutenant [William] Swain) to traverse his gun and open on them," reported Saunders. When Chase Whiting beheld the intrusion, he impulsively ordered a counterattack. Colonel Lamb remembered that Whiting lost no time in "calling on those around him to pull down those flags and drive the enemy from the works." Major Saunders, though slightly wounded in the fight with the naval column, collected what men he could to assist in the counterstroke.

Fresh from their victory along the Northeast Bastion, a host of Rebel defenders—General Whiting foremost among them—hurried westward down the battlements toward Shepherd's Battery. Major Saunders, weakened from his injury, collapsed at the foot of the fifth traverse and was soon

carried away. Atop the battlements, however, Whiting's defenders pitched headlong into the Federals at the fourth traverse, with enough momentum to temporarily wrench the mound from the enemy. The savage brawl escalated anew with the arrival of Whiting's contingent. The officers loaded and fired alongside their men, while other combatants bludgeoned each other or fought with their fists. It was "cold steel or the butt of the gun," recalled an observer in Curtis' brigade. As the Union horde jockeyed to keep its lodgment on the battlements, the men stumbled and trod upon the bodies of the dead and wounded of both sides.

Pushing boldly up the third traverse, the indignant Whiting reached for an enemy banner to snatch it down from the works. As the general grappled with the Union color bearer, Little Billy's shoulder insignia became apparent, and shouts arose for his immediate surrender. "Go to hell, you Yankee bastards!" screamed Whiting, who was promptly cut down with two bullets in his right thigh. Lieutenant Wiley H. Williford, one of Lamb's best officers, who had earlier commanded the Blakely rifles along the redan, was soon numbered among the slain.

Several comrades managed to pull the stricken Whiting from the mounds and drag him to relative safety on the plain below. As the general was being attended, Capt. Kinchen Braddy rushed over and blurted out that "all [is] confusion," with Hagood's South Carolinians "killing more of our men than the Yankees." The battle, however, was over for Whiting, and he could only offer encouragement: "Captain, for God's sake, try and stop it." The general was then hauled away to the hospital bombproof below the Pulpit on the Sea Face. Whiting, in a show of support for William Lamb, had cast his lot with the garrison of Fort Fisher, and the region for which he had spent so much time and effort to defend—and he would pay the ultimate price for it.

The Federals regained the fourth traverse, as the fighting reached its zenith along the land front of Fort Fisher. "The struggle for this traverse," observed N. Martin Curtis, "was the hottest and most prolonged single contest of the day." Sergeant T. A. McNeill of Company D, 1st North Carolina Heavy Artillery, remembered that "it was a deadly struggle with the foe . . . the enemy and [our men] firing into each other's faces at a few paces distance." The "killed and wounded," continued Curtis, "were set aside to make room for the comrades who came impetuously forward to support their respective sides." A member of the 203rd Pennsylvania agreed that "it was all too much for even demons."

As Whiting's contingent grappled with the enemy on the battlements, William Lamb assessed his options and sought to organize the garrison's remnants to defend the open plain behind the fort. The commandant raced through the center sally port and outside the work to better observe the condition of affairs at the western salient. From this vantage point Lamb witnessed the violent struggle for the fourth traverse, and observed the rear echelon of Bell's brigade pushing its way toward the riverside gate. "I saw the enemy pouring in by the river road apparently without resistance," remembered Lamb.

"*I doubt if ever before the commander of a work went outside and looked upon the conflict for its possession, but for the construction of the fort it was absolutely necessary for me to do so . . . and I was concealed from the [enemy] by a fragment of the palisade.*"

The colonel ordered Capt. Zachariah Adams to train his two Napoleons in the demilune upon the Federals still trying to enter the gate. Lamb then hurried back to collect as many reinforcements as possible to resist the Federal advance inside the fort. He rallied a small force and posted it behind a section of light breastworks in rear of the sally port, "*and behind every cover that could be found.*" From this new line Lamb hoped to punish the flank of the Federals atop the battlements, as well as deliver a more direct fire into the enemy then deploying behind the western salient.

As the defenders moved into position, Lamb's aide, Lt. Charles H. Blocker, approached to apprise his commander of the dismal situation now facing the garrison: many of Hagood's South Carolinians, the officer reported, had refused to join Reilly's men on the battlements; the galvanic torpedo-firing apparatus had been disabled by the naval bombardment;[4] the guns at the River Road were lost, and the Federals held Shepherd's Battery; worse yet, the enemy was pouring unchecked onto the parade ground.

The news "*was rather disheartening,*" admitted Lamb, but the colonel was undaunted. He believed that if the garrison could hold on until dark, and if Braxton Bragg would finally send Hoke's Division to the fort's relief, the enemy might yet be driven from the works. Whiting's adjutant, Maj. James H. Hill, once again wired Bragg at Sugar Loaf: "*We still hold the fort, but are sorely pressed. Can't you assist us from the outside?*"

Captain Braddy soon arrived to help rally the men, and Colonel Lamb hurried along the oceanside batteries looking for reinforcements. He also sent orders for the Mound Battery and the Columbiad Battery to bring their guns to bear upon the western salient. Lamb returned with about 100 men and added them to the force already engaged along the light breastworks. In this dire hour of need for the garrison, Lamb beseeched every group he could find to rally to the defense of Fort Fisher. He ordered Captain Adams to run the Napoleons through the sally port to the fort's interior, where they opened at close range upon the surging Federals. Lamb also implored the frightened South Carolinians to fire on the enemy, and dashed among the fort's internal passageways looking for additional help. "*I went along the galleries,*" the colonel remembered, "*and begged the sick and slightly wounded to come out and make one supreme effort to dislodge the enemy.*" Within half an hour he had gathered a sizable force.

As Lamb moved along in rear of the land front, however, the gravity of his situation began to sink in. The stunned commander beheld a scene that "*was indescribably horrible. Great cannon broken in two, their carriages wrecked, and among their ruins the mutilated bodies of my dead and dying comrades; others were partly buried in graves dug by the shells which had slain them.*" Worst of all, he lamented, there were "*still no tidings from Bragg.*"

To the west, the parade ground of the fort was teeming with Federal infantry. The troops of Bell's brigade, however, with elements of Pennypacker's, were entirely exposed on the open plain south of the land front. As heavy artillery rounds from three Confederate batteries and a hot frontal fire from the fort's interior rained upon them, the bluecoats hugged the ground for cover. The men closest to the Confederates hastily carved out a trench in the sand in an effort to shield themselves from enemy fire. Lieutenant William Walling, who had recovered somewhat from his earlier anxiety, observed his comrades massed on the open ground: "*acres of men lying on their faces crowded together so thickly there was no room to lie down.*" Union officers who tried to rally their men for a charge were often ignored, noted Walling. It was difficult for the prone soldiers to load and fire their weapons, and some further back in the ranks accidentally shot their comrades in front while trying to fire upon the enemy. The Federal advance had stalled. "*Our hands were full,*" stated Col. Nathan Johnson of the 115th New York, "*but we held on.*"

The Tide Turns

Monitoring the progress of the assault from his command post at Battery Holland, Alfred Terry made a decision that would begin to erode the enemy resistance. "*Just as the tide seemed to have turned in our favor,*" noted William Lamb, "*the remorseless fleet came to the rescue of the faltering Federals.*" Thus far during the ground attack the fleet had been dueling with the oceanside batteries of the fort; but at Terry's request Admiral Porter directed his ironclads to resume their bombardment of the northern battlements. It was a risky proposition, but the overwhelming firepower of the combined land and sea forces would tip the scale decisively in favor of the attackers. The massive shells from the *New Ironsides* and monitors, bursting on and around the land front, proved more than the defenders on the ramparts could withstand. Their organized resistance deteriorated, and many were driven back in confusion toward the Northeast Bastion. Like the Confederate rounds from Battery Buchanan, however, the erratic naval gunfire killed friend and foe alike. "*At the fifth traverse,*" complained Curtis, "*a shot went wide of its mark and killed or disabled all but four men in our front line.*" To quell the panic of his own comrades, and to help discourage a counterattack, the determined Curtis began collecting the weapons of the killed and disabled and discharging them at the enemy. Amid the thunderous shellfire, as the Confederates pulled back, the Union advance gained the remaining traverses with greater ease.

The tide of battle was turning, and Colonel Lamb had few remaining options. The mass of Federals on the open plain had made little forward progress, and were rapidly entrenching against a possible counterattack. Now was the time for decisive action, reasoned Lamb, and he made the decision to play his final card. "*I believed a determined assault with the bayonet would drive them out,*" he explained, and the commander sent word to Fisher's gun crews not to fire if the garrison became closely engaged with the enemy. "*The head of the [Federal] column was not over one hundred feet from the portion of our breastwork where I stood,*" he continued, "*and I could see their faces distinctly, while my men were falling on either side of me.*"

Lamb beseeched his garrison to rally one last time: "*I passed quickly down the rear of the line, and asked [my] officers and men if they would follow me. They all responded fearlessly that they would.*" With that, the colonel shouted the order "*charge bayonets*" and sprang upon the top of the breastwork. Waving his sword, William Lamb called above the din of battle: "*forward, double quick, march!*" The men rose, but at that moment their commandant was sent sprawling to his knees with a bullet in the left hip. Lieutenant Daniel Perry (who had commanded the upper oceanside batteries during the December 1864 attack) fell mortally wounded at Lamb's side. The countercharge fell apart immediately, and a heavy volley from the enemy sent the men scrambling back behind the breastwork. Expecting to return to the field, Lamb ordered Capt. Daniel Munn to assume command and to keep the enemy in check. By the time he reached the hospital beneath the Pulpit, however, Lamb had lost so much blood that he was incapacitated for further action. His hip was broken.

In the hospital bombproof Lamb found General Whiting "*suffering uncomplainingly.*" It was shortly after 4:30 p.m. As Fisher's two senior officers lay bleeding in the dark confines of the Pulpit, Whiting confided that he was certain Braxton Bragg had no intention of committing Hoke's Division to their relief. Bragg had ignored his presence in the fort, lamented Whiting, and had ignored his many pleas and messages. Lamb became despondent. Outside it seemed that the garrison's fire had slackened, and time was short. The colonel sent his adjutant, John M. Kelly, in search of Maj. James Reilly[5]. When Reilly arrived at the hospital the major promised his commander that he would continue the fight as long as possible. "*I being the Senior Officer there for duty,*" remembered Reilly, "*the Command devolved on me, and under the Circumstances I was placed in a very disagreeable situation [but] I assumed it with all its responsibility and with a small number of brave men.*"

Major Reilly formed a force of about 150 men in the open space behind the sally port and, like Lamb before him, attempted to mount a counterattack on the enemy. Though the major was able to rally some of Hagood's South Carolinians, the Confederate advance was squelched immediately. Two-thirds of Reilly's force was cut down by a destructive fire from the enemy, and the survivors fell back toward the Northeast Bastion. When Reilly took a new position behind a sand berm at the main magazine (in rear of the redan), he counted less than 60 defenders around him. From this new station, those who stayed on the line returned the Federal fire as best they could.

By 4:45 p.m. the Union attackers on the mounds had captured seven traverses, which brought them near the center sally port. As Reilly's men fell back, the Federals on the parade ground gained an advanced position even with their comrades atop the ramparts. With heavy naval ordnance bursting with impunity among the defenders, the Confederate will to fight was dwindling by the minute. At one point Reilly spied a white flag of truce waving from the sally port. Thinking at first that it might be of Federal origin, he sent Captain Braddy to investigate. Braddy, his sword draped with Reilly's handkerchief, approached the postern; but the pocket of flag wavers quickly scampered for Union lines and gave themselves up. Reilly was mortified, and remembered that his men fought with more determination than ever after the "*dastardly conduct of their comrades.*"

From his position at the seventh traverse, N. Martin Curtis sensed that victory was within his reach. The Federal advance was now within musket range of the Northeast Bastion, where Curtis found that "*our best marksmen could drive the gunners from the Columbiad [in the redan].*" He quickly formed a plan to silence this heavy weapon, and storm the redan. Curtis proposed to capture the "*sea-bastion*" by sending a force between the palisades and the outer wall of the land front. By this time, however, the Federals on the parapet were exhausted—and casualties were severe. Curtis needed more men, and he sent a corporal from the 117th New York back to the western salient to request reinforcements. With the Federals on the verge of victory, the bad blood between Curtis and General Ames would reach its boiling point.

Curtis and Ames

The courier returned to Curtis with news from General Ames that no reinforcements would be forthcoming. The men were exhausted, the division commander had explained, and preparations should be made to entrench for the night. Curtis ignored this information and immediately sent his orderly, A. D. Knight, to the rear to bring forward the necessary manpower for attacking the Northeast Bastion. Observing this young orderly, Ames asked Knight what he was trying to do, and repeated his order for Curtis to stand down for the night. When Knight returned to the front with Ames' directive, Curtis became angry. He sent the orderly back a second time to ask specifically for members of the First Brigade (Curtis') to come to the front. Again the orderly was accosted by Ames: "*I told you to go and tell Gen. Curtis to fortify,*" he said to Knight, "*and not to attempt any further movement tonight.*"

Ames, accentuating the order with sarcasm, gestured to a pile of entrenching tools on the ground nearby, and directed Knight to carry a few to Curtis. The orderly grabbed an armful of shovels and returned to Curtis, who became enraged by Ames' illustrative gesture. Curtis—"*inflamed with the magnificent rage of battle*"—snatched up a few of the shovels and threw them over the traverse toward the Confederates. "*Dig, Johnnies,*" he shouted, "*for I'm coming for you.*"

In an effort to sidestep Ames' authority, Curtis sent a messenger to General Terry at Battery Holland. Silas W. Kempton was *one* member of the Federal navy who saw action inside Fort Fisher. He had approached Curtis early in the engagement and asked to serve in whatever capacity he might be useful. As a volunteer aide, Kempton was dispatched to tell Terry that the Federals needed more men. The enemy were now offering slight resistance, insisted Curtis, and "*a bold push would secure a victory already substantially won.*"[6] Leaving the advance in charge of Capt. David Magill, 117th New York, Curtis stormed off toward the western salient to round up as many of his own men as possible. Magill had orders to continue the struggle for the next traverse with the first men who should come up.

A color sergeant of the 4th New Hampshire rushed forward and planted his banner on the eighth traverse, "*so near the rebel flag*," noted a comrade, "*that the stars and stripes actually flapped against the southern cross.*" The standard bearer, however, paid for the endeavor with a severe wound, and Captain Magill soon lost a leg to a fragment of shell from the fleet.

At the western salient, Curtis descended to the parade ground in rear of Shepherd's Battery. Predictably, as he sought volunteers for the push on the Northeast Bastion, Curtis encountered General Ames in person. It was their first face-to-face meeting of the day. "*I have two or three times sent you word to fortify your position and hold it*," barked Ames, "*until reinforcements can be sent to aid us; the men are exhausted and I will not order them to go forward.*" Curtis pointed to two steam transports visible in the Cape Fear River, which he feared were loaded with Confederate troops awaiting nightfall to land and reinforce the garrison. Darkness was minutes away. "*Should they succeed in landing,*" rebutted Curtis, "*they may drive us out.*" The enemy was on the verge of giving up, insisted Curtis: "*I informed [Ames] that the garrison was resisting with less spirit than earlier in the day, and asserted that complete victory was within our grasp if we roused ourselves and pushed the advantage we surely had.*" Curtis then sought to gain a better view of the bastion he intended to attack. As he ascended a small sand dune for a better vantage point, a shell detonated nearby, and two hot fragments of iron tore into the First Brigade commander's skull. "*Curtis fell senseless at my feet,*" recalled Ames.

Though he had received several slight wounds during the battle, these knocked Curtis out of action for good. One shell fragment destroyed his left eye, and the other carried away a portion of his frontal bone. They appeared to be mortal wounds, and Curtis was borne from the field about 5:30 p.m. It is a wonder that the hulking brigade commander was not struck down or killed long before he was incapacitated by the shell fragments. At age 29, the man was a towering six feet, seven inches tall, and weighed 225 pounds—an easy mark, one would suppose, for enemy bullets. Indeed, he had been seriously wounded during the Peninsula Campaign of 1862, and Fort Fisher was his first real action since his recovery.[7]

"*Gen. Ames stood there amid the fragment of his Division,*" recalled an observer, "*every commander of Brigade and almost every commander of Regiments having fallen.*" It was getting dark. "*As the sun sank to the horizon,*" noted Ames, "*the ardor of the assault abated. Our advance was but slow. Ten of my officers had been killed, forty-seven wounded, and about five hundred men were killed and wounded . . . . I now requested General Terry to join me in the fort. It was dark before he and [Colonel] Comstock arrived.*"

"During the day [our] chief of artillery was busily engaged in landing artillery . . . so that if the assault failed siege operations might at once be commenced." —**Bvt. Maj. Gen. Alfred H. Terry**

Abbott's Advance

"*When Bell's brigade was ordered into action,*" reported Alfred Terry, "*I foresaw that more troops would probably be needed.*" Consequently, the commanding general requested that Lt. Cmdr. William B. Cushing reform the broken ranks of sailors and marines at the Union northern line. By 4:30 p.m., the naval contingent had replaced Col. Joseph C. Abbott's brigade, which Terry ordered southward to the support of Ames' division. Abbott's men reached Battery Holland a short time after sunset, and Terry soon sent the 1,400-man brigade to Fort Fisher. Abbott's troops poured through the riverside gate around 6:00 p.m., and the brigade commander reported to General Ames.

As night fell the ferocity of the contest diminished significantly. At intervals the bursting naval rounds illuminated the darkness, and sporadic gunfire crackled along the battlements. The Federal advance was clearly at a standstill, and General Terry ordered Charles J. Paine to dispatch one of his best regiments to the front as an added reinforcement. Terry also proposed to visit Fort Fisher in person to assess his options for continuing the attack. As Paine sent Gen. Albert M. Blackman's 27th U.S. Colored Troops southward, Terry arrived at the fort with chief engineer Cyrus Comstock around 7:00 p.m.

Adelbert Ames had done nothing thus far with Abbott's troops, having formed them in reserve upon their arrival. Ames, in fact, was still planning to entrench for the night and resume the battle in the morning. Terry, however, had plans of his own. Concurring with Curtis' assessment, Terry reasoned that the Confederates were nearly beaten and that they should be overwhelmed before any reinforcements could arrive. The Provisional Corps commander conferred with his subordinates, and decided not to compromise the strength of the northern line by committing Paine's division to the assault. Instead, at Comstock's suggestion, Terry would finish the job with Abbott's men.

By 8:00 p.m. the Confederate resistance was on its last legs. An aide found a suffering Colonel Lamb at the Pulpit Battery hospital, and reported with grim tidings: the men were running low on ammunition, he said, though efforts had been made to gather extra rounds in a blanket from the dead and wounded; the enemy had possession of nearly all of the land front; it would be "*impossible to hold out much longer,*" continued the aide, who suggested that "*it would be wise to surrender, as further struggle might be a useless sacrifice of life.*" William Lamb, however, was unwilling to accept defeat: "*I replied that so long as I lived I would not surrender the fort; that Bragg must soon come to the rescue, and [he] would save us.*" Chase Whiting, though he held no illusions about assistance from Braxton Bragg, sided firmly with his young friend. "*Lamb,*" he said, "*when you die, I will take command, and I will not surrender the fort.*" Nevertheless, the stubborn determination of Fisher's two senior officers would not be enough to save their bastion from the clutches of the enemy.

At this same time (8:00 p.m.), Braxton Bragg was reporting from Sugar Loaf to authorities in Wilmington that all was under control at Fort Fisher. Rumors were circulating that Fisher

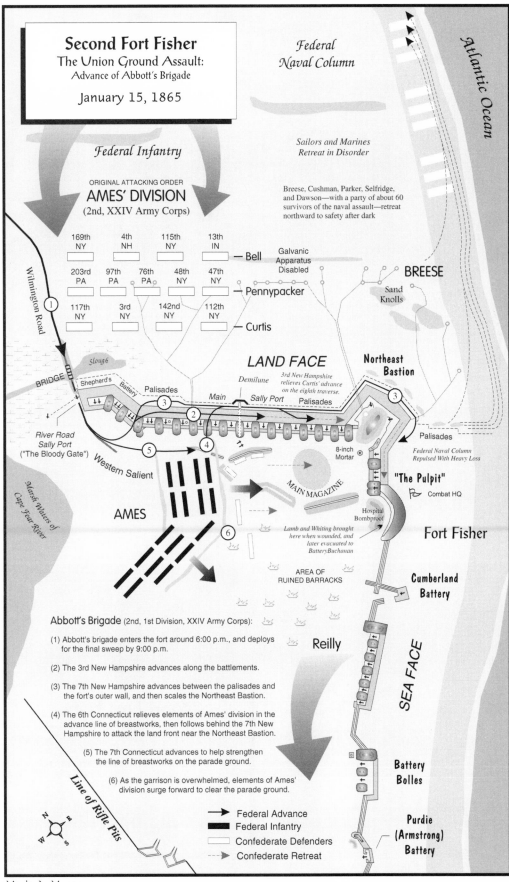

Second Fort Fisher
The Union Ground Assault:
Advance of Abbott's Brigade

January 15, 1865

Federal Naval Column

Atlantic Ocean

Federal Infantry

ORIGINAL ATTACKING ORDER
AMES' DIVISION
(2nd, XXIV Army Corps)

*Sailors and Marines
Retreat in Disorder*

Breese, Cushman, Parker, Selfridge,
and Dawson—with a party of about 60
survivors of the naval assault—retreat
northward to safety after dark

| 169th NY | 4th NH | 115th NY | 13th IN | — Bell | Galvanic Apparatus Disabled |

BREESE

| 203rd PA | 97th PA | 76th PA | 48th NY | 47th NY | — Pennypacker |

Sand Knolls

| 117th NY | 3rd NY | 142nd NY | 112th NY | — Curtis |

Wilmington Road

(1)

Slough

LAND FACE

Northeast Bastion

BRIDGE

Shepherd's Battery Palisades

Demilune   Main   *Sally Port*   Palisades

*3rd New Hampshire
relieves Curtis' advance
on the eighth traverse.*

(3)

(3)

(2)

*River Road
Sally Port
("The Bloody Gate")*

(5)   (4)

Western Salient

8-inch
Mortar

Palisades

*Federal Naval Column
Repulsed With Heavy Loss*

"The Pulpit"
Combat HQ

*Marsh Waters of
Cape Fear River*

AMES

MAIN MAGAZINE

*Hospital
Bombproof*

Fort Fisher

(6)

*Lamb and Whiting brought
here when wounded, and
later evacuated to
Battery Buchanan*

AREA OF
RUINED BARRACKS

**Cumberland
Battery**

Reilly

SEA FACE

Abbott's Brigade (2nd, 1st Division, XXIV Army Corps):

(1) Abbott's brigade enters the fort around 6:00 p.m., and deploys
for the final sweep by 9:00 p.m.

(2) The 3rd New Hampshire advances along the battlements.

(3) The 7th New Hampshire advances between the palisades and
the fort's outer wall, and then scales the Northeast Bastion.

(4) The 6th Connecticut relieves elements of Ames' division in the
advance line of breastworks, then follows behind the 7th New
Hampshire to attack the land front near the Northeast Bastion.

(5) The 7th Connecticut advances to help strengthen
the line of breastworks on the parade ground.

(6) As the garrison is overwhelmed, elements of Ames'
division surge forward to clear the parade ground.

Line of Rifle Pits

→ Federal Advance
■ Federal Infantry
□ Confederate Defenders
⇢ Confederate Retreat

**Battery
Bolles**

**Purdie
(Armstrong)
Battery**

Mark A. Moore

"The 3rd New Hampshire is ordered to the extreme front traverse held by our men, to reach which position we crawl through bomb-proofs and traverses, clambering over the dead, wounded and dying—literally piled upon one another—and arriving there we open fire at once with our Spencers [seven-shooters], soon silencing the enemy in our immediate front. We then charged and drove them from one traverse to another, until nine more are in our possession. The brigade was now placed in proper positions and charged the whole line, with a momentum no power could stop. Gen. Ames' whole force, cheered by the presence of fresh troops, rallied once again, and made a general advance, and the stronghold was ours." —**Capt. William H. Trickey**, commanding the 3rd New Hampshire, Abbott's brigade

"The contending forces would blaze away in the darkness. They would throw themselves on the ground and then come alternately crawling or running for position. Hoarse voices were shouting orders, and from the huge round traverses, that looked like great sea-billows toppling over to engulf all before them, shadowy forms of friend and foe were seen in confused masses . . . . The outlines of the work could now and then be seen by the flash of exploding shell or blaze of musketry, but indistinct as the creation of some hideous dream." —**Federal Survivor** of the attack on Fort Fisher

"Thus ended the greatest bombardment ever known in modern warfare [and] the largest hand-to-hand fight during our civil war, and the struggle inside the fort was unsurpassed in stubbornness. Our casualties were not known as the roll was never again called . . . . After the battle was over, seeing so many of our comrades alive and able for duty, was a cause of deep gratitude to Almighty God." —**Sgt. T. C. Davis**, 40th North Carolina Regiment, garrison of Fort Fisher

"The garrison, though in good heart, was sadly worn out by the hard work they were called upon to perform by day and night, but . . . a feeling of much disappointment existed that the long-looked-for co-operation from the forces outside, which they expected would have been rendered, failed to assist them in their hour of need." —**Lt. Col. George T. Gordon**, Assistant Inspector General, staff of Gen. W. H. C. Whiting

"The future historian, in light of all the facts and circumstances connected with the fall of Fort Fisher, will place the blame upon those who merited it . . . . The loss in the garrison in killed and wounded was severe. The detachments of the Tenth suffered quite as heavily in proportion to numbers as any other command in the fort." —**Lt. John W. Sanders**, 10th North Carolina Regiment, garrison of Fort Fisher

"The land forces on our [right] . . . in no instance broke nor exhibited any cowardice . . . .

"At one time I thought they could never stand it, neither do I believe they would have stood, but for the fact that they knew the black troops were in the rear, and if [the white troops] failed, the colored troops would take the fort and claim the honor. Indeed, the white troops told the rebels that if they did not surrender they would let the ne-groes loose on them . . . .

"The battle raged amid the terrific fire of deadly missiles until after dark . . . . I retired some distance from the scene of conflict and lay down until about 10 o'clock, when the news spread that Fort Fisher had surrendered . . . At this news I jumped up and went to survey the fort and behold the results of our conquest.

"The fort had been ploughed by our shells until everything looked like a heap of destruction . . . . Several rebels had been utterly buried by our shells . . . . The soldiers were ransack-ing every nook and corner in search of trophies and other memorials . . . .

"After walking around the fort for some time, viewing it by the light of the moon, I found myself shot at from some unknown quarter. This led me to believe there were rebels still secreted in some undiscovered spot whom we had not found . . . .

"I asked several rebel officers if they killed the colored prisoners they took. They told me they did not. They also told me if they were free men from the north, or even from any slave State in our lines, they were treated as other Yankee prisoners are; but if they were slaves, whose owners were in the Confederate States, and such colored men could be identified, they were treated as house-burners and robbers. And as for you, said they, you would get the same treatment as other Yankee officers."

—**Chaplain Henry M. Turner**, 1st United States Colored Troops, Wright's brigade [3rd, Paine's (Third) Division, XXV Army Corps]. The 27th USCT also belonged to Wright's brigade.

During the fight at Fort Fisher, Chaplain Turner served as an aide to surgeon Norman S. Barnes, medical director for Gen. Alfred H. Terry's Provisional Corps.

"Through the whole evening, until long after darkness closed in, [the Confederates] had offered the most stubborn defense. Never did soldiers display more desperate bravery and brilliant valor."

—**Capt. George F. Towle**, 4th New Hamp-shire, acting Assistant Inspector General, staff of Gen. Alfred H. Terry. Captain Towle was often close to the front during the fighting, and was kept busy delivering orders and messages for General Terry.

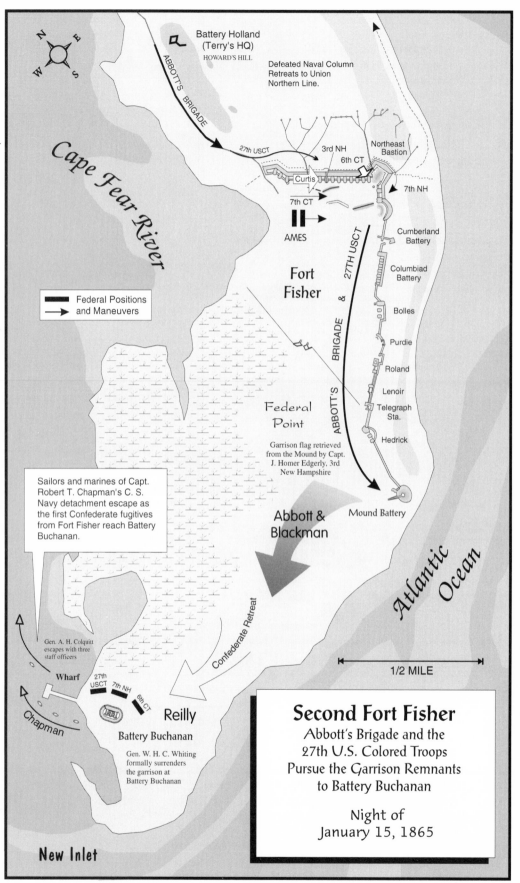

Sailors and marines of Capt. Robert T. Chapman's C. S. Navy detachment escape as the first Confederate fugitives from Fort Fisher reach Battery Buchanan.

Gen. A. H. Colquitt escapes with three staff officers

Gen. W. H. C. Whiting formally surrenders the garrison at Battery Buchanan

Federal Positions and Maneuvers

Garrison flag retrieved from the Mound by Capt. J. Homer Edgerly, 3rd New Hampshire

1/2 MILE

Second Fort Fisher
Abbott's Brigade and the 27th U.S. Colored Troops Pursue the Garrison Remnants to Battery Buchanan

Night of January 15, 1865

Mark A. Moore

had already fallen to the enemy. "*The sensational reports about Fisher are entirely unfounded. Official information from General Whiting of later hour reports enemy's attack unsuccessful.*"[8] Just one and one-half hours earlier, however, Whiting had sent his final desperate plea to Bragg for assistance: "*The enemy are assaulting us by land and sea. Their infantry outnumber us. Can't you help us? I am slightly wounded.*"

By 9:00 p.m. the Federal mop-up operation was underway, as Colonel Abbott deployed his brigade for a final thrust against the beleaguered garrison. The 3rd New Hampshire Infantry, commanded by Capt. William H. Trickey, advanced along the battlements to the eighth traverse. The newcomers relieved the advance elements of Curtis' command stationed there, and proceeded to capture the ninth traverse. The 7th Connecticut moved up to the vicinity of the eighth traverse on the parade ground, while the 7th New Hampshire and 6th Connecticut advanced between the palisades and the fort's exterior slope. The 7th passed around the Northeast Bastion and ascended the upper oceanside batteries, and the 6th charged over the north wall near the redan. Abbott's troops, many of whom were armed with Spencer repeating rifles, made short work of the few remaining defenders on the mounds. Those who were not killed, wounded, or captured escaped southward along the Sea Face. As the last resistance broke, the men of Ames' division surged forward with a shout toward the angle behind the Northeast Bastion.

Major James Reilly barely had time to evacuate his wounded superiors. "*When we left the hospital,*" recalled Lamb, "*the men were fighting over the adjoining traverse, and the spent balls fell like hail-stones around us.*" The fort's new commander had Lamb and Whiting hurried away on litters to Battery Buchanan, at the base of the peninsula. Reilly was sure that Capt. Robert T. Chapman, whose naval contingent was stationed there, would see that the fallen officers were evacuated to safety across the Cape Fear River. As Lamb was hauled away Capt. Edward B. Dudley, of 2nd Company C, 36th North Carolina, secured the colonel's saber and sword belt. Determined not to let these symbols of honor fall into the hands of the enemy, Dudley hurled them into the Atlantic Ocean.

The final Union push "*compelled me to fall back from one position to another,*" lamented Major Reilly, "*until we were driven from the Fort [and] with saddened Hearts marched away from the fort we defended with all our might.*" When the major reached Battery Buchanan, however, he was stunned to find the post empty, save for about 500 refugees from Fort Fisher who were crowded around the imposing shore installation. As rumors circulated that the fort was about to fall, Captain Chapman beat a hasty retreat with his small command, and vanished with the boats that had been docked at Buchanan's wharf. "*I thought him too good a soldier to abandon us,*" a furious Reilly later wrote of Chapman, "*for we were all sailing in the same ship and let us all go down together.*" Chapman had spiked Buchanan's guns before departing. Not only had the garrison been left to its fate by Braxton Bragg, but its last line of defense and meager means of escape had disappeared as well. The Confederates were stranded on the Federal Point

peninsula, with a victorious enemy rapidly bearing down upon them from the north.

Victory

When Albert Blackman's 27th U.S. Colored Troops finally reached the bridge at the riverside gate of Fort Fisher, they found the way obstructed, with too many soldiers crowded in rear of the western salient to allow a passage. By 9:30 p.m., however, the 27th had orders to advance. Joining the regiments of Abbott's brigade by way of the center sally port, the 27th advanced southward, helping to secure the fort's lower seaside batteries. At the towering Mound Battery, Capt. J. Homer Edgerly of the 3rd New Hampshire spied the coveted Rebel banner waving high above the beach. As Pvt. Christopher Bland had done during the Christmas 1864 engagement, the young captain scaled the Mound's flagstaff—but this time the Confederate colors, now a prize of war, were cut down by a victorious enemy.

The sweep southward had netted the Federals a sizable cache of prisoners, and from these Abbott learned that the garrison had fled to Battery Buchanan. The colonel then formed two regiments in line of battle, flanked on the right by the 27th U.S. Colored Troops, and advanced toward the base of the peninsula. A bright moon was rising over the sandy plain, increasing visibility as the Federals followed close on the heels of the fleeing remnants of the garrison.

James Reilly was out of options. "*I saw there was not a possible chance of defending ourselves,*" he concluded. Reilly had hoped for one last defensive stand with the aid of Buchanan's guns, but it was not to be. With Maj. James H. Hill of Whiting's staff, and Capt. A. C. Van Benthuysen of the C.S. Marine Corps, Major Reilly advanced some 300 yards northward to await the inevitable confrontation with the enemy. The trio of officers brandished a small white flag of surrender. Soon the dark mass of the enemy became discernible on the white sandy plain. "*It was as bright as day,*" remembered Reilly, with "*the enemy advancing on the two fronts of the Battery.*"

At length Reilly was approached by Capt. E. Lewis Moore, adjutant of the 7th Connecticut. The major offered his sword in surrender, and asked for a reassurance that his defenseless troops would not be fired upon. Captain Moore accepted Reilly's saber unceremoniously, and would keep the artifact as a cherished souvenir. When Abbott and General Blackman arrived, they were conducted by Major Hill to the base of Battery Buchanan, where Lamb and Whiting lay suffering with their wounds.

To the right of Abbott's men, the 27th U.S. Colored Troops advanced upon the riverside portion of Battery Buchanan. "*As we came into close proximity of the battery,*" noted 20-year-old Lt. Albert G. Jones of the 27th, "*we could dimly discern men on top of it. As soon as they saw us, they disappeared. We continued to advance, and as we neared the wharf leading out into the Cape Fear River, we could hear the sound of oars [in the water] . . . but continued on our way, and suddenly came into the presence of the enemy.*" "*The fresh soldiers of the 27th USCT,*" asserted surgeon Francis Weld, "*aggressively pushed*

Brig. Gen. Alfred H. Colquitt

forward, ahead of [Abbott's] two other regiments . . . . Our skirmishers rushed forward and captured [Buchanan]." Indeed, Lieutenant Jones confronted a Confederate officer and demanded the immediate surrender of the garrison.

The splashing of oars heard by Lieutenant Jones was occasioned by the narrow escape of Gen. Alfred H. Colquitt, of Hoke's Division, whom Bragg had sent to assume command of Fort Fisher. Weary of Whiting's caustic pleas for assistance, Bragg had determined to remove the general from Fisher altogether. Early that afternoon Bragg's adjutant, Archer Anderson, had sent a message from Sugar Loaf informing Whiting that Colquitt would arrive that night to take command. Anderson added that *"General Bragg directs you [to] report in person at these headquarters this evening for conference and instructions."* Whiting ignored the message, if indeed he ever received it.[9]

By 7:00 p.m. "unpleasant" reports had begun to reach Bragg from Battery Lamb, across the Cape Fear River, stating that *"the enemy have the fort."* Rumors notwithstanding, the district commander held fast to his conviction that all was right. *"My mind was easy,"* he wrote. *"General Colquitt [was] hurried forward."*

Colquitt set out in a small rowboat around 9:00 p.m. The general was accompanied by Lt. George L. Washington of Hoke's staff, together with Lt. Hugh H. Colquitt and ordnance officer Lt. Harry Estill of his own staff. By this time Abbott's brigade was clearing the fort of its last defenders. The boat's crewmen refused to land directly at Fort Fisher, despite Colquitt's insistance, and instead put in about 500 yards north of Battery Buchanan. The waning conflict for possession of the fort rumbled in the distance. Some 50 yards inland, Colquitt and his aides approached an old blacksmith's shanty on the wastes of the lower peninsula. The building was occupied, and smoke and sparks floated from the chimney. *"We called,"* reported Lieutenant Colquitt, *"and a man, who was either a mulatto or a badly smoked white man, made his appearance."* The shack, noted Estill, was *"filled with negroes."*

General Colquitt inquired of the man the route to Fort Fisher. *"The man replied very unconcernedly that the Yankees were up there."* The fort, he said, had been captured. The general immediately discredited the news, and insisted that a guide lead him to Fort Fisher. Colquitt then saw his first evidence of the Confederate evacuation. Captain Daniel Munn approached with 15 or 20 disheveled Confederates. Colquitt hailed the cap-

tain, who excitedly explained the situation. His squad was about the last to leave the fort, Munn exclaimed, and the enemy were in full possession of the fort. Whiting and Lamb had been wounded and evacuated to Battery Buchanan. The skeptical general remained unconvinced of the fort's capture, but his entourage became uneasy. *"These men were without guns,"* noted the younger Colquitt, *"without accouterments, some of them without hats, and all in a very bad state of demoralization."* Worse yet, they were eyeing the party's rowboat with keen interest. After a brief conference with his aides, General Colquitt decided to travel to Buchanan to meet with Lamb and Whiting before going to Fort Fisher. *"Fortunately, the general concluded to keep the boat in sight,"* and the little party rowed down river to within 40 yards of Battery Buchanan.

Here the signs of defeat were unmistakable. *"The beach was crowded with a disorganized, demoralized rabble,"* reported Lieutenant Colquitt, *"and it was with the utmost difficulty that we prevented them from taking our boat."* Lieutenant Estill noted that the garrison remnants were *"wandering about in confusion [and] at once confirmed the capture of Fisher."* Leaving his aides to guard the boat, the general was led by an officer to where Colonel Lamb lay at the foot of Battery Buchanan. Colquitt promptly asked Lamb if anything more could be done to save the fort.

By this time, the shouts of triumph from the enemy were rolling along the peninsula, and the fleet had begun to launch fireworks in celebration. *"I was accosted by General A. H. Colquitt,"* recalled Lamb, who hastily outlined the unsuccessful defense of the fort. Downplaying his own wound, he also requested that Whiting be evacuated across the river. Steadfast to the last, Lamb requested reinforcements: *"I assured [Colquitt] that if Bragg would even then attack, a fresh brigade landed at Battery Buchanan could retake the work."* Colquitt, of course, had disappointing news. *"I told [Lamb] there was no brigade with me, and wished to know of him the condition of the men who had escaped."*

The condition of the men, however, was obvious. *"No officer seemed to be in command,"* noted Lieutenant Washington. *"They appeared to have given up all idea of making resistance, and there was no possible means of escape. No boat of any character was on the beach except the one in which we came. There was no alternative except capture."* The general's aides were engaged in trying to glean information from the mass of stragglers when the enemy suddenly came into view. They quickly sent one of the boatmen to fetch their leader.

Alfred Colquitt was turning from Lamb to find Whiting when he was approached by the messenger, who warned that the enemy was upon them, *"and that in a minute longer we could not escape."* The skirmish line of the 27th U.S. Colored Troops was not more than 100 yards away, followed closely by its main line of battle. *"In the moonlight it was distinctly visible,"* remembered Harry Estill, and it was moving toward them. The general could see the enemy's battle flags, and determined it was time to beat a hasty retreat. All thought of Lamb, Whiting, and Fort Fisher was lost as Colquitt and his entourage scrambled for the boat, whose crewmen paddled frantically in the darkness. As the little boat finally pulled away, the battle line of the 27th USCT passed within 30 yards of the wharf. The younger Colquitt, worried by the notion that he might "*spend the winter North*," was flooded with relief upon their narrow escape: "*I saw no body of organized men while I was near the battery, except the enemy. All of our men were in a state of panic . . . nothing but confusion and dismay. The only man I saw with a gun was a drunken Irish marine, who cocked it and presented it at me.*"[10] "*Self-preservation*," agreed Lieutenant Washington, "*prevented our gaining any further information.*

As the troops of Abbott and Blackman surrounded Battery Buchanan, Gen. Alfred H. Terry arrived to receive the formal surrender of Fort Fisher. The Federal commander was directed to where Fisher's senior officers lay at the foot of Buchanan's outer slope. Whiting inquired for the commanding officer, and Terry stepped forward and spoke his name and rank. Captain Adrian Terry, the general's brother and a member of his staff, overheard Whiting's reply: "*I surrender, sir, to you the forces under my command, I care not what becomes of myself.*"[11] Terry assured "Little Billy" that the prisoners would be treated with respect. As the captured officers and enlisted men were separated, Whiting bid his men farewell for the last time: "*Goodbye, boys,*" he said, waving to the troops. "*They have got us but you have done your duty well.*" Lamb was despondent. "*Colquitt made a precipitate retreat,*" he complained, "*leaving our beloved Whiting a captive, to die in a Northern prison.*"

When it was over, General Terry mounted a captured horse and sped northward toward Fort Fisher. He soon encountered Captain Edgerly, who was brandishing the garrison flag he had filched from atop the Mound Battery. Terry proudly accepted the trophy, recalled the 3rd New Hampshire's Sgt. M. L. Holt. "*Gen. Terry entered the fort with the flag . . . wound around his body. We gave him three cheers, and he made this remark: 'Boys, rather than that you should for cheer me, I ought to cheer for you.'*"

Terry lost no time in conveying the tidings of victory to Adm. David D. Porter. The navy, however, was already onto the notion, for the army troops onshore were cheering wildly. On the bridge of the flagship *Malvern*, Lt. William Clemens watched as a signal torch flashed a brief but telling message from atop the ramparts of Fort Fisher: "*The fort is ours.*" Admiral Porter was beside himself. He summoned his crew to the *Malvern*'s quarterdeck, and bellowed excitedly for his men to give three cheers for the capture of Fort Fisher. The sailors—officers and men alike—all heartily complied. Overcome with both exhaustion and joy, Porter would need assistance that night in returning to his stateroom.

The contagious celebration ran rampant among the fleet, and the moonlit sky above the Atlantic was resplendent with a vast array of multicolored flares and rockets. "*At the signal,*" remembered surgeon C. MacFarlane, "*thousands of rockets and colored lights went up from the fleet which were reflected again and again in the mirror-like water.*" It was a "*grand pyrotechnic display,*" marveled William Lamb, who had witnessed the fireworks begin even as he pleaded with Colquitt to save the fort. The revelry would continue into the small hours of January 16, 1865. "*Such another noise you never heard,*" boasted a proud William Cobb. Cobb and his fellow seamen and marines on the northern line were thankful to be alive. Though their contingent had met with disaster below the parapets of Fort Fisher, they felt they had played a role in the fort's capture. As they grieved for their fallen comrades, their ears were filled with "*men hurrahing, steam whistles screaming. Rockets, the air was alive with rockets of all colors.*" And Fort Fisher belonged to the Union.

Evacuation of the Lower Cape Fear

When Alfred Colquitt reached Battery Lamb on the west bank of the Cape Fear River, he wired General Bragg with the official news: "*Fort Fisher is evacuated; troops rushed in confusion to Battery Buchanan . . . . There is no mistake in this information.*" General Louis Hébert, in command at Smithville, confirmed the loss at midnight on January 16, 1865: "*Last information is that Fort Fisher has surrendered. I await orders.*" His complacency jolted by the news, Braxton Bragg had no choice but to pass it on to his superiors. At 1:00 a.m. he wired Gen. Robert E. Lee at Petersburg, Virginia: "*I am mortified at having to report the unexpected capture of Fort Fisher, with most of its garrison, at about 10 o'clock to-night. Particulars not known.*" The same message went out to President Jefferson Davis and Governor Zebulon Vance. Davis was stunned. "*The intelligence is sad as it was unexpected,*" replied the president. "*Can you retake the fort? If anything is to be done you will appreciate the necessity of its being attempted without a moment's delay.*" Bragg refused this notion, fearing the Federal fleet would cut any attacking column to pieces.

Instead, Bragg acted swiftly to evacuate the lower Cape Fear defenses. In the small hours of January 16, General Hébert was ordered to destroy the fortifications at Old Inlet, spike the guns, and retreat to a new defensive position at Fort Anderson. The installations abandoned included Fort Caswell, Fort Campbell, and Battery Shaw on Oak Island; Fort Holmes on Smith Island; Fort Pender at Smithville; and Battery Lamb at Reeves Point.

It was over. With the loss of Fort Fisher, there was little use in defending Old Inlet, and the withdrawal gave the Federals free access to both inlets into the river. There would be no more running the blockade at Cape Fear. The loss of Fort Fisher effectively sealed the port of Wilmington to contraband shipping, leaving only the formality of capturing the town itself. In little more than one month from Fisher's demise, this goal would be accomplished with negligible loss to the invading Federals.

Aftermath

At dawn on January 16, 1865, the awful carnage of the battle became more visible to the survivors of Fort Fisher. Many of the combatants had collapsed in exhaustion and fallen asleep among the dead and wounded. The victorious Federals, including officers of the United States Navy, were eager to get a closer look at the inside of the imposing bastion. The scene was not a

FORT FISHER.

DETAILS OF THE VICTORY.

Official Dispatch from Secretary Stanton.

REPORT OF ADMIRAL PORTER.

Full Particulars of the Assault.

THE BLOODY WORK ON THE RAMPARTS

A Nine Hours Struggle in the Fort.

" From Traverse to Traverse, and from Bomb-proof to Bomb-proof."

Heroic Gallantry of the Soldiers and Sailors.

Headline from the *New York Times*, Thursday, January 19, 1865

pleasant one. *"Within the fallen Fort,"* noted one naval observer, *"were sights sickening and dreadful."* Among the ruined machinery of war were numerous *"caps, clothes, bayonets, swords, muskets, rifles, scattered, battered, bloodstained."* Among the shell fragments and other debris lay several dead horses. *"And then the dead! Men in all postures, mangled in the head and body, with brains out, but with perfect features, covered with sand and grimed with powder."* The dead lay thickly strewn along the battlements, from bombproofs and traverses to green pools of water on the parade ground, *"here, there, everywhere .... The carrying past of the wounded, the groans of the dying, and the smell of blood and powder!"*

To make matters worse, the fort's main magazine exploded shortly after sunrise. The tremendous blast killed at least 200 men of both sides, and sparked a heated debate as to what caused the tragedy. Though the victors were eager to blame the Confederates for dastardly behavior, a court of inquiry ruled that the explosion was *"the result of carelessness on the part of persons unknown."* The giddy celebration of the night before had spawned many a drunken reveler, and the accident occurred despite the posting of guards at the fort's magazines.

The unexpected ending to the affair notwithstanding, the capture of Fort Fisher gave testament to the overwhelming might of the combined arms of the United States military. Despite a natural interservice rivalry, both General Terry and Admiral Porter were quick to extol the virtues of the other's command. Of Terry, the bombastic Porter wrote that *"He is my beau ideal of a soldier and general. Our cooperation has been most cordial. The result is victory, which will always be ours when the Army and Navy go hand in hand."* Terry expressed that *"nothing could surpass the perfect skill with which the fleet was handled by its commander. Every request which I made to Admiral Porter was most cheerfully complied with, and the utmost harmony has existed between us from the outset to the present time."*

When Secretary of War Edwin M. Stanton arrived at Fort Fisher unexpectedly on the afternoon of January 16, the peninsula was *"quiet as a Sabbath day,"* despite the busy work of burying the dead and caring for the wounded. Stanton was on his way back to Washington following a visit with William T. Sherman in Georgia, and enjoyed a six-hour layover at Cape Fear. Alfred Terry proudly presented the secretary with Fisher's captured garrison flag, and Stanton was overjoyed with the triumph. *"You will be pleased to know,"* he told President Abraham Lincoln, *"that perfect harmony and concert of action existed between the land and naval forces .... Admiral Porter and General Terry vied in their commendation each of the other."* Stanton also proposed that the gushing good will between Terry and Porter *"may perhaps be attributed in some degree [to] the success of an attack."*

As is often the case for the losing side, there had been no such harmony among the Confederate high command. The conflicting notions of Fort Fisher's impregnability shared by Bragg and Whiting severely undermined a defensive effort that was disadvantaged from the outset. Embittered by defeat, William Lamb would spend the rest of his life denouncing Braxton Bragg and defending the honor of his garrison:

"North Carolina need cross no ocean to search amid Roman and Grecian story for examples of self-sacrifice in defense of home and country, for here among our own sons, upon her own soil, the valor of Pharsalia and of Thermopylae were reproduced, and no correct history of this grand old State can be written unless the defense of Fort Fisher by North Carolinians in January, 1865, be placed among the most heroic deeds in the drama of our civil war."

STEAMER S. R. SPAULDING
Off Fort Fisher, January 16, 1865

The Secretary of War has the honor to acknowledge the receipt of the flag of Fort Fisher, and in the name of the President congratulates you and the gallant officers and soldiers, sailors, and marines of your commands, and tenders you thanks for the valor and skill displayed in your respective parts of the great achievement in the operations against Fort Fisher and in its assault and capture. The combined operations of the squadron and land forces of your commands deserve and will receive the thanks of the nation, and will be held in admiration throughout the world as proof of the naval and military prowess of the United States.

Edwin M. Stanton
Secretary of War.

Major-General TERRY and
Rear-Admiral PORTER,
Commanding, etc.

In Washington, no one was more excited than Secretary of the Navy Gideon Welles. Welles had lobbied long and heavily for this expedition and fretted over its implementation, and he reveled in the *"glorious news"* of the capture of Fort Fisher. *"At the Cabinet-meeting there was a very pleasant feeling,"* Welles wrote on January 17. *"The President was happy. Says he is amused with the manner and views of some who address him, who tell him that he is now reëlected and can do just as he has a mind to.*" Welles would comment on the victory for days to come. "*The congratulations over the capture of Fort Fisher are hearty and earnest,*" he gloated. "*Some few whom I have met are a little out of humor. General [Benjamin F.] Butler is not gladsome, and it is not in human nature that he should [but] the congratulations and hearty cheer of the people over the victory at Fort Fisher are most gratifying.*"[12]

For an analytical discussion of the loss of Fort Fisher and why it fell, as compared to the loss of the fortress of Sebastopol during the Crimean War, see Appendix A, page 137.

[1] On that same day, at the opposite end of the Federal battle line from Ames' position, Joshua Lawrence Chamberlain and the 20th Maine won immortality for their gallant defense of Little Round Top at the Battle of Gettysburg, Pennsylvania.

[2] The Federals knew the palisade fence would be a difficult obstacle. General Terry reported that, in addition to the employment of axmen, bags of powder fitted with fuses had been prepared to blow holes in the fence. The powder bag scheme was dropped on the morning of the assault, when it appeared that the naval gunfire had sufficiently damaged the fence. When the attackers reached the fence, however, they found the openings more narrow than anticipated.

[3] Had the Confederates manned the crest of the parapet, they would have enjoyed a much closer range, and an easier field of fire than that experienced by their comrades at the Northeast Bastion.

[4] Lamb had ordered the mines to be exploded when the Federal advance passed over the torpedo field, but the fort's electrician had been unable to detonate them. The connecting wires had been plowed up and broken by naval gunfire.

[5] James Reilly was Lamb's second in command on this day, Maj. James M. Stevenson being too ill for duty. Stevenson would soon die a prisoner of war. Lamb, agreeing with N. Martin Curtis, would later criticize Reilly's defense of the western salient.

[6] This errand was Kempton's second trip to Terry's headquarters. Curtis, after capturing the fourth traverse, had sent Kempton to request that the naval gunfire be increased. Curtis wanted the fuses cut shorter, so the shells would explode nearer the parapet. Many of the rounds were errant, and either exploded among the Federals or crashed into the marsh or river to the west. Said Curtis: "*Mr. Kempton commanded my warmest admiration.*"

[7] Abraham Lincoln—himself of long stature at six feet, four inches—had met Curtis before the war. Curtis was so tall that the president quipped: "*Mr. Curtis, how do you know when your feet are cold?*"

[8] Bragg was referring to a terse report from Whiting early in the engagement, in which he pointedly asked Bragg if he would allow the Federals to besiege Fort Fisher, or if he would attack them instead. Whiting ended the message with the following statement: "*The fire on the fort from iron-clads heavy, but casualties so far during the fight 3 killed and 32 wounded.*" Moreover, Adjt. James H. Hill's afternoon dispatch began with the line: "*We still hold the fort.*" Bragg apparently latched onto such phrases in adhering to his own conviction that Fisher was impregnable against an infantry assault. In response to Whiting's missives, the Confederate commander sent a message to Fisher at 2:30 p.m.: "*Hoke is moving on enemy, but I am confident you will repel him with your infantry.*" Robert F. Hoke's 4:00 p.m. movement, however, amounted to nothing more than a half-hearted reconnaissance. He pulled back to Sugar Loaf after a brief engagement with Paine's skirmishers.

[9] On January 20, 1865, Bragg wrote his brother, Thomas: "*During Saturday [January 14] I was greatly disturbed by the tone and phraseology of General Whiting's dispatches, and by reports of others from him in town . . . . I ordered General Whiting on Saturday evening to report to me in person. This order he declined to obey . . . . My mind was now made up as to his*

Fort Fisher: From a drawing by Frank Vizetelly, *Illustrated London News*

condition and I felt that the safety of the fort required his prompt relief."

[10] Following the battle, Braxton Bragg seized upon this incident and claimed that many of the garrison remnants were drunk at the time of their evacuation to Battery Buchanan. William Lamb was both saddened and angry by Bragg's assertion, and stated that "*the charge that my brave men who, for sixty hours had withstood a furious bombardment and who for six hours had engaged in a hand to hand fight, and who had not retreated until their ammunition was gone and with it all hope, were drunk, is too absurd to require a denial.*"

[11] Whiting, though the senior officer, was not in command at Fort Fisher, and wished to spare his young friend Lamb the painful duty of surrendering.

[12] Gideon Welles had been openly critical of Butler's involvement in the first expedition against Fort Fisher.

SECOND EXPEDITION

From a J. O. Davidson Lithograph

Bombardment

Fort Fisher is engulfed in smoke and flames as Federal warships pummel the bastion prior to the ground assault. The Mound Battery is visible at the far left. Note that the fort's palisade fence along the Northeast Bastion extends nearly to the water line.

The navy's four ironclad monitors are positioned between the fort and the line of conventional warships in the foreground. The airbursts around the vessels and whitecaps in the water show evidence of Confederate return fire.

The double-turreted monitor is the USS *Monadnock*. The remaining monitors are the *Mahopac, Saugus,* and *Canonicus.*

January 13: "Soon after we had taken position it became evident that since the previous attack a reinforcement of experienced artillerists had been received in the fort, as its fire was much more accurate and spirited than before. They soon obtained our range and struck the ship frequently, while many shots fell close alongside. Upon one occasion two shots out of three, fired simultaneously, struck the side armor, abreast of the turret. We count 36 hits this day, and everything about the deck not shot proof was badly cut up."
—**Lt. Cmdr. George E. Belknap,** commanding the USS *Canonicus*

January 14-15: On the second and third days, the Confederate fire was less severe, but errant rifle balls and grapeshot aimed at their "gallant fellows" onshore pattered against the ship. During the three days' bombardment the *Canonicus* expended 297 15-inch shells on Fort Fisher. In return, the ironclad suffered extensive, if not serious, damage. The vessel received three shots on the turret, one on the turret's base ring, one in the forward side armor, five in the side armor abreast of the turret, one in the side armor abreast of the smokestack, three on the deck plating, seven through the upper part of the smokestack, and four on the stack armor. The stack was badly cut up by pieces of broken shot and fragments of shell. In addition, a hole was knocked in the turret rifle guard by a piece of the ship's side armor.

Many of the hostile rounds punched holes in the ship's armor, and its compass and both of its flagstaffs were shot away. One gig and one cutter on board were shot to pieces, and another cutter received a large shot through its side. On top of all this, the ship lost many of its support guys and other small fittings. The monitors cut a low profile in the water, and were not easy targets.

Harper's Weekly, February 4, 1865

Attack

Federal infantry forces storm the western salient of Fort Fisher, January 15, 1865. In the left background, Fleet Capt. K. R. Breese's naval column is engaged at the Northeast Bastion.

"At the very outset of the attack, while rapidly forming my regiment for the charge on the works, I was severely wounded in the right shoulder. Notwithstanding this I continued in the fight from first to last, about seven hours, having secured a lodgement in the northwest angle of the fort. With a few others of my regiment, I advanced from traverse to traverse . . . . having been in very close contact with the enemy during the whole time, and in several hand to hand encounters with them."

—**Lt. John Wainright**, 97th Pennsylvania Infantry, Pennypacker's brigade. Medal of Honor recipient at Fort Fisher.

SECOND EXPEDITION

North Carolina Division of Archives and History

Resistance

Confederate gunners atop Fort Fisher's Mound Battery answer the fire of the Federal fleet. The view of the fort from the Mound was impressive. It was from this lofty position that Confederate president Jefferson Davis once received a 21-gun salute from the fort's Sea Face artillery. Sprawling along the beach to the north, the oceanside batteries extend to meet Fisher's massive land front in the background. When Federal troops gained a lodgment at the western salient, the guns on the Mound joined those of the Columbiad Battery and Battery Buchanan in firing upon the attackers. A Confederate officer monitored the final stages of the battle from his post at Battery Lamb across the Cape Fear River: "4.20 p.m. - Enemy still hold east part of land face of Fisher. Mound and Buchanan still firing. Flag still waving over the Mound . . . . 4.50 p.m. - The enemy still hold same position . . . . 10:30 p.m. - All at once firing has ceased; also signals; and the whole fleet are now throwing rockets up—all colors. It is fully believed that the fort has surrendered."

—**Lt. John J. Bright**, telegrams to Gen. Louis Hébert at Smithville, January 15, 1865

Celebration

A portion of Adm. David D. Porter's fleet celebrates the capture of Fort Fisher. As the ecstatic sailors and marines stage an elaborate fireworks show, one young naval officer is consumed with thoughts of home. "We have taken Fort Fisher by a bombardment and a combined assault of soldiers and sailors. It has been a dreadful Sunday, but we have done something toward ending the war. I led one of the divisions and was shot through the left arm and shoulder . . . Our men were driven back with heavy loss[,] nearly all the leading officers being killed or wounded. . . . God and your prayers and love were with me during those dreadful hours. I love you more than ever, and will come to you as soon as I can."
—**Lt. Roswell H. Lamson**, USS *Gettysburg*, to fiancée Kate Buckingham, night of January 15, 1865

Harper's Weekly, February 4, 1865

SECOND EXPEDITION

Aftermath

This sketch of Fort Fisher's Mound Battery was made following the battle by Acting Ens. Francis P. B. Sands, of the USS *Gettysburg*. A United States flag flies in place of the Confederate garrison flag, as Federal soldiers stand guard. Note the spent shot and shell fragments lying on the beach, and on the slopes of the Mound itself. "*On Sunday [January 15, 1865] the fire of the fleet reached a pitch of fury to which no language can do justice,*" reported Gen. W. H. C. Whiting. "*The fleet surpassed its tremendous effort upon the previous attack [December 1864].*" The Mound was Fisher's most visible landmark and a testament to the capabilities of its engineers, and the structure drew much attention and comment from its adversaries. Miles M. Oviatt, a young marine stationed aboard the USS *Brooklyn*, joined his comrades in a tour of the fort on January 17. "*The celebrated mound battery,*" he noted, "*which commands the channel for 7 miles which they said was Ironcladed, was not, but mounts two heavy guns.*" The view faces the Atlantic Ocean and New Inlet, with a few vessels of the fleet visible in the background.

Official Records of the Union and Confederate Navies

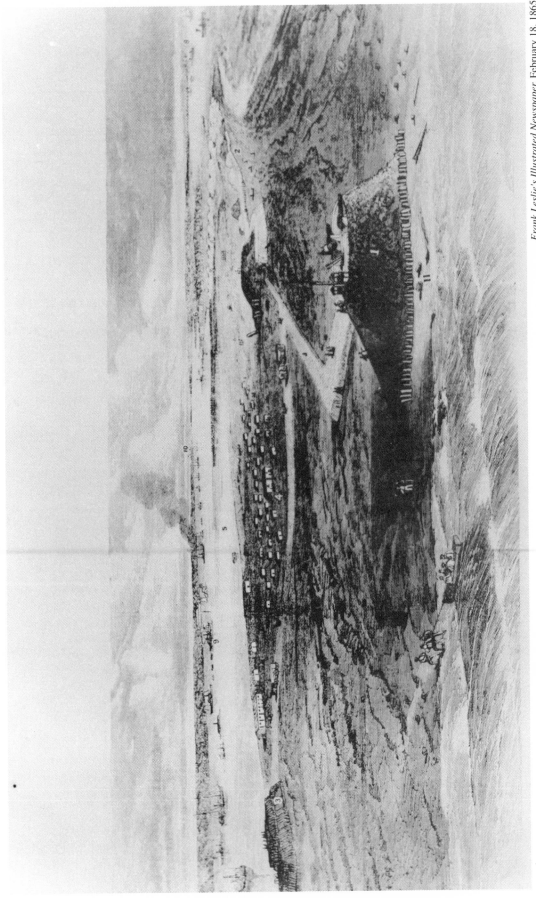

Frank Leslie's Illustrated Newspaper, February 18, 1865

Occupation

This aerial view of Fort Fisher includes Battery Buchanan, though spatially the scale is incorrect. The view faces north from the Mound Battery, toward the port of Wilmington on the horizon. KEY: **(1)** Mound Battery — **(2)** Fort Fisher — **(3)** Battery Buchanan — **(4)** Camp for Federal Troops — **(5)** Cape Fear River — **(6)** Gen. Alfred Terry's Headquarters — **(7)** Abandoned Blockade Runner *Condor* [upper right] — **(8)** Gunboats of the Fleet Protecting the Union Northern Line [upper right] — **(9)** Admiral Porter's Flagship *Malvern*, in the Cape Fear River — **(10)** Port of Wilmington, 20 miles to the north — **(11)** Cylindrical torpedoes on the beach below the Mound Battery. From this staging point east of the river, the Federal army would begin its campaign to capture Wilmington. The advance would involve ground forces on both sides of the Cape Fear, and a squadron of Porter's gunboats in the river.

Casualties and Other Numbers
January 13-15, 1865

FORT FISHER GARRISON

Forces Engaged:

Command	Effectives
Garrison	Approx. 1,550
Reinforcements January 15:	
Elements of the 11th, 21st, and 25th South Carolina Infantry	350
Approximate Total:	**1,900**

Casualties:

Killed and Wounded (approximate)	500
Captured (approximate)	1,400
Approximate Total:	**1,900**

Guns in Position When Captured:

No.	Weapon	Condition	Carriage
		LAND FACE	
1	10-inch columbiad	Unserviceable	Unserviceable
2	6⅜-inch rifle (old 32)	"	Serviceable
3	8-inch smoothbore - 1841	Serviceable	Unserviceable
4	8-inch smoothbore - 1841	Unserviceable	"
5	8-inch columbiad	Serviceable	Serviceable
6	4½ -inch Parrott rifle	"	"
7	6⅜-inch smoothbore (32)	Unserviceable	"
8	5⅞-inch smoothbore (24)	"	Unserviceable
9	6⅜-inch smoothbore (32)	"	"
10	5½-inch Coehorn mortar	Serviceable	Serviceable
11	6⅜-inch smoothbore (32)	Unserviceable	Unserviceable
12	5½-inch Coehorn mortar	Serviceable	Serviceable
13	6½-inch smoothbore (32)	"	"
14	8-inch smoothbore (32)	"	Unserviceable
15	6⅜-inch smoothbore (32)	"	Serviceable
16	6⅜-inch smoothbore (32)	"	Unserviceable
17	6⅜-inch smoothbore (32)	Unserviceable	"
18	6⅜-inch rifle (32)	Serviceable	"
19	7-inch Brooke rifle	"	Serviceable
20	6⅜-inch rifle (32)	"	Unserviceable
21	6⅜-inch rifle (32)	Unserviceable	"
22	10-inch columbiad	"	"
23	8-inch mortar	Serviceable	Serviceable
24	8-inch smoothbore	"	"
		SEA FACE	
25	8-inch Blakely rifle	Serviceable	Serviceable
26	10-inch columbiad	"	Unserviceable
27	6⅜-inch rifle (32)	"	"
28	10-inch columbiad	"	"
29	----------	----------	----------
30	10-inch columbiad	"	Serviceable
31	8-inch columbiad	"	"
32	8-inch columbiad	"	"
33	8-inch columbiad	"	Unserviceable
34	8-inch columbiad	"	Serviceable
35	7-inch Brooke rifle	Unserviceable	Unserviceable
36	8-inch columbiad	Serviceable	Serviceable
37	6⅜-inch rifle (32)	"	"
38	6⅜-inch rifle (32)	"	"
39	150-pdr. Armstrong rifle	"	"
40	10-inch columbiad	"	"
41	10-inch columbiad	"	"
42	7-inch Brooke rifle	Serviceable	Serviceable
43	6⅜-inch rifle (32)	"	"
44	10-inch columbiad	"	"
45	10-inch columbiad	"	"
46	10-inch columbiad	"	Unserviceable
47	6⅜-inch rifle (32)	"	Serviceable

See map of Fort Fisher, page 12.

HOKE'S DIVISION

Forces Engaged:

Command	Effectives
Hoke's Division	Approx. 6,400
Casualties: None reported for Hoke's demonstration on the Union northern line on January 15, but the division probably lost a few men on the skirmish line (Kirkland's and Clingman's Brigades).	

UNITED STATES ARMY

Forces Present:

Command	Effectives		
From official returns for January 10, 1865[§]			
	Officers	Men	Aggregate
General Headquarters	12	12	24
Ames' division (2nd, XXIV)	192	3,787	4,243
Paine's division (3rd, XXV)	160	3,149	3,683
Abbott's brigade (2, 1, XXIV)	65	1,385	1,494
16th New York Battery	3	42	45
3rd U.S. Artillery (E)	4	55	61
Detachment Signal Corps	4	27	31
Ambulance Corps	-----	-----	51
Total:	440	8,457	**9,632**

[§]Officers and men reported as present for duty. Aggregate reported as aggregate present.

Casualties:[¤]

Unit	Killed	Wounded	Missing	Total
Second Division, XXIV Army Corps: Ames'				
XXIV A.C. HQ	-----	1	-----	1
Division Staff	-----	4	-----	
(1) Curtis	39	184	5	228
(2) Pennypacker	51	227	2	280
(3) Bell	16	97	2	115
First Division, XXIV Army Corps:				
(2) Abbott	4	23	4	31
Third Division, XXV Army Corps:				
(3) 27th USCT	1	4	-----	5
Total:	111	540	13	**664**

[¤]From official returns. In addition, 1 officer and 4 men, 112th NY; and 1 man, 142nd NY were wounded on January 14; for a total of **670**.[†]

[†]Unofficial army returns place the total at **955** battle victims (184 killed, 749 wounded, and 22 missing), with at least another 104 casualties from the magazine explosion on January 16 (25 killed, 66 wounded, and 13 missing).

See **Orders of Battle**, Appendix B, page 157, for complete command listings

UNITED STATES NAVY

Forces Present:

Number of Warships:	**58**
Naval Shore Contingent	**2,261** sailors and marines

Casualties:

Command	Totals		
From official returns.			

Sailors	Officers	Men	Aggregate
Killed:	6	75	81
Wounded:	24	198	222
Missing:	-----	29	29
Marines			
Killed:	-----	7	7
Wounded:	2	47	49
Missing:	-----	5	5
Total:	32	361	**393**

Rounds Expended:

Projectiles	Weight
19,682	1,652,638 pounds

Combined with numbers from the December 1864 bombardment, the projectiles expended equal 39,953—with a weight of 2,927,937 pounds. See page 33 for December 1864 returns. The projectile numbers are officially suffixed with this statement: "*It is estimated that the above statement includes between 90 and 95 percent of the projectiles actually expended.*"

TOTAL FEDERAL CASUALTIES: 2nd Fort Fisher

The combined army and navy losses range somewhere between 1,167 and 1,452 killed, wounded, and missing—based upon published figures available, as listed above.

COMBINED UNION & CONFEDERATE CASUALTIES
for the December 1864, and January 1865
Engagements at Fort Fisher

Command	Killed	Wounded	C/M	Total
— December 1864 —				
Federal Army	1	11	1	13
Federal Navy	20	63	-----	83
Fort Fisher	3	58	-----	61
Hoke's Division	5	16	307	328
— January 1865 —				
Federal Army	209	815	35	1,059‡
Federal Navy	88	271	34	393
Subtotal:	326	1,234	377	1,937
Fort Fisher		500	1,400	1,900
Aggregate:	2,060		1,777	**3,837**

‡Unofficial army figure of 955, plus 104 from the magazine explosion. (Based upon the "official" tally of 670, this figure would equal 774). The navy, however, also reported a loss of eight men in the magazine explosion. It is unclear whether these men are included in the total for this tragedy. (It is thought that about 200 men, both Union and Confederate, were lost in the explosion. It is further unclear whether the Confederate losses in the explosion are included in the often-cited approximate figure of 500 killed and wounded for the garrison).

Approximate Total Federal Casualties for both engagements equal 1,548. (Based upon the "official" army tally of 670, this figure would equal 1,263).

Approximate Total Confederate Casualties for both engagements equal 2,289.

Combined Union and Confederate Casualties for both engagements equal 3,837. (Based upon the "official" Federal army tally of 670, this figure would equal 3,552).

The exact number of casualties in the battles for Fort Fisher will never be known. Confederate records are sketchy, and wide discrepancies exist between the various Federal numbers published. In addition, the figure for the magazine mishap is incomplete.

The Federal infantry attack on January 15, 1865 initiated perhaps the most prolonged hand-to-hand engagement of the Civil War. The close-quarters nature of the fight, together with the unprecedented bombardment from the Federal fleet, produced casualties of an unusually grave character. Considering the amount of ordnance expended upon the fort, it is a wonder that the number of killed and wounded (especially among those of the garrison who manned their weapons to return the naval fire) was not much greater.

Frank Vizetelly, of the *Illustrated London News*—one of the most famous combat artists of the era—braved the storm to sketch the interior of Fort Fisher during the height of the bombardments. His drawings would later provide a first-hand view of the death and destruction wrought by the heavy ordnance of the fleet. It was unlike anything he had ever witnessed.

For official figures, see *OR*, 42, Pt. 1, pp. 1007-1008, 1023; *OR*, 46, Pt. 1, pp. 403-405; *ORN*, 11, pp. 442-444; and "The Opposing Forces at Fort Fisher, N.C.," in Robert U. Johnson and Clarence C. Buel, eds., *Battles and Leaders of the Civil War*, 4, pp. 661-662. 4 vols. New York: The Century Company, 1884-1889.

The Land Front of Fort Fisher, as seen from the fort's interior. The view faces toward the western salient, with the Cape Fear River in the background. This drawing appeared in the published histories of several Union regiments who participated in the attack on Fort Fisher.

Bvt. Brig. Gen. N. Martin Curtis (1st Brigade)

Col. Galusha Pennypacker (2nd Brigade)

As the lines formed for the assault on Fort Fisher on January 15, 1865, the irascible N. Martin Curtis eyed the Federal navy's shore contingent with disapproval. When Lt. Benjamin Porter approached Curtis to coordinate the particulars of the assault, the young naval officer received a prompt admonishment from the army brigade commander. Curtis warned Porter that the naval column was too *"closely massed . . . your formation is bad, and your front is too narrow for the depth of your column."* Porter expressed his regret that the army found fault with the navy. *"I condemn your formation as a landsman,"* Curtis assured the younger officer. *"I would not criticize nautical matters."*

Before nightfall on the 15th, Porter would be dead and Curtis would lie grievously wounded. Curtis later asserted that *"It was just as absurd to have expected beneficial results from [the naval attack] as it would be to put our landsmen at the masthead of a ship in a storm."*

Curtis was awarded a Medal of Honor for his conduct in the assault in November 1891. His feud with Adelbert Ames continued, and the two nearly came to blows at a veterans' meeting in 1897. Ames wanted credit for the victory at Fort Fisher—*"that palisaded Malakoff fortress,"* as he called it. Curtis, of course, refuted Ames' claim, and the incident prompted him to write a detailed account of the battle. •

The Federal Brigade Commanders of Ames' Division in the Attack on Fort Fisher, January 15, 1865

Not long before the attack on Fort Fisher, Louis Bell wrote a heartfelt letter to his wife in New Hampshire: *"God knows I will not shrink from any necessary danger. If I live through the conflict I will live far more for my wife and children than for myself. If I die, do not forget, my own precious wife, that I die in defense of our country. Teach our children to die for it, if need be, and to regard death with it as far beyond life without it, be that life surrounded by however many blessings. Teach our children, darling Mollie, that liberty and freedom are first freedom for all, and that for it we are bound to lay down our lives. Should I be killed, do not mourn me, precious wife. Let me be as one absent, soon to return, and while away gaining a history that will be remembered while history lives . . . . My last thought will be for the future of our children, and for the happiness of my own precious, darling wife, my own loved Mollie."*

When he was shot at Fort Fisher, a stunned Bell first thought his arm was broken. Lieutenant Hugh Sanford of Bell's staff, however, had heard the bullet strike his commander, and he knew immediately that it was a body wound. As the men of the Third Brigade rushed past to enter the fort, Bell asked those who were attending him: *"Lift me up a little, if you please."* He was then borne to the rear. Bell managed to ask if his wound was mortal. *"I am fearful it is, colonel,"* replied a surgeon. *"Well,"* admitted Bell, *"I thought as much myself."*

Bell's men were crushed by the loss of their commander. He was loved and admired for his ability to lead the men firmly, without losing his pleasant demeanor and gentle disposition. In his final hours Bell became delirious, in turns murmuring the names of his wife and children. *"When first brought in he recognized me,"* noted surgeon C. MacFarlane, but Bell soon faded. *"See the rebels!"* he agonized. *"Here they come—one, two, three, four."* Bell lingered through the night, *"and before the sun had risen on the sixteenth, our Colonel was no more."* •

Col. Louis Bell (3rd Brigade)

As he lay suffering at the Federal field hospital at Fort Fisher on January 16, 1865, Galusha Pennypacker was informed by General Terry that he would receive the brevet rank of brigadier general. His wound, however, was considered fatal, and Pennypacker would spend the next ten months in painful convalescence at Fortress Monroe, Virginia. By April 1865, his promotion was official, and the 20-year-old officer found himself the youngest general in United States military history. He was too young to vote for the president who appointed him.

Pennypacker arrived at home in West Chester, Pennsylvania, that November, where an acquaintance noted that he was *"handsomely received by his friends, and the citizens generally."* He had returned a hero, but as Pennypacker continued to recover, the "boy general" found himself plagued by severe depression and self doubt.

Pennypacker shared his feelings with a trusted friend, Capt. William Wayne. Wayne had known the young officer since their service together in the 97th Pennsylvania Infantry. Though Wayne had resigned his commission in January 1863, the two friends remained close.

In 1866, an attorney named Rees Davis, unbeknownst to the general, queried Wayne on the prospect of Pennypacker's running for Congress. The notion so troubled the insecure youngster that he refused, fearing Davis was trying to humiliate him. *"Blue, Blue, Blue! That's what's the matter . . . . My wits, what few I have, are, I don't know where to-day,"* Pennypacker confided to Wayne. *"I wonder, my best friend, if there ever lived another mortal, as unhappy, as weak, as am I. I can never do right, and feel that I've done right, and be cheerful thereat like others . . . . Do you think Rees Davis made a fool of me? Is he honest, strictly? . . . . I am too young for the position now . . . . I make so many good resolves [but] keep so few promises that I make to myself. I am ashamed to send you this letter. But, you are so kind to me—you have, always, apologies for me. God knows, I am not much in this world; but, I do feel that I owe much of what I am, (be it very little, or little) to the influence for good you exerted over me—teaching me to be a man—during our one year's constant and daily intercourse. Why shouldn't I believe in you?"*

The United States army was reorganized in 1866, and despite his insecurities, Galusha Pennypacker recovered sufficiently from his wound to serve until 1883. He served as a regimental commander with the rank of colonel in the Regular Army, and was one of the few Reconstruction-era commanders to gain the respect of postwar Southerners. Complications from his wound at Fort Fisher troubled Pennypacker for the rest of his life, and he was awarded the Congressional Medal of Honor in August 1891 for his part in the capture of Fort Fisher. He continued to shun the notion of political office. •

*For a discussion of the Malakoff and Crimean War fortifications at Sebastopol, Russia, see Appenix A, page 137.

The Commander of Fort Fisher

William Lamb was spared the fate of his captive garrison, whose members were sent to prison camps in the North. On January 23, 1865, the wounded colonel arrived at Federal-held Fortress Monroe, Virginia, aboard the steamer *California*. One of his Fort Fisher adversaries, Lt. James Parker of the United States Navy, had obtained permission for Lamb to be put ashore in his home state. Lamb's long recovery would begin at Monroe's Chesapeake Hospital.

On March 12, Lamb received the *"great shock"* of General Whiting's death two days earlier. Recovering from his wound in a Northern prison, "Little Billy" had contracted dysentery and died. Before his death, however, Whiting had penned a series of scathing reports demanding an investigation of Gen. Braxton Bragg and his conduct in the defense of Fort Fisher. Lamb mourned his friend and mentor, and he never forgot him.

The colonel suffered intense discomfort and sickness in the months following his injury. He endured bouts of colic, and his hip wound became abscessed. To quell the pain he ingested liberal doses of morphine and other anodynes, and the drugs often left him in a state of mental befuddlement—*"very stupid from the effects of chloroform,"* he complained on March 29. Nineteenth-century doctors could offer little relief from the agony of battlefield wounds to the extremities.

Following General Lee's April 9 surrender at Appomattox and the assassination of President Abraham Lincoln, Lamb took the oath of allegiance to the United States of America on April 22, 1865. The colonel pledged to support the federal Constitution and its laws, *"deeming further resistance useless & wrong & believing a life in prison could do no one good & that it would result in my death."*

On April 29, Lamb dressed for the first time since his injury, and on May 1 he left for Providence, Rhode Island, aboard the steamer *Adelaide*. By the time he reached his wife's family home in Providence, however, another painful abscess had formed under his thigh. Lamb's doctors began a close scrutiny of the lesion to determine the cause of the continued problems. Though there was no exit wound, the physicians were apparently unsure whether the damaged thigh contained fragments of bone or a Federal bullet.

By the middle of May, Lamb was able to sit up on his own for the first time, while his doctors continued to puzzle over his injury. In late June Lamb, able to move a little more, was carried downstairs for the first time, and was soon taking carriage rides with his wife and others. During this period, the colonel read William Makepeace Thackeray's *The Adventures of Philip*,[1] and wrote letters to pass the time. He also received a *"handsome pair of crutches"* from his mother-in-law the following month.

By August, Lamb's wound had begun to yield small bits of woolen cloth, which had been carried into his hip by the bullet that felled him. Whenever doctors probed the hole in his upper thigh, Lamb became desperately ill. By September, however, they had determined that the object inside the wound was ready to be extracted. On September 25, a team of four

physicians *"performed an operation on me,"* recalled Lamb, *"& extracted a large conical musket ball. It had particles of red woolen fibre [sic] attached to it—from the red flannel lining of my [military] overcoat."*

Though the wound continued to emit fragments of wool from his uniform, Lamb's hip began to heal after the surgery. Relieved, he gave the Federal bullet to one of his surgeons as a souvenir, and soon immersed himself in *"Abbott's Life of Napoleon"* to help occupy his hours of inactivity.[2]

Col. William Lamb, of Norfolk, Virginia

Battles and Leaders

On October 10, 1865, William Lamb, supported by a family member, took his first steps with the aid of a crutch. Gradually, he improved to the extent that he could sit with the family at the dinner table, and move about more easily. The crutches would be a part of Lamb's life for the next seven years.

On November 7, the colonel finally set out for his home town of Norfolk, Virginia, where he arrived two days later. At *"sweet home"* he was able to complete his recovery, and make arrangements to get his business affairs in order. Capitalizing on his old blockade running contacts, Lamb engaged in the shipping business, did a bit of writing, and in 1880 was elected as mayor of Norfolk. As mayor, Lamb held the job that both his father and grandfather had once held, and he was eager to introduce improvements to the city.

In his later life, William Lamb was active in reunions of Confederate and Union veterans at Fort Fisher, and at the urging of friends he penned several detailed histories of the fort's defense and capture. He denounced his former Democratic Party and became a Republican, and at that party's national convention in 1888 he met his former adversary, N. Martin Curtis. The two became fast friends, and Lamb referred to Curtis as *"my friend the enemy"*—for they had once been locked in mortal combat against one another. In the 1890s, the two former enemies toured the aging ruins of Fort Fisher together, each explaining to the other his exploits in the battle. They pointed out topographical landmarks, structural locations, discussed the battle, and remembered the names of their fallen comrades. Their efforts to save the fort as a national park, however, failed. William Lamb died in March 1909, after a period of declining health. He was 73 years old. His vision of preserving Fort Fisher for posterity would not be realized for another 50 years. •

---

[1] Originally published in the magazine *The Cornhill*, 1861-1862.

[2] John S. C. Abbott was a renowned historical author of the era, best known for his works on European history. He penned several biographies of Napoleon, as well as studies of the French emperor's military campaigns. Abbott also published a history on the American Civil War.

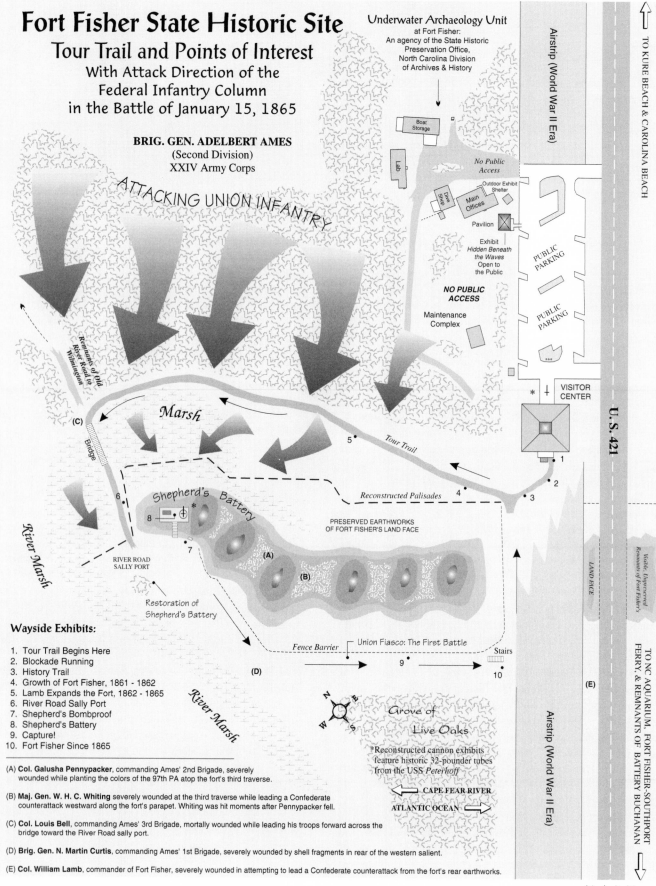

Fort Fisher State Historic Site
Tour Trail and Points of Interest
With Attack Direction of the Federal Infantry Column in the Battle of January 15, 1865

BRIG. GEN. ADELBERT AMES
(Second Division)
XXIV Army Corps

ATTACKING UNION INFANTRY

Underwater Archaeology Unit at Fort Fisher:
An agency of the State Historic Preservation Office, North Carolina Division of Archives & History

Boat Storage

Lab

No Public Access

Dive Shop

Main Offices

Outdoor Exhibit Shelter

Pavilion

Exhibit
Hidden Beneath the Waves
Open to the Public

NO PUBLIC ACCESS

Maintenance Complex

PUBLIC PARKING

PUBLIC PARKING

VISITOR CENTER

Airstrip (World War II Era)

TO KURE BEACH & CAROLINA BEACH

U.S. 421

Marsh

Remnants of Old River Road to Wilmington

(C)

Bridge

Tour Trail

5

Reconstructed Palisades

4

3

2

1

6

Shepherd's Battery

8

7

PRESERVED EARTHWORKS OF FORT FISHER'S LAND FACE

(A)

(B)

River Marsh

RIVER ROAD SALLY PORT

Restoration of Shepherd's Battery

(D)

River Marsh

LAND FACE

Visible, Unexcavated Remnants of Fort Fisher's

Fence Barrier

Union Fiasco: The First Battle

Stairs

9

10

(E)

Wayside Exhibits:

1. Tour Trail Begins Here
2. Blockade Running
3. History Trail
4. Growth of Fort Fisher, 1861 - 1862
5. Lamb Expands the Fort, 1862 - 1865
6. River Road Sally Port
7. Shepherd's Bombproof
8. Shepherd's Battery
9. Capture!
10. Fort Fisher Since 1865

Grove of Live Oaks

*Reconstructed cannon exhibits feature historic 32-pounder tubes from the USS *Peterhoff*.

CAPE FEAR RIVER ⟵

ATLANTIC OCEAN ⟶

Airstrip (World War II Era)

TO NC AQUARIUM, FORT FISHER-SOUTHPORT FERRY, & REMNANTS OF BATTERY BUCHANAN

(A) **Col. Galusha Pennypacker**, commanding Ames' 2nd Brigade, severely wounded while planting the colors of the 97th PA atop the fort's third traverse.

(B) **Maj. Gen. W. H. C. Whiting** severely wounded at the third traverse while leading a Confederate counterattack westward along the fort's parapet. Whiting was hit moments after Pennypacker fell.

(C) **Col. Louis Bell**, commanding Ames' 3rd Brigade, mortally wounded while leading his troops forward across the bridge toward the River Road sally port.

(D) **Brig. Gen. N. Martin Curtis**, commanding Ames' 1st Brigade, severely wounded by shell fragments in rear of the western salient.

(E) **Col. William Lamb**, commander of Fort Fisher, severely wounded in attempting to lead a Confederate counterattack from the fort's rear earthworks.

Mark A. Moore

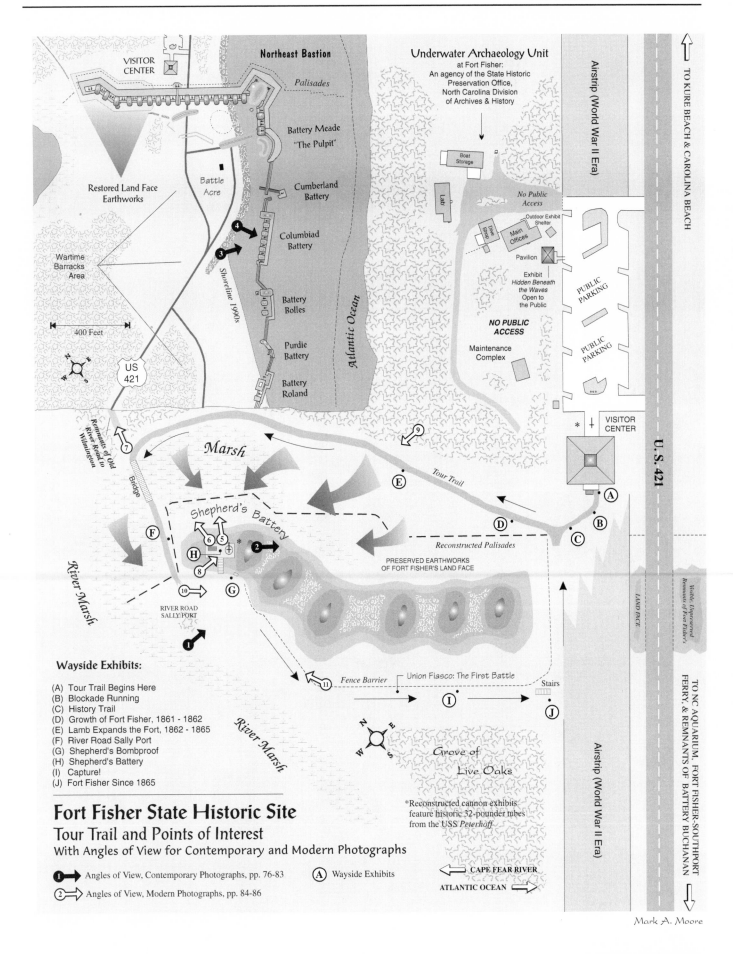

Fort Fisher State Historic Site
Tour Trail and Points of Interest
With Angles of View for Contemporary and Modern Photographs

Wayside Exhibits:

(A) Tour Trail Begins Here
(B) Blockade Running
(C) History Trail
(D) Growth of Fort Fisher, 1861 - 1862
(E) Lamb Expands the Fort, 1862 - 1865
(F) River Road Sally Port
(G) Shepherd's Bombproof
(H) Shepherd's Battery
(I) Capture!
(J) Fort Fisher Since 1865

Angles of View, Contemporary Photographs, pp. 76-83

Angles of View, Modern Photographs, pp. 84-86

Wayside Exhibits

CAPE FEAR RIVER

ATLANTIC OCEAN

*Reconstructed cannon exhibits feature historic 32-pounder tubes from the USS *Peterhoff*

Mark A. Moore

SECOND EXPEDITION

1. The Western Salient: (Shepherd's Battery). First Three Gun Chambers of Fort Fisher

An interior view of the fort's western salient, or Shepherd's Battery. It was here that the attacking brigades of Adelbert Ames' division gained a lodgment on Fort Fisher.

On the open plain behind this installation, stretching south and west toward the Cape Fear River, the massed columns of Federal infantry were subjected to Confederate artillery fire from Battery Buchanan, the Mound Battery, and the fort's Columbiad Battery—in addition to a frontal fire from stubborn Confederate defenders positioned further south and east on the parade ground. *For approximate angle of view, see map on page 75.*

Image by T. H. O'Sullivan

Contemporary Views of Fort Fisher

Following the capture of Fort Fisher in January 1865, Timothy H. O'Sullivan arrived to capture the fort yet again—through the lens of a camera. O'Sullivan, a native of Staten Island, New York, recorded a remarkable series of images of the battle-ravaged fort. These detailed photographs provide a telling visual chronicle of Fort Fisher's main structures and components. O'Sullivan made the negatives for his more famous employer, the photographer Alexander Gardner. Both Gardner and O'Sullivan had once worked for the Civil War's most renowned photographer, Mathew Brady. Gardner had since left Brady to open a gallery of his own in Washington.

As a field photographer, T. H. O'Sullivan provided negatives to Gardner, who then created positive images. In 1865 and 1866, Gardner published 100 photographs, many of which were taken by O'Sullivan, in his two-volume collection titled *Gardner's Photographic Sketch Book of the War.* Two of O'Sullivan's images of Fort Fisher—the one pictured opposite and one of the Pulpit Battery—were included in the Gardner book. Four are reproduced for this volume.

1. The Western Salient *(Shepherd's Battery): Land Front.*

This interior view of the western salient shows the location where Federal troops gained a lodgment on the fort, and the gate through which the bulk of them gained access to the rear of the structure. Three Federal soldiers stand near the gate at the left of the photograph, where a portion of the palisade fence is visible.

In the first gun chamber can be seen a rifled and banded 32-pounder seacoast gun, which is mounted on a wooden center-pintle carriage. The muzzle of its tube appears to have been knocked off, while the remains of the 10-inch columbiad to its left are not in view.

A testament to the fury of the Union naval bombardment, the second chamber—which once housed two 8-inch smoothbore cannon—is a wreck of demolished gun carriages and tubes. The tube of the right piece lies propped against the embrasure, while the tube of the left piece appears to be lying at the base of the rear slope of the battery, just to the left of the access ladder. For a detailed, closeup view of the second gun chamber, see page 78.

Visible in the third gun chamber is a 30-pounder Parrott rifle. This siege weapon is mounted on a wheeled carriage similar to a piece of field artillery. To its left sits an 8-inch columbiad, the rear of which appears to be visible beyond the second traverse.

At the base of the first and third traverses are the entrances to the western salient's bombproofs and magazines. To the rear, on the parade ground, lies the wheel and broken axle of a caisson, or perhaps a field artillery carriage, or wagon. A flagstaff or telegraph pole stands where the Wilmington Road enters the fort through the riverside gate. •

Light Weapons of the Land Front

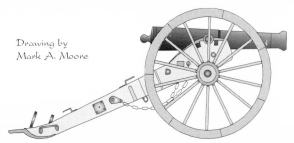

Drawing by
Mark A. Moore

Field Artillery: The sally ports of Fort Fisher were defended with four light fieldpieces similar to the one pictured above: two in the center sally port, one at the riverside gate, and one near the river marsh west of the gate. These weapons rendered crucial service in slowing the Federal infantry attack. The fort's garrison, however, lacked sufficient manpower to adequately serve the riverside pieces. Moreover, many of the cannoneers refused to leave the safety of the fort's bombproofs during the attack.

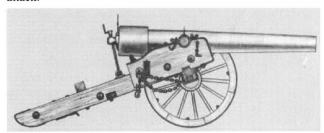

4½-inch Parrott Rifle: A Parrott rifle, similar to the 30-pounder siege weapon pictured above, was stationed in the third gun chamber of Shepherd's Battery. This gun is visible in the photograph opposite. —*Arms and Equipment of the Civil War*

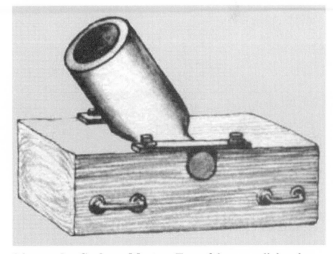

24-pounder Coehorn Mortar: Two of these small, hand-carried mortars were stationed on the land front: one each in the fifth and sixth gun chambers. Fort Fisher's chief of artillery, Maj. William J. Saunders, noted that Confederate gunners were able to service these small weapons on the night of January 14, 1865, when the incessant fire of the Federal fleet prevented the garrison from remounting the damaged heavier pieces on the land front. —*Arms and Equipment of the Civil War*

2. Second Gun Chamber of Shepherd's Battery: Western Salient

This view of the fort's battle torn Land Face, taken from the traverse between the first two gun emplacements, looks eastward toward the Atlantic Ocean. Beyond the main sally port the Northeast Bastion looms in the background. Note the damaged palisade fence.

The accurate gunfire of the Federal navy is well evidenced by the ruins of an 8-inch smoothbore and its wooden barbette carriage, seen at the right of the photograph. Knocked from its shattered carriage, the heavy tube lies propped against the wall, crushing the embrasure beneath it. *For approximate angle of view, see map on page 75.*

Image by T. H. O'Sullivan

2. Second Gun Chamber of Shepherd's Battery *(Western Salient): Land Front.*

This closeup view of the second gun chamber offers details of the fort's construction, as well as evidence of the power of the Federal naval bombardment. The walls of the gun emplacement are revetted with wooden planking, and the parapet is lined with a triple row of sandbags. The traverses are sodded with marsh grass to help reduce erosion from the constant ocean breeze.

The two 8-inch smoothbore cannon stationed here, mounted en barbette, were knocked to pieces by naval gunfire. Between the two gun emplacements, several stands of grapeshot lie propped against the embrasure below the parapet. Also nearby are several ammunition or equipment boxes, and a sponge bucket. A banquette—upon which gun crew members would stand to service the muzzle-loading weapon—appears to be visible at the embrasure in front of the destroyed carriage at the right of the photograph. The sandy floor of the battery is dotted with hundreds of footprints, from attackers and defenders alike.

Looking toward the Atlantic Ocean in the background, the Northeast Bastion protrudes in the distance. The palisade fence, interrupted by the center sally port, lies mangled by naval gunfire—and by holes chopped in the fence by attacking Federal infantry forces. •

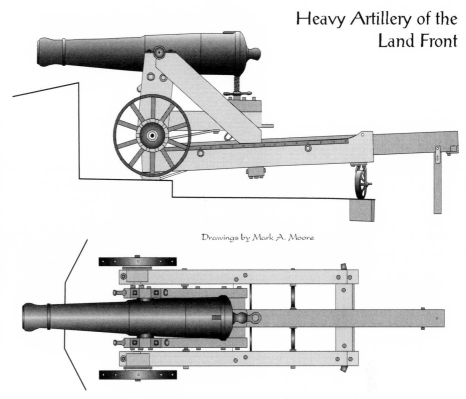

Heavy Artillery of the Land Front

Drawings by Mark A. Moore

Barbette Carriage: A wooden, front-pintle carriage like the one pictured above is an example of how the disabled guns in the second chamber of Shepherd's Battery were mounted.

Fort Fisher, N.C.
January 16, 1865

Stillman K. Wightman
195 Broadway
N.Y.C.

On board the steamship "Atlantic"
Near Fort Fisher, N.C.
January 12, 1865

Dear Father, Mother, Fred, Abbie, Jim, Lillie, Chas, Mary, Ell, and the babies:

Your Christmas family letter dropped into camp on New Years Day like a five hundred pound Parrot[t] shell and administered such a shock of homesickness and hunger that I came near being annihilated. What had I, a free going, half starved soldier to do with your savory turkey, and mealy sweet potatoes and lu[s]cious plum pudding and hot mince pies and foaming lager? . . . . Well, well, if we all do see another Christmas, maybe it will be a jolly one.

I am glad to hear that you all had such a pleasant time. Our family is very fortunate, indeed, to have preserved thus far its circle unbroken and to be able to meet and enjoy quietly an occasional holiday. You will readily believe, without much assurance from me, that I long to rejoin you and assume my place in your midst. Let us hope that the year 1865 will restore peace in the country and to all Americans the rights and privileges of respectable citizens

As ever your Affectionate son, brother, and uncle,
Ed. K. W. [**Edward King Wightman**, 3rd New York Infantry, Curtis' brigade]

One of the most terrible battles of the war has just been terminated in our favor, but not without removing suddenly from among us our beloved "comrade" Edward K. Wightman, whose long association with us has deepened [our] every sentiment into the warmth of earnest attachment. In him our country has lost a true soldier, always faithful in the discharge of his duties and unflinching in the hour of danger; your family an affectionate son and brother; and we a worthy example, and an associate, who had endeared himself to us by his many virtues and by the open frankness of his character. He died while gallantly charging at the head of our regiment and was among the "first" to enter the fort.

He was buried this morning and the grave marked so that it can be found any time if needed. He was hit on the right side and expired immediately.

I have a few things, found in his knapsack, which I have taken charge of. I shall send them on to you at the earliest opportunity [and] any further particular you wish to hear of you can learn from [me].

With much sorrow for your untimely loss,

Your Obdt. Servt.
1st Sergt. John W. Knowles
Co. C, 3rd N.Y. Vol.
Fort Fisher, N.C.
Via Fort Monroe, Va.

SECOND EXPEDITION

3. Columbiad Battery: (Sea Face), Largest of Fort Fisher's Oceanside Gun Batteries

An interior view of the fort's six-gun Columbiad Battery.

The Sea Face guns of Fort Fisher engaged the Federal fleet as defenders on the land front prepared for the enemy ground assault. The guns of the Columbiad Battery slowly and deliberately answered the fire of the fleet, until called upon to reverse their trajectories to the north—to fire upon Fort Fisher's western salient. Rounds from the surviving guns of this installation helped slow the Federal advance on the open plain behind the land front.

Image by T. H. O'Sullivan

3. Columbiad Battery: *Sea Face.*

This view, facing the Atlantic Ocean, reveals the six gun chambers and six traverses of Fort Fisher's Columbiad Battery. This installation housed five 8-inch columbiads and one 7-inch Brooke rifle. The Brooke rifle was stationed in the second gun chamber from the right.

Spent rounds from the Federal naval bombardment—either solid shot or unexploded shells—lie scattered on the sandy plain behind the battery, while thousands of footprints mark the steps of the victorious and the vanquished alike.

Unlike those of the Land Face, the traverses and gun emplacements of the Columbiad Battery were revetted with masonry. Battle damage to the brickwork is evidenced in the second, fourth, and fifth traverses from the left. Wooden banquettes—stepping platforms—are visible in the second, third, and fourth chambers from the left. A bombproof entrance can be seen at the inner base of the battery's first traverse.

Note the missing guns in the third and fifth chambers from the left. These weapons were dismounted or destroyed by naval gunfire—an 8-inch columbiad and the 7-inch Brooke rifle. The tubes and shattered gun carriages (of the wooden, center-pintle variety) lie in pieces behind the battlements. Two men can be seen standing in this photograph, one each behind the third and fourth gun chambers from the left. An overturned wagon is also visible.

There is a noticeable absence of turf on the first, fourth, and fifth traverses of the battery. This may suggest that these mounds were damaged during the December 1864 bombardment, and were topped off, or repaired, between then and the January 1865 bombardment. The sixth traverse (or first from right) appears to have been leveled off to some degree by naval gunfire.

One of the most interesting aspects of this image is the direction in which the guns of the second and fourth chambers are facing. The guns are pointing toward the western salient of Fort Fisher—in the direction they faced when the battle ended. These weapons, their crews having been ordered to reverse their fields of fire by Col. William Lamb, helped slow the Federal infantry advance on the open plain behind the fort. The remaining two guns of the battery are still facing the ocean.

For a detailed close-up view of the battery's third and fourth traverses, viewed from a different angle, see the photograph on page 82. •

"I was in command of the fort after the chivalrous [Gen. W. H. C.] Whiting and the brave Colonel [William] Lamb were wounded . . . . I being the Senior Officer there for duty the command devolved on me [and] with a small number of brave men (I never had over one Hundred men fighting after the first assault, and that number dwindled to about thirty-two (32) before 8 o.C. p.m.) Kept the Heavy assaulting Column of the enemy in check all that memorable afternoon . . . . [T]he men that did fight fought as well as any men ever fought. Shortly after the enemy got possession of the western angle of the work the fleet slacked its fire to a very great extent. This encouraged our men and I revived considerable enthusiasm and determination amongst them and it showed plainly that they meant business and the few that did come out of the [bombproof] chambers where they were seeking protection from the destructive and murderous fire of the enemy fleet all day fought as men ought to fight for the protection of Hearths and Homes."
—**Maj. James Reilly**, on assuming command of Fort Fisher

"A foothold having been secured on the parapet troops were sent to re-enforce the advanced lines, and slowly but irresistibly the rebels were driven from one position after the other. Hand-to-hand fighting of the most desperate character took place, the huge traverses of the land face being used successively by the enemy as breastworks, over the tops of which the contending parties fired in each others' faces.

"The scenes toward the close of the battle were indescribably horrible. Great cannon lay in ruins, surrounded by the bodies of their defenders; men were found partly buried in graves dug by the shells which had slain them. The outlines of the works could now and then be seen by the flash of an exploding shell or the blaze of musketry, but indistinct as the creation of some hideous dream. Soldiers were falling everywhere, shot in the head by rifle-balls . . . . There arose now and then an agonizing clamor of wounded men, writhing in the sand, beseeching those near them to end their suffering. A color-bearer had fallen, and though choked by blood and sand, he murmured: 'I am gone. Take the flag.' An officer who had been shot through the heart retained a nearly erect position, leaning against a gun-carriage. Some lay face downward in the sand, and others who had been close together when struck by an exploding shell had fallen in a confused mass, forming a mingled heap of broken limbs and mangled bodies. At times a grim and uncanny sense of humor seizes a wounded man. Captain A. G. Lawrence, of General Ames' staff, lay on his back; one arm had been amputated, and the other arm as well as his neck had been pierced by rifle-balls. He had told the chaplain to write his father that he could not live, and then, calling another officer to him, whispered, as he held up the stump of his amputated limb: 'Isn't this a devil of a bob-tail flush?'" —"**Historic Incidents from the Fall of Fort Fisher**." Beyer, W. F. and O. F. Keydel. *Deeds of Valor: How America's Heroes Won the Medal of Honor.* 2 volumes. Detroit, Mich.: The Perrien-Keydel Company, 1903

The Mound Battery at Fort Fisher: Federal soldiers confer before the fort's most notable landmark. This artist's rendering appeared in the published histories of several Union regiments who participated in the attack on Fort Fisher.

4. Columbiad Battery: (Sea Face), Third and Fourth Traverses, Facing the Atlantic

A close-up view of a portion of the Columbiad Battery.

The Sea Face batteries and traverses of Fort Fisher were not built on the same massive scale as the fort's land front. These modest structures served to protect men and equipment while engaged with enemy vessels in the Atlantic.

Image by T. H. O'Sullivan

4. Columbiad Battery: *(Detail) Sea Face.*

This view provides a detailed look at the third and fourth traverses of the Columbiad Battery. Two 8-inch columbiads, one at the extreme left and one at the extreme right of the photograph, sit atop their wooden, center-pintle carriages—facing toward the western salient of Fort Fisher.

The gun chamber in the center of the image is the third from the left. Its destroyed weapon lies in pieces on the ground. The tube is on the floor of the chamber, while fragments of the shattered carriage lie scattered behind the chamber and third traverse. A second columbiad tube lies in the sand before the gun chamber on the extreme left of the photograph. A close inspection reveals that this weapon used the "notch and pawl" system for raising and lowering the gun's angle of fire. The thin row of notches is visible on the breech (or back) of the tube.

A wooden banquette is clearly visible, along the embrasure below the parapet, in the third gun chamber (center of image). Note the significant shot damage to the masonry revetment of the fourth traverse. The wall appears to have taken a direct hit during the Federal bombardment.

For a wide-angle shot of the entire Columbiad Battery and the open plain behind it, viewed from a different angle, see the photograph on page 80. •

"After taking Fort Fisher I think our troops could storm hell itself. But our navy rather done the business for them. One of the most powerful fleets the world ever saw concentrated its fire upon the fort raining a perfect storm of iron from six hundred guns on their heads for three days. From the morning of the 13th to 10 o'clock the night of the 15th the awful war never stopped.

"The nights were made hideous by the terrible screams of shell and shot and the light from burning buildings, bursting missiles and glaring signals radiating on the horizon combined to make one of those fearfully sublime scenes which can only be witnessed in a night bombardment."

"Visited Fort Fisher today and took a view of its wonders. After a pleasant little sail of half an hour we landed just below the fort. Before entering the woods, I went over the grounds where our men advanced to the final charge. The many little pits scarcely deep enough to cover a person show with what persevering energy and determination our troops advanced. After getting within 200 yards of the fort volunteers were called for to cut the palisades at the base of the embankment. It is almost needless to say that plenty were found and the work was done effectually.

"The charge was made and the summit of [the] immense [fort] gained. Here [our troops] were screened from the fire of Mound [Battery] and Ft. Buchanan. But on advancing to the left they would be exposed between the traverses. The ditches on the parapet from one traverse to another indicate how they avoided it. How our troops escaped the torpedoes planted in front of the works is wonderful. There being a complete line

across the northern front about 15 feet apart, not one of them exploded and they have been carefully taken up since the capture of the fort.

"The sally port where we entered is near the back of the [Cape Fear] river at N.W. angle of the fort. [H]ere, two brass field pieces in position done our boys up badly. Inside the fort everything susceptible [sic] of injury seems to have received its share of rough handling. Barges, small boats, guns and gun carriages, wagons, carts, wheelbarrows, etc., were scattered in fragments or piled in promiscuous confusion. Huge old Columbiad were bursted and their colossal debris thrown hundreds of feet apart.

"We walked down in the inside and came back on the parapet. The inside comprising an area of at least 150 acres were literally covered with whole and fragments of missiles of every caliber and description from the 6 pound Parrot[t] ball to the large 15 inch shell with its terrible entrails of brimstone, powder, and grape.

"The magazine which exploded on the 16th inst. was in the N.E. corner, and was the principal one in the fort. The great mound of earth which covered it was spread out for hundreds of yds. on all sides. It was an awful misfortune . . . . The traverses on the N and E sides which serve at the same time for a protection to the gunners, and bombproof quarters for the troops, are near 40 ft. high. Many of the guns are disabled, muzzles broken, trunnions knocked off or carriages demolished. The innumerable holes and furroughs [sic] plowed in the parapet bear witness to the storm of iron which our fleet rained upon the place.

"On the N.E. angle there is a splendid Blakely gun that has escaped without a scar: halfway down the eastern side there is a fine Armstrong gun mounted on a richly finished black walnut [mahogany] carriage, and said to have been presented to Jeff Davis by his English admirers: it also escaped unhurt and will now do service in a better cause.

"A quarter of a mile down from Fisher is a Mound Bat'ry mounting two heavy guns and a beacon light. A mile still further down is Fort Buchanan the neatest earthwork I have ever seen mounting 4 heavy pieces, commanding both the channel through New Inlet which is within 100 yds of the fort, and the channel of the Cape Fear River.

"I noticed the blockade runners lying off in the river that have been decoyed in and captured since the fort fell into our hands." —**Lt. Joseph J. Scroggs**, 5th United States Colored Troops, Wright's brigade; letter to his wife, Maggie, January 23, 1865; and diary entry, January 20, 1865.

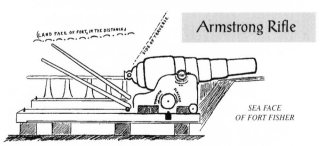

This sketch appeared in Capt. Daniel Eldredge's *The Third New Hampshire and All About It.* Boston: E. B. Stillings and Company, 1893.

Author's Collection

◄ 5. A Defender's View from Shepherd's Battery

This view, slightly east of north, shows the focal point of the Federal attack from a Confederate vantage point. Thousands of Union troops attacked from the background toward the foreground of this image, which was taken from the parapet of the restored gun battery.

"The occupants of the fort felt no uneasiness at the presence of the enemy, owing to their former repulse [in December 1864]. The assault was made, and the men of the fort fought bravely, but in vain. Overpowered by vastly superior numbers, they were at last compelled to yield. Never was a more heroic defence made than that of Fort Fisher. Even after the fort was entered and the citadel captured the men refused to yield, and for hours resisted the fierce assault of three splendid brigades of Federal soldiers, contesting every inch of ground until pushed by the force of irresistible numbers to the very brink of the sea, and then surrendered—their ammunition expended and all hope lost." —**Col. Stephen D. Pool**, 10th North Carolina Regiment

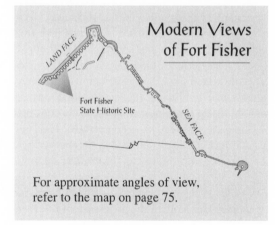

Modern Views of Fort Fisher

Fort Fisher State Historic Site

For approximate angles of view, refer to the map on page 75.

Author's Collection

Author's Collection

THE CAUSEWAY AND THE RIVER ROAD TO WILMINGTON

Author's Collection

▲ 6. A Defender's View of the Access Bridge

This view, facing north from the observation platform in the restored gun battery, shows the modern bridge leading to the River Road sally port. From this distance, the marsh grass on either side of the bridge gives the ground a solid appearance. This ground today, however, is as swampy and forbidding as it was during the battle.

As the attacking Federal soldiers became mired in the slough around the original bridge, they became easy marks for Confederate field artillery thundering up the road, and for riflemen atop the parapet. The mock sandbags revetting the parapet are visible in the extreme foreground. The wooded area in the background was open ground in 1865.

◄ 7. Remnants of the River Road

Today, gnarled live oak trees shade the trace of the old river road to Wilmington. This road entered the fort at the western salient, and gave the garrison access to points north on the peninsula. Unlike the First and Second Brigades of Brig. Gen. Adelbert Ames' division, the majority of the Third Brigade—Col. Louis Bell's—was able to enter the fort by crowding onto this road to cross the bridge. Colonel Bell was mortally wounded in the vicinity of this view.

"The time had come when it was to be decided whether this, perhaps the strongest of the rebel works, on which the wealth of England and the best engineering skill of West Point had been expended, could be taken . . . . Curtis's brigade dashed forward upon the angle near the Cape Fear River . . . . The gate and one mound were gained, though the road to the former lay over a broken bridge, enfiladed and crossed by a murderous fire." —**Lt. M. Van Buren Richardson**, 4th New Hampshire, Bell's brigade

Author's Collection

8. The 32-Pounder Replica at Shepherd's Battery

This authentic replica, positioned on the right of the fort's first gun chamber, sits where Fisher's original rifled and banded 32-pounder seacoast weapon once guarded the western salient. An observation platform, to the left of this gun, now stands in place of the chamber's original 10-inch columbiad.

The gun carriage, of the wooden center-pintle variety, is identical to the original carriages that were mounted in the oceanside Columbiad Battery. Compare this image with T. H. O'Sullivan's photographs on pages 80 and 82.

While the reconstructed carriage is fully operational, the gun itself is a non-functioning original weapon. The tube was pulled from the wreck of the USS *Peterhoff* and preserved in the 1960s. Before being mounted atop the new carriage in Shepherd's Battery, this gun sat for many years behind the restored mounds of the land front. The cannon mounted in front of the Fort Fisher Visitor Center also came from the *Peterhoff*.

9. An Attacker's View of the Western Salient

Beyond the trees in this photo lie the massive walls and traverses of the western salient. Following the line of the original fence, the reconstructed palisades stretch westward toward the Cape Fear.

"*I was through the whole of it from the time the first gun was fired . . . and didn't get hurt except to be knocked down several times by pieces of timber and clods of earth flying in the air.*"
—**Hermon Clarke**, 117th New York, Curtis' brigade

THE WESTERN SALIENT (SHEPHERD'S BATTERY)

Author's Collection

"*The brigade advanced to the charge, obliquing to the right, so as to strike the sally port (that having been deemed the only vulnerable point of the work), and after a desperate struggle the advance of the brigade reached the parapet of the fort and scaled it to the first traverse . . . . The great confusion consequent upon the peculiar character of the assault, and the confined position of the troops on the parapet, render a more particular report of the progress of the brigade after reaching the work impossible.*" —**Col. Rufus Daggett**, commanding the First Brigade, Second Division (Ames'), XXIV Army Corps, after the wounding of Gen. N. Martin Curtis.

Author's Collection

10. In Rear of the Western Salient

This photo, taken from a vantage point just inside the gate, provides a prominent view of the second and third traverses of the fort, with a portion of the first visible at the far left. Also visible are the reconstructed ladder leading to the first gun chamber, and a reconstructed bombproof entrance. Compare this image with O'Sullivan's photograph on page 76.

For the area of the second gun chamber, just above the reconstructed bombproof entrance in this image, see O'Sullivan's photograph on page 78.

Colonel Galusha Pennypacker, commanding the Second Brigade, Second Division, XXIV Army Corps, was grievously wounded at the third traverse.

Major James Reilly's small contingent of Confederates struggled vainly to defend this area—the fort's most vulnerable point. Thousands of Federal attackers swarmed around the end of the fort in this area, and formed a strongly entrenched battle line that stretched across the open plain to the Cape Fear River.

SECOND EXPEDITION

Author's Collection

◄ 11. A Defender's View of the "Bloody Gate"

Immediately to the left of the first gun chamber lies the break in the palisades known as the River Road sally port. Note that the palisades continue westward into the river marsh.

Visible on the right are the fort's first and second traverses. As the attackers swarmed atop the mounds and parapet at right, masses of Union infantry poured through the gate to the left and toward the foreground of this image.

FEDERAL TRIUMPH AND CONFEDERATE SURRENDER

"The regiment was again formed [following Federal mop-up operations on the land front] and advanced by the right flank down the peninsula to Mound Battery, where line of battle was formed, with Sixth Connecticut on our left, and an advance ordered to Battery Buchanan. Within a mile of the battery I ordered forward a skirmish-line of ten men, armed with Spencer rifles, under command of an officer . . . . The battery, with its guns and 1,300 prisoners, was surrendered without resistance." —**Lt. Col. Augustus W. Rollins**, commanding the 7th New Hampshire, Abbott's brigade

Author's Collection

◄ 12. Remnants of Battery Buchanan

Today the hulking, unpreserved remnants of Battery Buchanan are still visible at the tip of Federal Point. The top view at left was taken from across U.S. Highway 421, just south of the present-day ferry landing.

The bottom view looks toward Buchanan from the deck of the Fort Fisher-Southport Ferry, as it departs Federal Point. As the final surrender loomed, Fort Fisher's wounded senior officers—William Lamb and Chase Whiting—were laid at the foot of Buchanan's walls to await the inevitable.

"But what surprise and mortification came upon me when Capt. Powell returned and informed me that Capt. [Robert T.] Chapman and command was gone with few exceptions, the Battery [Buchanan] abandoned and the guns spiked. And on my arrival I found about six hundred officers & men perfectly disorganized. With considerable effort of myself and several officers we succeeded in getting their Battery re-organized but three fourths of them had no arms, & we had no means . . . of defending our position against an organized and victorious enemy. We had a splendid opportunity to Retrieve our defeat and get away, If the armament of the Battery had been serviceable . . . . We would have regained courage, and the enemy would not have captured us, not that night at all events, for the position was very strong, and I always have been confident we were able to hold it. I could have Communicated with Genl. [Louis] Hebert and got means for there was plenty at his disposal at Fort Pender, for to get all the troops across the river. I knew from the activity the enemy displayed in the latter part of the attack on the fort that they would soon advance upon and attack Buchanan and as soon as they would Come within range they would fire upon a defenseless mass. When I saw there was not a possible chance of defending ourselves, I took Maj. Hill and Capt. Van Benthusen [sic] of the Marine Corps and went some distance in advance of the Battery and awaited their Coming. We had a white Flag with us and met the enemies [sic] Skirmish line." —**Maj. James Reilly**, senior commanding officer at Fort Fisher after Lamb and Whiting fell.

Antagonists and Irreconcilable Differences

THE WAR OF WORDS BEGINS...

— BRAXTON BRAGG —

WILMINGTON
January 20, 1865

The unexpected blow which has fallen upon us is almost stunning, but it shall not impair my efforts. Two hours before hearing of the certain fall of the fort I felt as confident as ever man did of successfully defending it. The responsibility is all mine, of course, and I shall bear it as resolutely as possible, but time will make known some matters which may as well be told you now in confidence. No human power could have prevented the enemy from landing, covered as he was by a fleet of ships carrying six hundred heavy guns . . . .

During Saturday [January 14] I was greatly disturbed by the tone and phraseology of General Whiting's dispatches, and by reports of others received from him in town . . . .

At 7:00 p.m. [on January 15] a dispatch from General Whiting reported: 'We still hold the fort but are hard pressed.' Soon after another from his Adjutant said: 'We are still in possession of the fort,' &c. My mind was easy. General Colquitt and his reinforcements were hurried forward. The bombardment continued heavily until about 10:00 p.m., when all became quiet. Unpleasant reports continued to reach me, but nothing worthy of credit until an escaped officer reported to me from across the river by telegraph that the fort was captured. General Colquitt soon returned and reported. He [had] found everything in confusion, hundreds of men without arms, *many of them drunk*, and no one apparently in command . . . . Colquitt barely had time to escape in his small boat . . . .

Blockade running has cured itself. I knew its demoralizing influence, and even before I came here, had urged on the President to remove these officers and troops, replacing them by veterans. I was at work on these evils, gradually correcting them, but meeting with the usual denunciation. Time was not allowed.

The defense of the fort ought to have been successful against *this* attack, but it had to fall eventually—the expedition brought against it was able to reduce it in spite of all I could do. The fleet after dismounting our guns, could have arranged itself above their land forces, and no spot of ground for six miles above Fort Fisher could have been held by our land forces. Owing to the depth of water they could get nearer to us than they could to Fort Fisher, and could sweep everything to the middle of the river.

The same operation, on a much smaller scale was entirely successful against the forts at the mouth of Charleston harbor, except that they were well defended by sober, resolute men, until it was necessary to evacuate, and the harbor was closed by the fall of Fort Wagner. But enough for the present. I am both tired and sad. — **Gen. Braxton Bragg**, letter to his brother Thomas Bragg, Governor of North Carolina, 1855-1859 •

— CHASE WHITING —

HOSPITAL, GOAT ISLAND
March 2, 1865

Col. Blanton Duncan:

My dear Duncan—I am very glad to hear from you on my bed of suffering. I see the papers have put you in possession of something of what has been going on. That I am here and that Wilmington and Fisher are gone is due wholly and solely to the incompetency, the imbecility and the pusillanimity of Braxton Bragg, who was sent to spy upon and supersede me about two weeks before the attack. He could have taken every one of the enemy, but he was afraid.

After the fleet stopped its infernal stream of fire to let the assaulting column come on, we fought them six hours from traverse to traverse and parapet to parapet, 6,000 of them. All that time Bragg was within two and a half miles, with 6,000 of [Gen. R. E.] Lee's best troops, three batteries of artillery and 1,500 reserves. The enemy had no artillery at all. Bragg was held in check by two negro brigades while the rest of the enemy assaulted and, he didn't even fire a musket.

I fell severely wounded, two balls in right leg, about 4 P.M. Lamb, a little later, dangerously shot in the hip. Gallant old Reilly continued the fight hand to hand until 9 P.M., when we were overpowered.

Of all Bragg's mistakes and failures, from Pensacola [Fla.] out, this is the climax. He would not let me have anything to do with Lee's troops. The fight was very desperate and bloody. There was no surrender.

The fire of the fleet is beyond description. No language can describe that terrific bombardment, 143 shots a minute for twenty-four hours. My traverses

*The Youth's Soliloquy,
Or A Tale of Fort Fisher*

How delightful a country
  Where peace reigns
  supreme,
Where if War ever existed
  It seems like a
  dream,
I've a faint recollection
  When but a mere
  youth,
Of hearing tales of a war
  Too startling for
  truth.

I have no doubt some writer
  Of blood curdling lore
Wrote falsely to take the
  charm
  From our quiet shore.
Not so, says a veteran
  Whose leg was of
  wood,
'T would be pleasure to for-
  get,
  I wish that I could.

It was so horribly real
  That terrible fight,
With the cannon a-boom-
  ing
  Long into the night,
Oh! The anguish I suffered,
  The sorrow and pain,
For 'twas in this battle
  My brother was slain.

Oh how well I remember
  With what a sad heart,
We beheld at the station
  Dear mother depart.
"Go, my sons, and fight
  bravely
  Your country to free,
From this yoke of oppres-
  sion,
  This dread slavery."

On the eve of each battle
  My spirits would sink,
Of my mother's parting
  words
  How oft I would think.
I shall always remember
  The look in her eye,
As she uttered those words
  And bade us goodby
  [sic].

The battle of Fort Fisher
  Raged fiercely
  around,
The dead and the dying
  Lay strewn o'er the
  ground,
Our brave leader naught
  heeding
  Pressed frantically

on,
Determined Fort Fisher
    His colors should don.

When this noble victory
    Was nearly attained,
The dread rebel sharpshoot-
    ers
    Their guns at us aimed,
A bullet pierced the breast
    Of brave Colonel Bell,
And thus mortally wounded
    In action he fell.

Tenderly, sorrowfully,
    Bore we to the rear,
Our brave valiant Colonel
    We all loved so dear.
His dying wish was granted
    For plainly in view,
On the fort waved his colors
    The Red, White, and
    Blue.

Young man, many a struggle
    Was thus dearly
    bought,
Ere peace and freedom
    In our land was
    wrought,
Through the courage and
    valor
    Of earth's noblest and
    best,
Through the life blood of he-
    roes
    Thus gone to their rest.

May the roar of the cannon,
    The hiss of the shell,
Never more to the people
    Proclaim their death
    knell.
That the flag of our nation
    Float proudly in air,
Will always be remembered
    As a veteran's prayer.

M. E. W. Colomy
Farmington, N.H.

stood it nobly, but by the direct fire they were enabled to bring upon the land front they succeeded in knocking down my guns there.

I was very kindly treated and with great respect by all of them.

I see that the fall of Fisher has attracted some discussion in the public prints in London. So clever a fellow as Captain Cowper Coles, R[oyal] N[avy], ought not to take Admiral Porter's statement and reports *au pied de lettre*, and he ought to be disabused before building theories on what he accepts as facts and which are simply bosh.

The fight at Fisher was in no sense of the word a test for the monitor *Monadnock* (over which Porter makes such sounding brags), or of any other monitor or iron-clad.

W. H. C. Whiting
Major-General (prisoner of war).

FORT FISHER
January 18, 1865

I am sorry to have to inform you, as a prisoner of war, of the taking of Fort Fisher on the night of the 15th instant, after an assault of unprecedented fury, by both land and sea, lasting from Friday morning until Sunday night . . . . Making every allowance for the extraordinary vigor and force of the enemy's assault, and the terrific effect of the fire of the fleet upon the garrison, and the continual and incessant enfilading of the whole point from Battery Buchanan to the fort, thereby preventing to a great extent the movement of my troops, I think that the result might have been avoided, and Fort Fisher still held, if the commanding general [Braxton Bragg] had have done his duty. I charge him with this loss; with neglect of duty in this, that he refused or neglected to carry out every suggestion made to him in official communications by me for the disposition of the troops . . . . I charge him further with making no effort whatever to create a diversion in favor of the beleaguered garrison during the three days' battle, by attacking the enemy, though that was to be expected, since his delay and false disposition allowed the enemy to secure his rear by works, but works of no strength. I desire that a full

investigation be had of this matter and these charges which I make; they will be fully borne out by the official records. I have only to add that the commanding general, on learning the approach of the enemy, would give me no orders whatever, and persistently refused from the beginning to allow me to have anything to do with the troops from General Lee's army. I consequently repaired to Fort Fisher as the place where my own sense of duty called me.

W. H. C. Whiting
Major-General (prisoner of war).

General R. E. LEE
Commanding Armies Confederate States

HOSPITAL, FORT COLUMBUS, GOVERNOR'S ISLAND
New York Harbor
February 19, 1865

I went to the fort with the conviction that it was to be sacrificed, for the last I heard General Bragg say was to point out a line to fall back on if Fort Fisher fell. In all [Bragg's] career of failure and defeat . . . there has been no such chance missed, and no such stupendous disaster . . . . I demand, in justice to the country, to the army, and to myself, that the course of this officer be investigated . . . . I do not know what he was sent to Wilmington for. I had hoped that I was considered competent. I acquiesced with feelings of great mortification. My proper place was in command of the troops you sent to support the defense; then I should not now be a prisoner, and an effort at least would have been made to save a harbor on which I had expended for two years all the labor and skill I had. I should not have had the mortification of seeing works which our very foes admire, yielding after [three] days' attack, given up and abandoned without even an attempt to save them. •

W. H. C. Whiting
Major-General (prisoner of war).

General R. E. LEE
Commanding Armies Confederate States

A Call for a Fort Fisher Reunion: Veterans Respond - 1875

"It was the greatest artillery battle of the war, if not of history. The truth about it has yet to be printed. No statement that I have seen even approaches accuracy. During the engagement I was acting as volunteer aide to Gen. Whiting and have an imperfect diary of the battle up to 2 o'clock Sunday evening when I was disabled by wounds. While two soldiers were engaged in bearing me to a [bombproof], General Whiting was shot. I saw him fall, and soon afterwards supported by his gallant Adjutant, Major Hill. I never saw him afterwards." —**J. B. Hussey**, veteran of Fort Fisher

"I hope that Col. Lamb will be present at the appointed time, and how glad would be the hearts of all if Gen. Whiting too could be present, but he fills a soldier's grave." —**Veteran** of Fort Fisher. *Whiting Papers, N.C. Division of Archives & History*

Occupation of the Lower Cape Fear

"In case of disaster at [Fort] Fisher, Sugar Loaf and Fort Anderson will be our line."
— **Lt. Col. Archer Anderson**, Assistant Adjutant General, staff of Gen. Braxton Bragg, to Gen. Louis Hébert at Smithville, 6:00 p.m. January 15, 1865

Confederate troops began evacuating the defenses at Old Inlet before dawn on January 16, 1865. Col. John J. Hedrick's contingent of the 40th North Carolina abandoned Fort Holmes on Bald Head, while Col. Charles H. Simonton, a South Carolina officer from Hagood's Brigade, oversaw the evacuation of Oak Island. Colonel John D. Taylor at Fort Caswell and Col. Alexander MacRae at Fort Campbell relinquished their positions and fell back accordingly. The retreating garrison troops spiked their guns, set fire to the gun carriages, and exploded the powder magazines to render this matériel useless when captured by the enemy. Fort Holmes was fired on January 16, followed by the defensive posts at Oak Island the next day. In the panic and confusion that characterized the evacuation, however, Gen. Louis Hébert allowed his men to needlessly destroy equipment and provisions that would be sorely missed later.

The Federals wasted little time in moving in after the Confederate withdrawal from Old Inlet. On January 18 Admiral Porter sent his daring young commando, Lt. Cmdr. William B. Cushing, across the Western Bar to reconnoiter the area. After raising the American flag at Fort Caswell, Cushing traveled to Smithville, where he arrived in a launch at the wharf at Fort Pender. The naval officer was here accosted by the mayor of Smithville, who promptly surrendered the little town to the Union. Cushing quickly called in reinforcements from his ship, the *Monticello*—which lay nearby in the river channel. Detachments of the 2nd South Carolina Cavalry were still in the streets when Cushing came ashore, but he immediately took possession of a building at the end of the wharf and waited for his men to arrive. That night the confident Cushing, with some 200 of his sailors onshore, appointed himself "Military Governor" of Smithville—where a sizable cache of Confederate small arms were confiscated.

Following the capture of Fort Fisher, Admiral Porter dispersed his large fleet of ships, sending a few to aid in operations on the James River in Virginia, and others to convey wounded Federal soldiers and Confederate prisoners northward. Porter deployed his remaining vessels to guard both inlets, and assembled a flotilla of about 30 lighter draft gunboats—steamers that could navigate the Cape Fear River—to participate in the inevitable advance on Wilmington. Porter also employed naval crews to mark the channel and remove Confederate torpedoes from New Inlet, so that his gunboats would have unobstructed access to the harbor. A naval contingent from the gunboats *Wilderness* and *Pequot* also moved ashore to occupy Bald Head on January 19.

Full control of the inlets of the lower Cape Fear gave the Federals a strong starting base for future operations against Wilmington, and the troops settled in to solidify their foothold on the harbor. Many inbound blockade runners, however, were still ignorant of the loss of Fort Fisher. Captain John N. Maffitt, aboard the blockade runner *Owl*, somehow managed to cross the bar undetected on January 16 and pulled in at Smithville. When he finally realized Fisher had been captured, Maffitt was lucky enough to escape into the Atlantic, where he quickly set sail for Bermuda. When John Wilkinson arrived off Cape Fear aboard the *Chameleon*, as well as Capt. M. P. Usina aboard the *Rattlesnake,* the pilots became suspicious of the numerous campfires behind Fort Fisher, and the absence of signal lights atop the Mound Battery. Both Wilkinson and Usina, like Maffitt, beat a hasty retreat.

The wily Admiral Porter, however, was eager to set a trap for the contraband shippers. He ordered the signal lamps on the Mound to be burned in an effort to lure them over the bar—where his gunboats and boarding parties might then pounce upon the unsuspecting blockade runners. William B. Cushing employed a similar tact at Old Inlet, and threatened to hang a few river pilots unless they agreed to burn the signal lights on Oak Island—*"the signal lights by which ships ran in and out,"* he explained.

The scheme worked to perfection. In the small hours of January 20, the blockade runner *Stag* pulled in at Smithville, followed closely thereafter by the swift English steamer *Charlotte*—both inbound from Bermuda with supplies and munitions of war. Cushing, enjoying the game with malicious delight, soon stepped aboard the *Charlotte*. *"When we boarded and informed the captain [Thomas E. Cocker] that his vessel was a prize,"* remembered Cushing, *"he was not the only one astonished. A champagne supper was in progress in honor of successfully running the blockade; at which several English army officers were making merry, confident that they were in the friendly and hospitable bosom of the Southern Confederacy. As we sat down amongst them and ordered the steward to bring another case of champagne, their tongues were loosed and one in accents of English disgust, exclaimed 'Beastly luck!' 'A most unmitigated sell!' responded number two.' Aye! gentlemen,"* chided Cushing, *"and may you never meet better luck on the same errand!"*

The *Blenheim* suffered a similar fate five days later at New Inlet. Captain Maffitt, however, was able to warn other vessels at Bermuda that the harbor below Wilmington was now closed to the outside world, and slowly the word spread that Fort Fisher had been captured.

The Sugar Loaf - Fort Anderson Lines

General Braxton Bragg struggled to cope with the loss of Fort Fisher, and assessed his few and unpromising options for defending Wilmington. Confederate authorities admonished the district commander that Wilmington must be held—at least until all government stores could be removed; and, hopefully, until naval constructor John L. Porter could oversee completion of the ironclad *Wilmington* at Beery's Shipyard on Eagles Island.

Before long, as Gen. William T. Sherman's army was preparing to launch its overland campaign northward through the

Carolinas, Federal prisoners and deserters confirmed for Bragg that the city of Wilmington would be attacked in support of Sherman's campaign. Confederate authorities in Richmond urged Bragg to somehow prevent the Federals from using the port of Wilmington to supply or reinforce Sherman's army in the Carolinas.

Consequently, Bragg ordered the city's inner and outer defenses to be strengthened, and employed both slaves and Confederate soldiers to accomplish the task. Additional torpedoes were placed in the river channel, and derelict vessels were sunk below Eagles Island, opposite the Mt. Tirza batteries, to further obstruct the river. Strong works and river obstacles aside, however, Bragg could muster only about 7,600 men—representing all branches of the service—to defend the city.

General Robert F. Hoke remained in his entrenched position at Sugar Loaf with three brigades of infantry and three batteries of artillery; plus a small scouting detachment from the 2nd South Carolina Cavalry. Hoke's strong position was manned by roughly 4,400 troops. Across the Cape Fear, directly opposite the Sugar Loaf line, Confederate troops west of the river were holed up at Fort Anderson. Upon his return from a recruiting trip to South Carolina, Brig. Gen. Johnson Hagood, of Hoke's Division, was placed in command of the defense of Fort Anderson—the largest interior installation in the Cape Fear defensive network.

Hagood's Brigade had been at Fort Anderson since its unsuccessful attempts to reinforce Fort Fisher during the recent battle. At Anderson Hagood's men were bolstered by the North Carolinians originally stationed at the fort, as well as the Confederate refugees from the lower Cape Fear, now led by Col. John J. Hedrick. Thanks to Hagood's recruitment trip his brigade now numbered about 1,200 men, and when these were added to the other units at his disposal, Hagood counted a force of about 2,300 troops with which to defend the western approaches to Wilmington. General Hébert, who had recently been in overall command of Confederate forces at Old Inlet, was relieved of field command and reassigned to the post of chief engineer for the Department of North Carolina.

The defensive positions on both sides of the river were formidable, but the Confederates lacked sufficient numbers to defend the sprawling approaches west of the river. Moreover, it would soon become evident that Braxton Bragg would not be the only Confederate officer to exercise poor command judgment during the defense of Wilmington.

Federal Reconnaissance of the Sugar Loaf Line

General Alfred H. Terry was eager to resume the campaign to capture Wilmington following the conquest of Fort Fisher, but Admiral Porter urged caution. The naval commander explained that he needed time to resupply his ships, and felt that measures should be taken to safeguard Fort Fisher against a Rebel attempt to reclaim the bastion. Terry agreed, and immediately employed the 15th New York Engineers in rebuilding Fisher's palisades and mending its battered earthworks. The Federals also remounted some of the workable guns along the land front of the fort.

Terry faced General Hoke on Federal Point with roughly 8,500 men, minus two infantry regiments that were stationed across the river to guard Fort Caswell and Smithville. Recent battle casualties, disease, and attrition had dwindled this force from its original strength of approximately 9,600.

On January 18, 1865, three days after the fall of Fort Fisher, General Terry ordered a reconnaissance of Hoke's position at Sugar Loaf. Terry knew that Hoke's line blocked the shortest route to Wilmington, and the Federal commander wanted to find out whether the position could be carried by assault. The reconnaissance fell to the African American troops of Col. John W. Ames' brigade (of Gen. Charles J. Paine's division). After a brief skirmish with Hoke on the 18th, in which the Federals lost two men, Ames moved on Hoke's line in force the following day.

On January 19, Colonel Ames deployed his four regiments—the 4th, 6th, 30th, and 39th United States Colored Troops—in line of battle across the peninsula and advanced on Hoke's well-entrenched line. The black units were supported on the right by 291 men from the 7th New Hampshire and 7th Connecticut regiments, of Bvt. Brig. Gen. Joseph C. Abbott's brigade. The Federals engaged Hoke's three brigades in a lively and heated skirmish around 2:00 p.m., while the Union gunboats *Governor Buckingham* and *Montgomery* shelled the Sugar Loaf line from the Atlantic. On the plain below Myrtle Sound, General Abbott climbed atop the James Burriss house to better survey the Confederate position. From this lofty vantage point, Abbott could see that the Confederate line was formidable—the earthworks stretched unbroken from the Cape Fear River to the Atlantic, and the line was strong in men and artillery.

The Federals soon withdrew from the hot Confederate fire with a loss of one man killed (Capt. N. J. Hotchkiss of the 6th USCT), 29 wounded, and five missing. This tentative movement, however, convinced Terry of the strength of Hoke's position, and he was now content to await reinforcements before attempting a full advance on Wilmington.

Admiral Porter conducted a reconnaissance of his own on January 22, sending the gunboat *Pequot* up the river to engage Fort Anderson. The *Pequot*, under command of D. L. Braine, exchanged a few artillery rounds with Anderson's guns, while Commander Braine assessed the feasibility of an attack from the river. Braine noted that the river channel below Anderson was narrow, and that only a few vessels could stand within range of the fort at one time. This report satisfied Porter that a ground force would be needed to cooperate with a naval bombardment of Fort Anderson. Like General Terry, Porter knew that such a movement would require reinforcements from Gen. Ulysses S. Grant's army in Virginia—or possibly from Sherman's army.

As the month of January 1865 drew to a close, the armies and navies of both sides tangled daily with one another, but no general engagement developed. Small arms fire crackled along the skirmish lines, and Federal gunboats lobbed occasional shells toward Confederate shore positions. The Confederate gunboat *Chickamauga* also steamed downriver to harass the Union positions on the peninsula.

Standoff on Federal Point

A timid Braxton Bragg worried over the menacing presence of the Federal army on the lower Cape Fear. To ensure a secondary line of defense, Bragg ordered a line of breastworks constructed below Wilmington, from Fort Meares (of the river batteries) eastward to Hewlitt's Creek near Masonboro Sound. West of the river another line was constructed north of Town Creek, a position about midway between Wilmington and Fort Anderson—and slightly south of the new line east of the river. These positions would give Bragg's troops a new defensive station to fall back upon if driven from the Sugar Loaf-Fort Anderson lines.

Bragg most feared a Federal siege of Wilmington, and was loath to pull his men back to man the city's defenses in force. And just as Gen. Chase Whiting had feared of Bragg during the battles for Fort Fisher, the district commander kept one eye on a line of retreat northward from Wilmington. He ordered a survey of the Duplin Road, which ran northward from the city across the Northeast Cape Fear River, and made arrangements for necessary repairs to the road in the event it was needed for a Confederate troop evacuation.

Bragg also ordered the government stores and private property of military value in Wilmington to be removed from the city. Most of these provisions were transferred to the capital city of Raleigh; but, predictably, a large amount of cotton was hoarded by speculators who hoped to sell it to the Federals if and when they captured Wilmington. These measures and preparations did not go unnoticed by the townspeople of Wilmington. It seemed to them that Bragg was ready to give up the city without a fight, and sharp criticisms of the Confederate commander soon ran rampant among the masses.

A repressive anxiety and gloom settled over the citizens of Wilmington, as most of them lost their trust in Braxton Bragg. To make matters worse, Bragg sought to keep the population ignorant of military news, especially from the lower Cape Fear. As a result, many became fearful of imminent disaster and fled the town. Economic austerity worsened, as local suppliers ceased to bring their products to town. Prices soared as a result, and the poorer citizens of Wilmington suffered severe hardship.

Many Confederate soldiers also began to desert the ranks. Hoke's command alone, as a result of casualties, attrition, and desertion, dwindled from 6,400 to about 5,500 in the month following the loss of Fort Fisher. The men of Hoke's Division, many of whom had been eager to pitch into the Federals during the attacks on Fort Fisher, were now largely demoralized.

It seemed that soldiers and civilians alike could sense that Union victory was beginning to settle like a pall over the land. Grant was enveloping Robert E. Lee's army in Virginia, Sherman stood poised to strike into the very heart of the South, and Britain and France had failed to recognize the sovereignty of the Confederate government. All the military setbacks, inflation, and other home front shortages were eroding the South's will to fight. Whether the soldiers and civilians at Cape Fear knew it or not, the Confederate nation was indeed in its death throes.

As the Federals prepared for the advance on Wilmington, both armies endured the hardships of life in the field during the harsh North Carolina winter of 1865. The frequent rains and freezing temperatures made for a winter more unbearable than usual, and the elements proved a formidable adversary to even the most hearty of men. To make matters worse, the Confederates were short on food and other provisions. In an effort to help relieve the monotony both sides fraternized with the enemy, trading coffee, tobacco, and newspapers for at least a minimal increase in the quality of life.

Confederate hopes for peace soared briefly as the month of February began—only to be dashed as quickly as they had arisen. When news of talks between President Abraham Lincoln and a high-ranking delegation of Confederate peace advocates reached the Rebels at Cape Fear, many of the men prayed earnestly that a peaceful end to hostilities might finally be at hand.

On the morning of February 3, 1865, the Hampton Roads Conference occurred aboard Lincoln's steamer *River Queen*, near Fortress Monroe, Virginia. Confederate president Jefferson Davis' delegation included his vice president, Alexander Stephens; Senator Robert M. T. Hunter, and Assistant Secretary of War John A. Campbell. The meeting proved a hollow gesture, however, as both sides came to the table unwilling to compromise their positions. Lincoln, as one might suspect, would accept nothing less than total restoration of the Union, while the Southern delegates were prepared to negotiate for nothing less than Confederate independence.

If it was not already apparent, the Hampton Roads Conference confirmed that the Civil War would continue indefinitely—until a clear military victor emerged somewhere on the battlefields of America. And it was becoming increasingly evident to many men of both sides that victory would belong to the Union.

When news of the failed conference reached Cape Fear, many of the Confederate soldiers became all the more deflated. *"Better a thousand times peace had not been mentioned,"* lamented Lt. William Calder of the 1st Battalion North Carolina Heavy Artillery, who was suffering the winter hardships at Fort Anderson. *"The relapse will be too much for the army to bear."*

Dashed hopes for peace notwithstanding, the Federals were eager to break the monotony and suffering of camp life on Federal Point. The bluecoats had their eyes on the city of Wilmington, and felt that victory was within their grasp.

"After taking Fort Fisher we spent several weeks between it and Wilmington in the woods and marshes and on the seashore. It was during the months of January and February; there were frequent and long continued rains; we had no tents or shelter of any kind, and sometimes for a week at a time we would not have a single article of dry clothing on our persons. How the cold east wind would pierce our wet garments and how our teeth would chatter on those ghostly night marches on the seashore." —**Surgeon C. MacFarlane**, Third Brigade, Second Divisioin, XXIV Army Corps

North Carolina Division of Archives and History

An older aerial view of Federal Point, showing the narrow neck where the land front of Fort Fisher spanned the width of the peninsula. The Cape Fear River is visible on the left of the image, with the Atlantic Ocean on the right.

The Advance on Wilmington

"Your movements are intended as co-operative with Sherman through the States of South and North Carolina. The first point to be attained is to secure Wilmington. Goldsboro will then be your objective point, moving from either Wilmington or New Berne, or both, as you deem best."
— **Ulysses S. Grant**, General-in-Chief, United States Army, to Maj. Gen. John M. Schofield, January 31, 1865

If the campaign to capture Fort Fisher had been waged to seal the port of Wilmington and cut off the flow of supplies to Confederate forces in Virginia, the capture of Wilmington itself was directly subordinate to the operations of Gen. William T. Sherman. By late January 1865, Sherman's "army group" of nearly 60,000 veterans stood poised to strike northward from Savannah through the Carolinas. Ulysses S. Grant had accepted Sherman's bold plan to join Federal forces in Virginia by means of a land campaign through the South, and Grant meant to assure that his friend and trusted subordinate would have a safe base for supplies in North Carolina. The hub of this base would be the port of Wilmington, and Grant was eager to have the place in Federal hands by the time Sherman approached the neighborhood of the North Carolina line.

Grant deemed the operation of such importance that he left the Virginia fighting front to travel in person to Cape Fear in late January. Here the general-in-chief sought to ascertain the state of military affairs in the region, and to outline with his officers a plan for capturing Wilmington. Accompanying Grant was Assistant Navy Secretary Gustavus Fox and Maj. Gen. John M. Schofield—a corps commander recently operating with George H. Thomas' army in Tennessee—whom Grant had called to the Eastern Theater. On the night of January 28, Grant, Fox, and Schofield conferred with Adm. David D. Porter and Gen. Alfred Terry aboard the flagship *Malvern* on the Cape Fear River.

The general-in-chief outlined Sherman's forthcoming campaign, and explained that the town of Goldsboro would be the ultimate destination for Sherman's army in North Carolina. The importance of Goldsboro, explained Grant, lay in its position as an inland junction of two coastal railroads: the Wilmington & Weldon, and the Atlantic & North Carolina. The former ran northward through Goldsboro from Wilmington, and the latter westward from Federal-held New Bern. At Goldsboro, Sherman's force could be supplied or reinforced by rail from, as Grant said, *"either Wilmington or New Berne, or both."*

Sherman's grand army would be operating on its own in hostile country, free of any supply base, and would thus be foraging off the land to sustain itself. By the time Sherman reached North Carolina, his army would no doubt be in dire need of provisions and refitting. From Goldsboro, Grant further explained, Sherman would be in a position to move on the capital city of Raleigh, and thence toward the rear of Robert E. Lee's army in Virginia.

The first step in securing a supply base at Goldsboro was the capture of Wilmington. Grant correctly assumed that Bragg's presence at Wilmington meant that the rail lines running out of the city were still operational. Those running inland from New Bern needed extensive repairs, and Grant reasoned that a quick strike on Wilmington might secure its rail facilities for the Union—before the Confederates could destroy them.

Ulysses S. Grant, lieutenant general, United States Army, and 18th President of the United States, 1869-1877

During the three-and-one-half-hour meeting aboard the *Malvern*, Porter and Terry suggested to Grant that the most feasible plan would be to land an infantry force at Smithville, and advance on Wilmington via Fort Anderson west of the Cape Fear River. The inland approaches would give the army plenty of room to maneuver. The navy would augment the ground forces with a flotilla of gunboats on the river, and Terry's troops would pressure the Confederate resistance on the east bank of the Cape Fear.

Grant approved of the plan, and to ensure its success he ordered Schofield to transfer his 21,000-man XXIII Corps, Army of the Ohio, to Cape Fear to augment Terry's force on Federal Point. Grant returned to Virginia on January 30, and on the following day asked Secretary of War Edwin M. Stanton to recreate the Department of North Carolina—with General Schofield as its commander.

John Schofield was one of Sherman's old subordinates, whose command of Westerners had participated in Uncle Billy's Atlanta Campaign of 1864, and in the destruction of Gen. John Bell Hood's Army of Tennessee later that year (as part of an army under Gen. George H. Thomas). Though inexperienced in combined operations, the 33-year-old Schofield was a tried and competent corps commander. He had also recently lobbied against Thomas, his commander in Tennessee, with personal complaints to U. S. Grant in Virginia.

The surprising new appointment understandably hurt General Terry, and it downright angered Admiral Porter. The conquerors of the South's greatest bastion—the commanders who had recently received the official thanks of Congress for the capture of Fort Fisher—were stunned. With the success of Sherman's operations in the Carolinas possibly hanging in the balance, however, Grant meant to insure that a competent officer of his own choosing was on hand to oversee the campaign for Wilmington. Moreover, Schofield was Terry's senior in rank.

After conferring with Stanton, Grant explained to Schofield

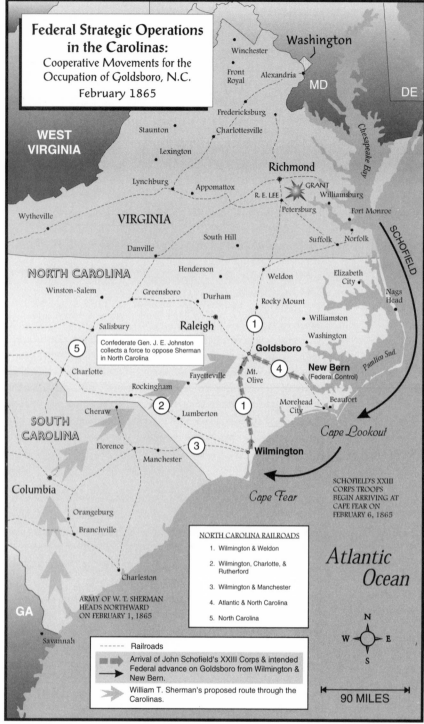

Federal Strategic Operations in the Carolinas:
Cooperative Movements for the Occupation of Goldsboro, N.C.
February 1865

Confederate Gen. J. E. Johnston collects a force to oppose Sherman in North Carolina

New Bern (Federal Control)

SCHOFIELD'S XXIII CORPS TROOPS BEGIN ARRIVING AT CAPE FEAR ON FEBRUARY 6, 1865

NORTH CAROLINA RAILROADS
1. Wilmington & Weldon
2. Wilmington, Charlotte, & Rutherford
3. Wilmington & Manchester
4. Atlantic & North Carolina
5. North Carolina

ARMY OF W. T. SHERMAN HEADS NORTHWARD ON FEBRUARY 1, 1865

Atlantic Ocean

Railroads

Arrival of John Schofield's XXIII Corps & intended Federal advance on Goldsboro from Wilmington & New Bern.

William T. Sherman's proposed route through the Carolinas.

90 MILES

Mark A. Moore

left to you. I would urge, however, if I did not know that you are already fully alive to the importance of it, prompt action."

Preparations

General Schofield set sail from Alexandria, Virginia, with Gen. Jacob D. Cox's Third Division, XXIII Army Corps, on February 4, 1865. The remainder of Schofield's force would ship out to Cape Fear over the next two weeks, as transports became available. A provisional corps was also detached from Sherman's Right Wing (Army of the Tennessee), and sent to New Bern. This force, under Brig. Gen. Thomas F. Meagher, had orders to advance on Goldsboro simultaneously with Schofield after Wilmington was captured.

At Cape Fear, both Porter and Terry readied their commands for the coming campaign. On Federal Point, General Terry's force was soon boosted to about 9,000 men as a Federal detachment, including a small force of cavalry, arrived from Virginia. To operate with advantage on the Cape Fear River, Admiral Porter secured the services of the shallow-draft monitor *Montauk*, which hailed from the Charleston blockading force.

Porter's gunboats shelled Hoke's position at Sugar Loaf, and the *Tacony* and *Shawmut* later engaged Fort Anderson with a few range-finding shots on the afternoon of February 3. Anderson's Whitworth rifles answered with keen accuracy, putting three bolts through the hull of the *Tacony*, and causing her to leak severely. *"We are expecting a fight here evry [sic] day,"* Anderson's Cabe L. Ray explained to his parents on February 5. *"The yankees threw a few bom[b]s at us the other day and wounded six men in our Regiment. There is a good deal of talk here about piece [sic]. I hope the time is not far off when I will be at home with you all."* Rumors of peace notwithstanding, it was clear to Confederate soldiers west of the river that a final confrontation with the enemy loomed close at hand.

The first of Cox's troops arrived off Fort Fisher on February 6, with the remainder—including Schofield and Cox themselves—pulling in the next day. The ocean journey proved a miserable and forgettable experience for Schofield's Westerners, many of whom had never seen an ocean until recently, let

on January 31 that he would ultimately be subject to the orders of William T. Sherman. Until such time as Sherman drew within communicating distance, however, Schofield would receive his orders directly from Grant. Once Wilmington was secure, Schofield was to immediately commence the accumulation of 20 days' rations and forage for Sherman's 60,000 men and 20,000 animals, and to get the materials to the interior base at Goldsboro in the most prudent manner possible. The general-in-chief left the particulars of the Wilmington march to Schofield's discretion. *"The details for carrying out these instructions,"* the commander told Schofield, *"are necessarily*

alone traveled upon one. The transports had weathered a gale off Cape Hatteras where, remembered Isaac C. Clark of the 63rd Indiana, the suffering began in earnest. Clark endured the ride aboard the steamer *Atlantic*, and *"the waves ran high and the vessel rocked like a cradle . . . and about this time three thousand of us got seasick. I thought that I would rather take my chances in battle on land than go through another spell of sea sickness."* Employing a bit of soldierly advice, Clark lay flat on the deck of the vessel to help relieve the queasiness. *"As I lay there pondering in my mind whether to live or die,"* he continued, *"one of the men on a bunk above me emptied the contents of his stomach into my face. [T]his somewhat aroused my fighting qualities, and I came to the conclusion that I would live long enough to thrash that fellow."*

The first of the newcomers—about 4,500 men—went ashore on Federal Point on a cold and rainy February 8, with the remainder following the next day. General Cox came ashore on February 10, and established his headquarters about two miles north of Fort Fisher, behind Terry's position.

From his vantage point at Fort Anderson, Brig. Gen. Johnson Hagood observed the Federal landings at the wharf at Battery Buchanan, and relayed the information to Braxton Bragg's headquarters. The Confederates, however, could do little more than watch, as there were no significant reinforcements to be had. Bragg, in fact, had recently suggested to Governor Zebulon Vance that the enemy was showing signs of advancing inland from Cape Fear and New Bern, where the Federals were busy repairing the railroad toward Goldsboro. Bragg reminded Vance that—just as it would soon be for the Federals—Goldsboro would be their concentration point for consolidating forces if Bragg was driven out of Wilmington. Bragg urged upon Vance that all available state troops be gathered and made ready to render aid at any point necessary.

In a strange development in defense efforts at Wilmington, just as the new Federal troop build-up was under way at Federal Point, Bragg was called to Richmond by President Jefferson Davis—for a conference on reorganizing the general's staff. Since the beginning of February Davis had been urging that Bragg resolve some mundane technicalities of his staff appointments, and though Bragg had suggested that his presence at Wilmington was more important, Davis insisted. Before leaving, Bragg admonished Hoke—who would assume command in Bragg's absence—that the *"utmost vigilance must be observed in the front on both sides of the river to secure timely notice of any [Federal] movement."* The district commander urged that a *"close and unremitting observation be kept up"* to guard against undue surprises from the enemy.

Most importantly, explained Bragg, *"An attempt by the [Federal] gun-boats to pass Fort Anderson must be resisted by all means in our power."* If that event should occur, however, the Confederates must be prepared for swift reactionary movements. To facilitate such movements, a steam ferry was proposed to run from the mouth of Town Creek on the west bank of the river, to the Old State Salt Landing on the east bank. *"By this route,"* Bragg's orders suggested to Hoke, *"reenforcements can be sent to and from both detachments of the command until [Fort Anderson] is passed [by the enemy]. Thus*

any land attack can be met."

On February 9 Bragg informed Robert E. Lee of the recent Federal build-up. The Confederate commander also warned Brig. Gen. Lawrence Baker, who was in command at Goldsboro, that a large enemy force was gathering at Cape Fear, and that any Federal movement toward Goldsboro from New Bern may be a mere demonstration. It was apparent that a major advance on Wilmington was at hand. Thus, with a large new enemy force ashore on Federal Point, Braxton Bragg departed Wilmington for Richmond on February 10. He would be gone for eleven days, and Wilmington would be all but gone when he returned.

The Federal Plan of Operation

On February 10, 1865, General Schofield began preparations for establishing the interior base at Goldsboro. He ordered his chief quartermaster to make requisition for 400,000 rations of forage and 20,000 pairs of shoes to be shipped to Beaufort, N.C., for eventual use by Sherman's army. These items would remain aboard the vessels in the harbor at Beaufort until operations at Cape Fear determined whether they would be deployed to Goldsboro via Beaufort, Wilmington, or both. Schofield also informed Col. William Wright, commanding the Federal railroad construction corps, that he should expend all efforts to get the railroad between New Bern and Goldsboro in running order as soon as possible. *"I shall endeavor to get possession of Wilmington,"* Schofield explained to Wright, *"and the railroad from that place to Goldsborough by the 5th of March, or earlier if possible."* The general added that the line to Goldsboro from Wilmington would likely need repairs once in Federal possession, and in that event a construction force should be ready if needed at Wilmington on short notice.

That same day Schofield, Terry, Cox, and Porter held a council of war aboard the *Malvern*, to discuss the march on Wilmington. Schofield was eager to proceed, and determined to begin the campaign with the relatively small force then on hand—about 13,500 men—before the rest of the XXIII Corps arrived. Before advancing in force on Fort Anderson, however, Schofield decided to test the strength of the Confederate line at Sugar Loaf. The Federal commander reasoned that applying pressure to the Sugar Loaf line might prevent Hoke's Division from reinforcing Fort Anderson. Moreover, if Hoke's position could be softened by Porter's naval gunfire, and Terry could develop some weak point in the line, there was a chance that Hoke's troops might be overrun—thereby opening the door to the shortest route to Wilmington. If Hoke's line broke, explained Schofield, *"the enemy will be pushed back as far as Wilmington with vigor."*

Barring a breakthrough at Sugar Loaf, Terry's force would then take up a strongly entrenched position as close to Hoke's line as practicable. Once Terry's line was firmly established, Cox's division would then be free to begin operations west of the river. Terry's advance on Federal Point was scheduled to commence at eight o'clock the following morning.

That night the Federal navy began its final preparations for the coming campaign. The adventurous commando Will-

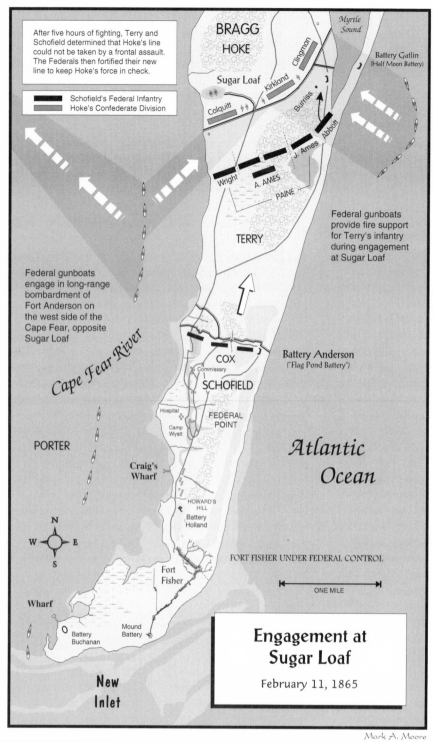

After five hours of fighting, Terry and Schofield determined that Hoke's line could not be taken by a frontal assault. The Federals then fortified their new line to keep Hoke's force in check.

▬ Schofield's Federal Infantry
▬ Hoke's Confederate Division

BRAGG
HOKE
Myrtle Sound
Clingman
Battery Gatlin ("Half Moon Battery")
Sugar Loaf
Kirtland
Colquitt
Burriss
Abbott
J. Ames
Wright
A. AMES
PAINE
TERRY

Federal gunboats provide fire support for Terry's infantry during engagement at Sugar Loaf

Federal gunboats engage in long-range bombardment of Fort Anderson on the west side of the Cape Fear, opposite Sugar Loaf

Cape Fear River

COX
Commissary
SCHOFIELD
Hospital
Camp Wyatt
FEDERAL POINT

Battery Anderson ("Flag Pond Battery")

PORTER

Atlantic Ocean

Craig's Wharf

HOWARD'S HILL
Battery Holland

N
W E
S

FORT FISHER UNDER FEDERAL CONTROL

Fort Fisher

ONE MILE

Wharf

Battery Buchanan
Mound Battery

New Inlet

Engagement at Sugar Loaf

February 11, 1865

Mark A. Moore

The United States Colored Troops "pushed the enemy with great gallantry, driving them from every stump and tree where they sought to make a stand. On this part of the line it was a sort of running fight, in which the colored soldiers seemed to pursue their enemy with relentless animosity, driving them at last to the cover of their main works . . . . [The black soldiers] behaved well, and secured the respect and admiration of all who witnessed their steadiness and courage." — **James C. Fitzpatrick**, war correspondent, *New York Herald*

iam B. Cushing, under orders from Admiral Porter and with a small group of sailors, conducted a reconnaissance up the Cape Fear toward Wilmington. Cushing's scouts, in search of obstructions and torpedoes blocking the river channel, managed to creep to within one mile of Wilmington before retiring. Cushing's adventures would prove much more interesting on the following night.

Engagement at Sugar Loaf— The March Begins

General Terry's force advanced toward Hoke's line at Sugar Loaf early on the morning of a mild, windy February 11, 1865. The right of the Federal reconnaissance force was held by Col. Joseph C. Abbott's brigade. Two brigades of United States Colored Troops from Gen. Charles Paine's Third Division, XXV Army Corps, also joined the advancing battle line. Colonel John W. Ames' brigade—consisting of the 4th, 6th, 30th, and 39th USCT—formed on the left of Abbott's brigade. Colonel Elias Wright's brigade—with the 1st, 5th, 10th, 27th, and 37th USCT—advanced upon the extreme left of the line, along the banks of the Cape Fear River. The gap of swampy ground between the brigades of Ames and Wright was occupied by Gen. Adelbert Ames' division—the captors of Fort Fisher. Having endured the hardships of life on Federal Point, the Federals were eager to leave behind the misery of their winter encampments. A soldier in Abbott's brigade remembered that "*it was a relief to start now for the interior, for the purpose of taking something. We were full of life and big with hope, superinduced perhaps by the fact of the large force of which we were a part.*" The newest arrivals on Federal Point—the ocean-weary troops of General Cox's division—were held in a supporting position behind Terry's main line.

While Terry's force moved toward the enemy, a contingent of Admiral Porter's fleet in the Atlantic opened the engagement, as the gunboats *Keystone State*, *Aries*, *Emma*, *Howquah*, *Montgomery*, and *Vicksburg* began lobbing explosive shells onto Hoke's position. Around 9:00 a.m., Porter's flotilla in the Cape Fear River also joined the action, as the *Lenapee*, *Mackinaw*, and *Unadilla* unleashed their guns on Sugar Loaf. The gunboats, soon joined by the ironclad *Montauk*, also engaged in a long-range bombardment of Fort Anderson across the river.

At 9:30 a.m., a severe skirmish erupted between Hoke's troops and the black soldiers of Paine's division, as Terry's battle line approached the sandy dunes of Sugar Loaf. During the recent attack on Fort Fisher, many of Hoke's troops—confident of success—had been eager to assault General Paine's defensive line across the peninsula. Consequently, when Hoke's feeble advance on Paine's position had been recalled on January 15, many of the Confederates were disappointed. "*I believe our charge would have been successful,*" complained Adjt. Charles G. Elliott of Kirkland's Brigade, "*because the troops in our front were blacks.*" Now those same black troops were attempting a reconnaissance-in-force of the Sugar Loaf line, and at this realization the fighting spirit of Hoke's Confederates reached its zenith for the campaign.

The United States Colored Troops of Paine's division were no strangers to combat. Though most of these units were scarcely a year old, they had seen ample action in Virginia in 1864. Their many encounters with the enemy included operations during the siege of Petersburg, and its famous mine explosion that July. Other engagements included the battles at Baylor's Farm, Chaffin's Farm and New Market Heights, Fort Harrison, and Fair Oaks. Consequently, Paine's black soldiers showed no signs of faltering as they approached Hoke's entrenched position—a fortified line every bit as strong as any they had encountered before Petersburg or Richmond. Indeed, Hoke's Division had already faced many of these same troops in Virginia.

The roar of heavy musketry rolled across the peninsula as the African Americans steadily pushed the Confederate skirmishers back to their sand dune defenses. The bulk of Hoke's three brigades hunkered down along their trenches and low traverses as shells from the Federal fleet continued to burst along the line, and in the interval between the opposing forces. An "*attack in considerable force was made upon us by a negro regiment in command of white officers,*" scoffed Adjt. George M. Rose of the 66th North Carolina. "*The fact of seeing those negro troops in front of us exasperated the men and they fought with great gallantry and easily repulsed the attack made upon us.*"

As Paine's troops pushed ahead, the men of Adelbert Ames' division struggled over difficult terrain. The swampy ground—much like the bog that had impeded their approach to the western salient at Fort Fisher—hindered the advance of General Ames' troops. And much like they had during the Fort Fisher fight, the men endured a withering Confederate fire while blundering through the swamp close to the enemy's outworks.

On the Federal right, Abbott's brigade found clearer ground to cross. General Ames ordered Abbott to advance his command up the beach to pressure the enemy outworks at the head of Myrtle Sound. The 3rd New Hampshire, under Capt. William H. Trickey, took the lead and rapidly advanced a skirmish line toward the Confederate outposts and rifle pits near the James Burriss House. The Federal skirmishers were led by Capt. J. Homer Edgerly, the same officer who had pilfered the Rebel garrison flag from the Mound Battery during the capture of Fort Fisher, 27 days earlier. Spreading their skirmish line to enfilade the enemy outpost from two sides, Edgerly's men were able to quickly overwhelm a small group of defenders. Captain

Members of Company E, 4th United States Colored Troops, pictured here at Fort Lincoln, defenses of Washington. The 4th USCT engaged the Sugar Loaf defenses as part of Col. John W. Ames' brigade. *Library of Congress*

Trickey ordered a charge, and the Federals soon bagged 64 prisoners from the 17th North Carolina of Kirkland's Brigade. Trickey, however, was under orders to avoid a general engagement, and thus no further advance was made. Moreover, the ground was difficult near the head of the sound, and the main Confederate line lay within 60 yards of the outposts, well manned with formidable breastworks. "*Here the undergrowth and swamp,*" reported Trickey, "*rendered it impossible for a farther advance with anything like concert or safety.*" Abbott's contingent came out of the action with a loss of one man killed and five wounded.

By 11:00 a.m., Terry's entire line was within musket range of Hoke's position. On Abbott's left, the troops of Col. John Ames' brigade were equally successful in forcing back the enemy. Lieutenant Col. George Rogers advanced a heavy skirmish line of the 4th U.S. Colored Troops, reported General Paine, and "*drove the enemy very handsomely from his entrenched picket-line into his main works.*" When Company A of the 6th U.S. Colored Troops lost its lieutenant in charge, Sgt. Richard Carter (colored) assumed command and conducted his men "*with great skill and courage until the company was relieved.*"

The loud and spirited contest raged until about 4:00 p.m., and after five hours of sustained action Terry became satisfied that Hoke's position would not be easily carried by assault. Terry, who felt poorly that day and directed operations from an old buggy in rear of the lines, decided to disengage his men. The line was pulled back to a position some 900 yards south of Sugar Loaf and entrenched for the night. John Schofield con-

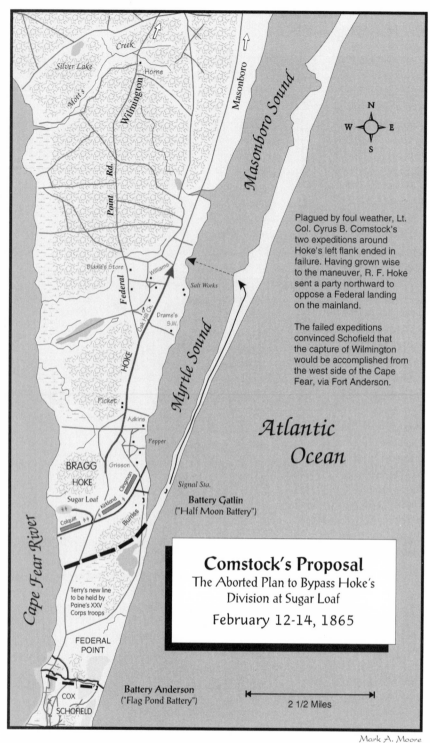

Plagued by foul weather, Lt. Col. Cyrus B. Comstock's two expeditions around Hoke's left flank ended in failure. Having grown wise to the maneuver, R. F. Hoke sent a party northward to oppose a Federal landing on the mainland.

The failed expeditions convinced Schofield that the capture of Wilmington would be accomplished from the west side of the Cape Fear, via Fort Anderson.

Comstock's Proposal
The Aborted Plan to Bypass Hoke's Division at Sugar Loaf
February 12-14, 1865

2 1/2 Miles

Mark A. Moore

that the men had faced Hoke's Division before—offered his own opinion as to the enemy's lack of aggressiveness: "*The Confederate commander evidently had a wholesome fear of encountering the Colored Division [again],*" he boasted. "*He possibly entertained the opinion expressed by one of his disgusted captives of the division on the 15th of June [1864] before Petersburg, who was credited with the remark, 'Damned if Southern gentlemen would fight with [Negroes], and the government ought not expect them to do it.'*"

Paine's black soldiers suffered 16 killed (including two officers) and 76 wounded (seven officers) during their tentative advance on Sugar Loaf. "*For a little while,*" observed Maj. John McMurray of the 6th U.S. Colored Troops, it had been "*a lively and interesting fight.*" As Terry's men returned to their main line that evening, one Southern captive found himself mortified to be the prisoner of one of his own former slaves, who was now a soldier in the United States Army. The captor paraded his former master for all to see, to the great amusement of the black soldier's white comrades.

The white soldiers of Terry's command had observed their colored comrades in the engagement with keen interest. Many of Cox's Westerners had never before seen African American troops, and were eager to judge their behavior in combat. From their vantage point in rear of Terry's position, Cox's men had watched the advance of the Colored Division, and admitted that its ranks maneuvered under fire in parade-like order. "*There is a division of Negro troops here,*" marveled Capt. Thomas Speed of the 12th Kentucky Infantry after the engagement. "*You must not turn up your nose when I say they fight splendidly. I saw them tried yesterday. And our regiment saw it and they all acknowledge that 'we have to give it up' . . . old [Negro] will fight.*"

Perhaps no officer then on Federal Point was more protective of his men, or more confident of their fighting qualities, than Lt. J. J. Scroggs. Lieutenant Scroggs, a company commander in the 5th U.S. Colored Troops, had been impressed with his men from the moment he joined the regiment in January 1864. He sang their praises openly, and on more than one occasion threatened to resign over the low pay and lack of respect his soldiers received. The young lieutenant himself found it hard not to become discouraged. "*There are other things also,*" he had complained bitterly to his wife, "*which will have an influence in making me wish myself out of this particular branch of the*

curred with Terry's assessment, and was satisfied that the new Federal position "*was close enough to the enemy's line to compel him to hold the latter in force.*" A stalemate was acceptable for the moment, reasoned Schofield, as long as Hoke could not easily send reinforcements to Fort Anderson.

Not surprisingly, the Confederates seemed disinclined toward a counterattack on Terry's force. Hoke was comfortable in his strong defensive position and sought to hold it in force, lest he should weaken the line and risk opening the door to Wilmington. Captain Solon Carter, of Paine's staff—who knew *service. That is the apparent unwillingness of the government to do these soldiers justice or even recognize them as soldiers, for neither they [n]or their officers are protected in any way from the inhuman barbarities of the rebels should they unfortunately fall into their hands. The men are not paid as soldiers: receive no bounty: [and] are looked upon with distrust by white soldiers.*" Scroggs noted of his men that the tense racial climate "*tends to greatly discourage them and they even loose [sic] confidence in themselves . . . . It is a burning shame to our government to permit colored soldiers to be butchered by the rebels without one retaliatory act or even a protest yet persist in pushing them to the front.*"

By September 1864, after the engagements at Chaffin's Farm and New Market Heights in Virginia, Scroggs' opinion of his soldiers had been solidified. In these fights the Colored Division of the Army of the James fought splendidly, absorbing several hundred casualties in the process. And the young lieutenant made special note of the valor displayed by members of his own bloodied regiment. "*I seen all this and more,*" he declared, "*and no man dare hereafter say aught in my [presence] against the bravery and soldierly qualities of the colored soldiers.*"

The only beings Lieutenant Scroggs loathed more than detractors of the "Sable Arm" were the wagers of the "*unholy rebellion*" themselves. He scoffed at the week-old Hampton Roads Conference, and predicted what was in store for all Union and Confederate armies in the field—"*some hard fighting yet.*" As for the present campaign, he wrote on the eve of the engagement at Sugar Loaf, "*There will likely be some fighting to do, but I have no fears as to the result. When we start we intend to go to Wilmington.*" If Paine's division of black soldiers had held the rear during the recent battle for Fort Fisher, it would constitute the vanguard of Federal forces east of the Cape Fear River for the remainder of the advance on Wilmington.

Comstock's Proposal—A Sidelight of the Campaign

While Terry's men were engaged at Sugar Loaf, the industrious engineer Cyrus Comstock had conducted a careful reconnaissance up the narrow strip of beach east of Myrtle Sound. Comstock—recently promoted to brevet brigadier general following the capture of Fort Fisher—became convinced that a Federal force could march up the beach under cover of darkness for a distance of about seven miles, and cross the sound via pontoons to gain the rear of Hoke's position. It was an ambitious scheme; but if this surprise landing could induce Hoke to split his force, the Sugar Loaf line might then be overwhelmed by the main body of Terry's command.

Reasoning that the planned attack on Fort Anderson and consequent flank movement around Orton Pond might prove costly and difficult, General Schofield embraced the plan and issued orders for its implementation. General Cox's division, together with a portion of Adelbert Ames' command, was detailed for the expedition, while Admiral Porter was ordered to ferry pontoons and some of the troops to the chosen landing site.

The plan was sound enough, but as the operation got un-

der way, the elements and a dose of bad luck intervened to hamper and finally doom the expedition. Strong winds whipped the Atlantic into a frenzy beginning on February 12, preventing Porter's full participation. Comstock had such confidence in the plan, however, that he suggested the pontoons be hauled on wagons up the beach. A bone chilling wind and rain made for less than optimal conditions for a night march, and the soldiers suffered extreme discomfort. The

Bvt. Brig. Gen. Cyrus Comstock, chief engineer, and trusted member of Grant's inner circle. *USAMHI*

wind was "*blowing a gale from the northeast,*" General Cox recorded in his journal, "*as searing and cold a blast as I have ever felt . . . . The sand, driving with the wind, cuts like a knife, and adds much to the unpleasantness of the march.*" Moreover, the high tides had softened the sandy spit to a point where it was difficult for the wagon teams to advance. The Federals, laden with sufficient rations and ammunition, tried unsuccessfully for two nights to gain the chosen landing zone before daylight. "*It was a perilous adventure,*" recalled an officer in the 12th Kentucky Infantry, "*and as we stood on the naked sand at the waters [sic] edge of the Atlantic shivering in the cold night wind, we thought with dread of the desperate business before us.*"

The second attempt had begun promisingly enough, but conditions quickly deteriorated. "*It was a beautiful night,*" observed a correspondent for the *New York World*, "*just dark enough to march by the enemy, and plant ourselves in his rear. Several things, however, conspired against us . . . . First, the mules gave out, and could not draw up the pontoons, as the sand was exceedingly heavy, even on the edge of the water. Then a storm was brewing which would unfit the men for immediate fighting, while the march told heavily on all. Though veterans from the army of the West and the East, and accustomed to long and severe marches, they all agree that this was the toughest march they ever made. For a while they bore up gallantly under their heavy loads, but human endurance has its limits . . . . In spite of their efforts to keep in line, the sand was too deep for them, and one after another fell down exhausted . . . . Now began the retreat, which had to be more rapid than the advance, in order to be out of sight of the enemy before day-light. With blistered feet and swollen limbs the veteran boys in blue wended their way back to their various rendezvous . . . . The next day many of them were on their way to their old camps, all blackened and begrimed by the sand and the smoke of the fat pine-wood fires kindled on the route. It*

FORT ANDERSON
Continued on page 101

Frank Leslie's Illustrated Newspaper

Union Earthworks and Winter Encampment — Federal Point, North Carolina, 1865

"Hoke is still in our front, remaining quietly behind his intrenchments. Fort Fisher is being put into defensible condition under the direction of Brevet Brigadier-General Comstock. The line toward Wilmington has been made much stronger, and additional guns from among those captured in the fort have been placed upon it . . . . The enemy are busily working on Fort Anderson, and from the number of camp-fires seen I think that they have some force there. I am inclined to think, however, that it is a part of Hoke's division." — **Maj. Gen. Alfred H. Terry**, to Brig. Gen. J. A. Rawlins, Chief of Staff (Gen. Ulysses S. Grant), City Point, Virginia, January 27, 1865

"Our regiment started from here yesterday morning and went towards Wilmington but I don't think they have got there yet. They fought yesterday all day but to day [sic] is Sunday and they haven't fought any. But they will probably commence tomorrow morning. But I am out of the reach of their guns. You need not fear that I will go any farther than I am obliged to for I have seen all I want to in this big show, & all I want now is for my turm [sic] of service to pass away as fast as possible. Father I can imagine how lonesome you and mother must be sitting there all alone, & to think how many there was of us only a short time ago. This war is terrible. Many a home has been made desolate. But thank god I am yet spaired [sic] & I have great hopes of seeing you all next October, & if I do get there I shall be a happy man. But Father seven months is a long time on the battle field." — **Robert Whitcomb**, Quartermaster Sergeant, 169th New York, Bell's (Bachman's) brigade, to Father, Mother, Brother, & Sister, February 12, 1865

will be many days before several of these will be fit for duty again, while some have even died from exhaustion. Two men were picked up on the beach in the morning, having fallen dead in their tracks."

Schofield, ever mindful of Comstock's position as a trusted member of Grant's inner circle, had genuinely liked the plan. The uncooperative weather, however, proved too much to overcome, and the Federal commander finally called a halt to the miserable affair. The withdrawal came none too soon for Admiral Porter, who had scoffed at the idea from the start. Porter had little good to say about Schofield, and in fact wished that he had never been assigned to oversee the Wilmington raid. While the caustic admiral was smart enough not to challenge Schofield—perhaps because he knew the general had Grant's ear—he grumbled freely of *"imbecile maneuverings"* and declared that *"Terry, myself, and the rebels laughed"* at the scheme. As it turned out, Hoke had indeed become wise to the plan, and had sent a small force to oppose the Federal crossing at Masonboro Sound.

With the failed flanking maneuver behind him, Schofield resolved to adhere to the original plan of operation. He was now convinced that the path to Wilmington lay through Fort Anderson, and the forbidding wastelands west of the Cape Fear River. *"This [flanking] plan was a favorite one with General Comstock,"* Schofield explained to Grant on February 15, *"and I believe, had the wind been favorable, would undoubtedly have been successful. At all events we have lost nothing by making the attempt. My second division [XXIII Corps] commenced to arrive yesterday, and I can now commence operations west of the river without further delay."*

Cushing's Narrow Escape

While General Comstock outlined his plan to bypass Hoke's Division at Sugar Loaf, 22-year-old Lt. Cmdr. William B. Cushing once again ascended the Cape Fear River for a secret inspection of the obstructions in the channel off Fort Anderson. On the bright, moonlit night of February 11, Cushing's little scouting party observed that the channel was blocked by heavy pilings, chains, and a line of submerged torpedoes. While investigating the obstructions under the imposing walls of Anderson, Cushing heard the muffled commotion of cheering Confederate voices onshore. The naval officer—who was destined to die a young man in a hospital for the insane—decided to row ashore for a closer look.

Cushing's boat crew quietly rowed to a small cove just north of the riverside walls of the fort, and the young officer crept alone to the massive earthen mounds to eavesdrop on the enemy. On the other side, a brass ensemble—the Eutaw Band of the 25th South Carolina Infantry—accompanied the cheering men as Col. John Douglas Taylor shouted encouragement to the garrison. Cushing listened intently to the patriotic spiel, noting that it *"pictured in glowing terms the victories of the chivalrous South."* The indignant Cushing, who had sunk the CSS *Albemarle* four months earlier, was less than amused. *"The Confederacy was about to tumble,"* he later scoffed, *"but they were blind to the fact. Their armies were all beaten, but one*

Lt. Cmdr. William B. Cushing, Admiral Porter's fearless, albeit reckless, operative on the Cape Fear River. *Harper's Weekly*

Southerner was still the sure conqueror of five Yankees."

"I enjoyed the music," Cushing confided smugly in his journal, *"but at length could not resist the temptation of sending a bullet amongst the crowd as a period to the speech making—at the same time consigning them, with a shout, to a place somewhat warmer than Dixie."*

As Cushing's crew rowed frantically away from the fort, Confederate sentinels hailed the Federal launch. They received no reply, and immediately sounded the alarm of *"Yankee boats in the river."* The defenders rushed to man their guns and parapets. As the riverside batteries of Fort Anderson roared to life, William Cushing stood among his frantic crew and squeezed off a succession of defiant pistol rounds toward the enemy. *"I succeeded in astonishing them,"* he observed, *"but the way the grape shot flew around . . . was far from pleasant."* Amid the thunder and hail of cannon and small arms fire, the little Union naval party managed to pull away unscathed.

His scrape with the enemy notwithstanding, Cushing returned with the information Admiral Porter was seeking. The channel obstructions, Porter was told, were *"too heavy to attempt to break through them with [our] vessels under full headway."* Mindful that his flotilla would need to keep abreast of Federal ground forces as they advanced northward, the admiral determined to destroy the obstructions once Fort Anderson was captured.

The eccentric Cushing lost no time in detailing—with great embellishment—his exploits at Fort Anderson to *New York Herald* correspondent Thomas M. Cook. Cook had stationed himself with Porter's squadron, and he quickly forwarded his own account of Cushing's narrow escape. On February 18, 1865, four days before Wilmington fell to the Union, the *New York Herald* published Cushing's wild story of a patriotic rally in the moonlight at Fort Anderson.

This imposing fort, the area's largest interior defensive

structure, was the last major military obstacle that stood between the invading army and the port of Wilmington. Its strength as a well-designed earthen fortification, however, would be squandered: first, by its very location, and second, by the ubiquitous lack of Confederate troop strength at Cape Fear.

The Push on Fort Anderson

Additional troops from Schofield's XXIII Corps began arriving at Cape Fear on February 14, 1865. The new arrivals from the Second Division were immediately ordered by Schofield to cross over to Smithville, in preparation for the coming advance. Arrangements were also made with Admiral Porter to ferry General Cox's Third Division to Smithville.

The following day, Col. Albert M. Barney led a reconnaissance force from the 142nd New York—on detached service from Ames' division—toward Fort Anderson. In a heavy rainstorm, Colonel Barney slogged northward from Smithville with 300 men to scout the approaches to the massive fort, which lay about nine miles north of the village. Having scarcely covered three miles, Barney's scouts encountered a small detachment of the 2nd South Carolina Cavalry, in the vicinity of the Wescott and Price houses. The small band of Confederate troopers quickly fell back to White Springs Branch, where Barney's men found a more substantial force of enemy cavalry waiting to contest a crossing. Barney, however, was not looking for a fight, and Gen. Johnson Hagood—in command at Fort Anderson—noted that the Federal scouting party "*retired at nightfall without pressing vigorously.*"

Though his small command did not advance beyond White Springs Branch, Colonel Barney did ascertain that the roads were in reasonably good shape, despite the heavy rain. Nevertheless, the topography west of the Cape Fear was anything but favorable for military operations. The area's dim roads led through forbidding swamps, bayous, and dense pine forests, and the Federals would find large-scale deployment difficult. Upon completing his reconnaissance, Barney also reported that many of the local citizens along the road to Wilmington had remained in their homes, despite the presence of the enemy.

The heavy downpour delayed the transfer of Cox's division to Smithville until February 16. Several large steam transports spent the day shuttling Cox's troops, artillery, and wagons to Smithville. When the remainder of the Second Brigade, Second Division pulled in at Smithville, Cox counted a force of about 6,000 men with which to advance on Fort Anderson.

As the troops came ashore, they were heartened by the return of clear and balmy weather. "*The storm had cleared away,*" relished a soldier in the 111th Ohio, "*the warm sunshine had mellowed the air into May-days, and we waded out to the lime-stone reefs, at low tide, and returned loaded with oysters in the shell. We built fires of drift-wood along shore, and soon had those oysters frying and sputtering on the coals.*" More than glad to be free from the recent hell of ocean travel, the men regaled in the opportunity to supplement their meager rations. And unlike the barrens of Federal Point, their new station offered an abundance of fuel for campfires. "*Meanwhile*

the odor of 40 first-class restaurants, penetrating the pine woods, beguiled us into contentment again." It was dark by the time the last of the divisional baggage made it across the river.

On the eve of the push toward Fort Anderson, John M. Schofield explained his situation to Gen. John G. Foster, commander of the Federal Department of the South. Schofield outlined his plans for gaining Wilmington—plans which assured his communication with William T. Sherman, regardless of the success or failure of the Wilmington march: "*I shall . . . move against Fort Anderson to-morrow, and hope to get Wilmington in a few days. If I succeed in this I will then open the railroad toward Goldsborough as far and as rapidly as practicable. Should I fail to get Wilmington, which is possible, if [the area] be re-enforced from Richmond, I would then secure possession of the west bank of the Cape Fear River, and open communication with General Sherman in the direction of Florence [South Carolina]. In any event, I will have supplies for General Sherman's army at the best point attainable.*" With Schofield's men about to launch their Wilmington raid, Sherman's grand horde of hard-bitten veterans stood poised to invest the city of Columbia, South Carolina—the very cradle of secession.

With his men camped just north of Smithville, Jacob D. Cox worried over rations for the troops. A flank march around Orton Pond, he reasoned, would take a large portion of his command inland—away from the river—and the men would need to be supplied before the march commenced. "*Rations are on the way to Smithville,*" Schofield's adjutant assured Cox, "*and the commanding general desires you to supply your command . . . before you start, but to go to Fort Anderson to-morrow as previously ordered.*"

FEBRUARY 17, 1865

At 8:00 a.m. on February 17, having been issued their rations, the four brigades of General Cox's command began the march northward along the west bank of the Cape Fear River. Cox's own Third Division, XXIII Corps, led the advance. The First Brigade, under Col. Oscar W. Sterl, marched in front, followed by the brigades of Col. Thomas J. Henderson and Col. John S. Casement. Rounding out the force was Col. Orlando H. Moore's Second Brigade, of the corps' Second Division, and Battery D of the 1st Ohio Light Artillery, under Lt. Cecil Reed.

As Cox set out to develop the approaches to Fort Anderson, he enjoyed the assistance of a free black man named Lem Brown—as well as several other local blacks—who helped the army probe the forbidding countryside. The advance was slow, and as the invaders slogged their way northward their presence stirred more than a little emotion from the local slave population. Cox also intended to find access to the river's edge somewhere in the vicinity of Reeves Point, in order to establish communication with General Schofield. The department commander was then overseeing the operation from the river itself, aboard the hospital transport *S. R. Spaulding*. General Cox noted that this arrangement allowed Schofield to monitor both halves of his advancing army, *"passing from one bank to the other as circumstances required."*

The inevitable clash with Confederate troopers began about three miles north of Smithville, just as it had with Colonel Barney's command two days earlier. The Rebel horsemen of Col. Thomas J. Lipscomb's 2nd South Carolina Cavalry fell back before the enemy, leaving the woods along the road in flames, and felling trees to slow the Union advance. The troopers made a brief stand at White Springs Branch, but were soon forced back by three companies of skirmishers from the 16th Kentucky Infantry.

Having advanced about five miles, the Federals reached a point where the road forked sharply, in the vicinity of Governor's Creek. The left fork continued north toward Fort Anderson, while the right fork led eastward in the direction of the river. At this intersection Cox divided his force. He ordered the brigades of Sterl, Casement, and Moore to continue northward along the Wilmington Road, while the general personally accompanied Henderson's brigade down the easterly byroad toward the river. Both of the forks bisected Governor's Creek, and Confederate troopers briefly contested these crossings, as the Federals fanned out in two directions. With the infantry thus occupied in a running skirmish with Confederate cavalry, the monitor *Montauk* and several other Union gunboats engaged in a noisy duel with the guns of Fort Anderson.

Around 2:00 p.m., Cox and Henderson reached the riverbank about midway between the fort and Reeves Point. Federal signal operators, moving up from their station at Smithville, soon joined Cox along the river and helped establish communication with Admiral Porter and General Schofield. With the day's seven-mile march at an end, Henderson's men threw up a line of defensive works, and sent out a picket line to establish connection with Cox's main force further to the north.

Having reached the intersection of the Brunswick (or British) Road—which forked sharply to the west along the southern edge of Orton Pond—the commands of Sterl, Casement, and Moore also stopped for the night and entrenched their position in the smoldering wilderness. From Henderson's position along the riverbank, the road bent sharply again to the north in the direction of Fort Anderson, and by nightfall the separated units of Cox's command had established a united skirmish front across both roads, and roughly one and one-half miles south of the fort.

Having engaged the Union gunboats all afternoon with little

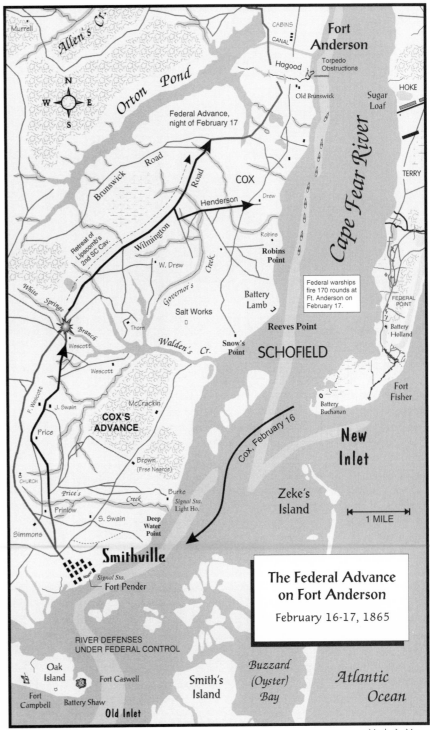

Mark A. Moore

effect, Gen. Johnson Hagood called a halt to Confederate return fire from Fort Anderson. His 12-pounder Whitworth rifle had exhausted its ammunition, and after dark the gun was pulled back to the lower Town Creek bridge to await the arrival of extra ammunition from Wilmington. In preparation for the coming scrap with the enemy's ground forces, Hagood placed his division under the immediate command of Col. Charles Simonton, and prepared to mass his small mounted force to the west of the fort near the head of Orton Pond.

With the enemy thus arrayed in his front, Hagood knew

FORT ANDERSON
Continued on page 105

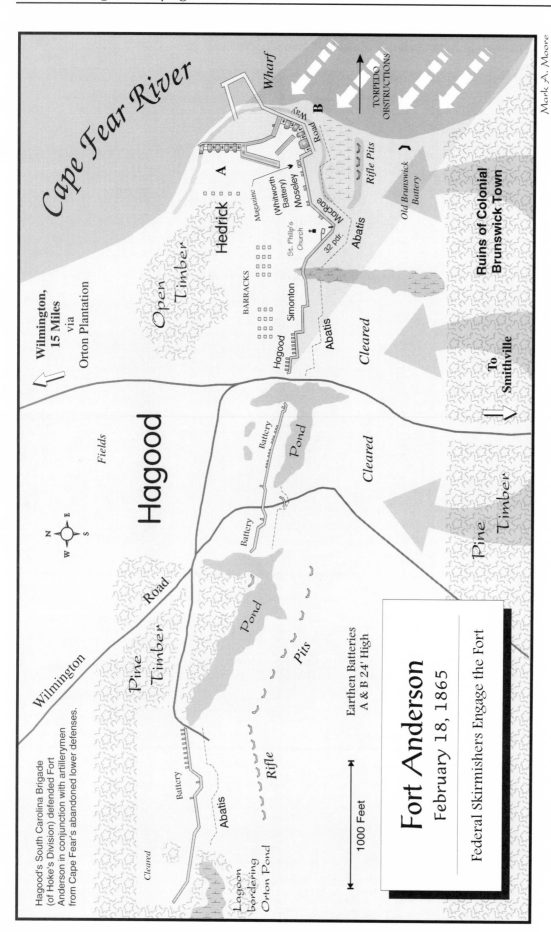

Mark A. Moore

Extract from the Journal of Commander John C. Beaumont, U. S. Navy, commanding the USS *Mackinaw*

U.S.S. MACKINAW, *Cape Fear River, North Carolina, February 18, 1865.*

Saturday. — Wind northward and westward.. 2; weather b.c. At 8:40 [a.m.] got underway and steamed up to within 1½ miles of Fort Anderson. Moored ship ahead and astern and opened fire on the fort with XI-inch pivot [gun]; fired 80 rounds. At 9:30 admiral [Porter] signaled to us, 7531. At 12:30 [p.m.] got underway and steamed up toward the fort and came to anchor. Opened fire on the fort with our IX-inch guns, doing splendid execution, the fort occasionally replying. One shot struck us below the water line on port side, inflicting no damage. At 6 ceased firing, excepting once every five minutes. Sent boat on picket.

that it was up to his force alone to block the enemy advance west of the river. He remembered with grim irony Braxton Bragg's warning—issued to Robert F. Hoke nine days earlier upon Bragg's departure for Richmond—that the enemy's attempt to pass Fort Anderson "*must be resisted by all means in our power.*" Hagood also recalled Bragg's ambitious plan for a steam ferry operation between the mouth of Town Creek and the old State Salt Landing on the east bank of the river, by which communications and reinforcements could be sent "*to and from both detachments of [our] command . . . Thus any land attack can be met.*" Hagood pondered this grand design now, with the enemy at his very doorstep, and he lamented that the scheme had never progressed beyond Bragg's proposal. "*It is well to remark in passing,*" he later noted in his memoirs, "*that this route of communication was never established.*"

As night fell on Federal Point, Robert F. Hoke—in command of the district in Bragg's absence—received distressing news from another theater of operation. A wire arrived bearing ill tidings from the Adjutant and Inspector General's office at Charlotte, North Carolina: "*The enemy have Columbia.*" Sherman's minions had captured the capital of South Carolina, and by the next morning much of the city would lie smoldering under smoke and ashes. And in the wake of this loss, as the retreating Southerners rushed to evacuate their stores, and Confederate authorities made plans to hold the city of Charlotte, requests would soon arrive at Cape Fear for men, supplies, and transportation. These rare commodities, however, were scarcely capable of sustaining the present operation at Cape Fear—let alone other theaters.

Hoke also informed Robert E. Lee in Virginia that he was in possession of a captured order from John Schofield, addressed to Gen. Alfred Terry. The plan of the enemy was clear: "*Their design is against Goldsborough,*" Hoke wired to Lee, "*and perhaps Greensborough in connection with Sherman.*"

That evening Schofield came ashore to confer with Gen. Jacob D. Cox, who suggested that Reeves Point be considered as a convenient landing zone for supplies and ammunition. If a fight developed at Fort Anderson, he reasoned, this landing site would be much closer to his troops than Smithville. Schofield reminded his division commander that Porter's gunboats would have difficulty silencing the guns at Anderson, due to the narrow channel and obstructions in the river. The bombardment would be long-range at best, he warned. After his discussion with Cox, Schofield drafted special orders allowing his division commander to determine how best to advance on the fort the following morning: "*He will attack or not, as may seem advisable after reconnaissance.*" If an attack proved impractical, Cox was to entrench and hold the line before Anderson. With his remaining force, the division commander would then "*move around the swamp which covers the enemy's right, and attack him in rear or force him to abandon his position [and] if practicable, cut off his retreat.*"

Across the way on Federal Point, opposite Hoke's position, Gen. Alfred Terry was under orders to be ready to follow up any success that might be gained on Cox's side of the river. Schofield had warned Terry to "*have a division ready to cross the river to-night, if it becomes necessary, which I expect it will.*" Having arranged for the disposition of his ground forces, Schofield also posted a request to Admiral Porter on the river: "*General Cox will move on Fort Anderson early in the morning. Please give it a good shelling.*"

FEBRUARY 18, 1865

Cox advanced his command at 7:00 a.m. on the clear morning of February 18. Henderson's brigade advanced on the right flank—along the riverbank—while Casement's brigade held the center, and Sterl's the left of the Federal battle line. Colonel Moore's brigade followed up in support behind the Third Division. Cox soon encountered a line of the enemy's infantry videttes about one-half mile below Fort Anderson, and the day's skirmishing began in earnest as the Federals pushed Hagood's picket force back toward the fort.

In Casement's front the 65th Indiana, under Lt. Col. John W. Hammond, pushed the Rebel videttes from their forward line of rifle pits, and advanced to within musket range of the massive fort. As the Confederates fell back along the riverbank, Henderson's advance regiment—the 63rd Indiana—rushed forward to follow up the retreat, and briefly held a position within 300 yards of the main batteries at Fort Anderson. It was a dangerous spot, where shells from the river squadron rained along the water's edge. The gunboats were firing from long range, and many of their rounds fell short of the fort and exploded among the Union infantry units onshore. Several members of the 63rd Indiana suffered injuries from this friendly fire, including James Harpin, who had one of his legs blown off by a shell from the squadron. The 63rd was forced to abandon its position.

As Fort Anderson came into view, Cox noted that the ground in front of the structure was cleared of brush for a distance of about 300 yards, where the Confederates had assured themselves an open killing field. A thick row of abatis guarded the earthen walls, and several light artillery stations dotted the works to the west. These light batteries roared to life as the main Union line advanced to within about 600 yards of the fort, and dared to push its skirmishers even closer. From this position the invaders beheld the fort's masterful construction.

Fort Anderson was enormous, built much like its larger and stronger sister on Federal Point. Two massive seacoast batteries formed an elbow-shaped bastion along the water's edge, with a sand curtain that stretched westward to a point beyond the ruins of colonial St. Philip's Church. The main river batteries of this eastern segment of the fort—which terminated on the road to Wilmington—were built on a scale similar to Fort Fisher's land front. The embrasures here mounted nine heavy seacoast weapons—32-pounder rifles and smoothbore cannons. A Whitworth battery was also in position between the seacoast batteries and the church.

It was while stationed here in 1861 that Col. William Lamb had begun to study the science of heavy siege fortifications, and it was here that he first put his acquired skills to the test. Indeed, many of the engineers and other officers who had helped

FORT ANDERSON
Continued on page 107

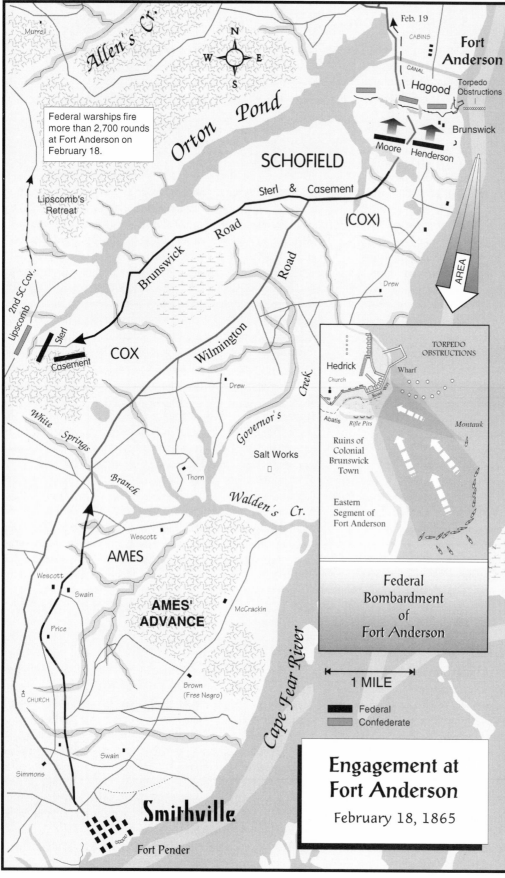

Federal warships fire more than 2,700 rounds at Fort Anderson on February 18.

Lipscomb's Retreat

Federal
Confederate

TORPEDO OBSTRUCTIONS

Hedrick
Wharf
Abatis Rifle Pits
Montauk
Ruins of Colonial Brunswick Town
Eastern Segment of Fort Anderson

Federal
Bombardment
of
Fort Anderson

1 MILE

Engagement at Fort Anderson
February 18, 1865

Mark A. Moore

"It was expected an assault would be made on the eighteenth of February, but owing to the difficulties the troops encountered in the way of dense woods, cane breaks, briars, and almost impassable swamps, they could not get in position before darkness set it.

"In the meanwhile the fleet were ordered to move up closer to the fort and open fire. The monitor [*Montauk*] took the lead and dropped anchor near the obstructions. The *Maratanza* soon followed and was joined by the *Pequot*, *Lenapee*, *Sassacus*, *Pontoosuc*, *Huron*, and *Chippewa*. A rapid fire was then commenced, and the enemy replied with great vigor; but when the vessels had obtained the exact range, they were compelled to retire to the bomb proofs where they were imprisoned the greater part of the day.

"[T]he fleet were having everything their own way when a rebel battery situated on a hill [Sugar Loaf] in front of General Terry's entrenchments opened fire; but was soon silenced by our heavier guns. As the assault could not take place that day, the vessels dropped down the river as darkness set in." —**Acting Ensign John Grattan**, clerk and aide to Admiral David D. Porter

"The country was nearly level and had a sickly growth of pines which had been boxed for turpentine until [they were] nearly dead. There were very few houses and no men to be seen. Often we had to wade marshes, which made it very unpleasant marching.

"Just before sundown we came to a halt at the edge of a swamp. On the other side the Johnnies had calculated to give us [a] fight, but a column of the 23rd Corps had moved around to come up on the flank. We had no communication with them and didn't know how matters stood . . . We went through all right: no Johnnies to oppose us, but we could see they had but just gone." —**Hermon Clarke**, 117th New York, Curtis' (Daggett's) brigade, Ames' division

Lamb in the construction of Fort Fisher had also worked on Fort Anderson.

The remaining two segments of the fort—little more than infantry breastworks—stretched westward toward Orton Pond, nestled brilliantly among the deep bayous and swamps of the area, and employing every advantage of the terrain. The last segment terminated on a lagoon bordering Orton Pond itself, a thin body of water that stretched south and westward for a distance of about six miles. With the seacoast batteries near the river, and the light artillery stations of the western segments guarding the difficult ground, a frontal assault on Fort Anderson would be costly, indeed.

Unlike Fort Fisher, however, Anderson was not situated on a narrow sand peninsula. Though the fort was roughly one mile in length, it was an *interior* defensive structure, and there was plenty of unguarded real estate to its west, beyond Orton Pond. Worse, the sprawling western approaches to Wilmington offered the invading Federals easy access to a good road that led around the head of Orton Pond. By this route Cox's force could, in effect, bypass Fort Anderson altogether. The Confederates did not have enough infantry to contest the approaches west of the pond—or anywhere else, for that matter—and absolutely nothing could stop the Federals from gaining access to the rear of Fort Anderson. Thus it was never a question whether Anderson would fall, but rather how soon it would come to grief. Moreover, Fort Fisher had ultimately fallen to an infantry force that was smaller than the 6,000-man army Cox now fielded west of the river—an army with more room to maneuver than Adelbert Ames' troops had been afforded on Federal Point. Combined with the riverine cooperation of Porter's squadron the Union thrust was unstoppable.

Anderson was a work best employed to engage enemy shipping in the river. Even now her bolts and shells, though few in number, were finding their marks among Porter's gunboats. But should these vessels ever gain a position far enough north—*behind* the fort—Anderson's nine heavy weapons would not be able to change their trajectories upriver for even a few parting salvos. "*This fort was a weak affair,*" scoffed a Confederate defender with little confidence in the structure, "*mounting only small, short-range guns.*" Thus, despite its formidable proportions, Fort Anderson was rendered useless as an obstacle to the capture of Wilmington from the moment Cox's infantry stepped ashore at the village of Smithville. From the outset, the Federals had planned for a flank march around the head of Orton Pond.

Inside Fort Anderson, Johnson Hagood's motley garrison weathered the storm of naval and infantry fire as best it could. Hagood, who seemed to have an uncanny knack for counting the incoming rounds, would tally the naval bombardment at 2,723 rounds by day's end, "*all of which struck the work or exploded within it.*" The general also asserted that his own guns fired 53 rounds of shot and shell—20 of which were expended on the ironclad *Montauk* alone. The fort's smoothbore weapons, admitted Hagood, were fired "*more in defiance than in the hope of injuring the enemy.*"

As his infantry engaged the skirmishers of Moore's and Henderson's brigades, the Confederate brigade commander sent word for Colonel Lipscomb to mass his small band of cavalry to defend the crossing at the swamp below Orton Pond. It was all that could be done under the circumstances, and it would merely delay the inevitable. These troopers, lamented Hagood, were little more than mounted infantry, brandishing an assortment of cavalry carbines and Enfield rifles.

By 2:00 p.m. on February 18, the brigades of Moore and Henderson were sufficiently arrayed in a semicircular line of works below Fort Anderson. The skirmishing was sharp, and

"I beg leave to bring to the favorable notice of the Department Lieutenant-Commander E. E. Stone, commanding the monitor Montauk.

"The officer has manifested proper zeal and spirit and been ready at all times to go into action.

"When ordered to attack Fort Anderson he did it handsomely; laid within 1,000 yards with the fire of the fort concentrated on him for over thirty-six hours and convinced the rebels that no work could be held where a monitor or monitors were brought against it." —**Adm. David D. Porter**, North Atlantic Blockading Squadron

Bombardment of Fort Anderson — Note the Ironclad *Montauk* on the right.

Harper's Weekly

Brig. Gen. Johnson Hagood, commanding a brigade in Hoke's Division, lacked enough defenders to hold Fort Anderson

Anderson's field-pieces—under Capt. Abner Moseley and Capt. William Badham—raked the woods south of the fort with a noisy fire.

With Moore and Henderson keeping the fort's gunners occupied, Cox rode westward with Sterl's and Casement's brigades on the Brunswick Road, toward the head of Orton Pond. Following the infantry was Lt. Cecil Reed's Ohio battery. After a march of about six miles, reported Cox, *"the head of the pond was reached and was found to be fed by a creek bordered by a deep marsh about 100 yards in width and crossed only by a narrow causeway."* A thin screen of Confederate troopers had fallen back before the Federal advance, and as the sun sank low in the pines, the main detachment of the 2nd South Carolina Cavalry stood in position and waiting as Cox's men approached the swamp. The troopers had erected several detached trenches on the rising ground above the crossing, forming a débouché—or opening in the works through which the causeway passed.

A lively skirmish erupted in the deepening gloam as Cox's troops attempted to force a crossing. Oscar Sterl's brigade had the lead, and its advance elements fanned out to find crossings through the marsh on both sides of the road. At the same time Lt. H. L. Reed, with a detachment of 15 men from the 104th Ohio, attempted a passage along the road itself. The men *"encountered the enemy's outpost strongly posted on the other side of an almost impassable swamp,"* reported Sterl. The Federals rushed headlong through the marsh and up the causeway *"man by man,"* asserted the brigade commander, *"under cover of the brush, to charge their rifle-pits."* After a brief struggle, the Ohioans gained a lodgment on the other side, with the loss of only one man killed and four wounded. Lieutenant Reed was among the latter, having been felled by wounds in both legs. With the Union attack up the causeway and upon both of their flanks, Lipscomb's troopers were forced to retire northward up the road above Orton Pond. Though Hagood had dispatched an artillery crew to aid the cavalry's defense of the western approaches, the gun did not arrive in time. The affair at the swamp had ended almost as quickly as it had begun, and this small action effectively brought a halt to the day's fighting.

"I have reached the point where the road turns Orton Pond," Cox notified Schofield. The enemy *"are slowly retiring by the road I purpose taking, which shows that we could gain nothing by taking [a] longer route. I have sent for [General] Ames to meet me here by the shortest and most practical route."* Having secured the crossing at Orton Pond, Cox's men went to work strengthening the causeway so that the artillery could pass without difficulty. The work was finished by 9:00 p.m., and both Sterl's and Casement's brigades encamped for the night on the opposite side—on the ground recently defended by the enemy. A party of Federal skirmishers had followed Lipscomb's retreat for about a mile northward following the clash at the swamp, but had developed no further force of the enemy. The western approaches to Wilmington, they found, were wide open. Jacob Cox could sense that a clear route to Wilmington was near at hand: *"We have one more difficult creek to cross [Town Creek] a short distance ahead."*

Several miles to the east, on Moore's and Henderson's front, the Union troops strengthened their positions south of Fort Anderson and settled in for the night. The naval bombardment slackened at nightfall, and Henderson reported that his picket line *"was as far [north] as it could be with safety."* The men fully expected a renewal of the action in the morning, and a member of the 111th Ohio noted that the regiment's skirmishers *"settled down for a night's watching."*

General Terry, as expected, had received Schofield's order late on February 17 to transfer a force to Smithville to reinforce Cox's command. The troops of Adelbert Ames' division—the captors of Fort Fisher—began their journey across the harbor before midnight, the last of whom pulled in at Smithville during the small hours of February 18. By noon, Ames' division was marching north, finding the road clogged with Cox's supply wagons. The guide Cox had sent to lead Ames to the head of Orton Pond succeeded in overtaking the column before it turned west on a longer interior route, and by early evening Ames' XXIV Corps troops had joined Cox on the upper side of the pond.

With the addition of Ames' division, Cox now had a sizable force threatening Fort Anderson, most of which was arrayed along the open approaches west of the fort. If the flanking force could bag the garrison at Fort Anderson and cross Town Creek, Wilmington would be theirs for the taking.

Despite the pummeling from naval gunfire, Confederate casualties inside Fort Anderson were surprisingly few—especially considering the number of projectiles that Hagood claimed had fallen upon the fort. Colonel John J. Hedrick narrowly missed serious injury, however, when a shell fragment clipped his sword from his belt. The night bombardment assured Anderson's defenders a peaceless existence. *"I don't think I ever passed such a night,"* remembered Lt. William Calder.

The structure itself was rather the worse for wear, but the garrison was holding up well. *"The damage to the earthwork was considerable,"* asserted Johnson Hagood. *"The wooden revetment had gradually given way; the epaulement was much torn up; in fact, in one place breached nearly to the level of the gun platform; and the traverses [were] knocked out of shape."* During the night the garrison—between the intermittent shells from Porter's gunboats—did what it could to repair the damages. As an added precaution, noted Hagood, "*an obstruction was made to the sally port of the fort on the river side in [case] of an infantry assault up the beach.*"

Around 10:00 p.m. Confederate sentries onshore observed in the moonlight a low, sleek craft approaching the line of obstructions in the river. It was a dangerous area, as recent Federal inspections had verified. The submerged torpedoes off Fort Anderson, explained Confederate ordnance officer E. S. Martin, "*were attached to floats of just sufficient buoyancy to keep them near the surface of the water and were provided with sensitive fuses, so that if touched they would explode.*" Fearing that the *Montauk* was attempting to force a passage to the north of the fort, however, Anderson's electricians—without waiting for the vessel to strike them—attempted to detonate the mines in an effort to sink the Federal ironclad. A few thunderous explosions notwithstanding, the little craft passed unscathed through the dangerous obstacles—and eventually ran aground just above Sugar Loaf on the eastern bank of the river. The warship had made no attempt to engage the fort—for, in fact, it was not a warship at all. The indefatigable William B. Cushing was once again employing a "cute" tactic assured to keep the campaign interesting.

Ever eager for a share in the action, Cushing felt that it had become "*necessary for the Navy to act.*" Knowing that Admiral Porter had used a sham gunboat during the Vicksburg Campaign of 1863, Lieutenant Cushing had several days earlier broached a similar subject with his commander. "*I therefore proposed,*" he explained, "*the construction of a mock monitor such as was used by [Porter] upon the Mississippi River.*" The adventurous Porter, of course, loved the idea—and Cushing hastily assembled a team of carpenters to construct the life-sized decoy. With the skillful and creative combination of a few barrels and "*an old flat boat and some canvas,*" the phony shipwrights fashioned a respectable counterfeit ironclad near Smithville. And when the work was finished they gazed upon their creation with pride. "*The* Mahopac," boasted Ens. John Gratton, "*was faithfully reproduced—smokestack and turret perfect imitations of the original.*" The proud Cushing agreed. "*When complete,*" he admired, "*it was not possible to distinguish it and the real [ironclad] nearby, at two hundred yards distance*"—especially at night.

Cushing calculated that the flood tide off Anderson ran at five knots—plenty of "*motive power*" for his engineless decoy. One end of the craft was purposely made heavier than the other so it would float straight with the tide. Shortly before 10:00 p.m. on February 18, Cushing towed the hulk to within 200 yards of the obstructions and cast her adrift, her black-painted canvas skin easily discernible in the brilliant moonlight. "*Up the river with the flood tide she went,*" relished Cushing, "*and in spite of everything passed successfully.*" The sailors waited expectantly for the fulfillment of the grand illusion. But it was not to be. Despite the apparent detonation of a few of the Confederate torpedoes, Ensign Grattan observed with dismay that "*nothing interrupted the silent course of the floating fraud.*" The obstructions remained intact—but Cushing, predictably, later claimed that the scheme had caused Hagood to evacuate Fort Anderson.

By 10:00 p.m., with Cushing's bogus warship ascending the Cape Fear River, and written dispatches arriving from Colonel Lipscomb and other scouts confirming the overwhelming presence of the Federal army, Johnson Hagood realized the game was up. He simply did not possess a force strong enough to contend with the enemy, which he feared was "*of the three arms [of the service].*" Shortly after 1:00 a.m. on February 19,

Maj. Gen. John M. Schofield commanded the raid on Wilmington, to the great displeasure of Admiral Porter. *USAMHI*

Hagood telegraphed Gen. Robert F. Hoke at Sugar Loaf—almost directly opposite Fort Anderson across the river—to explain his desperate situation:

"*The enemy are on my right and rear, in point of time three (3) hours' march. . . . It will take me three-quarters of an hour to hear of their advance, which reduces the time to two and a quarter hours. It is impossible for me to strengthen the small force opposed to them. You know its strength.*" Describing the Union position before the fort itself, Hagood continued: "*I have a very much larger force than my own 600 yards in my front, in full view by daylight, and with the fleet to cooperate. Therefore, when the force on my right rear moves, I must abandon this position, or sacrifice my command.*"

Hoke was fully aware that if Anderson was abandoned, he must also relinquish his own position at Sugar Loaf. Confederate forces east of the river would have to fall back on a line with Hagood's troops, in order to keep Porter's gunboats from gaining a position in their rear. Once the heavier earthworks and fortifications were abandoned, however, Confederate troops would have nothing of similar strength to fall back upon. Any defensive advantage enjoyed to this point—especially east of the river—would be lost, and it would be difficult to stand and fight at some point between their current position and Wilmington. The month-long defensive stand was over.

With hesitation, Hoke replied to Hagood's telegram: "*Dispatch received . . . . What do you think best?*" He knew the answer, of course, and for Hagood there was no question. At 2:00 a.m. Anderson's commander replied: "*I think this place ought to be evacuated and the movement commenced in half an hour.*" Hagood immediately made preparations to evacuate, and shortly before 3:00 a.m. Hoke's reluctant order arrived for the Confederates at Anderson to retire to the north. Hoke instructed Hagood to fall back roughly eight miles to the north side of Town Creek—the last natural obstacle of any substance west of the Cape Fear River, and a position that would constitute the infantry's final line of defense.

FEBRUARY 19, 1865

Having evacuated his field artillery and supply wagons, Johnson Hagood pulled the garrison out of Fort Anderson just before dawn on February 19, 1865. As the infantry trudged north on the Wilmington Road toward the Lower Bridge at Town Creek, Lipscomb's troopers took a more westerly route toward the Upper Bridge, several miles inland.

By first light the Federal troops of Moore's and Henderson's brigades were ready to storm the fort. The noise and commotion of the Confederate evacuation had been evident during the night, and the men were eager to push forward. The Federals dashed upon the fort without opposition, and managed to bag about 50 prisoners from Hagood's picket line, which had remained in position to help screen the Confederate retreat. Anderson's garrison flag was captured, and Colonel Moore planted the colors of the 26th Kentucky infantry on the battered ramparts of the fort.

Maj. Gen. Jacob D. Cox, *Oberlin College Archives*
commander of Schofield's forces west of the Cape Fear

Admiral Porter's gun crews were slow to realize that the Confederates had withdrawn, and their shells began to rain upon the fort—amid their frantic comrades. After sufficient chastisement from the ground forces, however, Porter's men got the message, and the *Montauk* hoisted a white flag to halt the bombardment.

Eager to size up the new prize, the admiral himself soon arrived aboard a small launch and stepped ashore with an entourage of officers. Porter glanced around hurriedly. A member of the 111th Ohio overheard the admiral as he surveyed the shot-torn remains of Fort Anderson: "*Be careful now men,*" Porter cautioned excitedly, "*be careful, this whole thing is probably mined; and wires stretched all around us, which would fire at the least touch and blow us all up.*" By this time, however, most of the structure had been thoroughly inspected by the men, "*above ground and below.*"

General Terry soon reported that Hoke had abandoned his stronghold at Sugar Loaf, and at 10:45 a.m. Jacob Cox—who was about halfway to Fort Anderson with Ames' division—was formally notified of the Confederate evacuation. Having left Sterl's and Casement's brigades at the head of Orton Pond to await the supply wagons, Cox sent Ames' division on to Anderson, and met with Moore's and Henderson's brigades north of the fort. The Federal pursuit of Hagood was delayed somewhat by damage to the bridge at Orton canal, the thin strip of water that connected the pond with the Cape Fear River. Hagood's men had cut the sluices at the pond, and set the bridge on fire as they fell back toward Town Creek.

Schofield was elated. "*I have the honor to report the success of our operations against Fort Anderson and the adjacent works on both sides of Cape Fear River,*" he informed Ulysses S. Grant in Virginia. The department commander was now confident that the end was near: "*Fort Anderson and its collateral works are very strong and rendered almost inaccessible by swamps. A small force could have held them until their supplies were exhausted. My information is that the rebels [now] have a line of defense behind Town Creek, where they propose to make a stand. If so, it can probably be only a short one.*"

Admiral Porter sent his own good tidings in a letter to Assistant Navy Secretary Gustavus Fox in Washington. The admiral could not resist an interservice jab at John Schofield, and proclaimed the navy's pivotal role in the capture of Fort Anderson. "*We are now within five miles of Wilmington,*" he explained, "*and would have been there long ago had Grant sent Terry men and kept Schofield away. We took Fort Anderson this morning, that is the gunboats whipped the Rebels clear out by sunset and they left afterwards taking their artillery with them, leaving us nothing but twelve large guns which they could not carry off. The Army claims the victory! of course, owing to their strategic movements when they were twelve miles away.*" Porter was referring to Cox's flank movement, without reference to Moore's and Henderson's commands.

That same day, Grant informed Schofield of William T. Sherman's progress through South Carolina, and reminded the general of the importance of securing an interior base at the rail hub of Goldsboro. Sherman had reached and passed Columbia, Grant explained, which would force the evacuation of Charleston. With regard to Wilmington, Grant asserted, "*You will either capture the place or hold a considerable portion of the enemy from Sherman's front . . . . Should you find an advance on Wilmington impracticable, keep up such a threatening attitude that the enemy will be compelled to retain there all the force he now has, and push on the [Federal] column from New Berne [toward Goldsboro].*" With or without Wilmington, Grant was determined to establish a base for Sherman at Goldsboro. The road to Wilmington, however, was now more open than it had ever been. The enemy had just relinquished its last major defensive strongholds, with nothing but creeks, rice fields, and a few thin lines of fieldworks left from which to defend the approaches to the city.

Thus began what Maj. John W. Moore, of the 3rd Battalion North Carolina Light Artillery, termed the "*perilous retreat to Wilmington*"—a movement occasioned less by force than by weight of numbers. Four days now lay between the Federal army and the port of Wilmington—and the vital rail lines linking the town with the rest of North Carolina. •

Pictured below is a portion of Gen. Jacob D. Cox's journal entry for February 19, 1865.

The bulk of this document was published in *War of the Rebellion: A Compilation of the Official Records of the Union and Confederate Armies*, Series I, Volume 47, Part 1, Reports.

Further from Fort Anderson — A Decoy Monitor.
In addition to the dispatch from Admiral Porter in relation to the surrender or evacuation of Fort Anderson, information was received at the same time, at the Navy Department, that Lieutenant Wm. B. Cushing constructed a mock monitor, so closely resembling one of those vessels that no difference could be detected at the distance of one hundred yards.

NORTH CAROLINA.

Capture of Fort Anderson on Sunday.

COMBINED NAVAL & LAND ATTACK.

Engagement With the Fort on Friday and Saturday.

CUTE TRICK OF LIEUT. CUSHING.

The Work Evacuated Saturday Night.

WILMINGTON A DOOMED CITY.

&c.,   &c.,   &c.

Above: Headline from the *New York World*, February 24, 1865

. . . As there was a strong flood-tide she moved up the river, and passed the fort as if under low steam . . . and the rebels, no doubt, thinking their communications would be cut off . . . hastily escaped by the only avenue open. — *New York World*

Sunday, Feby. 19th The trains of supplies which were to have come up last night did not report till 10 o'clock this morning. We resume our march up the west bank of Orton pond to turn the enemy's position at Ft. Anderson. March about ½ way when we meet Capt. Lord of Gen. Schofield's staff who informs us that the fort is evacuated—the enemy having left it in the night after hearing of our movement around the pond. Gen. Ames proceeds to the fort with his division, whilst I go on up the river road with my command, the two brigades left in front of the fort joining me. I put Henderson in advance & press the enemy rapidly to old Town creek where we find him in a strong line of works, the bridge being destroyed & the creek

Oberlin College Archives, Oberlin, Ohio

FORT ANDERSON

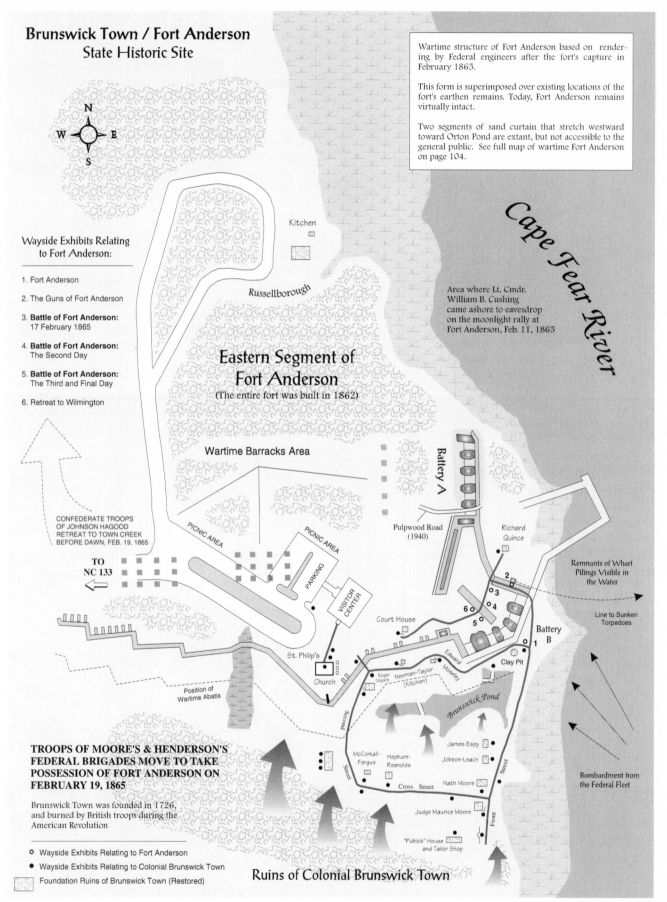

Brunswick Town / Fort Anderson
State Historic Site

Wartime structure of Fort Anderson based on rendering by Federal engineers after the fort's capture in February 1865.

This form is superimposed over existing locations of the fort's earthen remains. Today, Fort Anderson remains virtually intact.

Two segments of sand curtain that stretch westward toward Orton Pond are extant, but not accessible to the general public. See full map of wartime Fort Anderson on page 104.

Wayside Exhibits Relating to Fort Anderson:

1. Fort Anderson

2. The Guns of Fort Anderson

3. **Battle of Fort Anderson:** 17 February 1865

4. **Battle of Fort Anderson:** The Second Day

5. **Battle of Fort Anderson:** The Third and Final Day

6. Retreat to Wilmington

Kitchen

Russellborough

Area where Lt. Cmdr. William B. Cushing came ashore to eavesdrop on the moonlight rally at Fort Anderson, Feb. 11, 1865

Eastern Segment of Fort Anderson
(The entire fort was built in 1862)

Wartime Barracks Area

CONFEDERATE TROOPS OF JOHNSON HAGOOD RETREAT TO TOWN CREEK BEFORE DAWN, FEB. 19, 1865

PICNIC AREA

PICNIC AREA

PARKING

VISITOR CENTER

TO NC 133

Battery A

Pulpwood Road (1940)

Richard Quince

Remnants of Wharf Pilings Visible in the Water

Line to Sunken Torpedoes

Court House

Battery B

Clay Pit

St. Philip's Church

Roger Moore

Newman-Taylor (Kitchen)

Edward Moseley

Second Street

Position of Wartime Abatis

Brunswick Pond

TROOPS OF MOORE'S & HENDERSON'S FEDERAL BRIGADES MOVE TO TAKE POSSESSION OF FORT ANDERSON ON FEBRUARY 19, 1865

Brunswick Town was founded in 1726, and burned by British troops during the American Revolution

McCorkall-Fergus

Hepburn-Reanolds

Cross Street

James Espy

Jobson-Leach

Nath Moore

Front Street

Bombardment from the Federal Fleet

Judge Maurice Moore

"Publick" House and Tailor Shop

Ruins of Colonial Brunswick Town

○ Wayside Exhibits Relating to Fort Anderson

● Wayside Exhibits Relating to Colonial Brunswick Town

▣ Foundation Ruins of Brunswick Town (Restored)

Cape Fear River

Mark A. Moore

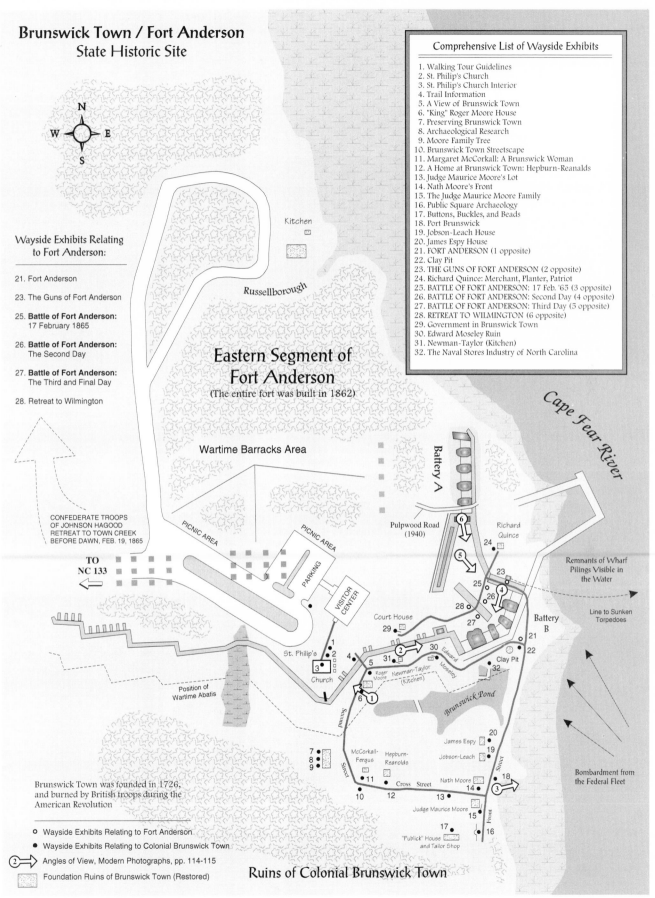

Brunswick Town / Fort Anderson
State Historic Site

N W E S

Comprehensive List of Wayside Exhibits

1. Walking Tour Guidelines
2. St. Philip's Church
3. St. Philip's Church Interior
4. Trail Information
5. A View of Brunswick Town
6. "King" Roger Moore House
7. Preserving Brunswick Town
8. Archaeological Research
9. Moore Family Tree
10. Brunswick Town Streetscape
11. Margaret McCorkall: A Brunswick Woman
12. A Home at Brunswick Town: Hepburn-Reanalds
13. Judge Maurice Moore's Lot
14. Nath Moore's Front
15. The Judge Maurice Moore Family
16. Public Square Archaeology
17. Buttons, Buckles, and Beads
18. Port Brunswick
19. Jobson-Leach House
20. James Espy House
21. FORT ANDERSON (1 opposite)
22. Clay Pit
23. THE GUNS OF FORT ANDERSON (2 opposite)
24. Richard Quince: Merchant, Planter, Patriot
25. BATTLE OF FORT ANDERSON: 17 Feb. '65 (3 opposite)
26. BATTLE OF FORT ANDERSON: Second Day (4 opposite)
27. BATTLE OF FORT ANDERSON: Third Day (5 opposite)
28. RETREAT TO WILMINGTON (6 opposite)
29. Government in Brunswick Town
30. Edward Moseley Ruin
31. Newman-Taylor (Kitchen)
32. The Naval Stores Industry of North Carolina

Wayside Exhibits Relating to Fort Anderson:

21. Fort Anderson

23. The Guns of Fort Anderson

25. **Battle of Fort Anderson:** 17 February 1865

26. **Battle of Fort Anderson:** The Second Day

27. **Battle of Fort Anderson:** The Third and Final Day

28. Retreat to Wilmington

Kitchen

Russellborough

Eastern Segment of Fort Anderson
(The entire fort was built in 1862)

Wartime Barracks Area

CONFEDERATE TROOPS OF JOHNSON HAGOOD RETREAT TO TOWN CREEK BEFORE DAWN, FEB. 19, 1865

TO NC 133

PICNIC AREA

PICNIC AREA

PARKING

VISITOR CENTER

Position of Wartime Abatis

Battery A

Pulpwood Road (1940)

Richard Quince

Cape Fear River

Remnants of Wharf Pilings Visible in the Water

Line to Sunken Torpedoes

Battery B

Court House

St. Philip's Church

Roger Moore

Newman-Taylor (Kitchen)

Edward Moseley

Clay Pit

Brunswick Pond

Bombardment from the Federal Fleet

McCorkall-Fergus

Hepburn-Reanolds

James Espy

Jobson-Leach

Cross Street

Nath Moore

Judge Maurice Moore

"Publick" House and Tailor Shop

Brunswick Town was founded in 1726, and burned by British troops during the American Revolution

○ Wayside Exhibits Relating to Fort Anderson
● Wayside Exhibits Relating to Colonial Brunswick Town
②➤ Angles of View, Modern Photographs, pp. 114-115
Foundation Ruins of Brunswick Town (Restored)

Ruins of Colonial Brunswick Town

Mark A. Moore

FORT ANDERSON

Author's Collection

1. Ruins of St. Philip's Church

Considering the number of explosive shells that Brig. Gen. Johnson Hagood claimed had landed on Fort Anderson, it is a wonder that the ghost of this colonial church is still standing. The structure was already nearly a century old in 1865, yet its thick and aged walls of brick remain solid even today. Note the fort's low sand curtain in front.

"The Fort is manned with heavy guns and built very strong so that it would withstand a heavy cannonade from the water . . . . The Fort is built on the site of the ancient town of Brunswick which was burned by Lord Cornwallis during the Revolutionary War . . . . The brick of which [St. Philip's Church] is built was brought from Europe . . . and it was the first church built in North Carolina. The walls are three feet thick and twenty feet high." —**Maj. Thomas C. Thoburn**, 50th Ohio Infantry, visitor to the captured fort as additional troops of Gen. John M. Schofield's XXIII Corps advaced on Wilmington in late February 1865. **For more commentary from Major Thoburn, see the section titled "Fort Anderson" on page 9.**

THE RIVERSIDE BATTERIES

Modern Views of Fort Anderson

Fort Anderson State Historic Site

For Approximate Angles of View, Refer to the map on page 113.

2. View Along the Sand Curtain Toward the Main Bastion—Battery B. ▶

This view looks eastward along the sand curtain between St. Philip's Church and the riverside batteries. In the distance "Battery B" (so named by Federal engineers) protrudes sharply to the south.

It was along this stretch of earthworks that Fort Anderson's Whitworth battery was positioned. These guns, and other fieldpieces stationed further west, engaged—from left to right across the photograph—the advancing Union infantry units of Col. Orlando H. Moore and Col. Thomas J. Henderson.

Following the Union occupation of the fort, Colonel Moore planted the regimental colors of the 26th Kentucky Infantry on the ramparts of Battery B.

Author's Collection

◀ 3. View of Sugar Loaf from Below Fort Anderson

This view faces eastward across the Cape Fear River toward Federal Point. The sandy bluff on the opposite bank, visible just to the right of the pine tree, is Sugar Loaf Hill.

This hill anchored the right flank of Gen Robert F. Hoke's Division, Army of Northern Virginia, as it spanned the width of the peninsula and blocked the eastern approaches to Wilmington. It was a formidable line of breastworks.

As they held the Federal forces of Gen. Alfred H. Terry in check, Hoke's men at Sugar Loaf had a good vantage point from which to view the bombardment of Fort Anderson. As the Federal gunboats shelled the fort, Hoke's artillery harrassed Admiral Porter's naval squadron by firing on the ships from the eastern bank.

When Hagood was forced to evacuate Fort Anderson, however, Hoke's position was rendered untenable, and his strong defensive line was relinquished without a fight. The loss of Anderson signaled the beginning of the end for the Confederate defense of Wilmington.

Author's Collection

Author's Collection

4. The Interior of Battery B

This shot affords a close-up view of the interior of the riverside gun emplacements, taken from atop the northern end of Battery B. The walls and traverses of Fort Anderson, as evidenced in this photograph, are in a remarkable state of preservation. Unlike Fort Fisher, most of the entire structure of Fort Anderson is still in existence today. The western segments of sand curtain, however, are inaccessible to the general public.

Thanks to its relative completeness, Fort Anderson offers a better example of nineteenth-century military engineering—seacoast fortification construction in particular—than the extant remains of the area's signature bastion on Federal Point.

The grove of trees to the south, beyond the gun chambers, surrounds the southern ruins of colonial Brunswick Town. In addition to the fort's reconstructed flagpole on the parade ground, this view shows two of the site's wayside exhibits relating to Fort Anderson.

5. Tour Trail Stairs Descending From Battery B

The riverside batteries of Fort Anderson bore the brunt of the Union naval bombardment, with explosive shells bursting furiously along the battlements pictured at right.

"The sight was most magnificent. The vessels moved into line splendidly . . . . The screaming of the shells, loud roar of the artillery, flashing of the guns, bursting of the shells, was well worth remembering." —**Stephen C. Bartlett**, surgeon aboard the Federal gunboat *Lenapee*

INTERIOR OF FORT ANDERSON - RIVERSIDE BATTERIES

Author's Collection

"Since then it has again relapsed into its former state, and the bastions and traverses and parapets of the whilom Fort Anderson are now clad in the same exuberant robe of green with which generous nature in that clime covers every neglected spot. And so the old and the new ruin stand side by side, in mute attestation to the utter emptiness of all human ambition, while the Atlantic breeze sings gently amid the sighing pines, and the vines cling more closely to the old church wall, and the lizard basks himself where the sunlight falls upon a forgotten grave." —**Alfred Moore Waddell**, author of *Some Memories of My Life*, on the ruins of Brunswick Town and Fort Anderson

Author's Collection

6. Interior View From Battery A

This wider shot of the interior, taken from the southern end of Battery A, reveals the large sand berm in rear of Battery B (visible on the right of the photograph).

"Our pickets and theirs, and light artillery were firing off and on all day, and with the shelling of the fort from the gunboats, made the place anything but comfortable." —**Lt. Zaccheus Ellis**, 1st Battalion North Carolina Heavy Artillery

Brunswick Town/Fort Anderson State Historic Site

Location:	**Hours:**
St. Philips Rd. in Winnabow, east of NC Hwy. 133	*April - October* Mon.-Sat.: 9:00 a.m.-5:00 p.m. Sun.: 1:00 p.m.-4:00 p.m.
Address: 8884 St. Philips Rd. SE Winnabow, NC 28479 **Phone:** (910) 371-6613 **Fax:** (910) 383-3806	*November - March* Tues.-Sat.: 9:00 a.m.-5:00 p.m. Sun.: 1:00 p.m.-4:00 p.m. Closed Monday *Closed most major holidays.*

FORT ANDERSON

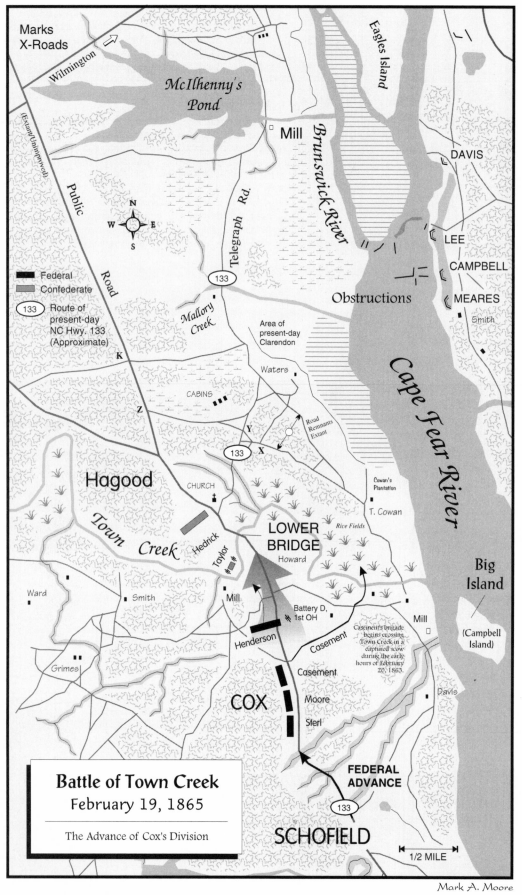

Marks X-Roads

Wilmington

(Extant/Unimproved)

McIlhenny's Pond

Mill

Brunswick River

Eagles Island

DAVIS

LEE

CAMPBELL

MEARES

Smith

Public

Road

N W E S

133

Telegraph Rd.

Obstructions

Mallory Creek

Federal
Confederate
133 Route of present-day NC Hwy. 133 (Approximate)

Area of present-day Clarendon

K

Waters

CABINS

Cape Fear River

Z

Road Remnants Extant

Y

133 X

Cowan's Plantation

CHURCH

T. Cowan

Hagood

Town Creek

Hedrick

Taylor

LOWER BRIDGE

Howard

Rice Fields

Big Island

(Campbell Island)

Ward

Smith

Mill

Battery D, 1st OH

Casement's brigade begins crossing Town Creek in a captured scow during the early hours of February 20, 1865.

Mill

Davis

Henderson

Casement

Grimes

Casement

COX

Moore

Sterl

Battle of Town Creek
February 19, 1865

The Advance of Cox's Division

FEDERAL ADVANCE

133

SCHOFIELD

1/2 MILE

Mark A. Moore

"Town Creek enters the Cape Fear River from the west about six miles above Fort Anderson and on the same side of the river. The upper and lower bridges had each been previously slightly fortified by General Hagood, his only communication with Wilmington being over them, and were held by bridge guards, the upper by eighty infantry and the lower bridge by twenty.

"The creek was forty or fifty yards wide . . . . The two bridges were the only regular crossings, and at both the high ground was on the southern bank . . . . Between the lower bridge and the mouth were bluffs on the north side with open rice fields and the usual dams to the highland opposite.

"At 9:45 a.m., on the 19th, the main column crossed the lower bridge and went inro position—Taylor's regiment, of Hedrick's brigade, in the entrenchments with three (3) pieces of artillery—[the] Eleventh South Carolina (under Captain Westcoat [sic]). picketing Cowan's—and the balance of Hagood's brigade, under Simonton and Hedrick's own regiment, the Fortieth North Carolina, with the balance of the artillery in reserve near the church.

"A patrol of twenty men were kept toward the front down the Fort Anderson road. Lipscomb arrived soon after at the upper bridge and reported himself in position with the balance of the cavalry, eighty infantry and one howitzer.

"The enemy appeared in front of lower bridge, at 3:30 p.m., and slight skirmishing ensued." —**Brig. Gen. Johnson Hagood**

The points marked X, Y, Z, and K match positions on Hagood's map, page 125.

The Final Obstacles: Town Creek, Forks Road, and the Evacuation of Wilmington

FEBRUARY 19, 1865

By 9:45 a.m. on February 19, Johnson Hagood's infantry and artillery—in full retreat from Fort Anderson—were crossing the lower bridge at Town Creek. "*My column is crossing Town Creek bridge and going into position,*" Hagood informed Adjt. Archer Anderson. "*Enemy charged my picket-line in heavy skirmish force just as we were about withdrawing it a little before day, and had to retire fighting. The bridges of the canal were, however, burned and the sluices of Orton Pond cut. No pursuit beyond.*" Observing the light breastworks above Town Creek, however, Hagood had little confidence in the new position. "*Ask General Hoke for orders for me,*" he requested of Anderson. "*This place needs much work if it is to be held for any length of time.*"

As General Hagood arrayed his forces along the creek, Col. John J. Hedrick took command at the lower bridge. Hedrick placed Col. John D. Taylor's North Carolinians west of the Wilmington Road, together with three pieces of artillery—including a Whitworth rifle under Capt. Abner Moseley. Taylor's entrenchments occupied a low bluff commanding the direct approach to the bridge. Along the rice fields of Cowan's Plantation, the 11th South Carolina was deployed to picket a two-mile stretch on the north bank of Town Creek, between the road and the Cape Fear River.

Approximately one-half mile in rear of Hedrick's line, the remainder of Hagood's Brigade—under Col. Charles Simonton—took position near a small white church. Seven miles to the northwest, Col. Thomas J. Lipscomb's cavalry—with a howitzer crew under Lt. John Jones—reached the upper bridge at Town Creek. The troopers scouted its southern approaches to guard against a flank attack by the enemy.

The clapboard church near Simonton's line stood where the road to Wilmington split into two forks. The eastern fork, a byroad known as the Telegraph Road, took a more direct route to Wilmington via McIlhenny's Pond. The western fork, known as the Public Road and the main artery leading into town, bypassed McIlhenny's Pond on a route further inland. Hagood's small force would have to guard both of these major avenues into the city of Wilmington.

As Hagood dug in at Town Creek, Hoke's Division pulled back to a position about three miles south of Wilmington, on the east bank of the Cape Fear River. Hoke placed his men in the previously constructed breastworks that stretched eastward from Battery Meares (on the river) to Hewlitt's Creek near Masonboro Sound. Most of this force went into position near the river batteries and across Forks Road, about two miles inland from the river. During the day Hoke received word from Department of North Carolina commander Braxton Bragg that he was finally on his way back from Virginia to Wilmington, via Raleigh and then Goldsboro. Around midday, Bragg had received word of the retired positions of both Hoke and Hagood,

and he sent Hoke a dismal wire from Raleigh: "*I shall leave for Goldsborough to-night. Advise me there if anything important. We can look for no assistance.*" At this point Robert E. Lee wanted Bragg to collect enough state forces to help Gen. Lawrence Baker resist an enemy movement inland from New Bern. Baker had reported that the Federals were demonstrating heavily, and feared an all out advance was at hand. When Bragg informed the Confederate general-in-chief that there were no state troops to be had, a concerned Lee queried General Hoke directly: "*Can you ascertain Schofield's strength?*"

With the Confederates apparently in full retreat toward Wilmington, the Federals advanced their forces on three fronts: Jacob. D. Cox's command followed Hagood and moved into position below Town Creek. Alfred H. Terry's contingent followed up Hoke's retreat on the Federal Point Road, and Admiral Porter's squadron of gunboats brought up the center by ascending the Cape Fear River abreast of the ground forces. General John M. Schofield once again established his headquarters with Porter's flotilla, aboard the hospital steamer *S. R. Spaulding.*

The pursuit of Hoke's Division began around midday on February 19. General Terry split his force into two columns in an effort to develop any further positions of the enemy, and to guard against a flank attack while on the march. General Charles J. Paine's division of African American soldiers—accompanied by Terry himself—led the way northward on the Federal Point Road, while Gen. Joseph C. Abbott's brigade veered eastward on the Military Road near Myrtle Sound. The 5th U.S. Colored Troops, of Col. Elias Wright's brigade, advanced a strong skirmish force in front of Paine's column. General Adelbert Ames' division, which had experienced no fighting in the past week but had done more than its share of maneuvering, was once again shuttled across the Cape Fear River from

Author's Collection

This battered monument, placed by the New Hanover Historical Commission in 1920, marks the vicinity of Hoke's Sugar Loaf line.

TOWN CREEK AND FORKS ROAD

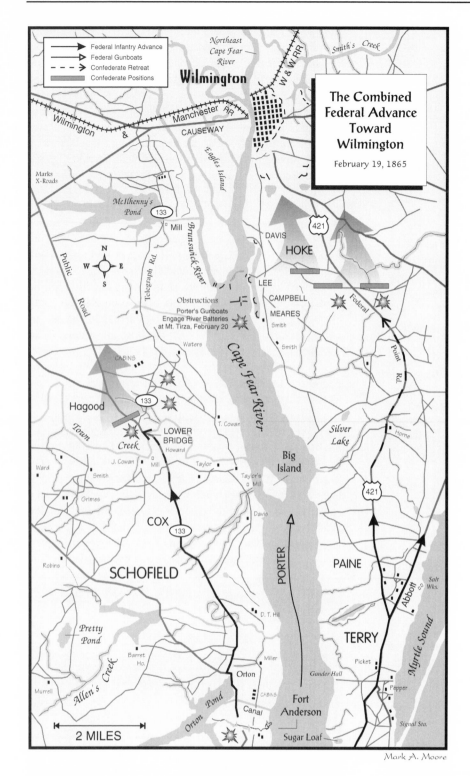

Federal Infantry Advance
Federal Gunboats
Confederate Retreat
Confederate Positions

The Combined
Federal Advance
Toward
Wilmington

February 19, 1865

Mark A. Moore

view, Hedrick's artillery opened fire. *"I at once formed the troops in line,"* reported Henderson, *"occupying the crest of a ridge running nearly parallel to the creek, and commenced fortifying."* Henderson sent a skirmish line forward, and soon assessed the difficult nature of the ground and stream that divided his command from the enemy. *"The creek was not wide,"* he reported, *"but deep, and could not be passed by troops without a bridge or boat, and between my line and the creek there was an almost impassable swamp."* Henderson determined that the only viable approach to Town Creek *"in front of the enemy's works, was the causeway constructed through it."* It was impossible to ford the creek, and the corduroy causeway was completely commanded by Hagood's artillery.

As Cox pondered his options for turning the Confederate flank, the brigades of Col. Oscar Sterl, John Casement, and Orlando Moore pulled in behind Henderson's command. These troops were not deployed, however, and Cox reported that he kept them *"out of sight and under cover"* for the remainder of the day.

General Hoke's response to Hagood's earlier request for orders had been noncommittal: *"Future operations will depend on circumstances."* Hagood, uncomfortable with the large Union force looming in his front, pressed his commanding officer with another dispatch at around 5:30 p.m. There were 13 Union gunboats in the river above Big (Campbell) Island, he warned Hoke, and small boat crews were sounding and marking the channel. *"Town Creek . . . can be held whenever occupied,"* continued Hagood. *"I have examined several miles of it today. From my observation it can be crossed almost anywhere that sufficient troops are not stationed. Let me know your views and intentions."* Hagood was looking for specific guidance, but Hoke had none to give. The interim district commander, after all, had a large enemy force in his own front, and the Southern objective was the same on both sides of the river: Keep the Union army out of Wilmington, or at the very least delay its advance as long as possible. Hoke's only reply was *"Hold Town Creek until you hear from me."*

Fort Anderson to the eastern side of the river. Ames' troops would follow in support of Paine and Abbott on the march toward Wilmington.

General Cox's advance units reached Town Creek at about 3:30 p.m. on February 19. As Hagood's mounted skirmishers fell back across the creek, they pulled the flooring from the bridge in an effort to impede the Federal advance. Colonel Thomas J. Henderson's brigade drew up on the high ground opposite the lower bridge, and when the Federals came into

As Porter's squadron ascended the river, naval crews busily cleared the way of torpedoes and, as Hagood observed, marked the narrow channel. Late in the day, 14 of Porter's launches approached to within sight of the river batteries three miles below Wilmington. Below these batteries—which mounted 16 heavy cannons commanded by Col. Peter C. Gaillard—the reconnoitering party found the waterway's main cluster of obstructions at the confluence of the Cape Fear and Brunswick rivers.

It was an elaborate system. The channel was blocked with a tangle of cheveaux de frise, several lines of sawyers (trees reaching from the bed of the river with their branches projecting to the surface), and a floating chain obstruction. Nestled among these obstacles lay the scuttled remains of the vessels *Arctic*, *Yadkin*, and *North Heath*, which further blocked the channel. The entrance to the Brunswick River was almost entirely barred by a double row of pilings, and the chain obstruction—fitted with a floating gate—extended from tiny Clark's Island to the riverbank below Battery Lee. This gated obstruction blocked the Cape Fear at the narrows below the river batteries, and was the last major obstacle in the river between Battery Lee and the Wilmington waterfront.

As the Federal launches approached, however, Battery Campbell opened fire, and the small craft were forced to retire. Admiral Porter wanted to bring the monitor *Montauk* up to engage the river bluff installations, but she ran aground at Big Island, and Porter decided to stand down for the evening. Despite this setback, preparations for the final push on Wilmington were progressing well, and by sundown both sets of ground forces had advanced to within nine miles of the city.

"*My advance is . . . close to the enemy's outposts,*" General Terry reported to Schofield. Terry was eager to receive reinforcements, and was assured that Ames' division would arrive sometime that night. Schofield then gave Terry his marching orders for the following morning: "*If you find the enemy in a fortified position this side of Wilmington, try to turn his left and force him back . . . or you may endeavor to cut him off from that place if your force appears sufficient. If the enemy fall back to the defenses of Wilmington, invest the place as far as practicable . . . . I will move up the river in the* Spaulding, *so as to keep in communication with the troops on both sides.*"

Schofield gave similar orders to General Cox on the west bank of the river. Turn the enemy's position at Town Creek, explained the Federal commander, and secure all of the western approaches to Wilmington. Schofield also expected Cox to be prepared to hold the approaches with a small force, so that a portion of his command could be transferred to the east bank of the river to reinforce Terry's men as they neared Wilmington. The city's outer defenses were arrayed along its eastern fringes; and if the Confederates chose to make a determined stand at these works, Schofield would need a sizable force on the eastern side of the river. Moreover, the department commander knew that Hagood's contingent of Hoke's Division numbered little more than 2,000 men, and reasoned that Cox had troops to spare.

Shortly after nightfall, General Cox received some timely news that would ultimately nullify the Town Creek dilemma. The break came when an elderly black man approached Colonel Henderson, and explained that there was an old warehouse downstream near the river. This facility, the man said, housed Confederate commissary stores, and "*there was also a flat-boat or scow in the creek by it, brought there for the purpose of moving the stores.*" Realizing the Confederates must not have had time to evacuate everything, Henderson dispatched a guard to take possession of the stores—and more importantly, the boat.

When Cox received word of the boat, he seized upon its importance immediately. The scow was his ticket to the north bank of Town Creek. "*I ordered it carefully secured and guarded by a strong picket,*" he explained, "*having learned that all the bridges on the stream were destroyed and that there was no ford for fifteen miles above.*"

At 8:30 p.m. Cox reported his situation to Schofield. He explained the disposition of Hagood's forces and the difficulty of forcing a crossing "*The creek is very crooked and deep,*" he explained. "*The water is said to be twenty or thirty feet deep, being deeper than the river. I learned of a flat-boat, capable of carrying near 100 men, a short distance below our camp, and ordered it secured and carefully protected . . . . If the enemy resist stubbornly and in force on the road [at the lower bridge], I think our only feasible way of crossing will be by the flat under cover of the fire of the gun-boats.*" Though Cox did not realize it, Hagood's position lay too far inland to be reached by fire from Porter's gunboats.

Schofield agreed that a 15-mile circuit in search of a crossing would be unfeasible, and welcomed the news of his division commander's good fortune. Three hours after Cox's dispatch went out, Schofield sent word to "*See what can be done with the flat-boat, as you suggest.*" Armed with the department commander's blessing, Cox began preparing for a bold flanking maneuver that would doom Hagood's ill-established line at Town Creek.

FEBRUARY 20, 1865

Before dawn on February 20, Casement's and Sterl's brigades began making their way eastward toward the warehouse on Town Creek, and their rendezvous with the small rice barge that would ferry them to its northern shore. If all went well, reasoned Cox, the movement would put the troops across the creek with little resistance, "*& thence around to the enemy's rear.*"

At first light—as Casement and Sterl prepared to make the crossing—Henderson's brigade moved forward "*to keep the enemy amused,*" explained Cox, "*by pressing as closely as possible in front.*" Henderson sent forward a strong skirmish line, which managed to approach within about 200 yards of the lower bridge at Town Creek. The ground in Henderson's front was open and afforded the men little cover, and the advance attracted the Confederates' attention almost immediately. The Federals endured "*a constant fire from the enemy behind his works,*" reported Henderson, but the men held onto their advanced position. It was a prudent maneuver, for it put the

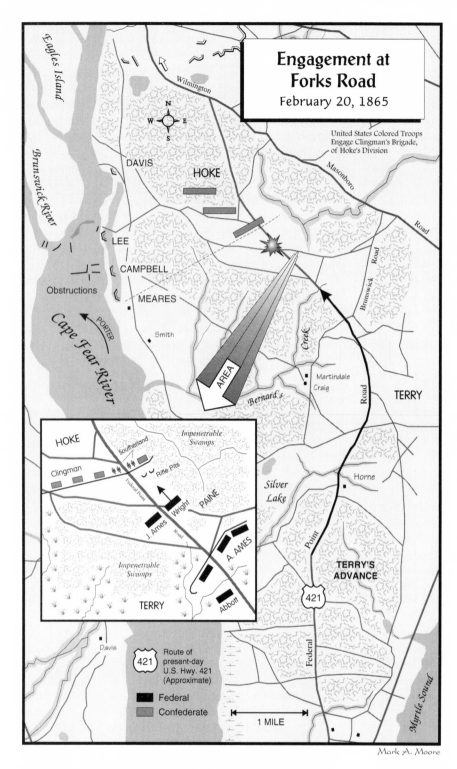

Engagement at Forks Road
February 20, 1865

United States Colored Troops Engage Clingman's Brigade, of Hoke's Division

Mark A. Moore

lery duel was carried on with the enemy by [our] left section, for several hours." During this action, the Ohio gunners erected slight works around their weapons as best they could—and waited for the results of Cox's flanking maneuver.

As disaster loomed for Hagood's Brigade, the Confederate situation at Wilmington reached a critical zenith. There were now more reasons than ever to keep the city out of Union hands—for just a little while longer, at any rate. The area was teeming with thousands of paroled Union prisoners of war who had begun arriving several days earlier—many of them from the notorious Andersonville, and the Confederate prison at Salisbury, North Carolina. They were to be exchanged, but Confederate authorities wanted time to evacuate them from the vicinity, to avoid their being liberated by the Union army. The rail lines leading from Wilmington—lines necessary for evacuating the prisoners— were already clogged from the effort to transport Confederate commissary and quartermaster stores from the city. To make matters even worse, Confederate troops under Lt. Gen. William J. Hardee—who were falling back rapidly before Sherman's army in South Carolina—had been ordered by Gen. P. G. T. Beauregard (in command at Charlotte) to fall back into North Carolina via Wilmington. Hardee's Corps was then about midway between Charleston and Florence. He needed immediate assistance, and looked to Bragg and Hoke to find it. Hardee hastily inquired of matters at the port city, and Hoke—determined to hold his position as long as possible—made plans to accommodate the erstwhile corps commander of the Army of Tennessee.

It was a gloomy predicament—and the fate of Wilmington hinged on the thin Confederate line west of the Cape Fear River. If this position held, it would buy time for an orderly evacuation of Wilmington. If the line crumbled, the back door to the city would be wide open.

At Town Creek, however, the situation was deteriorating rapidly for Johnson Hagood. Mindful of Hagood's propensity for wanting explicit orders, General Hoke reminded his bri-

Federals close enough to the bridge to keep Hagood's men from completely destroying it.

As Henderson moved into position, Lt. Cecil Reed's Battery D, 1st Ohio Light Artillery, unlimbered its 3-inch Parrott rifles on a knoll east of the road and opened fire. *"The enemy were alert,"* marveled one of the battery's gunners, *"and the first shot from their artillery showed us that they were no novices in artillery service. The position we held was scarcely a thousand yards from the enemy, who were behind heavy earthworks, and were thoroughly protected by them. An artil-*

gade commander that he was essentially on his own. "*You must move your command as you think best*," he admonished Hagood, "*[and] recollect the importance of your communication with Wilmington . . . . I leave the matter to your judgment.*" Hoke later accentuated his order with a warning to "*dispute [the enemy] advance at every available point.*"

Thus warned to fend for himself, Hagood immediately sought to gather information about the area's geography, in the event he was forced from his position at

Town Creek, the final Confederate line of defense west of the Cape Fear River. *Author's Collection*

Town Creek. The brigade commander envisioned a scenario where he might be cut off from the rest of Hoke's Division, and was anxious to find an avenue of escape across the Cape Fear River above Wilmington. He queried Bragg's adjutant, Colonel Anderson, for a detailed military map of the region, to be sent "*as soon as possible . . . . Enemy just opened on me with artillery.*"

By 11:00 a.m., Casement's brigade had gained a lodgment on the north bank of Town Creek, and early afternoon found Sterl's and Moore's brigades following close behind. Jacob D. Cox crossed with Moore's brigade, and would lead the Federal flanking maneuver in person. Fortune had smiled upon the Third Division commander. He had been allowed to sneak across the creek virtually unopposed—on an old barge whose slow-moving passage had consumed half the day. He was building a large force upon the enemy's left flank, and this time it appeared that nothing would prevent him from routing a woefully outnumbered foe. He had missed the opportunity at Fort Anderson, but Cox meant to bag Hagood's Brigade once and for all, along the diked rice fields of Cowan's Plantation. By the time Hagood's poorly-deployed picket force became wise to the Federal movement, it would be too late.

On the east bank of the Cape Fear River, General Terry's force was slowly bearing down on Hoke's position—and once again the United States Colored Troops of Paine's division had the lead. As the Union army passed a small residence on the Federal Point Road, about four miles below Wilmington, a young soldier asked permission to leave the ranks to visit the house. The man's commanding officer asked the purpose of the visit, and was surprised to learn that the house was the soldier's boyhood home. His name was Jacob Horne, a onetime Confederate who had deserted to the Union army.

At the house by the roadside, Horne greeted his overjoyed mother—who told her son that he had just missed his brother, Hosea, who had visited the house as Hoke's Division retreated toward Wilmington. Hosea Horne, an artillerist in Hoke's command, had narrowly missed a wartime confrontation with his

brother—the enemy—in their own mother's yard. It was a classic illustration of the brother-against-brother theme so often associated with the American Civil War. Both men would soon make it home alive—if not the best of friends.

By 3:00 p.m. Terry's skirmishers—the 5th U.S. Colored Troops of Elias Wright's brigade—had pushed Hoke's skirmishers back to their main line at Forks Road. The "*Southern chivalry speak with contempt of the 'smoked Yankee's,*'" gloated Capt. Elliott F. Grabill of the 5th USCT, "*yet they fell back with due respect before a well conducted skirmish line of 'colored Americans of African descent.*'" Paine's Colored Division was once again preparing to engage the enemy before a strong line of earthworks. While Hoke's new position did not rival the strength of the long-held Sugar Loaf line, it was well manned, with six pieces of artillery from Southerland's Battery commanding the road.

As Paine's division approached, Hoke's Confederates gave the attackers a stinging dose of small arms and artillery fire. A "*severe skirmish ensued,*" reported General Paine. "*The enemy's fire along our whole front was found to be that of a single rank or a little more, and his artillery fire was from six or seven guns.*" Eager to test the strength of the Rebel line, Alfred Terry ordered a probing attack. The task fell to Colonel Wright's entire brigade—the 1st, 5th, 10th, 27th, and 37th USCT—which advanced in force upon the works manned by Clingman's Brigade (under Col. William Devane). Hindered by swampy approaches and stiff resistance, however, the attack crested within 150 yards of the Forks Road entrenchments, and the men were unable to advance further. Hoke's infantrymen—veterans of many a battlefield in Virginia—were determined to hold their last line of defense before Wilmington.

The Confederates "*refused to be driven further,*" observed the pragmatic Lt. J. J. Scroggs of the 5th USCT. "*Gen. Terry ordered the 5th to charge the works and we done it, but were not able to take [them] . . . . Col. Wright who led the charge was wounded in the wrist. I suppose it was fun for Terry, but little for us.*" The brief tangle with Clingman's Brigade cost Paine two men killed (including one officer) and 51 wounded

A Flag of the 6th United States Colored Troops, of Col. John W. Ames' brigade, Paine's division, XXV Army Corps

United States Army Military History Institute

(three officers)—Colonel Wright and his aide-de-camp numbering among the latter. The brief nature of the fight and comparative strength of their defenses afforded the Confederates few casualties. A soldier in Hoke's command, however, acknowledged that the recent engagements and running skirmishes with the enemy were "*approaching closely the dignity of battles.*"

Terry ordered the African Americans to entrench on the front line, and Paine's division was soon joined by Ames' troops and Abbott's brigade. The confrontation settled into an extended skirmish, which would continue at intervals for the next 36 hours. The Federal advance on the east side of the river had been checked for the day, and Terry patiently awaited news from General Cox's side of the river.

On the Cape Fear itself, as the Colored Division sparred with Hoke's command two miles to the east, Admiral Porter's gunboats engaged in a spirited duel with the riverside batteries below Wilmington. The Union ground forces lay too far inland for Porter's vessels to provide fire support, so Porter concentrated on the installations crowning the eastern bluffs of the river. The upriver advance was slow and difficult. The *Montauk* lay grounded off Big Island, and several of the heavier gunboats also bottomed out in the shallows. A handful of ships with a lighter draft—including the *Lenapee* and *Sassacus*—cruised to within firing distance, and at 3:00 p.m. unleashed their guns on the Confederate shore installations.

In an artillery duel that would last for three hours, Porter's flotilla poured a concentrated fire onto the shore batteries—but were unable to silence them. Confederate return fire was brisk, and the *Sassacus* took several hits which "*set her to leaking badly,*" noted Porter.

While Confederate forces at Forks Road and the river batteries continued to hold their own, Johnson Hagood was in deadly peril at Town Creek. Jacob Cox's troops had clawed their way through the marshes onto dry ground, and were pushing Hagood's skirmishers back to the north. The Confederate brigade commander had earlier dispatched the 21st South Carolina to reinforce his 11th Regiment along the north bank of the creek, but now both units were retiring slowly before the Federal advance. Captain Joseph J. Wescoat notified his superiors that the enemy was coming on in large numbers.

Hagood immediately sent Colonel Simonton with the 25th and 27th South Carolina regiments to Cowan's Plantation to help stall Cox's advance. Above the plantation house, the farm road leading from Town Creek to Cowan's forked into two

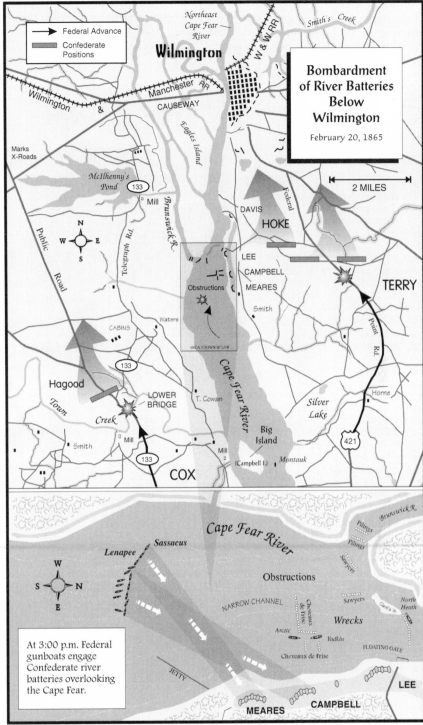

lanes—both of which fed into the Telegraph Road. Hagood ordered Simonton to guard the north and south lanes, and block the enemy advance.

With the 65th Indiana deployed as skirmishers, Casement's and Sterl's brigades advanced in line of battle toward the forks above Cowan's, followed by Moore's brigade in column upon the road. Colonel Simonton realized the predicament of his small command almost immediately. "*The enemy are in my front and appear to be extending on the north road,*" he reported frantically to Hagood. "*From my position I cannot guard*

"I could plainly see a number of transports in the Cape Fear River . . . . I stood there watching them for some time, thinking I was in no special danger, believing myself fairly well concealed, when the smoke, crack, of a rifle and striking of minie ball very near me caused me to think it advisable, like poor Jo, to 'move on, and not know nothink.' The enemy soon formed in line of battle and with skirmishers thrown out well in front, commenced the advance movement towards our position.

"We skirmished all day, till near sunset, when the enemy charged the very small force under Colonel Simonton, which was drawn up in line of battle, and supported by a section of artillery under Lieutenant [John] Rankin, of North Carolina. I was then on the skirmish line, about two hundred yards to the right of our line of battle. The firing ceased so suddenly that I concluded at once that the Confederates had all been captured, which became evident to me after we approached near enough to see the Confederates and Yankees mingling together.

"Having satisfied myself that the day was lost . . . I halted, and said to the those who were with me, that I did not propose to surrender without making an effort to escape, and all those who would follow me I would take back to the turnpike where we had left the brigade in the morning, supposing I would still find it there.

"After working our way through a dense swamp, sometimes waist deep in slush and water, we reached the hill on the opposite side in safety, and exactly at the desired point, but judge of our consternation when we stepped into the turnpike to find ourselves in the midst of a brigade of Yankees, instead of Confederates.

"One of them in a very jollifying manner called out: 'Hello, Johnnie, how deep have you been in!' I tried to hide my mortification and disgust and replied: 'Just so deep,' at the same time indicating with my hand the height around my waist reached by the water. I felt terribly chagrined at this *denouement* to my plans, but quiet submission was the only alternative." —**Sgt. William Izlar**, 25th South Carolina Infantry, Hagood's Brigade

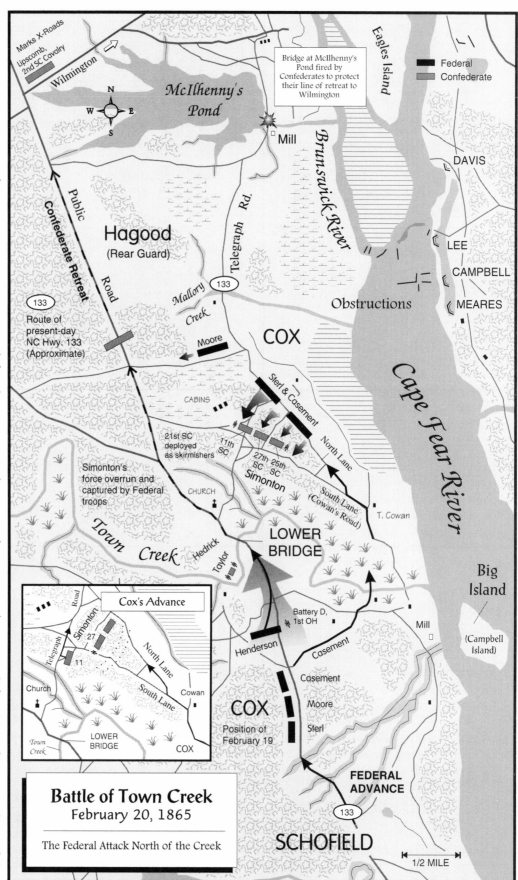

Bridge at McIlhenny's Pond fired by Confederates to protect their line of retreat to Wilmington

■ Federal
■ Confederate

McIlhenny's Pond

Eagles Island

DAVIS

LEE

CAMPBELL

MEARES

Brunswick River

Mill

Hagood
(Rear Guard)

Telegraph Rd.

133

Mallory Creek

Moore

COX

Obstructions

Cape Fear River

133

Route of present-day NC Hwy. 133 (Approximate)

Confederate Retreat   Public Road

CABINS

21st SC deployed as skirmishers

11th SC

Sterl & Casement

27th 25th
SC   SC

Simonton

North Lane

South Lane (Cowan's Road)

T. Cowan

Simonton's force overrun and captured by Federal troops

CHURCH

LOWER BRIDGE

Big Island

Town Creek

Hedrick

Taylor

Battery D, 1st OH

Mill

(Campbell Island)

Cox's Advance

Telegraph Road

Simonton

27

11

Church

North Lane

South Lane

Cowan

Town Creek

LOWER BRIDGE

COX

Henderson

Casement

Casement

Moore

Sterl

COX
Position of February 19

FEDERAL ADVANCE

133

SCHOFIELD

Battle of Town Creek
February 20, 1865

The Federal Attack North of the Creek

1/2 MILE

Marks X-Roads
Lipscomb, 2nd SC Cavalry

Wilmington

N W E S

Mark A. Moore

both roads." Hagood rushed to Cowan's in person, and watched as Cox moved in force upon Simonton's feeble left flank. The dreadful scene convinced Hagood then and there that all was lost. Thinking quickly, the South Carolina aristocrat-turned-soldier devised a scheme to extricate the rest of his scattered command from the doomed position at Town Creek—while Simonton's force bought time by stalling Cox's advance.

Hagood hurried back to his headquarters at the clapboard church, and sent orders for Colonel Lipscomb's troopers to retire from the upper bridge to Marks Crossroads, several miles above Hagood's position. The general also fired off a message to Adjt. Archer Anderson: "*Inform General Hoke that the enemy are landing at Cowan's house, north of Town Creek. It makes it necessary for me to prepare to leave this line . . . . I will send my baggage at once across the pontoon bridge at Wilmington . . . . Hurry the guides and maps for the event of my having to go higher up.*" As the sounds of battle swelled from the direction of Simonton's position, the brigade's wagons, artillery, and sick and wounded were swiftly evacuated toward Wilmington.

At 3:00 p.m., just as the action in General Terry's front was reaching its peak, Johnson Hagood ordered Colonel Hedrick to abandon his position at the lower bridge. "*I am now evacuating,*" he messaged Hoke. "*Enemy are turning my flank and are pushing me too strong.*" As if to underscore that he had no choice in retiring, Hagood added that he was "*obliged to do so.*"

The skirmishing intensified at the lower bridge as Hedrick pulled out, leaving a strong rear guard at the entrenchments to cover the withdrawal. "*About 3:00 p.m. the enemy made an effort to drive our little [skirmish] line back,*" remembered one of Reed's Ohio gunners. "*In short, to put it out of existence. It was a signal failure. In the next half hour one of their guns was dismounted; a caisson was rendered useless; three of the enemy were killed, and four were wounded. This stopped their firing, and in the meantime the flanking column had surrounded them.*"

While Cox pushed his command around Simonton's flank, the Confederates changed front to the north to meet the threat. The Federal advance reached the intersection with the Telegraph Road around 4:00 p.m. Here, Cox's good fortune received yet another boost when the division commander was approached by several members of the local black population. They had useful news—the kind of information from which Cox had benefited since the beginning of the march on Wilmington. There was another road—the Public Road—leading northward from Town Creek, they told the general. Cox reasoned that this road would provide an added means toward completely surrounding his foe. He immediately sent Moore's brigade across country toward the Public Road, with orders to

---

Johnson Hagood left a detailed account of the engagement at Town Creek—an account in which he blames Col. Charles Simonton for the Confederate disaster, while crediting him with saving the portion of Hagood's command that managed to escape to Wilmington.

X - Hagood marks this spot as the location of Simonton's reserves and two pieces of artillery, at the time the general arrived to assess the situation near Cowan's house.

Y - Having issued elaborate instructions to Simonton regarding his posting of reserves, Hagood designated this point as the location where Simonton should consolidate his reserves, after falling back to the Telegraph Road. Simonton had orders to engage in an "*obstinate skirmish fight*"—but not a general battle.

Y-Z - The road designated for Simonton's orderly withdrawal from Cowan's Plantation.

K-Z - Hagood posted a reserve force—the 7th South Carolina and 40th North Carolina regiments—between these points. He expected this line to cover Simonton's withdrawal.

By the time Capt. William E. Stoney reached Simonton—via road **Z-Y**—with orders to retreat, the colonel reported he was too heavily engaged to withdraw. Hagood claimed he intended for Simonton "*to throw away his artillery and make a run for it; that a line of battle was formed in his rear to protect him.*" But it was not to be. Charles Simonton and his entire command were overrun and captured by two brigades of Federal infantry from Cox's division.

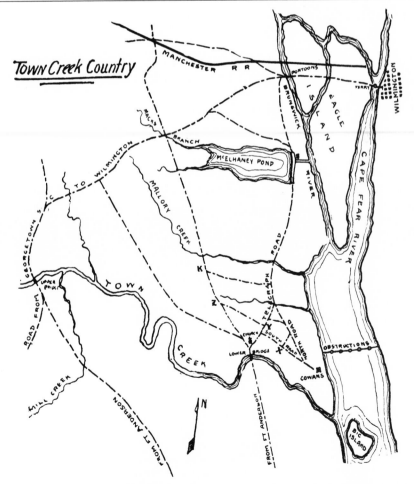

This map appeared in *Memoirs of the War of Secession, from the Original Manuscripts of Johnson Hagood* (1910). Compare the points marked X, Y, Z, and K with the map on page 116.

TOWN CREEK AND FORKS ROAD

Maj. Gen. Robert F. Hoke

move in upon the enemy's rear.

As Moore's troops headed for the interior road, Casement and Sterl formed a strong line of battle facing southwest along the North Lane, and prepared to strike a hammer blow against their beleaguered enemy. The sun was setting when the Federals launched their attack. They rushed forward with a shout, some three thousand strong, upon the incomplete breastworks of the enemy, and all but devoured Simonton's pitiful command. It was "*a hot little engagement*," observed Capt. Thomas Speed of the 12th Kentucky. "*We were in a level pine woods, [and] as we advanced we were a fair mark for small arms and two pieces of artillery.*"

As the attackers rushed upon the Rebel artillery, Captain Speed observed a fellow Kentucky officer demand the surrender of one of the guns. The cannon was "St. Paul," a prized possession of Company B, 3rd Battalion North Carolina Light Artillery—otherwise known as the Edenton Bell Battery. Just as St. Paul's crew was about to discharge the weapon, the Federal lieutenant seized the gun's commander, Sgt. Benjamin F. Hunter, and screamed "*if you shoot that gun I will kill you.*" "*Kill and be damned,*" retorted Hunter, who promptly ordered his gunner to jerk the lanyard to fire the weapon. The resulting blast of case shot tore through the ranks of the 104th Ohio Infantry at point-blank range, causing more than half of the total Union casualties for the engagement. "*It was a terribly effective shot,*" admitted Captain Speed. "*The enemy stood to the last, and did not surrender until their guns were snatched out of their hands.*" Stunned by Sergeant Hunter's defiance, the Kentucky lieutenant spared the man's life. "*He's too brave a man to be killed.*"

The Confederates had staged a brief but valiant resistance with close-quarters artillery and small arms fire, but the result was never in doubt. It was over nearly as quickly as it had begun, leaving the Federals with 375 prisoners, two pieces of artillery, and three Confederate battle flags.

At the lower bridge, the last of Col. John D. Taylor's command retired under fire about 5:00 p.m., and the men of Henderson's brigade stormed the bridge in pursuit. A party of skirmishers from the 63rd Indiana made it across in time to bag about 30 Confederate prisoners, but most of Taylor's force escaped up the Public Road. Moore's brigade had failed to reach this interior road in time to cut off Hagood's retreat, but the battlefield belonged to the Union. Hagood had escaped by the seat of his pants—sacrificing Simonton's men in the pro-

cess. While disappointed that part of Hagood's Brigade had gotten away, Cox was pleased to have captured a sizable chunk of the Confederate general's command—including Colonel Simonton.

Of Simonton's 400 to 500 men, the engagement claimed about 20 killed and wounded, with the bulk becoming prisoners of war. The Federal attack had come just as Simonton was about to retreat, and a few fortunate souls managed to escape—among them Capt. William E. Stoney, of Hagood's staff, who fled on foot after his horse was shot from beneath him. The Federals emerged with a loss of three killed and 31 wounded. The men had "*behaved with great gallantry,*" noted Colonel Casement, and had emerged relatively unscathed. Captain Thomas Bible, of the 8th Tennessee Infantry, Sterl's Brigade, summed the day up concisely: "*Our Brigade and the 2nd . . . crossed Town Creek and captured a boatload of sweetpotatoes, then charged a battery and captured it with about 400 prisoners, then camped on the battlefield.*"

At 6:00 p.m., Cox informed Schofield of the success of his flanking maneuver at Town Creek. He also instructed Henderson to strengthen the lower bridge, to allow the men and artillery easy passage to the north side of the creek.

With his command in full retreat, Johnson Hagood reached Wilmington about 8:30 p.m. His troops followed over the next three hours, via the pontoon bridge over the Brunswick River, and then by steam ferry across the Cape Fear to the city's waterfront. Hagood did not join Hoke near Forks Road, but rather camped at Hilton, along the northern skirts of the city. It was a temporary station, for the loss of the Town Creek position had sealed the fate of Wilmington. Four days after Cox's advance had begun, the western approaches to the city were clear at last, and Wilmington would belong to the Union.

On the Cape Fear River, as the evacuation of provisions continued at Wilmington, the Confederates had one last surprise in store for Porter's gunboats. That evening the Rebels floated some 100 torpedoes down the river in an effort to disperse the flotilla. Once again, however, a slave provided valuable information, and warned the sailors of the approach of the floating bombs. Though the naval crews took precautions against their arrival—scooping them up with nets and destroying others with musket fire—the Federals did not emerge unscathed. One torpedo detonated near a launch from the *Shawmut*, resulting in two deaths and two other injuries. A second device found its mark at the expense of one of the gunboats. "*One got in the wheel of the Osceola,*" lamented Admiral Porter, "*and blew her wheelhouse to pieces, and knocked down her bulkheads inboard, but there was no damage to the hull.*" By morning Porter would employ two large fishing nets to collect the remaining explosives, and dispose of them safely.

On the eastern side of the Cape Fear, the Federal forces of Alfred Terry's command settled in for the night, as occasional outbursts of gunfire illuminated the darkness between Paine's division and Hoke's line. During the day, John Schofield had received word of the pending exchange of prisoners from General Grant—indeed, they were already arriving at Wilmington.

Underscoring the importance of securing the city for Federal use, however, Grant cautioned his subordinate: "*Do not allow this exchange of prisoners to interfere in any way with your proposed military operations.*" Grant concluded his communication with news of William T. Sherman's progress through South Carolina. "Uncle Billy" and his 60,000 veterans were approaching the vicinity of Winnsboro, and would soon be crossing into North Carolina. By all accounts, the campaign was progressing well, and the interior base at Goldsboro would soon be established.

Robert F. Hoke had received news of his own that day, and none of it was good. Hagood had opened the door to Wilmington, Braxton Bragg—with the enemy at his very doorstep—was returning to the city by rail, and Gen. Lawrence Baker at Goldsboro had wired with fears of impending doom from the direction of New Bern. Despite gloomy reports from all fronts, however, Hoke kept a measure of confidence. "*The general expects to hold this position,*" reported adjutant J. L. Cross, and the interim district commander spent the evening supervising efforts to strengthen his left flank.

Hoke also communicated with Gen. Robert E. Lee in Virginia, passing ill tidings up the chain of command. He acknowledged General Baker's dilemma at Goldsboro, but was powerless to alleviate it. "*I cannot help him,*" he explained. "*Enemy in strong force against me.*" Hoke broke the news to Lee that Fort Anderson had fallen, but tried to reassure the general-in-chief in answering his earlier query regarding the strength of the Union Army: "*Schofield has 15,000 men. We will dispute every point.*"

By now General Bragg was en route from Goldsboro to Magnolia, a little rail stop on the Wilmington & Weldon about 60 miles north of Wilmington. He had sent word for Hoke to telegraph his "*condition*" that evening to Magnolia, and at 10:30 p.m. Hoke offered his commander a simple line that belied the true situation: "*All quiet now.*" Relative quiet notwithstanding, the situation was now hopeless for the Confederate defense of Wilmington.

On top of everything else, Hoke realized that if William J. Hardee's troops were to use Wilmington as a rail link to points inland, they would probably have to help fight for the city. At 11:00 p.m., he wired Hardee at Kingstree, South Carolina: "*Assisted by two brigades from you, we may succeed in forcing the passage of your force by this point.*"

The Federals on General Terry's front were also busy strengthening their works. The men had gone into position un-

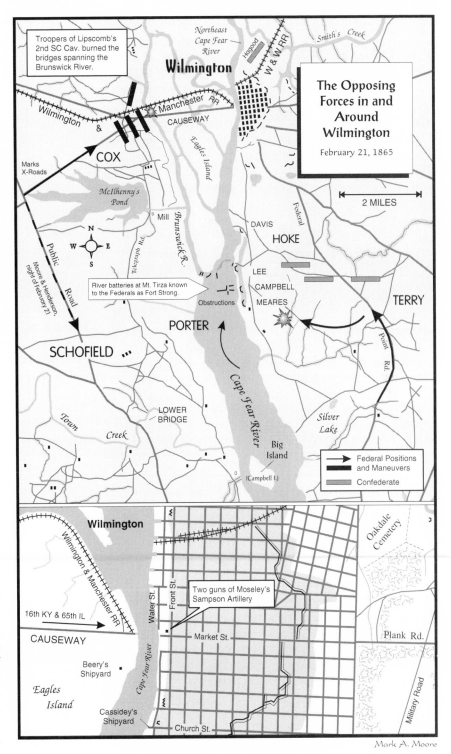

der fire, "*and by the use of our shovels,*" noted a soldier in Abbott's brigade, "*made our position secure for the night.*" And as the skirmish fire crackled occasionally in the darkness, the men knew that they were close—that Wilmington was within their grasp. "*We were then within about three miles of the prize,*" observed a member of the 3rd New Hampshire Infantry. "*Would we obtain it with, or without, bloodshed? Time alone would tell.*"

EVACUATION

The Evacuation of Wilmington

FEBRUARY 21, 1865

Gen. Braxton Bragg

Before dawn on February 21, Colonel Lipscomb's Confederate troopers burned the Wilmington & Manchester Railroad trestle and dismantled the pontoons over the Brunswick River. With Cox's troops fast approaching, the Rebels burned all of the bridges along the western approaches to Wilmington.

General Braxton Bragg, absent for the past 11 days, arrived in Wilmington that morning to find many of its residents fleeing the city. Pandemonium reigned in the streets. Even a few homes and businesses were looted, as refugees vied with Confederate military stores for egress out of the doomed city.

When the department commander learned the depressing state of military affairs at his post, he immediately conveyed the unwelcome news to Robert E. Lee: "*I find all our troops on this side [of the] Cape Fear [River]. The enemy in force on the west, and our communication [to the] south cut. We are greatly outnumbered. General Schofield in command with two corps. He refuses to receive prisoners and they are being sent north.*" The Union prisoners had become such a burden that the Confederates were now eager to be free of them. General Hoke had devised a plan to hand them over directly to the Union army, but Schofield rejected the plan. General U. S. Grant did not want the prisoner exchange to interfere with, or delay, Schofield's capture of Wilmington and its vital rail facilities.

Lee now understood that Wilmington was lost—that Bragg would evacuate the city immediately. The Confederate commanders were out of options. "*Destroy all cotton, tobacco, and naval stores,*" Lee wired Bragg, "*that would otherwise fall into the hands of the enemy.*" Many of the town's storehouses, foundries, shipyards, and vessels were set ablaze, and much of what was not burned was thrown into the river. The nearly-completed ironclad *Wilmington* and other small vessels—including a submarine—were all lost in the destruction of Beery's Shipyard on Eagles Island. The gunboat *Chickamauga*, which had harassed Adelbert Ames' troops on Federal Point during the attack on Fort Fisher, was also scuttled.

Confiscating all available modes of transportation, Bragg sought to expedite the evacuation by employing about 200 slaves and a force of able-bodied civilians to help hurry along the removal of government property and Union prisoners. Those prisoners who were strong enough to walk were led away on foot. As the city's streets emptied, a stiff easterly wind fanned the flames, and many structures were thus destroyed unintentionally.

By 3:00 p.m. Jacob Cox's men had arrived in force at the Brunswick River, having advanced via the Public and Telegraph roads. Gazing across Eagles Island, they could see the waterfront and church spires of Wilmington—and ample evidence that the enemy was hurriedly evacuating the city. "*There was a dense column of smoke arising from cotton and resin that was burning on the opposite side of Cape Fear River,*" observed an Ohio artillerist. "*The smoke from this fire made a column so marked that it could be seen for many miles away.*" Undaunted by the wrecked bridge, Cox's men gathered enough undamaged pontoons to ferry a scouting force of the 16th Kentucky and 65th Illinois regiments over to Eagles Island. Cox's resourceful engineers also began to repair the bridge, which would soon allow easy access to the island.

The Federal reconnaissance party pushed across the island's causeway, sparring with the rear elements of Lipscomb's troopers. Two artillery pieces of Capt. Abner Moseley's battery, however, opened upon the Federals from both sides of Market Street, on the Wilmington waterfront. Thus caught in the open, the two Union regiments were forced to halt and erect breastworks for protection. To help delay the inevitable, Colonel Hedrick sent a howitzer over to the island itself, where an extended artillery duel erupted as Cox's gunners lobbed their own shells directly into the city. As a result, noted one Federal gunner, Wilmington's market house suffered several direct hits, and "*hospital flags were run up upon nearly every building in the city.*" As panic ensued among the town's remaining citizens, and hoping for relief from the Union bombardment, Hagood ordered Moseley's artillery to cease firing.

Three miles below Wilmington, Gen. Robert F. Hoke's force spent the day stoutly resisting a series of attacks from Alfred Terry's Federals. Beginning at 10:00 a.m., a detachment from Ames' division had probed westward toward the river batteries, in search of a weak point in Hoke's line. They could not find one, however, and the skirmishing remained brisk throughout the day. At the same time, Admiral Porter's gunboats hammered away at the Cape Fear shore installations. That evening Schofield ordered Cox to send a portion of his command to the east bank of the river to reinforce Terry. The Federal commander wanted a force on Terry's front that was strong enough to push the enemy out of Wilmington.

As Bragg oversaw the final, frantic, and destructive evacuation of the city, Hoke clung defiantly to his entrenched position. He was confident that, with the aid of Hardee's Corps, they might yet hold Wilmington long enough to allow the lieutenant general's command to pass through. But it was not to be. Bragg sent word to Hardee that Confederate forces had been driven to the east side of the Cape Fear River, and that the Wilmington & Manchester line had been cut. "*You had better follow your original plan,*" Bragg warned Hardee, "*as the movement this way is no longer practicable.*"

When Bragg learned that a detachment of Cox's command had crossed onto Eagles Island, he ordered Hoke to prepare his men for a general retreat. At 10:45 p.m. Bragg explained to Robert E. Lee that the Federals were now pressing Wilmington closely from both sides of the river. *"This compels me to cross the Northeast [Cape Fear] River or they will be in my rear to-morrow,"* Bragg wired Lee. *"Our small force renders it impossible to make any serious stand. We are greatly embarrassed by [Union] prisoners."* Bragg assured Lee that his order regarding the destruction of provisions had been carried out, and at 1:00 a.m. on February 22, 1865, the department commander gave the formal order for Confederate forces to withdraw from Wilmington.

For Hoke's men, who had been largely squandered during the entire feeble effort to defend Wilmington, it was a bitter pill to swallow. With Kirkland's Brigade serving as rear guard, the men *"marched sadly and leisurely through the streets of our 'City by the Sea,'"* lamented Wilson G. Lamb of the 17th North Carolina, *"and Wilmington passed under Federal control."*

Notes on the Loss of Wilmington

The fall of North Carolina's once lucrative blockade-running seaport was inevitable following the January 1865 capture of Fort Fisher—a storied bastion which, in itself, never stood a realistic chance of remaining in Confederate hands. Indifferent Confederate authorities and lack of Southern manpower had conspired with overwhelming Union firepower and resources to render this structure untenable from the outset.

Despite this inevitability, from the planning stages of the attack on Wilmington through the capture of Fort Fisher, Ulysses S. Grant had shown little interest in the doomed port city. Indeed, it was not until his friend and trusted subordinate, William T. Sherman, embarked on a march through the Carolinas in February 1865, that the Union general-in-chief finally looked upon Wilmington with keen interest. The planning for Sherman's famous jaunt northward gave Wilmington a whole new relevance—an importance that for the first time rated Grant's personal attention. As plans were drawn for using Wilmington as the hub for Sherman's interior supply base at Goldsboro, Grant visited Cape Fear and sent Gen. John Schofield and a corps of veteran Westerners to take charge of the Wilmington march. This force, with Gen. Alfred Terry's Provisional Corps already stationed on Federal Point, gave the Union a formidable army with which to advance on Wilmington.

The outcome was never in doubt. If the beleaguered Confederates could not hold Fort Fisher, then certainly there was no hope—given their limited resources—of a successful defense of the "City by the Sea." Under the circumstances, however, it appears that Braxton Bragg and Robert F. Hoke could have employed a more prudent resistance—a defense which would have delayed the Federal advance long enough for a systematic and less destructive retreat from Wilmington.

It was the wide-open approaches west of the Cape Fear River that doomed the city. The Confederates managed to hold their own on the narrow sand spit east of the river. Hoke's peninsula-wide stronghold could not be outflanked, and it was held with a stout defensive line on par with any found outside Richmond or Petersburg in Virginia. Here, three brigades of Hoke's veteran division from the Army of Northern Virginia successfully stalled the advance of Terry's Provisional Corps.

West of the river, however, Fort Anderson—for all its immensity—proved useless as a defense against Union infantry. Johnson Hagood's single brigade of Hoke's Division was scarcely strong enough to hold the fort itself, let alone the open real estate to the west that offered the Federals a convenient avenue for outflanking the bastion. Given the physical strength of Hoke's Sugar Loaf line, the general would have been wise to evenly divide his force on both sides of the river: two brigades to hold the formidable Sugar Loaf earthworks, and two to defend the western side of the river. If Hagood had been given *two* brigades—one to hold Anderson itself, and one to block the approaches west of the fort—the advance of Jacob Cox's Federal command would have been greatly slowed. To be sure, this would have been a risky venture for the Confederates, but such a gamble might have paid the dividend of additional time.

Fort Anderson aside, Town Creek should have been the obstacle that halted Cox's advance, and assured a more orderly evacuation of Wilmington. In light of Hagood's small force, the Town Creek position was actually a better defensive location than Fort Anderson. Unlike Anderson, the deep, unfordable stream could not be outflanked—and the only bridges in the vicinity were miles apart, and severely damaged after the Confederates crossed to the northern bank. Cox found himself in a dilemma at Town Creek, but Union resourcefulness and an utter lack of cognizance on the Confederate side conspired to allow Cox's men to cross the stream unmolested.

Given Hagood's ideal position, it seems ludicrous that Cox would have been allowed to ferry several thousand men across Town Creek in a single rice barge. This cumbersome maneuver took half a day, and yet it went undetected by the Confederates until it was too late. Hagood's inexperienced field commander, Col. Charles Simonton, lacked the foresight to stage a proper vigilance with his small picket force stationed between the Wilmington Road and the riverbank. Vulnerable as they floated across the stream in the flatboat, Cox's Federals might have been seriously punished if Hagood's pickets had kept a proper watch for movements from the enemy. Hagood himself should have made certain that his skirmishers were properly posted. Perhaps the depth of the creek gave the Confederate brigadier a relaxed—and fatal—sense of security.

Thus, throughout the march on Wilmington, it was the retreat of Hagood's Brigade alone that forced the withdrawal of Hoke's command east of the river—first from the Sugar Loaf line, and then from the Forks Road entrenchments below the city. And from the moment the Town Creek line was turned, Wilmington belonged to the Union.

Interestingly, Johnson Hagood ascribed the loss of Town Creek to the support rendered Federal ground forces by the Union navy. His position, however, was too far inland to be affected by fire from Union gunboats. *"The propriety of making the obstinate stand at Town Creek at all rests with the direction of affairs,"* Hagood complained, shifting the blame to Robert F. Hoke. *"It delayed the evacuation of Wilmington but little and was a hazardous venture."*

The DeRosset House, *2nd and Dock Streets*.

North Carolina Division of Archives and History

Confederate army headquarters for the Cape Fear Region. During the occupation of Wilmington, the DeRosset family was ordered to pay rent for their own home. Unable to make payment, however, the family was forced to take on a Union boarder.

Downtown Wilmington, *Front Street and the waterfront*.

North Carolina Division of Archives and History

This wartime view faces north, with the Cape Fear River visible on the left. On the right of the image, note the four spires of St. James Church on Third Street.

Capture, Occupation, and Beyond

"I have the satisfaction of announcing the capture of Wilmington . . . . The enemy has gone toward Goldsborough, and General Terry is in pursuit."
— **Maj. Gen. John M. Schofield**, to Ulysses S. Grant, February 22, 1865

On the morning of February 22, 1865, General Alfred Terry's skirmishers pushed forward to find the Confederate position evacuated. The words *"They have gone,"* soon passed along the Federal lines, to the great relief of all.

That morning the curious citizens of Wilmington—those who had not fled—were treated to a grand spectacle, as the victorious Union army marched into town with glorious fanfare, their bands filling the air with martial tunes. Porter's squadron, decked with flags and pennants, slipped gracefully through the river obstructions and pulled in at the Wilmington waterfront. *"I have the honor to inform you,"* Porter told Navy Secretary Gideon Welles, *"that Wilmington has been evacuated, and is in possession of our troops."* The mood among Federal servicemen was one of rampant celebration, a fitting occasion for the 113th observance of President George Washington's birthday.

"The victorious entrance of Wilmington by Admiral Porter's fleet . . . with full colors flying on all war vessels, was the grandest celebration of the anniversary of the birth of Washington that was witnessed in the whole nation," beamed Adam Furnas, an orderly aboard the *S. R. Spaulding* with General Schofield. The waterfront docks were in shambles, but the scene was impressive. The sailors could see the *"steeples and tall factory chimneys"* of the town, remembered Furnas, *"through the clouds of smoke arising from smoldering ruins upon the wharves and river front where many ware houses [sic] and factories were destroyed by the retreating enemy, hulls of steamers, machinery, saw mills, etc."* Furnas and his comrades were soon amazed by the curious gaggle of citizenry lining the *"nice streets"* of the waterfront. *"First [a] small group of citizens all waving white flags, black persons, though females, farther along larger groups and a few whites in the town, farther see tastily green and red dressed damsels in fine houses, see nice well shaded streets. The main wharf becomes literally lined with citizens as we arrive, of all colors, sizes, conditions and sexes, variously attired, nothing showing marks of injury but the wharves . . . nearly burned to the water's edge, being now saved by citizens pouring on water."* Despite its role as a blockade-running seaport, there had remained in Wilmington's population an element of strong Unionist sentiment.

As Gen. Jacob D. Cox's men ferried themselves in flatboats from Eagles Island to the waterfront, Alfred Terry's Provisional Corps marched into Wilmington from the south. *"The people welcomed us,"* marveled Stephen Walkley of the 7th Connecticut Infantry, *"even the whites, with every indication of joy. They filled the streets, some crying aloud, one man waving the United States flag from a window as we passed. How our boys did cheer that flag! The negroes outdid the whites in the manifestation of joy. The young ones danced to the music of the bands as they ran along at the head of the column, chattering and throwing up their ragged caps. The old ones, with all sorts of affectionate expressions, clapping their hands, bowing their heads, and embracing one another."*

Federal forces poured into Wilmington throughout the day, and Terry's advance units followed the retreating Confederates. A sharp skirmish ensued that morning at Smith's Creek—one-half mile above the city—as Federal skirmishers caught up with elements of the 2nd South Carolina Cavalry.

As Confederate forces retreated northward on the Duplin Road, they destroyed the Wilmington & Weldon Railroad trestle over Smith's Creek, and set fire to the nearby wagon bridge. Their aggressive pursuers, however, managed to save the bridge and continued the chase toward the Northeast Cape Fear River. The running fight went on for a distance of nine miles, until the Federals reached Northeast Station. Here, as night fell, Gen. William W. Kirkland's Brigade fought a sharp rear guard action with the Federals while Braxton Bragg's troops struggled to cross the river. The Confederates fired the railroad trestle over the Northeast Cape Fear, and cut loose one end of the pontoon bridge after crossing. Exhausted, the Confederates collapsed on the north bank of the river, their skirmishers sparring with the Federals until well after dark. Before dawn, however, Bragg's weary troops resumed their retreat toward Goldsboro. Though disheartened at the loss of Wilmington, many were glad to leave the region. *"Our campaign in the barren turpentine peninsula [on Federal Point],"* complained Charles G. Elliott, *"was very uncomfortable. Food was scarce, and we all got smutted by lightwood fires."*

Since the fall of Fort Fisher, Hoke's Division and the surviving remnants of the Cape Fear coastal garrisons had escaped relatively unscathed. Their unsuccessful defense of Wilmington was now behind them, and they would live to fight another day. Indeed, that day was close at hand, for the army of William T. Sherman was fast approaching North Carolina. On the day following the fall of Wilmington, Gen. Joseph E. Johnston was assigned to command of all Confederate forces in the Carolinas. In the coming weeks, Johnston's efforts to collect his far-flung resources—including troops under command of Braxton Bragg—would bring together a motley conglomerate of Confederate forces, resulting in a final and desperate confrontation with the enemy. Hoke's Division would not fare as well in the coming campaign as it had on the sandy wastes of Federal Point.

Thus, as Wilmington passed from Confederate hands, it became a major tool in the destruction of the government of its former defenders. This grand seaport—so recently drunk with contraband provisions of every sort—gave the Union a river that was navigable by boat as far inland as Fayetteville, and three rail lines stretching to key points across North Carolina. An interior base for Sherman's army at Goldsboro was now assured, and it was only a matter of time before Schofield's forces united there with Sherman's Grand Army of the West.

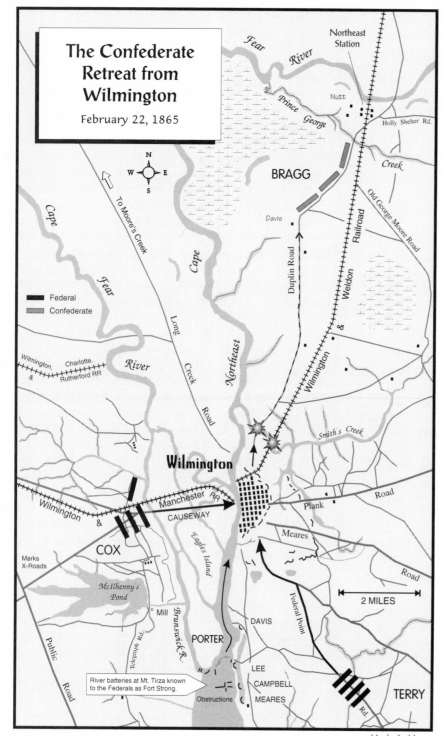

The Confederate Retreat from Wilmington

February 22, 1865

Federal
Confederate

River batteries at Mt. Tirza known to the Federals as Fort Strong.

Mark A. Moore

A Jubilant Liberation

In the confusion of moving thousands of Union prisoners inland from Wilmington, Samuel T. Haviland and a comrade managed to escape from their captors about 20 miles outside the city. After several grueling days of traversing the swampy countryside and dodging enemy picket posts, Haviland—a member of the 15th New York Cavalry—found himself at the bridge near Northeast Station. Hiding from the nearby enemy

the ailing Haviland, a recent inmate at Andersonville, Georgia, had arrived at the Northeast Cape Fear River just as the Confederate army began its retreat toward Goldsboro.

Weak and flushed with relief, the soldier approached a Union sentry at the bridge. The startled guard was shocked by the man's appearance. "*In the name of God what are you?*" he asked in disbelief. "*I was certainly a horrible looking object*," admitted the escapee. Haviland was taken a short distance to General Terry's headquarters, and when it was learned that the man was a Union soldier, "*there was not a dry eye in the crowd*," remembered Haviland. Delirious, the former prisoner came unglued: "*All I could do was laugh. You can imagine how I looked. Six foot one and one-half inches tall; weighing only 114 pounds [down from 200]; had not seen a piece of soap in nine months; my coat and pants hanging in strings; my feet and legs swollen and covered with sores; hair long and matted and beard the same; it was no wonder that I looked scarcely human.*"

The appearance and behavior of the hordes of former Union captives arriving for exchange universally horrified the conquerors of Wilmington. Most had never witnessed in person the effects of wartime prison life on human beings, and the soldiers gazed upon these poor wretches with a mixture of awe and pity. "*They were a hard looking set*," recalled F. B. Sherburne of the 103rd Ohio. "*We hardly knew them.*" Observing the "*walking skeletons*," Joseph Nicely of the same regiment declared that "*I cannot describe . . . my sympathy for them.*"

It was "*the most abject, pitiful mass of humanity the mind could conceive*," explained Dr. C. MacFarlane, "*their faces vacant, cadaverous and staring and their minds gone to the verge of dementia. Their presence haunted you and you wondered if these could be the strong, brave, hardy men who formed our army. But among this pitiful mass were a few strong, well-nourished and intelligent men . . . . and horrible and ghastly were the tales they told.*"

Some of the captives were overjoyed to find themselves reunited with their former commands—units that had just captured Wilmington for the Union. "*The sun shone out from the clouds*," remembered Lt. Freeman S. Bowley of the 30th United States Colored Troops, "*and there, in a beautiful little valley, was the Union flag. How we cheered when we saw it! . . . . A beautiful arch of evergreens had been erected in our honor, and on it were the words, 'Welcome Brothers.'* The young lieutenant arrived to a boisterous welcome from the men of his regiment. With "*happy tears running down my dirty cheeks*," recalled Bowley, the captive found himself in a welcoming embrace, as his former commander planted a kiss squarely upon the visitor's mouth. *"God bless you, old fellow,"* exclaimed the major, *"you are the boy I'm looking for! Your mother will be glad to know of this."* There was a round of hearty hand-shaking and joking between Bowley and the black soldiers of his regiment. *"Why, Carter, I thought I saw you killed at Petersburg!"* quipped the officer to one of the colored soldiers. Amid a chorus of laughter, one comrade retorted that a grape shot had indeed hit the man in the head at Petersburg, but that the projectile had received the worst of the encounter. The subject in question doffed his hat to show a large white scar where the shot had grazed his left temple. The man had been hit four times in combat, including a wrist injury received in the recent engagement at Sugar Loaf on Federal Point.

Later, before the young officer departed for Wilmington and points north, the soldiers of Company H, 30th USCT, tried to see their former lieutenant off in style. They *"would have clothed me in new, clean clothes from their scanty stock,"* Bowley recalled, *"and pressed me to take all the money they had. I could only say, 'Thank you, boys, but in three days I shall be up in old Bay State, and then I can get everything I need. You will need your clothes more than I shall.' God bless their brave and generous hearts, every one of them."*

Between February 26 and March 4, 1865, nearly 10,000 former Union captives arrived in the Wilmington area from points inland to be exchanged. They poured in at a rate of about 1,400 men per day for an entire week. The released prisoners were cared for in a host of camps and hospitals in and around the city, but many of them would die before the war ended in April. A member of the 104th Ohio observed steamers unloading the exchanged captives at the Wilmington waterfront: *"A number of these victims were seen lying dead on the decks [of the vessels] and others are dying. In wretched condition many are being carried away on stretchers, living, half clad skeletons, demented, covered with filth and vermin, men to whom death is a welcome visitor. These prisoners have been confined in Florence [South Carolina] and other prisons and liberated by the rebel authorities on approach of Sherman's army.... After witnessing these victims of rebel atrocity we are again reminded of Sherman's comparison of war with hell and now are almost ready to believe that, after all, the General may have maligned the fiery regions."*

It would be the end of March before the majority of the survivors were well enough for the journey home. The relief efforts also received a setback in mid-March as thousands of civilian refugees—former slaves and disillusioned whites—

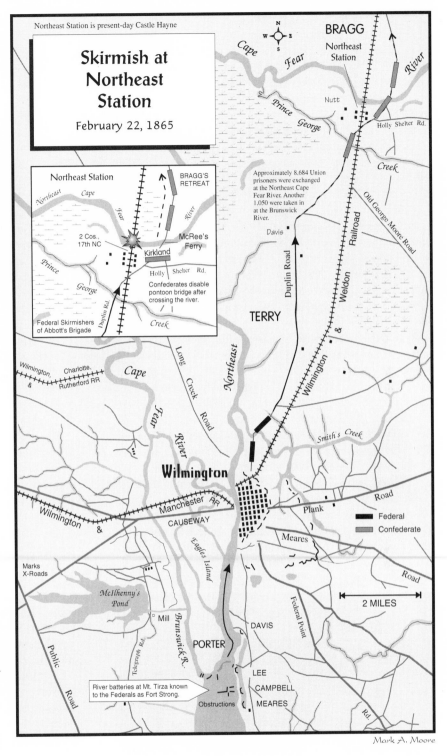

Mark A. Moore

descended upon Wilmington. Like the exchanged prisoners, this horde was a direct result of Sherman's march. The refugees, who had attached themselves to Sherman's columns, had become such a burden to the army's progress that Sherman dispatched them to Wilmington when his army reached Fayetteville on March 11, 1865.

Occupation and Beyond

Like other vanquished towns in the South following the

Civil War, North Carolina's once-active port of Wilmington saw its share of hardship and misery during Reconstruction. Most of the remaining residents, both white and black, were destitute. The great loss of life among white males, together with an exodus from the city as Federal troops approached in February 1865, left few to carry on the business of farming—let alone the revitalization of industry. The state's railroad system lay in shambles, and the labor system was now severely disorganized. Consequently, much of the population was dependent upon Union army commissaries, or hastily assembled outposts of the Freedmen's Bureau, for provisions. It was a trying period of demoralization and economic stagnation.

During the Union occupation, Brig. Gen. Joseph R. Hawley imposed a harsh, "Radical Republican" approach to Reconstruction in Wilmington. The post commandant was satisfied with nothing less than an oath of allegiance to the United States of America. A range of Southern belongings, ranging from food to houses and plantations, were confiscated. Many estates were soon resettled with squatters, or the wronged people who may have once been forced to work at such places. Not surprisingly, citizens who sympathized with the Confederate cause suffered more than others. Many poor whites and disillusioned blacks, however, were granted privileges and were supported in their efforts to obtain work. Though there was little crime in the city, there remained a *"constant danger of a collision between the races"* within the Union army. The white and black units had been segregated during the campaign against Wilmington, but as both converged about the town, there was a palpable racial tension among the ranks.

In May 1865, Salmon P. Chase, Chief Justice of the U.S. Supreme Court, paid a visit to the beleaguered port city. Chase, whose approach to abolishing slavery had been more realistic than moralistic, had served as Secretary of the Treasury under President Abraham Lincoln. He was on a trip to the South to test its political waters, and to provide President Andrew Johnson with facts on which to base his Reconstruction poli-

cies. The Chief Justice, in the company of *Cincinnati Gazette* correspondent Whitelaw Reid and others, was heartily greeted in Wilmington by General Hawley.

Chase was intent upon a reorganization that *"should proceed from the people,"* and contended that President Johnson *"would be grateful to have all loyal citizens participate in this work without reference to complection [sic]."* Though many Union commanders, including William T. Sherman and John M. Schofield, were dubious about immediate political rights for African Americans, the stern-minded Hawley—a journalist and politician before the war—embraced Chase's ideas for Reconstruction. The general took the Chief Justice through town, allowing him to meet various segments of Wilmington society, including its newly freed blacks.

Chase told the new president that, despite its *"old conservatives"* and fence-straddlers who longed for a stable society, the Southern population was showing a hint of a new element of *"progressives"*—citizens who saw a new social order, and supported biracial male suffrage. Though he admitted that the progressives were a distinct minority—and that *"few of the few have heretofore been conspicuous"*—Chase contended that *"in the end, they will control."*

As author Chris Fonvielle has noted, *"there was much suffering in Wilmington, and the road toward and through Reconstruction [was] a long and hard one."* For many, the road beyond proved equally forbidding as jubilation turned to Jim Crow, and another uphill battle was begun.

Through it all, Wilmington has survived and prospered. Recovering from the economic hardships of civil war and Reconstruction, Wilmington once again became a center of commerce, and regained a measure of its former culture. The town's waterfront was once again replete with tall-masted ships, as a large coastwise trade of lumber, naval stores, and cotton was resumed with Europe and the West Indies. By the 1880s Wilmington had regained its status as one of the busiest seaports on the Atlantic coast.

The new prosperity brought a period of growth and expansion that lasted through the early years of the twentieth century. The Second World War saw the return of shipbuilding as an important economic boost to the area, and the 1960s brought new industry to the town.

The roots of historic preservation also took hold in the 1960s, and by 1974 much of the older section of town had been listed in the National Register of Historic Places. Today, Wilmington includes a population of more than 60,000 people, a major university (UNC-Wilmington), fabulous shops and restaurants, and a thriving tourist industry. The city also remains an active seaport.

Preservation efforts are ongoing in a large historic district that covers more than 200 city blocks. Visitors can enjoy horse-drawn carriage or walking tours of historic downtown Wilmington, as well as riverboat cruises and the World War II battleship USS *North Carolina*.

Of particular interest to Civil War enthusiasts, the road network downtown has virtually the same layout as it did during the war, making it easy to identify locations and extant structures—many of which are still in use today. •

The Wilmington Theater (Thalian Hall), where performances were staged for the benefit of exchanged Federal prisoners during the occupation of Wilmington. From *Wilmington: Past, Present, and Future*, 1884.

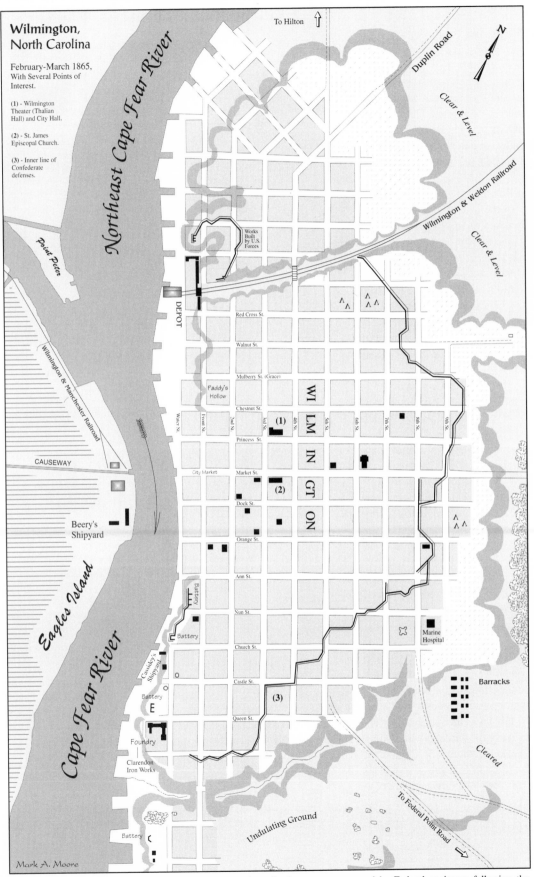

Wilmington,
North Carolina

February-March 1865,
With Several Points of
Interest.

(1) - Wilmington
Theater (Thalian
Hall) and City Hall.

(2) - St. James
Episcopal Church.

(3) - Inner line of
Confederate
defenses.

To Hilton

N

Duplin Road

Clear & Level

Northeast Cape Fear River

Wilmington & Weldon Railroad

Clear & Level

Works
Built
by U.S.
Forces

E

DEPOT

Red Cross St.

Walnut St.

Point Peter

Wilmington & Manchester Railroad

Mulberry St. (Grace)

Paddy's
Hollow

Chestnut St.

Water St.

Front St.

2nd St.

3rd St.

4th St.

5th St.

6th St.

7th St.

8th St.

9th St.

WI
LM
IN
GT
ON

(1)

CAUSEWAY

Princess St.

City Market

Market St.

(2)

Dock St.

Beery's
Shipyard

Orange St.

Eagles Island

Ann St.

Battery

Nun St.

Battery

Marine
Hospital

Church St.

Cassidey's
Shipyard

Battery

Barracks

Cape Fear River

E

Castle St.

(3)

Queen St.

Foundry

Clarendon
Iron Works

Cleared

Battery

C

Undulating Ground

To Federal Point Road

Mark A. Moore

"This city . . . is a nasty dirty hole; it is worse than West Troy or White-hall [New York] . . . .

"The worst sight I ever saw was our paroled prisoners that came in here. There was seven or eight thousand of them, and there was hardly a man of them that could walk. They were starved to death. It was horrible. No man could look at them & then say peace on any terms, but war to the end. We had ought to kill every [Rebel] that we come to for they hant [sic] human beings . . . I had rather Brother would lay where he is [killed in the Crater at Petersburg] than to have met him here in the condition that I met thousands. They are dieing [sic] here in the streets every day . . . . I hope I shall die before any Rebel gets me."
—**Robert Whitcomb**, Quartermaster Sergeant, 169th New York Infantry, to his family, March 7, 1865

"Wilmington is a city of sandy unpaved streets and is found almost deserted by its white inhabitants, they leaving the place in possession of old slaves with their women and children. Smouldering [sic] ruins of buildings, also cotton and other products intended for export are burning for several days after we occupy the city."
—**J. W. Gaskill**, 104th Ohio Infantry

"The country looks like a sandy deser[t], a purty town here tho."
— **Lorenzo W. Holder**, 91st Indiana (Second Division, XXIII Army Corps). Diary entry, February 23, 1865

Wilmington, February-March 1865: Based on a portion of a larger map prepared by Federal engineers following the capture of Wilmington. Note the abbreviated road layout. The original map accompanied an official letter of Col. William J. Twining, Chief Engineer, Department of North Carolina, June 20, 1865. Compare this image with the map on page 2.

CAPTURE

Lessons of the Crimea

In the last half-decade before the War for the Union, military men in America had an opportunity to study modern war on the largest scale, consider the role of new weapons and technologies, and profit from the intensive combat experience of major European armies. Only simpletons would have ignored such an opportunity and yet, despite the fact that hostilities in the Crimea ended only six years before Fort Sumter was fired on, Civil War historians have persisted in stressing the unique nature of the conflict, and have largely ignored the Crimean War (1854-1856).

The Crimea is the missing link in Civil War history—the conflict that connects the War for the Union with the Napoleonic era. In the Crimea important new technologies were used for the first time, from rifled muskets and cannon to submarines, submarine mines, armoured warships, the electric telegraph (connecting London and Paris with Balaklava), and the construction of the first tactical railway. Mark Moore has used this re-examination of the Fort Fisher campaign to demonstrate the importance of the Crimean War as the most recent conflict between major powers, and a key stage in the development of the modern earthwork fortification—largely the work of Russian engineer Franz Todleben.

Among the American officers to visit the Crimea in 1855-56 were George B. McClellan and David Dixon Porter. McClellan consciously repeated aspects of the Anglo-French attack on Sebastopol in his Peninsula Campaign of 1862, while Porter pressed Admiral David Farragut to employ mortar boats at New Orleans, citing his experience at Kinburn. Both men cited Crimean examples to justify or enhance their actions.

Every officer and politician in the United States had the opportunity to profit from the Crimean War through the Delafield Report, *The Art of War in Europe*, published by the government in 1860 and dedicated to the Secretary of War, Jefferson Davis. No aspiring officer, professional or amateur, could have ignored this key text, or its wealth of high quality drawings, plans, and maps. Similarly, Mark Moore has placed us all in his debt with his skilled cartography and clear exposition of the last great example of naval power projection in the American Civil War.

Just as in the Crimean War, this was a conflict in which the overwhelming naval power of one side was applied to the land, forcing the Confederates—like the Russians before them—to invest in massive earthworks, which owed so much to Todleben and the Malakoff bastion. After all, it was the glorious performance of the French army in taking the Malakoff that helps explain why some members of the armies went to war in French style uniforms! There can be no more sincere praise than imitation. The lessons of the Crimea were well known in America, as Mark Moore has shown.

Andrew D. Lambert
Department of War Studies
King's College, London
March 31, 1999

Fort Fisher and Sebastopol:
A Handful of Men and a Fight to the Death

A Comparative Analysis of the Capture of the South's Largest Earthen Fortification, and the Fall of Sebastopol during the Crimean War.

William Lamb, the Malakoff, and the Viability of Fort Fisher

"When Sebastopol has been demolished and the fleets of the Czar destroyed or taken in its harbours, the Black Sea will cease at once to be a Russian lake, Constantinople will be relieved from danger, the mouths of the Danube will be secure, and all the apprehensions entertained of Russian encroachment in the Mediterranean—that is to say, in the direction most alarming to Europe—will vanish at once and altogether . . . . But can Sebastopol be destroyed? We can only say that, if it cannot, it must resemble no other fortress under the sun." —*The Times*, London, August 7, 1854

Appendix A

William Lamb, the Malakoff, and the Viability of Fort Fisher

Born to a life of privilege and affluence in Norfolk, Virginia, on September 7, 1835, William Lamb received a gentleman's education. The boy was instilled with deep religious faith and an abiding love for books, and Lamb spent many youthful hours immersed in military biographies and other histories. He also enjoyed the fiction of Nathaniel Hawthorne and other novelists. By the time he entered the College of William and Mary in Williamsburg, the young student had experienced a strong primary program, a Connecticut prep school and the Rappahannock Military Academy.

At William and Mary Lamb studied the classics, history, and biography—and graduated Phi Beta Kappa in 1855 with a degree in law. At the tender age of 19, the new graduate found himself too young to practice his chosen profession.[1]

By August 1855, the city of Norfolk had fallen under the ravages of a severe yellow fever epidemic, and its citizens began dying by the hundreds. To escape the dread disease, Lamb and his family traveled to the North and settled temporarily in Orange, New Jersey. From here young Lamb ventured to stay at various points nearby, including Newark, Elizabethport, and New York City. His hours here were ones of leisure, and he attended the theater, read books, enjoyed the sights of the city, and took walks with family and friends. The pleasant surroundings and cordial company, however, were tempered with distressing news from home. All through September the local papers brought the sad tidings of famine, pestilence, and death from tidewater Virginia. Family and friends were stricken with yellow fever at an alarming rate, and Lamb wept openly when the family's longtime servant, Daniel Grimes, fell victim to the illness. *"My first manly tears were shed today,"* he mourned on the 16th, *"on hearing [of] the death of this noble slave."*[2]

The family soon took up residence at the City Hotel in Newark, where Lamb fell into despondency and boredom—"ennui," as he termed it. To pass the time he devoured the memoirs of James Gordon Bennett, founder of the *New York Herald* newspaper. Lamb's father was a friend of Bennett's, and the new college graduate—himself a future journalist—took great interest in the man's life. *"I am very much pleased with the work,"* Lamb scrawled in his diary, *"& think every journalist & Statesman, should read it."*[3]

While the Lamb family waited for disease to abate back home, a bitter, faraway war was being waged against Russia by Great Britain, France, and their allies. The conflict caught Lamb's attention, and fueled his interest in military matters. Perhaps news of the war brought a welcome diversion from the list of yellow fever casualties coming in daily from Norfolk. *"I bought a map of the seat of War today,"* he noted on September 21. *"It is about the best I have seen."*[4]

On September 27, Lamb read of the fall of the great Russian fortress of Sebastopol, and he lamented the outcome. *"What*

wholesale slaughter. And all for what?" The following day he noted that *"Sebastopol is taken. At last the press groan to day [sic] with this (to my Russian sympathizing heart) bad news."* Even at this early age, Lamb's opinions—whether about acquaintances or events in the news—were firm and unforgiving.[5]

A host of family and friends called on the family at the City Hotel in Newark. William Lamb was anxious to return home to Norfolk, and his patience was thin. *"I have become very well acquainted with an old conceited Englishman named Grimsby,"* he explained early that October. *"He is very talkative & but for my having nothing better to do, than listen to his verbose conversation, I would vote him a bore."* The British friend, however, soon introduced a subject more to the boy's liking: *"Tonight Mr. Grimsby presented me with a beautiful little map of the Crimea [site of the recent war] & adjacent country. It is exquisitely engraved, & is certainly something neat. It has made his conversation 10 pr cent [sic] better, yea, improved it as much, as mustard does the cold meat we have saved from dinner & served at supper, at this Hotel."*[6]

Bored with his recent choice of books—he disparaged *Fashion and Famine* by the author Ann Stevens—Lamb became more enthralled with the local newspapers, and yearned to make his own difference through words. *"The more I read the Daily papers,"* he declared, *"so much the more I long to be a Journalist. I feel and see the influence of the Press, & long to exert an influence through its means."* Lamb soon turned to Shakespeare for better reading material—*Hamlet* and *King Lear*. He was quite taken with the theater, and a performance of *Hamlet* on October 8 gave him *"an indescribable glow of enthusiasm."*[7]

Lamb followed politics closely in the papers. *"The people of the North seem considerably stirred up on the Kansas Question, on the great question, Whether Kansas will be a slave state or a free state . . . . No doubt the Union will be dissolved half a dozen times during the next few years by the abolitionists,"* he predicted, *"but such a dissolution as the fire eaters of the south have always brought about—all smoke."* When not engaged in books, the papers, or the theater, William Lamb engaged those around him. He chided his English friend Grimsby, finding him an *"obstinate old fellow . . . . So thorough, that he won't own the English were whipped at New Orleans in the war of [18]12."*[8]

Throughout the month of October 1855, Lamb—fueled by his interest in journalism—continued to comment on the daily news. *"Sebastopol is to be blown up,"* he noted on the 18th. *"The Russians have been defeated in a Cavalry battle near Eupatoria [in the Crimea]. A money crisis is about to arise in England. Look out for a blow up!"*[9]

In late October Lamb journeyed to Providence, Rhode Island, with a letter of introduction to a family named Chaffee. He was soon introduced to the family's young daughter, Sarah—*"a charming girl who was very kind and attentive to me, as was her Mother."* Lamb was touched by the generous hospitality of the Chaffee family, and left refreshed after a week's visit. Upon his return to Newark, he found his family preparing to return to Virginia. The cold fall weather had finally checked the yellow fever epidemic. On November 14, with the Chaffee family there to see him off, Lamb left Newark and sailed from New York for Norfolk. As a parting gift, Sarah Chaffee had presented her new friend William with Henry Wadsworth Longfellow's *Song of Hiawatha*.[10]

Lamb was elated to be back in his disease-ravaged hometown. "*As we came up to the wharf,*" he recalled, "*a negro hackman yelled out, 'Sebastopol's done taken, but there's a few of us left.' Our servants were delighted to see us.*" His days in exile up North had been a time of sadness and frustration for Lamb, and he was eager to begin a career of his own.[11]

Lamb's father, a well-to-do attorney and three-term mayor of Norfolk, soon purchased for his son a half-interest in a fiery secessionist newspaper known as the *Southern Daily Argus*—a paper Lamb had followed during his extended visit to the North. At the age of 20, Lamb became a newspaper editor, and began his wished-for career in journalism. Influenced by his father and the "message" of the *Argus*, Lamb emerged as a

College of William and Mary

Fort Fisher's commander and chief engineer, Col. William Lamb, in later life.

staunch and outspoken Democrat. The paper denounced a perceived undue influence of the federal government, as well as a troublesome new political entity—the Republican Party. The young editor engaged in local politics, and regardless of his ill feelings toward northern politicians, Lamb married his lovely Yankee friend, Sarah Anne Chafee, in 1857. Though the new Mrs. Lamb hailed from Providence, Rhode Island, she loved the South and would soon devote herself to its cause.[12]

Exercising his interest in military matters, Lamb helped organize a militia company called the Woodis Rifles in 1858, and was soon elected its captain. By 1859, the storm clouds of civil war were gathering in earnest. A radical abolitionist named John Brown led an unsuccessful attack on the U.S. arsenal and armory at Harper's Ferry, and Captain Lamb, as an officer in the state guard, was present at Brown's public execution that December. The following year, an obscure Republican named Abraham Lincoln was elected to the presidency of the United States, hastening the country toward armed rebellion. Following the states of the Deep South, Lamb's native Virginia seceded from the Union—the "*ties which now link together the North and the South must be sundered,*" the *Argus* had predicted—and the youthful officer saw his first military action when the Woodis Rifles engaged in a skirmish at Sewell's Point on Hampton Roads. When his company mustered in as part of the 6th Virginia Infantry, Lamb was promoted and reassigned to Wilmington, North Carolina, as chief quartermaster for the District of the Cape Fear. He arrived in the port city in early October 1861. After serving briefly on the staff of Brig. Gen. Joseph R. Anderson, Major Lamb found himself in command of a fledgling defensive post on the west bank of the Cape Fear River, 15 miles south of Wilmington.[13]

When William Lamb assumed command of the defenses at Brunswick Town, the affable and optimistic major had little combat or command experience. Lamb's natural ability and competence, however, got him elected colonel of the 36th North Carolina Regiment in May 1862. It was here, as he began to strengthen the area's largest interior defensive structure, that the volunteer officer began to show aptitude for military engineering. Lamb's true genius would soon emerge.

On a paymaster's trip to Charleston, South Carolina, in December 1861, Lamb had purchased a book on the Crimean War—a conflict over territory in Europe and Asia that had ended just a few years before hostilities erupted in America, a conflict whose headlines Lamb had followed six years earlier while in New Jersey and New York.[14]

This volume would help sow the seeds of design for the South's most powerful defensive bastion, soon to be commanded by the newly promoted colonel. A knowledge-hungry Lamb immersed himself in the science of heavy siege fortifications. His readings no doubt schooled Lamb on a besieged Russian city that was able to fend off its allied enemies for nearly a year, along the heavily fortified naval base of Sebastopol on the Crimean Peninsula. Absorbing the principles of fort architecture, Lamb was profoundly intrigued by the Sebastopol defenses, including the city's key position: the White Tower—an earthwork-enhanced structure of stone known as the Malakoff. Lamb's quest to strengthen Fort Fisher to similar

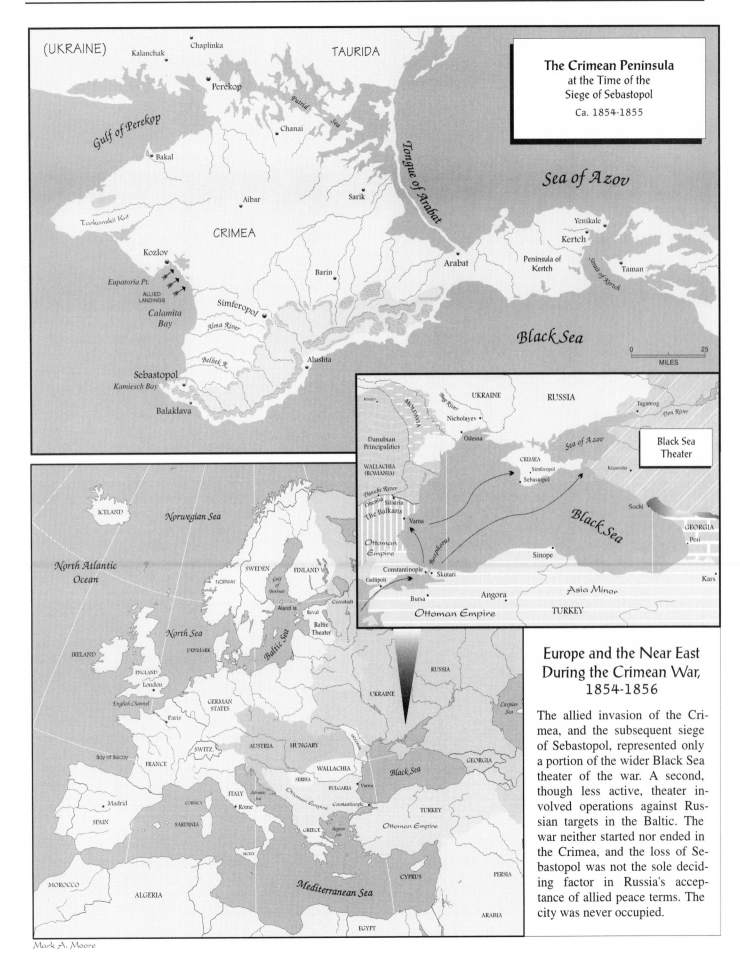

The Crimean Peninsula
at the Time of the
Siege of Sebastopol

Ca. 1854-1855

Europe and the Near East During the Crimean War, 1854-1856

The allied invasion of the Crimea, and the subsequent siege of Sebastopol, represented only a portion of the wider Black Sea theater of the war. A second, though less active, theater involved operations against Russian targets in the Baltic. The war neither started nor ended in the Crimea, and the loss of Sebastopol was not the sole deciding factor in Russia's acceptance of allied peace terms. The city was never occupied.

Mark A. Moore

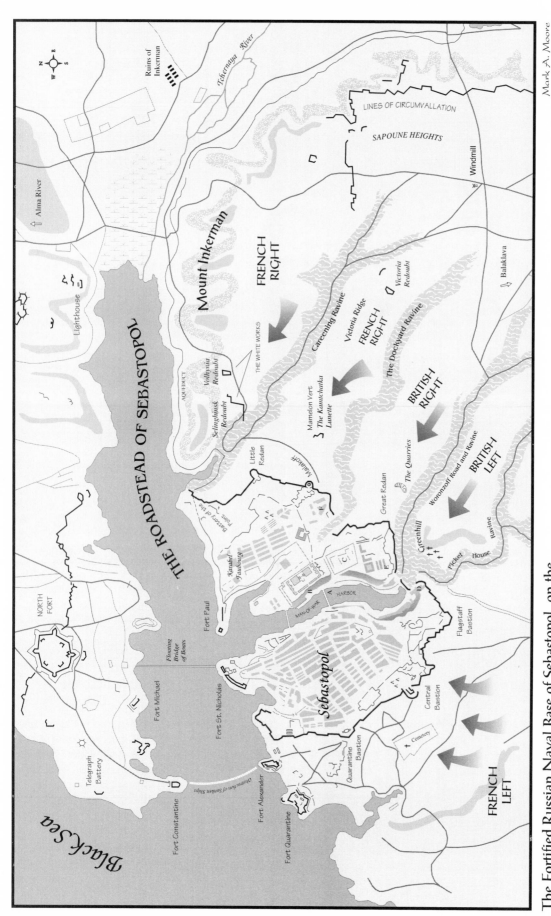

The Fortified Russian Naval Base of Sebastopol, on the
Crimean Peninsula (Ukraine), Ca. 1855

Mark A. Moore

(A) The Bridge of Boats — (B) Barracks — (C) Hospital — (D) Garden Battery — (E) Barrack Battery — (F) Gervais Battery

William Lamb gained inspiration for the construction of Fort Fisher from Frants E. I. Todleben's defensive works at Sebastopol.

"I heard to night [sic] by the evening paper, that Sebastopol had fallen, that the French had lost 15,000, the English 2,000 & the Russians about 15,000. What wholesale slaughter. And all for what? . . . Sebastopol is taken. At last the press groan to day [sic] with this (to my Russian sympathising heart) bad news."
—**William Lamb**, age 20; diary entries from Newark, New Jersey and New York City, September 1855.

proportions would not be the only comparison between the South's "Gibraltar" and the famed Russian fortress at Sebastopol.[15]

The War in the Crimea

In 1853, as militant Russia encroached upon a weakening Ottoman Empire, the Turks declared war against the regime of Czar Nicholas I. At issue was the czar's claim to protection of Orthodox Christian subjects in the Ottoman Porte. The Turkish Sultan rejected the czar's claim, and Ottoman forces opened the conflict in the Balkans by defeating the invading Russians at Oltenita along the Danube River that November. Czar Nicholas quickly retaliated by sending a fleet of warships across the Black Sea, where Russian vessels destroyed a small Turkish flotilla and the shore installations in the harbor of Sinope. Angered by the czar's aggression, and concerned over their own shipping interests in the area, England and France sent their fleets to the Black Sea region to protect Turkish shipping.

Early in 1854, Russian forces swarmed across the Danube from occupied Wallachia (now Romania). On the south bank, in what is now northeastern Bulgaria, the minions of Nicholas I lay siege to the Ottoman fortress of Silistria. The stubborn Turks managed to hold their position, inflicting about 10,000 casualties upon the invaders. The siege was abandoned that summer; but when Russia refused to withdraw from the Danubian Principalities, England and France—two nations capable of fielding the most powerful military forces in the world—joined the war in alliance with the Turks. Great Britain had an interest in upholding the *status quo* in the Near East, and feared that Nicholas I had aggressive designs on Constantinople, the "second Rome"—a city long desired by Russian rulers as a gateway to the Mediterranean. Thus England was obliged to support Turkey, and gained France as a consequential ally. The French government, which had seen its own standoff with Russia over Christian shrines in Palestine, was eager to restore itself as a dominant force in world politics following the setbacks of the Napoleonic era. Using the crisis with the czar to secure a British alliance, France hoped for an opportunity to call a European Congress to redraw the national boundaries of Europe.

With the exception of two British-French expeditions against Russia in the Baltic theater in 1854 and 1855, the primary focus of the war shifted to the Crimean Peninsula. Here the allied forces directed all of their efforts against the Russian fleet's base of operations at Sebastopol, on the southwestern tip of the peninsula.[16]

THE ALLIED INVASION

In mid-September 1854 the allied armies, some 50,000 strong, landed unopposed at Calamita Bay on the western coast of the Crimea. A few days later the forces began their march on the port of Sebastopol, 30 miles to the south. The terrain was difficult, and the armies had to negotiate a number of streams that ran westward to the Black Sea from interior regions of the lower peninsula. On September 20, as the allies reached the Alma River, they found the way blocked by a large Russian army under Alexandr Menshikov, drawn up on the heights to the south.

In order to keep contact with the allied fleet as it moved toward Sebastopol, and lacking sufficient cavalry for an inland flanking maneuver, the French and British armies forced a passage at the Alma. Marshal Armand St. Arnaud's Frenchmen, and the British forces of Gen. Lord Raglan (Fitzroy Somerset)—an officer in his first battle since Waterloo—pitched into the entrenched Russian position. Foreshadowing the butchery of the American Civil War, this engagement wrought the carnage inherent in fighting modern wars in the tactics and dress of the Napoleonic era. Armed with superior rifled muskets, which fired the new Minié bullet, allied troops slaughtered the ill equipped and poorly commanded Russians, who fell back in disorder on Sebastopol. The battle cost both sides more than 9,000 casualties.[17]

THE SEBASTOPOL DEFENSES

Lord Raglan was eager to pursue the defeated Russians after the allied victory at the Alma, but the ill and cautious St. Arnaud refused. Rather than investing the city from the north, the allies instead moved around to the south, skirting the town and establishing supply bases at the port of Balaklava and Kameisch Bay. Heavy siege guns and ammunition were soon landed, and the allies laid siege to Sebastopol. The English and French fleets also moved down to blockade the harbor and trap the Russian fleet within.[18]

While the allies were bogged down in preparing for the siege, a young military engineering genius, Frants E. I. Todleben, set out to modernize the city's long-standing defenses. Calling upon human and artillery resources far greater than those of the allies, Todleben oversaw the construction of an intricate series of well-designed batteries, earthworks, and defensive curtains. As early as September 27, the famed British war correspondent William Howard Russell—who would soon horrify the home front of a nation at war with details of horrendous casualties, disease, and command incompetence—observed a noticeable improvement in the defenses. "*A round tower of white stone,*" he predicted, "*on an eminence, over the extremity of the harbour, promises to be very troublesome.*" Having lost the element of surprise, the forces of Britain and France were in for a long struggle.[19]

The city's main defenses lay sprawled in a large arc, covering Sebastopol proper and the suburb of Karabel to the east. A series of forts guarded the northern and southern banks of the harbor. The key positions lay along the southeastern perimeter, a defensive wall marked by four major installations: the Great Redan, the Malakoff, the Little Redan, and the Battery of the Point. This line guarded the Karabel suburb, home of the important Russian dockyard and barracks. Most believed that the fall of the Round Tower of Malakoff would bring about the city's demise, but Todleben himself felt that the loss of other key positions, such as the Great Redan, might hasten the same result.[20]

Under Todleben's direction, the defenses soon grew to formidable proportions. The empty spaces between the main defensive structures were enclosed with heavy batteries and sand curtains. The whole of the town's population, it seemed, turned out to aid the construction efforts, as children pushed wheelbarrows and women carried earth in their aprons. The impressment of Cossacks and convicts lent a more bizarre element to the defense force.[21]

The works quickly materialized from simple earthen structures to stout breastworks and embrasures, revetted with gabions (cylinders of wickerwork filled with earth) and fascines (large bundles of sticks bound together). If defensive positions were not strengthened, new ones were erected elsewhere, and many of the embrasures and angles of fire were constantly changed to meet the latest threats from the besieging allies. A vast network of casemates and bombproofs, covered with ship timbers and rigging, provided shelter for the defenders. Each of the Russian battery commanders had explicit instructions regarding directions of fire and guns to be used, and the defensive stations could communicate with others by means of a signal system. *"All these arrangements,"* noted a Polish defector from the Russian army, *"emanated from Todleben."*[22]

By far the largest of the defensive structures was the incredible network of earthen walls surrounding the Malakoff. Alexander W. Kinglake observed that this simple white tower *"was fast losing its height from the ground, for already the summit of the knoll where it stood had been so changed in shape . . . that it now closed high up round the centre or waist of the building, and had not only begun to take the form of a glacis annexed to the original work, but was also the site of a new semicircular battery, which covered the front of the tower. This last battery was connected by entrenchments with the other new works thrown up on both flanks of the Malakoff."*[23]

As Billy Russell would later note, it was not the stone tower itself that was important, for that edifice was soon knocked to pieces by allied artillery fire. *"The solid mass of stone of which the Malakoff Tower consisted,"* observed the correspondent, *"was smashed, rent up, and split from top to bottom at our very first day's fire. It is now a heap of ruins [but] the earthwork beneath is as firm as it was the very first day we fired at it . . . . The observation of this siege ought to produce an immense effect on fortifications, for it has been demonstrated, one would think, that earthworks properly constructed are far better perhaps than any masonry."*[24]

By the time the allies were ready to begin pounding the city with artillery fire, Todleben's defenses were more than equal to the task of weathering the storm. Moreover, the garrison, composed largely of sailors and marines, had received a large reinforcement of troops from the Russian field army.[25]

THE SIEGE

As the besieging armies settled in below Sebastopol, a cholera epidemic ravaged the British army. Hoping for a quick reduction of the city, the allies opened their first bombardment on October 17, 1854. A week-long cannonade, however, ended with less than expected results. *"Rome was not built in a day,"* lamented Russell, *"nor will Sebastopol be taken in a week . . . we have run away with the notion that it was a kind of paste-board city, which would tumble down at the sound of our cannon as the walls of Jericho fell at the blast of Joshua's trumpet."*[26]

To complicate matters, Prince Menshikov's field army introduced to the allies the vulnerability of the rear and flanks of their position before Sebastopol. On October 25, the Russian commander-in-chief launched a sortie from the Crimean interior with about 25,000 men, moving on the British base at Balaklava in an attempt to break the siege. The attack was beaten off by allied forces in rear of the siege lines; but the engagement gave history the Charge of the Light Brigade, one of the costliest and least consequential actions of the Crimean theater. More importantly, the battle briefly disrupted the siege of Sebastopol.[27]

Eleven days later, on the mist-shrouded morning of November 5, the Russians again struck the allied flank in force. This time the assault came on the right—along the valley of Inkerman—and unlike the sortie at Balaklava, it was a furious, all-out effort to drive the allies into the sea. Along the Tchernaya River the Russians, with 35,000 men (supported by another 22,000) and a heavy complement of artillery, struck the British right flank near Inkerman. Lord Raglan's forces prevailed with the aid of the French, but the contest was savage, and superior allied firepower told severely upon the attackers. Though there were pockets of confusion and hand-to-hand fighting, allied rifles were able to cut down the Russian columns from distances that precluded successful return fire from antiquated enemy muskets. Menshikov's forces absorbed a staggering 12,000 casualties, while British and French losses numbered about 3,500 men.[28]

The battles of Balaklava and Inkerman were harsh lessons for Lord Raglan and French commander François Canrobert (who had taken over after the death of St. Arnaud). Sebastopol was never completely surrounded by the allies. The north side of the harbor was wide open, and the city could be reinforced at will with troops or supplies by the main Russian army, which lay inland near Simferopol. Enemy troops could move from the city, or from interior regions, by way of the Tchernaya River to menace the rear of the allied siege lines. Menshikov's link between the field army and the fortress of Sebastopol would help keep the allies out of the city for nine long months.[29]

England and France were thus forced to fight a campaign of attrition, while dangling precariously at the end of a 3,000-mile-long supply line. The weather began to deteriorate by mid-November 1854, and the brutal Crimean winter that followed nearly destroyed the British army. A breakdown in logistics and lack of British resourcefulness made for severe hardships. The Russians fared little better, while the French, hardened from years of campaigning in North Africa, were less affected.[30]

When the weather improved early in 1855, the allies prepared to resume the siege. The French increased their presence in the Crimea to three times the British force, and took over the extreme right of the siege lines, a position that put them in front of the Malakoff and its outworks. Various attacks and sorties ebbed back and forth along the opposing lines, and the allied bombardment was resumed in April. That same month brought a new ally when the Kingdom of Sardinia joined the

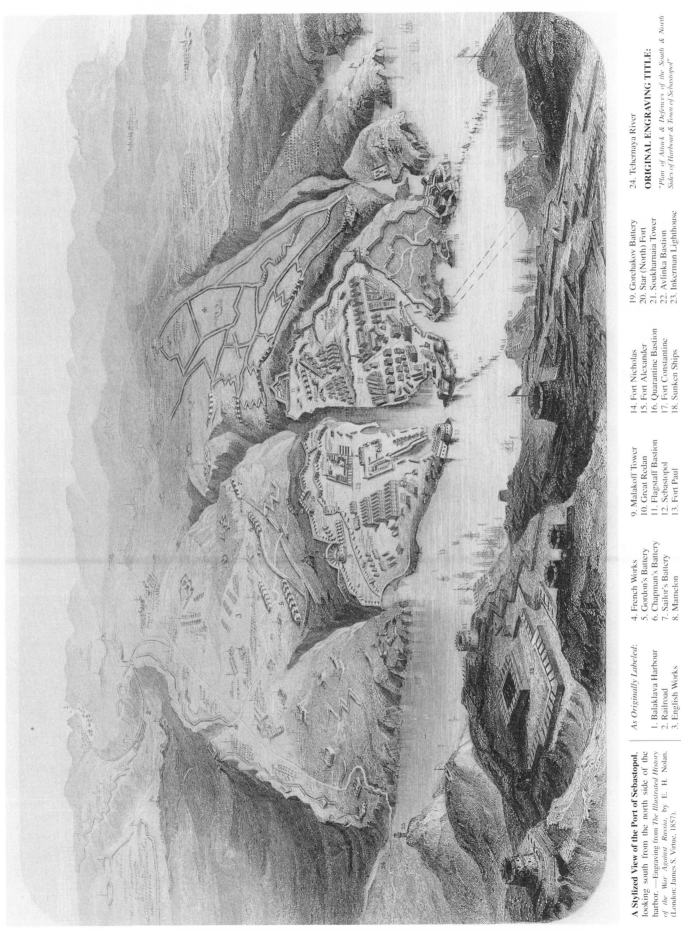

A Stylized View of the Port of Sebastopol, looking south from the north side of the harbor. —Engraving from *The Illustrated History of the War Against Russia,* by E. H. Nolan. (London: James S. Virtue, 1857).

As Originally Labeled:

1. Balaklava Harbour
2. Railroad
3. English Works
4. French Works
5. Gordon's Battery
6. Chapman's Battery
7. Sailor's Battery
8. Mamelon
9. Malakoff Tower
10. Great Redan
11. Flagstaff Bastion
12. Sebastopol
13. Fort Paul
14. Fort Nicholas
15. Fort Alexander
16. Quarantine Bastion
17. Fort Constantine
18. Sunken Ships
19. Gorchakov Battery
20. Star (North) Fort
21. Soukharnaia Tower
22. Avlinka Bastion
23. Inkerman Lighthouse
24. Tchernaya River

ORIGINAL ENGRAVING TITLE:

"Plan of Attack & Defences of the South & North Sides of Harbour & Town of Sebastopol"

APPENDIX A—Fort Fisher-Sebastopol

French Soldiers Storm the Malakoff, September 8, 1855. Note the flashy Zouave uniforms. Some American soldiers would adopt a similar mode of dress in the early stages of the Civil War.

Engraving from *The Illustrated History of the War Against Russia*, by E. H. Nolan, (London: James S. Virtue, 1857).

war against Russia, sending 15,000 men to the Crimea.[31]

May 1855, however, brought the turning point the allies desperately needed. After an abortive first attempt, a British-French expedition to Kertch, on the eastern shore of the Crimea, captured the straits into the Sea of Azov. Along with the amphibious assault at Kertch, a small squadron of allied gunboats penetrated into the Azov. The Russians quickly burned their forts in the area and retreated, leaving the allies control of the straits, as well as the freedom to blockade the Sea of Azov. This feat dealt a crippling blow to Russian logistics, which depended entirely upon waterborne transportation to bring supplies from the River Don into the Crimea. The forage depots around the Azov, its fisheries, and the flour mills at Kertch were all soon lost to the allies. The Russian position in the Crimea was thus rendered untenable, and Menshikov's field army—once able to hover about the allied right flank before Sebastopol—was severely restricted by lack of forage. Control of the Azov would ultimately seal the fate of the great Russian fortress.[32]

With the threat posed by the Russian field army significantly diminished, the allies were able to concentrate on taking Sebastopol. In June, British and French forces opened a third major bombardment of the city, and launched a successful attack upon the Russian outworks in front of the southeastern defensive perimeter. The British captured enemy works at the Quarries, while French troops stormed and took the Mamelon, a strong Russian lunette on a hill in front of the Malakoff. Slowly, the allied siege lines were creeping closer and closer to the main Russian line.

But the defenders of Sebastopol would not give up quietly. A fourth bombardment and an attack on the main Russian line on June 17-18, ended in disaster for the allies. British forces were repulsed with severe loss in front of the Great Redan, while the French suffered a similar fate before the Malakoff. The defensive lines were well manned, and the Russians fought furiously. "*Their parapets were lined with a triple rank of men,*" remembered a Frenchman in the 2nd Zouaves, "*who kept up a murderous file-fire upon our defenceless columns . . . . to advance in the teeth of such a terrible cross-fire, as that with which the enemy raked all the ground in front of their works, seemed downright madness.*" The 2nd Zouave Regiment was nearly annihilated in the fighting of the 18th, "*reduced to a perfect skeleton.*"[33]

THE FALL OF SEBASTOPOL

In August, the Russian field army, wasting away under the allied blockade of the Sea of Azov, staged a last desperate scheme to break the siege. But when two assault columns, under Prince Mikhail Gorchakov, attempted a crossing of the Traktir Bridge on the Tchernaya River, they were slaughtered by French and Sardinian troops. Gorchakov's forces suffered at least 10,000 casualties, with no positive result, and the Russian field army was repulsed for the third and final time. In this last great battle in the Crimean theater, the Russians were unable to prevent the fall of Sebastopol. The engineer Todleben was ordered to prepare for an orderly evacuation of the city,

and late in August a floating bridge of boats was built across the harbor to its northern shore.[34]

After the Battle of the Tchernaya, the allies once again prepared to storm Sebastopol. Heavy bombardments covered the advance units, as the French and British siege lines were pushed ever closer to the main Russian defensive wall. The rain of allied artillery fire upon the city was incessant. Finally, on September 8, 1855, the French made a mad dash on the Malakoff from their advance line, which by that time lay a scant 60 feet from the storied Russian bastion. The timing was perfect, for the enemy defenders were in the process of handing the station over to their relief. Within just a few minutes the French tricolor was flapping over the ramparts of the Malakoff, and the long-standing defenses were breached at last. Once they got in, the French troops "*threw open a passage to their own rear,*" observed Russell, "*and closed up the front and the lateral communications with the curtains leading to the Great Redan and the Little Redan. Thus they were able to pour in their supports . . . and to resist the efforts of the Russians, which were desperate and repeated, to retake the place.*" The British supporting attack on the Great Redan was punished unmercifully, as was the French advance against the Little Redan; but the Russians were unable to reclaim the Malakoff from the swarming and triumphant Frenchmen. The fate of the city had been decided.[35]

The Russian garrison soon retreated to the northern shore of the harbor and erected a series of batteries that commanded the city from the north. This precluded the allies from safely occupying Sebastopol, and the two sides frowned at one another across the harbor until the war officially ended in March 1856. The Crimean War, so named for its most active theater of operations, was successful in checking Russian designs on southeastern Europe and the Mediterranean, but it merely delayed the collapse of the Ottoman Empire.[36]

A Comparison

Much has been said of the likeness between the Malakoff and the American Civil War's Fort Fisher. Colonel William Lamb professed a fascination with the famed Russian bastion, and in truth was greatly influenced by the Sebastopol defenses in strengthening the South's largest fort. When the Confederate stronghold itself fell to a powerful combined force of the enemy, its captors then sang the fort's praises with lofty comparisons to the great fortress of Malakoff. Lamb, on the one hand, strove for a physical similarity between the two defensive works. The Federal conquerors, on the other, were quick to boast that their prize was stronger by far than the great Tower of Malakoff.[37]

The physical similarities are plainly discernible. In rear of the "*inglorious stump*" of the Round Tower, noted the correspondent Billy Russell, "*there is a perfect miracle of engineering. It is impossible to speak too highly of the apparent solidity, workmanship, and finish of the lines of formidable earthworks, armed with about [sixty] heavy guns, which the Russians have thrown up to enfilade our attack, and to defend*

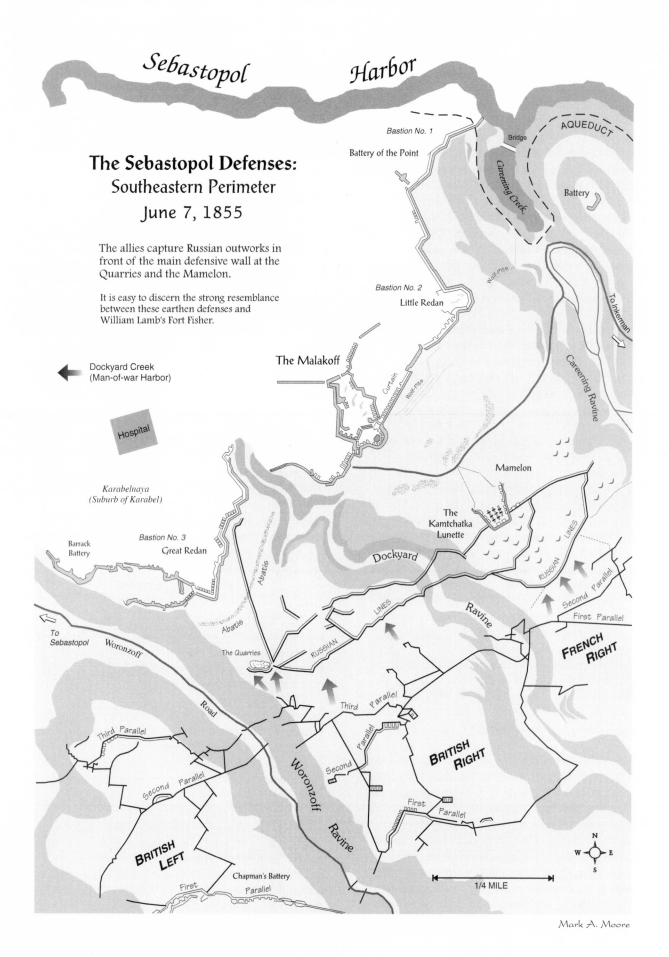

The Sebastopol Defenses:
Southeastern Perimeter
June 7, 1855

The allies capture Russian outworks in
front of the main defensive wall at the
Quarries and the Mamelon.

It is easy to discern the strong resemblance
between these earthen defenses and
William Lamb's Fort Fisher.

Sebastopol Harbor

Bastion No. 1

Battery of the Point

Bridge

AQUEDUCT

Careening Creek

Battery

Bastion No. 2
Little Redan

Wolf-Pits

To Inkerman

Careening Ravine

The Malakoff

Curtain

Wolf-Pits

Mamelon

Dockyard Creek
(Man-of-war Harbor)

Hospital

Karabelnaya
(Suburb of Karabel)

The
Kamtchatka
Lunette

RUSSIAN LINES

Second Parallel

First Parallel

Barrack
Battery

Bastion No. 3
Great Redan

Abatis

Dockyard

LINES

Ravine

FRENCH
RIGHT

Abatis

RUSSIAN

To
Sebastopol   Woronzoff

The Quarries

Third Parallel

Third Parallel

Road

Second Parallel

Woronzoff

Second

Ravine

First
Parallel

BRITISH
RIGHT

BRITISH
LEFT

First

Chapman's Battery

Parallel

1/4 MILE

N
W   E
S

Mark A. Moore

this position . . . the key to their works in front of us." These massive works were on a scale similar to Fort Fisher's Land Face and Northeast Bastion. "*The traverses are so high and deep,*" continued Russell, "*that it is almost impossible to get a view of the whole of the Malakoff from any one spot.*" Surgeon J. A. Mowris, of the 117th New York Infantry, observed a similar scene on the Federal Point peninsula: "*Fort Fisher presented a bold and heavy relief of sand bank . . . arranged in an irregular curve; from without, presenting a succession of heavy guns, separated by broad traverses, the tops of which were so regularly formed as to appear, in the distance, not unlike a row of large hay cocks.*" William Lamb, through his own study and advice from superiors, fellow officers, and engineers, had fashioned a formidable defensive work on a physical par with the great bastions of Todleben's design.[38]

Like the Sebastopol defenses, the main batteries at Fort Fisher were connected by long and formidable sand curtains. The Great Redan, Malakoff, and Little Redan each, in some way, resembled Lamb's own Northeast Bastion. Indeed, Maj. William J. Saunders, Fisher's Chief of Artillery during both attacks on the fort, and Colonel Lamb both made reference to the Northeast Bastion in some official correspondence as the "redan" or "redan battery."[39]

While Fisher lacked the extensive outworks that stretched before Sebastopol's southeastern perimeter, it did have a long row of palisades, not unlike the abatis which blocked the British approach to the Great Redan. Lamb's fort also employed a deadly sub-terra minefield, engaged by a galvanic firing apparatus which was disabled by the detonation of heavy ordnance from the Federal fleet.[40]

Both defensive structures were framed with heavy timbers, and each made use of a system of covered bombproofs and passages. While the Sebastopol lines were intricately revetted with anything from empty tin powder cases to numerous gabions and fascines, Fort Fisher's Land Face batteries and parapet were revetted with wooden planking. Interestingly, the interior sides of Fisher's Sea Face installations—at least along the Columbiad Battery—were lined with brick.[41]

Fort Fisher and the Malakoff differed in one important respect. Fisher was a two-sided work, shaped like the number "7," with one side commanding the ocean and inlet into the Cape Fear River, and the other covering the land approaches to the north. The Malakoff, however, was "*a closed work . . . only open at the rear to the town.*" While Fort Fisher mounted the heavy seacoast weapons of a later era in artillery design, the armament of the Malakoff, aside from "*a few old-fashioned, oddly-shaped mortars,*" was "*all ships' guns, and mounted on ships' carriages, and worked in the same way as ships' guns.*"[42]

By comparison, the length of Fort Fisher would be only slightly shorter than the wall of defenses south and east of the Karabel Faubourg at Sebastopol. This line stretched from the Great Redan (south of the suburb) to the Battery of the Point, which terminated on the harbor to the east.

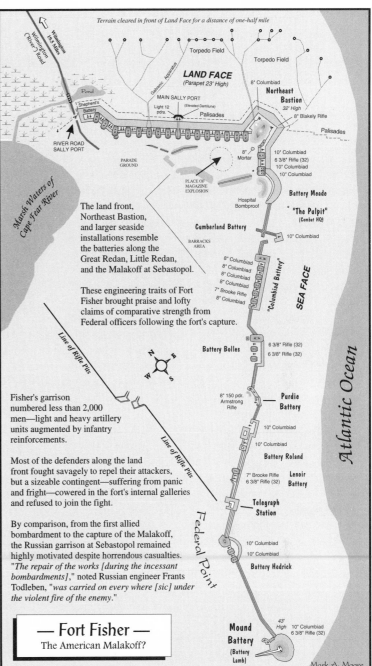

How Strong Was Fort Fisher?

In the aftermath of the fall of Fort Fisher on January 15, 1865, Union conquerors of the great bastion were quick to judge its strength as far greater than Todleben's Russian defenses. In 1865, news of the fall of Sebastopol was a recent memory, and the comparison was a natural one. William Lamb, himself influenced by the Russian fortress, remembered years after the war that Fort Fisher "*was styled by Federal engineers after the capture [as] the Malakoff of the South.*"[43]

On the day following the surrender, Adm. David D. Porter explained to Navy Secretary Gideon Welles that "*these works are tremendous. I was in Fort Malakoff a few days after it surrendered to the French . . . the combined armies of [Great*

Britain and France] were many months capturing that strong-hold, and it won't compare either in size or strength to Fort Fisher." On January 17, Porter again reported to Welles: "*I have since visited Fort Fisher and the adjoining works, and find their strength greatly beyond what I had conceived; an engineer might be excusable in saying they could not be captured except by regular siege. I wonder even now how it was done. The work . . . is really stronger than the Malakoff Tower, which defied so long the power of France and England, and yet it is captured by a handful of men under the fire of the guns of the fleet, and in seven hours after the attack commenced in earnest.*" In these statements, Porter seems to label the entire southeastern perimeter of the Sebastopol defenses—including the Great Redan opposite the British forces—as "the Malakoff." Moreover, he defines the Confederate bastion as "*Fort Fisher and the adjoining works,*" apparently referring to the area of the Northeast Bastion or land front alone as "Fort Fisher."[44]

To be sure, the Federal bombardment—"*which paved Fort Fisher with iron*"—was unparalleled. "*I wouldn't have missed seeing that bombardment of Fort Fisher for 10 years of my life,*" wrote Augustus Buell, who observed the battle from a Federal steam transport. "*It beat anything in history for weight of ordnance used—even greater than the bombardment of the Sebastopol forts by the English and French fleets, because the guns we used were so much heavier.*" Structurally, the mammoth fort weathered intact the second of the war's greatest bombardments up to that time. William Lamb had prepared diligently for just such an occasion. "*I had seen the effect of eleven-inch shell,*" he explained, "*and had read about the force of the fifteen-inch shell, and believed that their penetrating power was well ascertained, and could be provided against.*"[45]

Lamb commenced the transformation of Fort Fisher in July 1862, and by the time it was assaulted the heavy traverses and timber-framed earthen batteries were massive, indeed. The Land Face parapet towered 23 feet above the sand plain, the huge traverses reaching another nine to 12 feet higher than the parapet. The Northeast Bastion, little more than 100 yards from the crash of the surf, topped out at 32 feet above the beach, and the colossal Mound Battery on the Sea Face at 43 feet. Not only could the structure withstand the detonation of the era's heaviest ordnance, its sub-terra interior was a vast network of bombproofs, magazines, and connective tunnels. Lieutenant Col. Cyrus B. Comstock, Alfred Terry's chief engineer for the Wilmington expedition, noted that the fort's internal galleries comprised an impressive 14,500 feet of floor space, exclusive of the main magazine—which was located behind the main defensive structure. These compartments protected the garrison, between artillery duels with the fleet, during both Federal naval bombardments.[46]

Colonel Lamb remembered that his superiors "*did not altogether concur with me as to the value of elevated batteries, nor the necessity of such unprecedently [sic] heavy works.*" Nevertheless, the amateur engineer's notion of building "*a work of such magnitude that it could withstand the heaviest fire from any guns in the American navy*" proved successful. Colonel Comstock described the fort in detail to Federal authorities following the surrender. While the revetment of turf had been

skinned from the walls and mounds, he noted, "*all damage done to the earth-work can be readily repaired, its strength being about the same as before the bombardment.*" Despite the destruction of its heavy seacoast artillery pieces, portions of the palisades, and galvanic torpedo-firing apparatus, Fort Fisher's imposing walls showed little sign of material reduction to Federal ground forces as they made their attack. Why, then, did the fort fall to an infantry assault?[47]

After the war, Lamb—perhaps to underscore the fort's strong points—contended that Fort Fisher "*was built solely with the view of resisting the fire of the [Federal] fleet.*" But surely, in Lamb's interaction with an engineer so experienced as his friend and mentor W. H. C. Whiting, the contingent of a possible ground assault was considered. Whiting, in light of his official reports and correspondence for both attacks on the fort, seems to have deemed a ground attack as inevitable. As district commander, and later as a volunteer combatant at Fort Fisher, Whiting had fairly screamed for infantry reinforcements to ensure a successful defense of the fort and lesser works below Wilmington. The lack of adequate manpower to defend against an infantry assault ranks among three major reasons for the garrison's failure to repel the attackers.[48]

At the moment of crisis, Lamb and Whiting had a pitiful 1,900 men with which to defend nearly 2,000 yards of earthwork defenses. Along the 480-yard front between the western salient and Northeast Bastion, where the attacks occurred, the Confederates managed to deploy only about 750 defenders on the battlements. This force was divided into two groups, which were crowded to the extreme flanks at the main points of attack. Moreover, only a handful of the 350 South Carolinians sent in as reinforcements joined the battle on the parapet. While it was necessary for Robert F. Hoke's Division to keep a strong position on the Sugar Loaf line to protect the eastern approaches to Wilmington, Fort Fisher itself lacked enough musket-bearing defenders to man the parapet for the entire length of the Land Face. Even if the heavy artillery pieces here had not been destroyed by naval gunfire, they would have been of little use once Federal ground forces gained a position close enough to mount a charge. The limited downward angle of fire of these massive guns would have been ineffective against infantry at close range (though they might have made life difficult for the Union northern line). A sizable and willing garrison could have swarmed the gun chambers and parapet, training a formidable wall of rifle-muskets upon the attacking enemy. Colonel Lamb's light artillery rendered crucial service from both of the fort's sally ports, but lack of enough gunners at the riverside station proved costly.[49]

As it turned out, the larger group of defenders along the Northeast Bastion was able to sufficiently punish the head of the Federal naval column. The majority of the two-thousand-man naval contingent never got into the fight. The smaller of the two groups of defenders was arrayed along the western salient, and apparently was not deployed en masse atop the parapet. Federal infantry forces were able to breach the fort at the River Road sally port and Shepherd's Battery almost immediately. Thirty minutes after the attack began, more than 4,000 Federal troops were crowding atop the westernmost mounds and traverses, and onto the parade ground in rear of the fort.[50]

In describing the infantry attack on Fort Fisher, Lt. Martin Van Buren Richardson, of the 4th New Hampshire, astutely called attention to the structure's Achilles' heel. In a flippant nod to the post-battle Sebastopol comparisons, the young officer observed that "*the one weak point in the 'Malakoff' was the gate*." The half-bastion at Shepherd's Battery terminated shy of the river marsh, allowing the River Road from Wilmington to enter the fort at the western salient. This allowed the garrison convenient access to the road and points northward on the peninsula. While the massive earthworks stopped at the road, the palisades continued westward toward the river marsh. The "gate" where the road entered was blocked merely by a low wall of heavy sandbags, behind which frowned the muzzle of a single 12-pounder Napoleon fieldpiece. This gun commanded the direct approach to the "gate," across the bridge over a deep slough in front of Shepherd's Battery. A second fieldpiece stationed at the edge of the marsh was able to rake the bridge and road with an enfilading fire.[51]

The River Road sally port, however, gave the Federals almost immediate access to the rear of Fort Fisher. It was virtually the only defensive weakness inherent in the fort's design, and it was quickly exploited. The onrushing attackers, though fearfully punished at first, were able to knock down the sandbag wall and pour through the gate and around the western end of the palisades. By far the majority of Federal troops entered the fort by going around it, rather than scaling its outer walls. Once the men of Ames' division gained a foothold at the western salient, the attackers were able to overwhelm the outnumbered Confederates—who fought savagely—in one of the most terrible hand-to-hand engagements of the war. One by one, the Federals wrenched the Land Face gun chambers and traverses from the Confederates. No defense was mounted for the Sea Face, and the garrison capitulated after about seven hours of combat.[52]

Interestingly, William Lamb claimed after the war that "*Fort Fisher was far from complete when attacked by the Federal fleet.*" Whatever the commandant may have planned to further strengthen the bastion remains a matter of conjecture. If the western salient, however, had terminated at the extreme edge of the river marsh—rather than on the road—it would have been difficult indeed for attacking infantry to pass around the end of the structure. And any access to the rear of the fort, despite a numerically superior enemy, would have been dearly won—especially if the parapet had been defended with sufficient manpower. A gated and covered entrance, not unlike the center sally port, might have been plausible here. The road could have entered through the wall of the fort, perhaps with demilunes built up from the marsh on either side of the road at the gate—each armed with the light fieldpieces. All conjecture aside, the weak and poorly defended "Bloody Gate" at the River Road stands as the second primary reason for the fort's quick demise.[53]

The third reason is, of course, the presence of Admiral Porter's menacing armada of 58 warships, the second largest assembled for offensive operations during the Civil War. The inescapable rain of nearly 20,000 rounds of heavy naval ordnance understandably took its toll on the Confederates. Not only did this devastating fire maul a portion of the garrison, but the three-day exposure to the constant clamor and concussion of heavy ordnance strained the mental state of the defenders. Though drained both physically and emotionally, they mounted the best defense possible under the circumstances. The naval gunfire weakened the effectiveness of the palisades by knocking great holes in the fence, and did a huge service to the infantry by severing the buried wires of the torpedo-firing galvanic apparatus. Moreover, when the attack of Ames' division along the northern battlements was slowed due to stiff Confederate resistance, the well-practiced fleet once again unleashed a telling barrage on the Land Face, killing friend and foe alike.[54]

In the end, it would have been impossible for a Confederate garrison of *any* size to overcome the combined power of United States army and naval forces. Even if the attack of Ames' division had been repulsed, the Federals would have then laid siege to Fort Fisher. Given the importance of capturing Wilmington, it is doubtful that Gideon Welles would have recalled the fleet to other theaters of operation, as he had once feared might be necessary. At any rate, the Federals could probably have finished the job with half the number of warships then stationed off Federal Point. Porter's fleet would have renewed its bombardment, destroying the remaining guns on the Sea Face of Fort Fisher and Battery Buchanan, before training its sights on the defenses at Old Inlet. The lighter-draft gunboats would then have crossed the bar into the Cape Fear River, rendering any further inflow of supplies or reinforcements coming downriver to the fort impossible. The garrison would have been starved into submission; and any inbound blockade runners would have been turned away or captured by the fleet.[55]

"I WONDER EVEN NOW HOW IT WAS DONE"

Admiral David D. Porter boasted that Fort Fisher was stronger than the "the Malakoff," yet captured "*by a handful of men*" after a brief fight of seven hours. That the immense Confederate bastion was strong as a defensive earthwork should not be questioned. The comparison, however, to the long-held Sebastopol defenses—in light of the quick demise of Fort Fisher—is unfounded, and simply reflects a natural tendency by the victor to overstate the resistance of the vanquished.[56]

It took the allied armies, particularly those of France and England, nearly one year to capture the well-garrisoned fortress city of Sebastopol. By comparison, Fort Fisher (which was *thinly* garrisoned) fell to the largest combined Federal force assembled during the Civil War, after less than one week of action—and the deciding thrust was indeed accomplished in a single day, "*by a handful of men . . . in seven hours after the attack commenced in earnest,*" just as Porter had boasted. Sebastopol was defended to the death by an endless host of determined defenders. Casualties were horrendous. In the weeks prior to the city's fall, 400 allied guns and mortars inflicted more than 1,000 casualties a day upon the garrison and townspeople alike. The main defensive structures were pounded into "*matchwood and brickdust, only to be rebuilt at night*." Fort Fisher lost roughly 500 men killed and wounded during the second expedition, with the remainder of the garrison—about 1,400—being taken as prisoners of war. While the beleaguered defenders of Fort Fisher had fought, as one Federal attacker asserted, "*like savage dogs*," it was not enough. There were simply not enough defenders.[57]

Another important consideration to understand is that the allied armies in the Crimea were forced to contend with slashing attacks upon their flanks from the rear by the Russian field army, which was operating from the Crimean interior. This strategy disrupted the siege of Sebastopol, and helped keep the allies, who were struggling to sustain themselves at the end of a 3,000-mile-long supply line, out of the fortress city for nine long months.

Fort Fisher enjoyed no such outside assistance, though a large Confederate division of combat veterans, more than 6,000 strong, was ostensibly in a position to menace the rear of the attacking Federals. Nevertheless, neither Braxton Bragg nor Robert F. Hoke showed any inclination toward relieving the pressure on the doomed garrison of Fort Fisher—to the utter damnation and scorn of the fort's survivors. Even if this force *had* attacked, it would have found the Federals well prepared. The strong Union northern line across the peninsula, with entrenchments constructed for just such an occasion, was manned by a large force of United States Colored Troops—most of whom were combat veterans who had seen earlier action during the siege of Petersburg, Virginia. If the Confederates had attacked southward from the Sugar Loaf line, they may well have been repulsed. It is interesting to ponder, however, a Confederate engagement of the Union northern line.[58]

Having allowed nearly 10,000 Federal troops to come ashore on Federal Point unopposed—a force which boldly established a strong defensive position between Hoke's Confederate division and Fort Fisher—Department of North Carolina commander Braxton Bragg placed a woefully undermanned garrison at an insurmountable disadvantage. His feeble attempts to bolster the fort thereafter, with what would have been meager reinforcements at best, were a comedy of errors. When Adelbert Ames' Federal division finally attacked Fort Fisher, Bragg failed to engage the enemy's northern defensive line with Hoke's Division to help relieve the pressure on the garrison. Once that Federal position was established, however, the Confederates at Sugar Loaf found themselves in a losing situation: Bragg was caught between having to defend the land approaches to the port of Wilmington *and* being asked to reinforce the fort while applying pressure on the Federals to relieve the garrison. In the end, the most damning circumstance for the Confederates emerges in their lack of sufficient troop strength.[59]

Given the limited Confederate resources available for the campaign, however, Bragg did not make the most prudent use of these assets. At this point in the war it was a question of time for the Confederates. The effort to defend Fort Fisher was not engaged in by the supporting troops in the area. From a strictly military standpoint, a stronger defense of Federal Point—no matter the ultimate outcome—would have bought time for the Southern war effort. To delay as long as possible the Federal

occupation of Wilmington would have thrown a degree of uncertainty into the larger campaign of William T. Sherman, who was then on the verge of waging an overland campaign through the Carolinas, in an effort to join the forces of Ulysses S. Grant in Virginia. Sherman would be marching northward with an "army group" composed of 60,000 men, a force that would be foraging for provisions over ground already covered in some cases by Confederate foragers; and the general was counting on the use of the port of Wilmington as a safe base of supplies on the coast of North Carolina.[60]

"*The fort has fallen in precisely the manner indicated so often by myself*," the engineer W. H. C. Whiting told Confederate general-in-chief Robert E. Lee after the surrender, "*and to which your attention has been so frequently called, and in the presence of the ample force provided by you [Hoke's Division] to meet the contingency*." Two months later Chase Whiting, wounded and a prisoner of war, went to his grave cursing Braxton Bragg for the loss of Fort Fisher. "*I have been blamed for unnecessarily prolonging the fight*," explained William Lamb long after the war, "*[but] I had a right to believe that the troops which General Lee sent to our assistance would rescue us, and if Bragg had ordered Hoke to assault with his division late that afternoon we would have recovered the works*."[61]

While the district commander certainly bungled the defense of Federal Point, the Confederate president should ultimately share a portion of the blame. Jefferson Davis, a former army officer who thought the war would be decided by large armies upon the battlefield, lacked the foresight to adequately defend the major waterways of the Confederacy. The loss of Wilmington was, at least partially, the final result of this fatal policy. Abundant pleas for extra manpower from William Lamb, General Whiting, and North Carolina governor Zebulon B. Vance failed to produce significant results. Instead, Confederate authorities scoffed at the aggressive Whiting's vigilance, and grew to resent the requests.[62]

As previously stated, the issue of inadequate Confederate troop strength was obviated, ultimately, by the presence of the Federal armada on hand to assist the army ground forces. In light of this consideration, together with the exploitable flaw in the fort's land defenses, Fort Fisher was doomed from the moment Navy Secretary Gideon Welles concocted the grand scheme for "*a conjoint attack upon Wilmington*."[63]

The Delafield Report

Though his own writings reflected an interest in the Sebastopol defenses, William Lamb did not specify the title of the study which—along with advice from fellow officers and engineers—unquestionably influenced his design, reconstruction, and strengthening of Fort Fisher. The colonel simply recorded that he purchased a history on the "Russian War" while on a business trip to Charleston, South Carolina in December 1861. He paid $12.00 for the book "*frm Russel & Jones*."[64]

The Crimean War had not gone unnoticed in America. In 1855, Jefferson Davis (who would soon rise to lead the Confederate government in armed rebellion against the Union), was serving as Secretary of War under the administration of U.S. president Franklin Pierce. In an effort to gain knowledge for the United States military, Davis sent a group of officers abroad to study *"the practical working of the changes which have been introduced of late years into the military systems . . . of Europe."* Many important advances were occurring in mid-nineteenth-century warfare, and the best way to stay abreast of the latest technologies was to observe, first-hand, the military systems that were then employing them.

Davis' Commission to the Theater of War in Europe was tasked with studying all general aspects of European military institutions and development, with particular focus on the Crimean War. The commission included Bvt. Maj. Alfred Mordecai, Capt. George B. McClellan (who was within a few years of rising to lead the Union Army of the Potomac in the early stages of the Civil War), and Richard Delafield, of the United States Corps of Engineers.

The commission's tour of Europe included a three-week stay in the Crimea, during which its members enjoyed the hospitality of the British army. The Americans arrived at Balaklava on October 8, 1855—one month to the day after the fall of Sebastopol—and were assigned to camp on Cathcart's Hill. This locality afforded the visitors an extensive view of the area of recent field operations against the fortress city. Though the *"untoward formalities of diplomacy"* thwarted the group's efforts to secure a planned official meeting with French commander Aimable Pélissier—the "hero of the Malakoff"—the commission nonetheless gained access to the British, Sardinian, and Turkish camps. It also experienced a first-hand look at the confusing maze of siege lines and extensive Russian defenses before Sebastopol.[65]

There was much to see, and during the commission's visit *"an officer of the English army, under the authority of General [James] Simpson,"* wrote Delafield, *"was our daily companion to escort us wherever there was anything of interest to be seen, accompanied on several occasions by their engineer officers."* Access to the French camps was restricted to courtesy visits, despite the commission's original plan to spend half its time within French lines. The Americans were disappointed, but lost no *"profitable information"* as a result. Delafield noted with some dismay that their access privileges were no different than those of other United States officers on hand for a visit— one of whom was the navy's Lt. Cmdr. David D. Porter. Ten years later, Porter would be preparing a large Federal fleet for the massive bombardments of Fort Fisher.[66]

The commission members did tour Sebastopol, the Karabelnaya suburb, the Malakoff, and other defensive works. A French staff officer also provided welcome orientation with a detailed plan of the siege works, from their commencement through the capture of the Malakoff on September 8, 1855. This gave commission members *"a comprehensive idea of operations extended over many miles"* which, given the group's brief stay in the Crimea, was *"a favor that was duly appreciated."* The commission departed the Crimea on November 2, continuing its journey to other theaters of operation in Europe.

The tour ultimately produced an enormous volume of data,

and upon returning to America Richard Delafield compiled an official report to the Congress of the United States. This volume was nothing short of phenomenal, and would soon prove valuable to both Union and Confederate leaders during the early stages of the rebellion. The Delafield report provided American officers with not only an overview of European military developments, but numerous examples of Russian practice—including its system of defensive fortification.

USAMHI   **Richard Delafield**

In addition to its detailed textual descriptions, Delafield's work also provided rich illustrations and stunning, oversized maps (among them a comprehensive spread on the operations before Sebastopol). These graphical enhancements included diagrams on weaponry, details on fortification components, and even diagrams illustrating the explosion of mines via the use of electricity. William Lamb would employ just such a galvanic mine system along the northern front of Fort Fisher.[67]

While it is reasonable to assume that Colonel Lamb probably consulted more than one study on the Crimean War, Delafield's *Report on the Art of War in Europe* would have provided the amateur engineer a wealth of information on siege warfare and fort architecture. The report first appeared on the eve of the Civil War, and was thus available in the early stages of the conflict.[68]

NOTES

[1] "William Lamb," in Lyon G. Tyler, ed. *Men of Mark in Virginia: Ideals of American Life* (5 vols. Washington, D.C.: Men of Mark Publishing Company, 1906), I, 190-191.

[2] William Lamb Diary, August 28, September 16, 1855. Swemm Library, College of William and Mary, Williamsburg, Virginia. Lamb wrote much in his diary on the yellow fever epidemic throughout the months of August, September, and October 1855.

[3] *Ibid.*, September 19-20, 1855.

[4] *Ibid.*, September 21, 1855.

[5] *Ibid.*, September 27-28, 1855.

[6] *Ibid.*, October 3-4, 1855. Lamb, in daily anticipation of the worst news from Norfolk, scoured the papers for the names of friends and loved ones: "No news from the City of the Dead."

[7] *Ibid.*, October 5, October 8-9, 1855.

[8] *Ibid.*, October 16, 1855.

[9] *Ibid.*, October 18, 1855.

[10] *Ibid.*, October 27-28, November 14, 1855.

[11] *Ibid.*, November 15, 1855.

[12] Tyler, ed., *Men of Mark*, I, 191; Lamb Diary, October 20, 1855; Rod Gragg, *Confederate Goliath* (New York: Harper Collins, 1991), 14-15.

[13] Chris Fonvielle, *Last Rays of Departing Hope: The Wilmington Campaign* (Campbell, Cal.: Savas Publishing, 1997), 40-41;

Gertrude Elizabeth Baker, "The Diary of William Lamb, August 18, 1859-May 21, 1860" (Master's Thesis, College of William and Mary, 1960), x; Tyler, ed., *Men of Mark*, I, 191.

[14] William Lamb, "Thirty-Sixth Regiment (Second Artillery)," in Walter Clark, ed*., Histories of the Several Regiments and Battalions from North Carolina in the Great War 1861-'65* (5 vols., Goldsboro, N.C.: Nash Brothers, 1901), II, 630-631; William Lamb, "Fort Fisher, The Battles Fought There in 1864 and '65" (*Southern Historical Society Papers*, 52 vols., 1892), XXI, 259; Fonvielle, *Last Rays*, 41-42; Lamb Diary, December 21, 1861.

[15] Ava L. Honeycutt, "Fort Fisher: Malakoff of the South" (Master's Thesis, Duke University, 1960), 57.

[16] Andrew Lambert and Stephen Badsey, *The Crimean War* (Phoenix Mill, Stroud, Gloucestershire: Alan Sutton, 1994), 2-8. For an in-depth look at the origins of the war, see A. P. Saab's *Origins of the Crimean Alliance* (Charlottesville, Va., 1977).

[17] Lambert and Badsey, *Crimean War*, 55.

[18] *Ibid.*, 67-68.

[19] *Ibid.*, 77; William Howard Russell, *General Todleben's History of the Defence of Sebastopol, 1854-5. A Review* (New York: D. Van Nostrand, 1865), 64; Lambert and Badsey, *Crimean War*, 87-88. The ubiquitous Russell was a war correspondent for *The Times*, London.

[20] Alexander W. Kinglake, *The Invasion of the Crimea, Its Origin, and an Account of its Progress Down to the Death of Lord Raglan* (originally published, 8 vols., Edinburgh and London: William Blackwood and Sons, 1863-1869). This citation "Cheaper Edition Vol. IV," 1901, 243-244; an "abridged" version minus the amazing maps that accompanied other releases of this series. The Redan guarded the southern end of the Karabel faubourg, where the town was divided naturally from its suburb by Man-of-War Harbor (and the Woronzoff Ravine at the head of the harbor). My own maps of the Sebastopol defenses—the city overview and southeastern defensive perimeter—were derived chiefly from Kinglake's "New Edition Vol. IX," 1888, and Richard Delafield's *Report on the Art of War in Europe in 1854, 1855, and 1856* (Washington: George W. Bowman, 1861). Kinglake's sweeping narrative is the classic account of events in the Crimean Theater. My own map of the Crimean Peninsula is based on a lithograph published in the *Illustrated London News*, September 23, 1854.

[21] David Wetzel, *The Crimean War: A Diplomatic History* (New York: Columbia University Press, 1985), 117; Russell, *Todleben's History*, 65-66, 195-196; Philip Warner, *The Crimean War: A Reappraisal* (London: Arthur Baker Limited, 1972), 134.

[22] Warner, *A Reappraisal*, 130, 135-136, 215; Lambert and Badsey, *Crimean War*, 254. For a fascinating view of Sebastopol from a defender's perspective, see R. A. Hodasevich's *A Voice from Within the Walls of Sebastopol* (London: John Murray, 1856).

[23] Kinglake, "Cheaper Edition Vol. IV," 151-153.

[24] Lambert and Badsey, *Crimean War*, 197; Russell, *Todleben's History*, 132, 224. Todleben thus described the effect of allied fire upon the tower: "The guns of the Malakoff tower were silenced, and its parapet knocked to pieces, the stone splinters striking the men so severely that they were soon compelled to abandon it." The bombardment was so concentrated, explained Todleben, that the deadly flying shards "were constantly hitting the men."

[25] Lambert and Badsey, *Crimean War*, 87-88; Russell, *Todleben's History*, 64. The Sebastopol garrison had been severely weakened by Menshikov's concentration at the Alma. To bolster the defense force, a contingent of naval crewmen was formed into battalions for service onshore.

[26] Lambert and Badsey, *Crimean War*, 88-90; 196-102. This enlight-

ening history of the Crimean War strings together extracts from the voluminous reportage of Billy Russell and other correspondents, and molds their limited views into the context of not only the Crimean Theater, but the larger war as well.

[27] *Ibid.*, 102-103. Russell's account of the Battle of Balaklava, which included the original reference to "the thin red streak," made him a household name.

[28] *Ibid.*, 118-119.

[29] *Ibid.*, 7-8, 133; For an overview of the major field actions in the Crimea, see W. Baring Pemberton's *Battles of the Crimean War* (London: B. T. Batsford, Ltd., 1962). Russell, in addition to his dispatches for *The Times*, published widely on the war—including *The British Expedition to the Crimea* (London: George Routledge and Sons, 1858), a "New and Revised Edition" of which appeared in 1877. This volume provides many interesting maps of the various pitched battles of the campaign.

[30] Lambert and Badsey, *Crimean War*, 7, 134; Russell, *Todleben's History*, 216-217. A significant Turkish force was also in the Crimea, but was not used in the siege operations.

[31] Lambert and Badsey, *Crimean War*, 168, 196.

[32] *Ibid.*, 196-197, 211.

[33] *Ibid.*, 211; Jean Joseph Gustave Cler, *Reminiscences of An Officer of Zouaves*. Translated from the French (New York: D. Appleton and Company, 1860), 284, 286-287, 296. These concerted actions put the allies in position to creep ever closer for a deciding thrust upon the Russian defenses. "Not only were the besiegers enabled to sweep the harbor with a direct [fire]," noted this French officer, "they were also brought within only a few hundred metres of the Malakoff, that Gordian knot of the whole defence." Felix Maynard, ed., *Recollections of a Zouave Before Sebastopol*. Translated from the French. (Philadelphia: Hayes & Zell, 1856), 184-187, 213. Maynard recounts the story of another Frenchman who experienced the horrors of combat before the Malakoff. As his captain shouted "Forward *Jackals*! Forward!" the soldier and his fellow Zouaves stormed the Malakoff, only to be cut to pieces—including the captain: "Bullets, musket-shots and balls came flying through the air, crossing and intersecting each other, so countless, incessant and rapid, as to form a thicket of grape-shot, which it was as impossible to penetrate without being struck, as to penetrate a wooden thicket without being scratched by the branches." Many of the wounded French survivors lay motionless among the heaps of dead, feigning death themselves to escape the notice of the Russians—who sent parties out upon the contested plain to pilfer the bodies of the enemy.

[34] Lambert and Badsey, *Crimean War*, 220-221. In the Battle of the Tchernaya, British forces were commanded by Sir James Simpson, who assumed command when Lord Raglan died of cholera on June 28, 1855. The French were commanded by Aimable Pélissier, General Canrobert having stepped down in May 1855.

[35] *Ibid.*, 229, 256. Wetzel, *Diplomatic History*, 172; Warner, *A Reappraisal*, 214-217; Nicolas Bentley, ed., *Russell's Dispatches from the Crimea, 1854-1856* (London: Andre Deutsch, 1966), 253-259. Russell likened the relentless French attack to "a swarm of bees." The French advanced with some 30,000 men, and were supported by a force of about 5,000 Sardinians. While the leading French units had negligible ground to cover in the assault, the British troops had to cross more than 200 yards of difficult terrain to storm the Redan. Their ranks were quickly savaged. For an interesting account from the English perspective, see Douglas Arthur Reid's *Memories of the Crimean War, January 1855 to June 1856* (London: St. Catherine's Press, 1911), 103-109.

[36] Lambert and Badsey, *Crimean War*, 11, 247; Bentley, ed., *Russell's*

Dispatches, 263; Warner, *A Reappraisal*, 214. See also John Codman's *An American Transport in the Crimean War* (New York, 1896). Following the Russian evacuation, Sebastopol and its environs constituted a scene of devastation and ruin. The approaches leading to the city were literally covered with balls, shell fragments, and the debris of extended battle. In the city itself, scarcely a structure had escaped the damage wrought by the incessant artillery barrages. And the scenes along the southeastern defensive perimeter were unlike anything Russell had ever seen: "The interior of the Malakoff was dark and foul. Crammed with debris and corpses, it was a hideous sight . . . . The Russians lay inside the work in heaps, like carcasses in a butcher's cart; and the wounds—the blood—the sight exceeded all I had hitherto witnessed." The Crimean War left Russia in shambles—both militarily and financially—and cost the nation its dominant influence in Central Europe. The Ottoman Empire would cling to a tenuous existence until broken apart during the First World War. Russia would not regain its dominance in Europe until the Red Army destroyed Adolf Hitler's Third Reich in 1945.

[37] Honeycutt, "Malakoff of the South," 57; Fonvielle, *Last Rays*, 41-42. Charles M. Robinson III, *Hurricane of Fire: The Union Assault on Fort Fisher* (Annapolis: Naval Institute Press, 1998), 33; Adelbert Ames, "The Capture of Fort Fisher," *Civil War Papers of the Commandery of the State of Massachusetts, Military Order of the Loyal Legion of the United States*, 1 (1900), 290.

[38] Bentley, ed., *Russell's Dispatches*, 211; Lambert and Badsey, *Crimean War*, 164, 255; J. A. Mowris, *A History of the One Hundred and Seventeenth Regiment, N. Y. Volunteers* (Hartford, Conn.: Case, Lockwood and Company, 1866), 171-172; Lamb, "Fort Fisher, The Battles Fought There," 257, 260; Tyler, ed., *Men of Mark*, I, 193. Though Lamb would go on to a life in business and politics after the Civil War, he would be linked indelibly to the fort and its defense: "The reputation I acquired in the construction of Fort Fisher, North Carolina, and its outworks, in the protection of blockade running and in the defence of the fort, was more than I expected."

[39] United States War Department, *War of the Rebellion: A Compilation of the Official Records of the Union and Confederate Armies* (128 vols., Washington, 1880-1901) Series I, Vol. XLII, Pt. 1, pp. 1001, 1002 (hereinafter cited as *OR*; unless otherwise indicated, all references are to Series 1); *Ibid.*, Lamb's Report, p. 1006.

[40] Lamb, "Fort Fisher, The Battles Fought There," 263; Gragg, *Confederate Goliath*, 18-21; Fonvielle, *Last Rays*, 43-45.

[41] Russell, *Todleben's History*, 196-197; Lamb, "Fort Fisher, The Battles Fought There," 261-262; Lambert and Badsey, *Crimean War*, 164; See also R. A. Hodasevich's *A Voice from Within the Walls of Sebastopol* (London: John Murray, 1856). Fisher's revetment features are discernible in the photographs of Timothy H. O'Sullivan, prints of which are available at the United States Army Military History Institute, Carlisle Barracks, Carlisle, Pennsylvania.

[42] Lamb, "Fort Fisher, The Battles Fought There," 261-262; Lambert and Badsey, *Crimean War*, 255-256.

[43] Lamb, "Fort Fisher, The Battles Fought There," 260.

[44] United States War Department, *War of the Rebellion: A Compilation of the Official Records of the Union and Confederate Navies in the War of the Rebellion* (30 vols., Washington, 1900-1901) Series I, Vol. XI, p. 436 (hereinafter cited as *ORN*; unless otherwise indicated, all references are to Series 1); *Ibid.*, Porter's Report, 440. Porter's confusing statements stem, in part, from the initial Federal assessment that Fort Fisher was a four-sided work. Indeed, the fort began as a quadrilateral work in the vicinity of what became the Northeast Bastion.

[45] John G. Hutchinson, *History of the Fourth Regiment New Hampshire Volunteers* (Manchester, N.H.: John B. Clarke Company, 1913), 119; Augustus Buel, *"The Cannoneer." Recollections of Service in the Army of the Potomac. By "A Detached Volunteer" in the Regular Artillery* (Washington: The National Tribune, 1890), 328-333. The diversionary bombardment of Sebastopol by the allied fleet was greatly restricted, due to an obstruction of sunken ships across the entrance to the harbor. The Russians were so concerned over the threat posed by the Royal Navy as to sink their own fleet; Lamb, "Fort Fisher, The Battles Fought There," 260.

[46] United States War Department, *Atlas to Accompany the Official Records of the Union and Confederate Armies* (Washington, 1891-95), LXXV, 2; Comstock's Report, *OR*, vol. XLVI, Pt. 1, pp. 405-408.

[47] Lamb, "Fort Fisher, The Battles Fought There," 260; Comstock's Report, *OR*, vol. XLVI, Pt. 1, p. 408.

[48] Lamb, "Fort Fisher, The Battles Fought There," 260; Whiting's pleas for reinforcements at Cape Fear, and for Braxton Bragg to attack the rear of the Federal battle lines to relieve the pressure on Fort Fisher—during both attacks on the fort—were numerous. For examples, see Whiting to James A. Seddon, *OR*, vol. XXIX, Pt. 2, p. 670; Whiting to Seddon, *OR*, vol. XLII, Pt. 3, pp. 1146-1147, 1281; *Ibid.*, to R. E. Lee, pp. 1151-1153; *Ibid.*, to J. F. Gilmer, p. 1297; *Ibid.*, to Bragg, pp. 1201-1202, 1306-1307, 1312, 1357; Whiting to Seddon, *OR*, vol. XLVI, Pt. 2, pp. 1000-1001; *Ibid.*, to Bragg, pp. 1019, 1024, 1055, 1056, 1064.

[49] William Lamb, "The Defense of Fort Fisher," in Robert U. Johnson and Clarence C. Buel, eds., *Battles and Leaders of the Civil War* (4 vols., New York: The Century Company, 1884-1889), IV, 650.

[50] *Ibid.*, pp. 650-651; Fonvielle, *Last Rays*, 275.

[51] Hutchinson, *Fourth New Hampshire*, 120. Any supplies received by land also arrived through this gate. Provisions arriving at Fort Fisher by water were received via the wharf at Battery Buchanan, at the southern tip of the peninsula.

[52] The Federals were well aware of Fisher's defensive weakness. During the first Federal reconnaissance in December 1864, Lt. George W. Ross, with others, got close enough to the River Road sally port to assess the feasibility of an infantry assault: "The curtain does not extend all the way to the Cape Fear River," he explained. "I think that troops could march into the work through this interval. I saw Fort Wagner [on Morris Island, South Carolina]; I would rather assault Fort Fisher from what I saw [and] was sanguine that the work could be taken." Ross, an aide-de-camp on the staff of Bvt. Brig. Gen. N. Martin Curtis, correctly assessed the fort's Achilles' heel. See Cyrus Comstock to J. A. Rawlins (return of statements), *OR*, XLII, Pt.1, p. 976; Gragg, *Confederate Goliath*, 168-229; Fonvielle, *Last Rays*, 261-297.

[53] Lamb, "Fort Fisher, The Battle Fought There," 260.

[54] The largest fleet assembled—64 warships—was employed just three weeks earlier, during the December 1864 bombardment of Fort Fisher; For rounds expended, see *ORN*, vol. XI, 441; Cyrus Comstock's Report, *OR*, vol. XLVI, Pt. 1, p. 407; The palisade fence, however, was less damaged in front of the attacking infantry forces than it was further east toward the Northeast Bastion. Explosive devices constructed to blow holes in the fence were not used in the end, and a contingent of pioneers, or axmen, was employed to knock larger holes in the fence. See Terry's Report, *OR*, vol. XLVI, Pt. 1, p. 398. Similarly, the abatis in front of the Redan at Sebastopol were severely damaged by British artillery fire, weakening their effectiveness. See Reid, *Memories of the Crimean War*, 106; Lamb, "Fort Fisher, The Battles Fought There," 282, 285;

Even similar incoming rounds from Fisher's Columbiad Battery, Mound Battery, and Battery Buchanan—aimed at the western salient—could not stop the determined Federal advance.

[55] In preparing for the attack, Maj. Gen. Alfred Terry had ordered plenty of artillery and ammunition put ashore, "so that if the assault failed siege operations might at once be commenced." See Terry's Report, *OR*, vol. XLVI, Pt. 1, p. 399; Gideon Welles, *Diary of Gideon Welles, Secretary of the Navy Under Lincoln and Johnson* (3 vols., Boston and New York: Houghton Mifflin Company, 1911), II, 221.

[56] Porter's Report, *ORN*, vol. XI, 441; Robinson, *Hurricane of Fire*, 188-189.

[57] Lambert and Badsey, *Crimean War*, 229; Fonville, *Last Rays*, 306-307; Russell, *Todleben's History*, 217. Todleben, Sebastopol's engineer, recorded a staggering 89,142 casualties among the fortress city's garrison—and this figure *does not* include casualties from the field engagements at the Alma River, Balaklava, Inkerman, the Tchernaya, and other places. These losses reflect the losing side in a conflict of proportions far exceeding that of Fort Fisher.

[58] William Lamb, "Defence and Fall of Fort Fisher" *(Southern Historical Society Papers*, 52 vols., 1882), X, 346-368. In this article, Lamb vehemently disputes the claims and reasoning of Braxton Bragg regarding the loss of Fort Fisher. See also Bragg's Report, *OR*, vol. XLVI, Pt. 1, pp. 431-435; Charles Paine's Report, *OR*, vol. XLVI, Pt. 1, pp. 423-424; Fonville, *Last Rays*, 221-223.

[59] Bragg's Report, *OR*, vol. XLVI, Pt. 1, pp. 431-435; Lamb, "Defence and Fall of Fort Fisher," 346-349; Fonville, *Last Rays*, 234-236; Alfred Terry knew his operation would be successful from the moment his troops began constructing the Union northern line. "It was much improved afterward," he noted, "but from this time our foothold on the peninsula was secured." See Terry's Report, *OR*, vol. XLVI, Pt. 1, p. 397.

[60] The campaign to capture Wilmington itself was entirely subordinate to the operations of William T. Sherman in February 1865. Ulysses S. Grant took pains to assure Sherman a viable base for reinforcements and supplies in North Carolina. Grant even went so far as to place one of Sherman's old subordinates, Gen. John M. Schofield, in command of the Wilmington raid—usurping Terry's authority, as well as his status as the captor of Fort Fisher. Moreover, Schofield was subject to direct orders from Sherman. See Grant to Sherman, *OR*, vol. XLVII, Pt. 2, pp. 101-102, 859; See also Grant to Schofield, *OR*, vol. XLVII, Pt. 2, pp. 189-190.

[61] Whiting's Reports, *OR*, vol. XLVI, Pt. 1, pp. 440, 442; Lamb, "Fort Fisher, The Battles Fought There," 287-288; In his mortification at having lost Fisher—with no help from Bragg—Whiting was beside himself with anger and resentment. His post-battle reports to R. E. Lee demanded an investigation of Bragg's conduct during the campaign. See also Whiting to Blanton Duncan, W. H. C. Whiting Papers, North Carolina Division of Archives and History, Raleigh.

[62] Ironically, Davis's "strategic blindness" was born of his policy of defending every inch of Confederate soil, his defensive-offensive strategy toward managing the Union invaders (as opposed to a more consolidated policy of deploying more resources over less ground). Though Davis's choice was the most viable under the circumstances, there simply were not enough resources to go around. Moreover, once it became clear that England and France would not intervene on behalf of his nation, Davis showed little concern for the Federal blockade. By 1865 the blockade had indeed failed to squelch the inflow of goods and munitions of war into the Confederacy—and by then the most important Southern resource lacking was manpower. Just as Britain and France had

known that it was not a question *whether* they would defeat the Russians in the Crimean War, but rather how and when, it was also a question of time for the Confederacy. In this light, a better defense of Southern waterways would not have won the war for Jefferson Davis—for his was a war unwinable. For Davis, rather, it was a matter of how best to delay the inevitable. While his policy decisions helped prolong the life of his nation in the Eastern Theater (Virginia), they only served to hasten its destruction in the West. And somewhere in between the two, clouded by complacency, Davis's loyalty to Braxton Bragg, and perhaps by apathy toward the blockade, lay Wilmington and her defenses. See William C. Davis, *Jefferson Davis: The Man and His Hour* (New York: Harper Collins, 1991), 690, 696-699; James A. Seddon to Whiting, *OR*, vol. XLII, Pt. 2, pp. 1236-1237; See also Vance to Jefferson Davis, *OR*, vol. XLII, Pt. 3, p. 1214; *Ibid.*, Davis to Vance, p. 1222. Davis and the War Department were quick to buck the pleas for extra manpower at Cape Fear to Robert E. Lee. Sadly for Whiting, however, the Confederate high command—including Lee—had deemed the enthusiastic engineer an alarmist during his tenure as commander of the District of the Cape Fear. Thus it was not purely an issue of the unavailability of extra manpower for the defense of Wilmington. The Confederate War department simply did not take Whiting seriously, and Braxton Bragg—a successor with nothing approaching the understanding of the region that Whiting possessed—tacitly accepted the *status quo* at Cape Fear. For his part, Lee appreciated and valued Whiting's engineering talents, but questioned his capacity for district command. See Lee to Vance, *OR*, vol. XLII, Pt. 3, p. 1141-1142.

[63] Gideon Welles, *Diary of Gideon Welles, Secretary of the Navy Under Lincoln and Johnson* (3 vols., Boston and New York: Houghton Mifflin Company, 1911), II, 127, 146-147.

[64] Lamb Diary, December 21, 1861.

[65] Richard Delafield, *Report on the Art of War in Europe in 1854, 1855, and 1856* (Washington: George W. Bowman, 1861), xix-xxi. Delafield would later predict failure for Ben Butler's powder boat scheme in December 1864.

[66] *Ibid.*, xix-xx; Davis, *Jefferson Davis*, 233; Paul Lewis, *Yankee Admiral: A Biography of David Dixon Porter* (New York: David McKay Company, 1968), 88; Secretary Davis took a special interest in events in the Crimea, and plotted the course of the war on a wall map in his office at the War Department. He also followed the press and diplomatic dispatches with careful attention. Porter had sailed to the Mediterranean to bring back camels to be studied for their feasibility as military mounts. From Constantinople, Porter accepted an invitation from the British to visit the Crimea, where he toured Sebastopol and was also fascinated by a French "floating battery" sheathed with armor plating. Porter was so taken with the vessel that he constructed a model of it, and sent back voluminous notes to the Navy Department.

[67] Delafield, *Report on the Art of War in Europe*, xx. See oversized folding maps at the end of the work.

[68] Another interesting similarity between the combined assault on Fort Fisher and events of the Crimean War can be seen in the allied attack on the Russian fortress of Kinburn, October 17, 1855. Kinburn guarded Dnieper Bay, at the confluence of the Bug and Dnieper rivers—and commanded the approaches to Nicolayev, the shipbuilding yard of the Russian Black Sea fleet. Like Fort Fisher, Kinburn (a moderate structure of earth and stone) was constructed at the tip of a narrow peninsula, and consisted of a main structure with lesser batteries connected by sand curtains. Its garrison was roughly equal to Fisher's. On October 15, a British-French force of about 9,000 troops (which included nearly 1,000 marines) landed

on the peninsula south of the fort and dug a double line of trenches across the spit. Seventy warships—half from each navy, and including ironclads, mortar vessels, gunboats, and battleships—moved into position opposite Kinburn and into the bay behind it. On October 17, in the best handled operation of the war, the allied fleet demolished the fort. It is interesting to consider that this operation, though accomplished by naval gunfire, may have inspired David Dixon Porter—an observer in the Crimea—to put ashore a force of sailors and marines to share in the glory of capturing Fort Fisher on January 15, 1865. See Andrew Lambert's, *The Crimean War: British Grand Strategy, 1853-56* (Manchester and New York: Manchester University Press, 1990), 251-268.

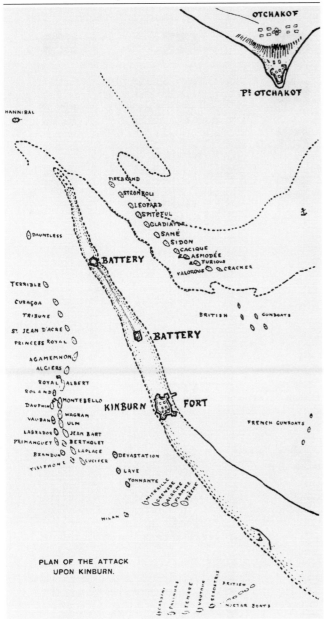

Bombardment of Kinburn, October 17, 1855.
From a drawing by a French officer. From *Life of Admiral Sir William Robert Mends*. The amphibious operation at Kinburn bears a strong resemblance to the Federal attack on Fort Fisher. Kinburn demonstrated the decisive edge in strategic mobility and advanced weapons that the allies held over the Russians. At Fort Fisher, nearly ten years later, the combined Union forces would hold the same advantages over Confederate defenders.

— Fort Fisher and Kinburn —

Like the attack on Fort Fisher, the Kinburn engagement was largely a one-sided affair. By the time this bombardment occurred, Great Britain and France—as a result of earlier experiences in the war—had devised new tactics for engaging Russian coastal installations. Their mortar vessels and gunboats would open the action and usually avoid damage by engaging the enemy while underway. The "floating batteries"—armored forerunners of ironclad warships—would also move in, followed by the larger ships-of-the-line.

At Kinburn, the French floating batteries were stationed off the spit in roughly the same proximity to the fort as David D. Porter's ironclads were arrayed off the Northeast Bastion of Fort Fisher. The three armored batteries anchored within 900 to 1,200 yards of Kinburn under a steady fire.

"The floating batteries opened with a magnificent crash," observed the war correspondent William Howard Russell, *"and one in particular distinguished itself for the regularity, precision, and weight of its fire throughout the day."* The batteries lobbed more than 3,000 rounds of shot and shell onto Kinburn. Just as Confederate gunners at Fisher had drawn an accurate—though ineffective—bead on the Union ironclads, the defenders of Kinburn responded with a lively fire. *"The enemy replied with alacrity,"* continued Russell, *"and the [floating] batteries must have been put to a severe test, for the water was splashed into pillars by shot all over them."* These early armored vessels had a profound impact on Admiral Porter.

Though their importance in reducing Kinburn has been exaggerated in the past, the floating batteries were seen as an important new technology. The aggressive British theater commander Sir Edmund Lyons noted that *"floating batteries have become elements in amphibious warfare, so the sooner you set about having as many good ones as the French the better it will be."* Rear Adm. Sir Houston Stewart agreed that *"in every conceivable case of 'Assault & Battery' they must be formidable and valuable."*

Though a large force of allied soldiers and marines moved ashore and entrenched across the peninsula, this action was decided solely by naval power. The allied fleet demolished the fort and the lesser batteries on the spit, and the Russian garrison was forced to surrender. *"Kinburn was ours,"* reported Russell, *"as far as the flames and smoke would allow us to occupy it."* Nevertheless, the larger prize of Nicolayev, which lay 30 miles up the Bug River from Kinburn, was abandoned due to conflicting war aims between Great Britain and France.

By contrast, the Union navy—after a bombardment unequaled in Civil War history—was unable to reduce Fort Fisher on its own. The inescapable presence of Porter's armada, however, ultimately assured the capture of Fort Fisher and Wilmington for the Union. *See note 68 above.* •

Kinburn and Fort Ochakov were constructed to protect riverine shipping from allied warships. Before the construction of railroads in the 1860s, the Bug and Dnieper Rivers were the main avenues of transportation in southern Russia.

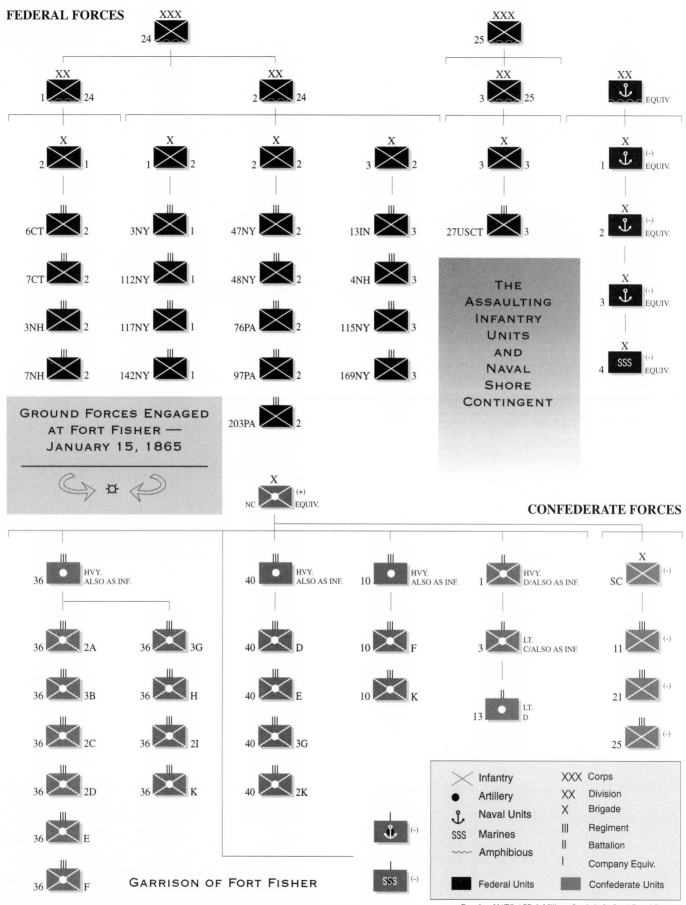

FEDERAL FORCES

GROUND FORCES ENGAGED
AT FORT FISHER —
JANUARY 15, 1865

THE
ASSAULTING
INFANTRY
UNITS
AND
NAVAL
SHORE
CONTINGENT

CONFEDERATE FORCES

GARRISON OF FORT FISHER

	Infantry	XXX Corps
•	Artillery	XX Division
⚓	Naval Units	X Brigade
SSS	Marines	‖‖ Regiment
〰	Amphibious	‖ Battalion
		I Company Equiv.
■	Federal Units	▨ Confederate Units

Based on NATO APP-6, Military Symbols for Land Based Systems
MARK A. MOORE

Appendix B—The Opposing Forces in the Wilmington Campaign

ORGANIZATION OF CONFEDERATE FORCES

Department of North Carolina, Third Military District
(District of the Cape Fear),
Gen. Braxton Bragg, commanding

First Expedition Against Fort Fisher
December 24-27, 1864

DEFENDERS OF FORT FISHER
Maj. Gen. William Henry Chase Whiting,
observer, adviser, combatant

Col. William Lamb
36th North Carolina Regiment
(2nd Artillery), commanding

1st Battalion North Carolina Heavy Artillery
Co. D, Capt. James L. McCormic

1st Battalion North Carolina Junior Reserves
Cos. A, B, C, Maj. D. T. Millard

3rd Battalion North Carolina Light Artillery
Co. C (Sutton's Battery), Capt. John M. Sutton

4th Battalion North Carolina Junior Reserves
Cos. A, B, C, D, Maj. John M. Reece

7th Battalion North Carolina Junior Reserves
Cos. A, B, C, Maj. William F. French

8th Battalion North Carolina Junior Reserves
Cos. A, B, C, Maj. James Ellington

10th North Carolina (1st North Carolina Artillery)
Maj. James Reilly, commanding
Co. F, Capt. Edward D. Walsh
Co. K (Shaw's Company), Capt. William Shaw, Jr.

13th Battalion North Carolina Light Artillery
Co. D, Capt. Zachariah T. Adams

36th North Carolina Regiment
(2nd Artillery)
Col. William Lamb, commanding
3rd Co. B (Bladen Stars), Capt. Daniel Munn
Co. E (Powell's Artillery), Capt. Oliver Powell
Co. F (Hunter's Company), Capt. Samuel B. Hunter
Co. H (Clarendon Guards), Capt. Daniel Patterson
Co. K (Brunswick Artillery), Capt. William Brooks

40th North Carolina Regiment
(3rd Artillery)
Co. E (Scotch Greys), Capt. Malcomb McBride
2nd Co. K (Bladen Artillery Guards),
Capt. Daniel James Clark

Detachment of C. S. Navy
Lt. Robert T. Chapman

Detachment of C. S. Marines
Capt. A. C. Van Benthuysen

TROOPS STATIONED AT WILMINGTON
Lt. Gen. Theophilus Hunter Holmes, post commandant

6th Battalion North Carolina Troops
(Fayetteville Armory Guards)
Cos. A, B, C, D, E, F, G, Lt. Col. F. L. Childs

Hahr's Battalion North Carolina Infantry
Maj. Franz J. Hahr

Capt. Henry P. Allen's Company
North Carolina Local Defense Troops

Bass' (unattached) Company

Capt. E. D. Sneed's Company
North Carolina Local Defense Troops

Detachment of C. S. Engineers and Coast Guard

DEFENDERS OF THE SUGAR LOAF LINE
Hoke's Division
(From the Army of Northern Virginia)
Maj. Gen. Robert Frederick Hoke

Hagood's Brigade
Brig. Gen. Johnson Hagood
7th South Carolina Battalion, Lt. Col. James H. Rion
11th South Carolina, Col. F. Hay Gantt
21st South Carolina, Col. Robert F. Graham
25th South Carolina, Capt. James Carson
27th South Carolina

Kirkland's Brigade
Brig. Gen. William W. Kirkland
17th North Carolina, Lt. Col. Thomas Sharp
42nd North Carolina, Col. John E. Brown
66th North Carolina, Col. John H. Nethercutt

Artillery
10th North Carolina Regiment (1st North Carolina Artillery)
Lt. Col. John P. W. Read, commanding (W)
2nd Co. I (Southerland's Battery)

Capt. Thomas J. Southerland

Staunton Hill Artillery (Paris' Battery)
Capt. Andrew B. Paris

Connally's Brigade of North Carolina Reserves (224)
Col. John K. Connally
4th Battalion North Carolina Junior Reserves
Cos. A, B, C, D, Maj. John M. Reece
7th Battalion North Carolina Junior Reserves
Cos. A B, C, Maj. William F. French
8th Battalion North Carolina Junior Reserves
Cos. A, B, C, Maj. James Ellington
8th North Carolina Senior Reserves
Cos. B, C, D, E, F, Col. Allmond McKoy

TROOPS STATIONED AT FORT ANDERSON
40th North Carolina Regiment
(3rd Artillery)
Co. A (Lenoir Braves), Capt. Ancram W. Ezzell

TROOPS STATIONED AT FORT PENDER, SMITHVILLE
3rd Battalion North Carolina Light Artillery
Co. A (Northampton Artillery), Capt. Andrew J. Ellis

TROOPS STATIONED AT FORT CASWELL, OAK ISLAND
36th North Carolina Regiment
(2nd Artillery)
Lt. Col. John Douglas Taylor, commanding

1st Battalion North Carolina Heavy Artillery
Co. A (Clark Artillery), Capt. Robert G. Rankin
Co. C (Brown's Battalion), Capt. William H. Brown
Capt. Abner A. Moseley's Company (Sampson Artillery)

TROOPS STATIONED AT FORT CAMPBELL, OAK ISLAND
Col. John J. Hedrick, commanding

1st Battalion North Carolina Heavy Artillery
Co. B (River Guards), Capt. John W. Taylor

40th North Carolina Regiment
(3rd Artillery)
Co. F, Capt. John C. Robertson

Second Expedition Against Fort Fisher
January 13-15, 1865

DEFENDERS OF FORT FISHER
Maj. Gen. William Henry Chase Whiting,
adviser and volunteer combatant

Col. William Lamb
36th North Carolina Regiment
(2nd Artillery), commanding

1st Battalion North Carolina Heavy Artillery
Co. D, Capt. James L. McCormic

3rd Battalion North Carolina Light Artillery
Co. C (Sutton's Battery), Capt. John M. Sutton

10th North Carolina Regiment (1st Artillery)
Maj. James Reilly, commanding
Co. F, Capt. Edward D. Walsh
Co. K (Shaw's Battery), Capt. William Shaw, Jr.

13th Battalion North Carolina Light Artillery
Co. D, Capt. Zachariah T. Adams

36th North Carolina Regiment
(2nd Artillery)
Col. William Lamb, commanding
2nd Co. A (Murphy's Battery), Capt. Robert Murphy
3rd Co. B (Bladen Stars), Capt. Daniel Munn
2nd Co. C (Braddy's Battery), Capt. Kinchen Braddy
2nd Co. D (Anderson Artillery), Capt. Edward Dudley
Co. E (Powell's Artillery), Capt. Oliver Powell
Co. F (Hunter's Company),
Acting Capt. Exum Lewis Hunter
3rd Co. G (Russell's Battery), Lt. William Swain
Co. H (Clarendon Guards), Capt. Daniel Patterson
2nd Co. I (Bladen Artillery), Capt. John T. Melvin
Co. K (Brunswick Artillery), Capt. William Brooks

40th North Carolina Regiment
(3rd Artillery)
Co. D (Bay River Artillery), Capt. James Lane
Co. E (Scotch Greys), Capt. Malcomb H. McBride
3rd Co. G, Capt. George Buchan
2nd Co. K (Bladen Artillery Guards),
Capt. Daniel James Clark

Detachment of C. S. Navy
Capt. Robert T. Chapman

Detachment of C. S. Marines
Capt. A. C. Van Benthuysen

Hagood's Brigade
11th South Carolina (detachment)
21st South Carolina (detachment), Capt. D. G. DuBose

25th South Carolina (detachment), Capt. James Carson

DEFENDERS OF THE SUGAR LOAF LINE
Hoke's Division
(From the Army of Northern Virginia)
Maj. Gen. Robert F. Hoke

Clingman's Brigade
Col. Hector McKethan
8th North Carolina, Lt. Col. Rufus A. Barrier
31st North Carolina, Lt. Col. Charles Knight
51st North Carolina, Capt. James W. Lippitt
61st North Carolina, Col. William S. Devane

Colquitt's Brigade
Brig. Gen. Alfred H. Colquitt
6th Georgia, Col. John T. Lofton
19th Georgia, Col. James H. Neal
23rd Georgia, Col. Marcus R. Ballenger
27th Georgia, Capt. Elisha D. Graham
28th Georgia, Capt. John A. Johnson

Hagood's Brigade
Col. Robert F. Graham
7th South Carolina Battalion, Lt. Col. James H. Rion
11th South Carolina, Col. F. Hay Gantt
21st South Carolina
25th South Carolina
27th South Carolina

Kirkland's Brigade
Brig. Gen. William W. Kirkland
17th North Carolina, Lt. Col. Thomas H. Sharp
42nd North Carolina, Col. John E. Brown
66th North Carolina, Col. John H. Nethercutt

Cavalry
2nd South Carolina, Col. Thomas J. Lipscomb

Artillery
3rd Battalion North Carolina Light Artillery
Co. A (Northampton Artillery), Capt. Andrew J. Ellis

10th North Carolina Regiment
(1st Artillery)
2nd Co. I (Southerland's Battery), Capt. Thomas Southerland

Staunton Hill Artillery (Paris' Battery)
Capt. Andrew B. Paris

The Advance on Wilmington
February 11-22, 1865

DEFENDERS OF THE SUGAR LOAF LINE
Hoke's Division
(From the Army of Northern Virginia)
Maj. Gen. Robert F. Hoke

Clingman's Brigade
Col. William S. Devane
8th North Carolina, Lt. Col. Rufus A. Barrier
31st North Carolina, Lt. Col. Charles W. Knight
51st North Carolina, Capt. James W. Lippit
61st North Carolina

Colquitt's Brigade
Col. Charles T. Zachry
6th Georgia, Lt. Col. Sampson W. Harris
19th Georgia, Col. James H. Neal
23rd Georgia, Col. Marcus R. Ballenger
27th Georgia, Capt. Elisha D. Graham ?
28th Georgia, Capt. John A. Johnson ?

Kirkland's Brigade
Brig. Gen. William W. Kirkland
17th North Carolina, Lt. Col. Thomas H. Sharp
42nd North Carolina, Col. John E. Brown
66th North Carolina, Col. John E. Nethercutt

Artillery
3rd Battalion North Carolina Light Artillery
Co. A (Northampton Artillery), Capt. Andrew J. Ellis
Co. C (detachment), Lt. Alfred M. Darden

10th North Carolina Regiment
(1st Artillery)

2nd Co. I (Southerland's Battery)
Capt. Thomas J. Southerland

Staunton Hill Battery (Paris' Battery)
Capt. Andrew B. Paris

Cavalry
2nd South Carolina Cavalry (detachment)
Col. Thomas J. Lipscomb

DEFENDERS OF FORT ANDERSON
Hagood's Brigade
(Detached from Hoke's Division)
Brig. Gen. Johnson Hagood

7th South Carolina Battalion, Lt. Col. James H. Rion
11th South Carolina, Col. F. Hay Gantt
21st South Carolina (remnants), Col. Robert F. Graham

25th South Carolina (remnants), Col. Charles H. Simonton
27th South Carolina, Capt. Allston

Artillery
3rd Battalion North Carolina Light Artillery
Co. B, Capt. William Badham, Jr.
Capt. Abner A. Moseley's Company (Sampson Artillery)

Hedrick's Brigade
Col. John J. Hedrick
40th North Carolina Regiment
(3rd Artillery)
Maj. William Holland, commanding

Co. A (Lenoir Braves), Capt. Ancram W. Ezzell
Co. B (McMillan Artillery),
Lt. Macon Bonner, Lt. Selby Harden
Co. C (Bridger's Artillery), Capt. John E. Leggett
Co. F, Capt. John Robertson
2nd Co. H (Barnes' Battery), Capt. Calvin Barnes
Co. I, Capt. Charles C. Whitehurst

Taylor's Battery
Lt. Col. John Douglas Taylor
36th North Carolina Regiment
(2nd Artillery), remnants

1st Battalion North Carolina Heavy Artillery
Co. A (Clark Artillery), Capt. Robert G. Rankin
Co. B (River Guards), Capt. John W. Taylor
Co. C (Brown's Battalion), Capt. William H. Brown
Co. D (remnants), Lt. John T. Rankin

71st North Carolina Regiment
(2nd North Carolina Junior Reserves) Co. B

Capt. W. J. McDougald's Unattached Company
North Carolina Troops

Coast Guard Company (unattached)

Cavalry
2nd South Carolina Cavalry (detachment)
Col. Thomas J. Lipscomb

TROOPS STATIONED AT WILMINGTON
Col. George Jackson, post commandant

Armory Guards
Co. B, Capt. Armand L. DeRosset

7th Regiment Home Guard
Cos. A, B, Col. James G. Burr

8th North Carolina Senior Reserves
Col. Allmand M. McKoy

Engineers
2nd Engineers Co. A, Capt. John C. Winder

Signal Corps
Lt. George C. Bain

Cape Fear River Batteries
(Forts Davis, Lee, Campbell, Meares)
Col. Peter C. Gaillard, commanding

13th Battalion North Carolina Light / Heavy Artillery
Co. D (Adams' Battery), Lt. Samuel H. Forbes ?

68th North Carolina, Co. C (detachment)

McDougald's Company (detachment)
Capt. W. J. McDougald

Naval Detachment

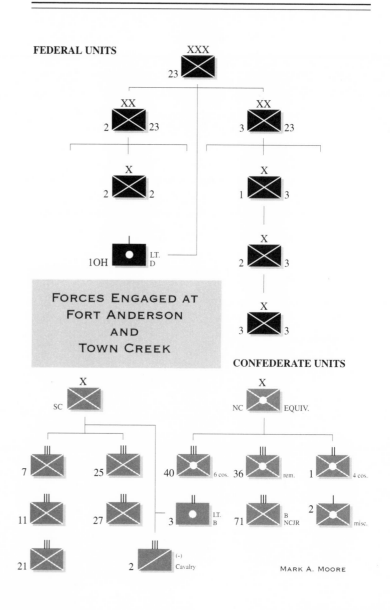

FORCES ENGAGED AT FORT ANDERSON AND TOWN CREEK

FEDERAL UNITS

CONFEDERATE UNITS

MARK A. MOORE

ORGANIZATION OF UNION FORCES

First Expedition Against Fort Fisher
December 24-27, 1864

Department of Virginia and North Carolina
Maj. Gen. Benjamin F. Butler and Maj. Gen. Godfrey
Weitzel, commanding

FORT FISHER EXPEDITIONARY FORCE

XXIV Army Corps
Second Division
Brig. Gen. Adelbert Ames

First Brigade
Bvt. Brig. Gen. N. Martin Curtis
3rd New York, Capt. George W. Warren
112th New York, Lt. Col. John W. Smith
117th New York, Col. Rufus Daggett
142nd New York, Col. Albert M. Barney

Second Brigade
Col. Galusha Pennypacker
47th New York, Capt. Joseph McDonald
48th New York, Lt. Col. William B. Coan
76th Pennsylvania, Col. John S. Littell
97th Pennsylvania, Lt. John Wainwright
203rd Pennsylvania, Col. John W. Moore

Third Brigade
Col. Louis Bell
13th Indiana, Capt. Samuel M. Zent
4th New Hampshire, Capt. John H. Roberts
115th New York, Maj. Ezra L. Walrath
169th New York, Col. Alonzo Alden

Artillery Brigade
Capt. Richard H. Lee
16th New York Independent Battery Light Artillery

XXV Army Corps
Third Division
Brig. Gen. Charles J. Paine

Second Brigade
Col. John W. Ames
4th U.S. Colored Troops, Lt. Col. George Rogers
6th U.S. Colored Troops, Lt. Col. Clark Royce
30th U.S. Colored Troops, Lt. Col. Hiram A. Oakman
39th U.S. Colored Troops, Col. Ozora P. Stearns

Third Brigade
Col. Elias Wright
1st U.S. Colored Troops, Lt. Col. Giles H. Rich

5th U.S. Colored Troops, Col. Giles W. Shurtleff
10th U.S. Colored Troops, Lt. Col. Edward H. Powell
37th U.S. Colored Troops, Col. Nathan Goff, Jr.
107th U.S. Colored Troops, Lt. Col. David M. Sells

Artillery Brigade
3rd U.S., Regular Army, Battery E
Lt. John Myrick

UNITED STATES NAVY
North Atlantic Blockading Squadron
Fort Fisher Task Force
Rear Adm. David D. Porter, commanding

Ship's Name / Number of Guns / Commanding Officer

Ships of Line No. 1
Canonicus (ironclad) / 2 / Lt. Cmdr. George Belknap
Huron / 5 / Lt. Cmdr. Thomas 0. Selfridge
Kansas / 8 / Lt. Cmdr. Pendleton G. Watmough
Mahopac (ironclad) / 2 / Lt. Cmdr. Edward Potter
Monadnock (ironclad) / 4 / Cmdr. Enoch G. Parrott
Neurus / 9 / Cmdr. John C. Howell
New Ironsides (ironclad) / 20 / Cmdr. William Radford
Nyack / 8 / Lt. Cmdr. L. Howard Newman
Pequot / 8 / Lt. Cmdr. Daniel L. Braine
Pontoosuc / 12 / Lt. Cmdr. William G. Temple
Saugus (ironclad) / 2 / Cmdr. Edmund R. Colhoun
Unadilla / 6 / Lt. Cmdr. Frank M. Ramsay

Ships of Line No. 2
Bigonia / 3 / Acting Vol. Lt. Warrington D. Roath
Brooklyn / 26 / Capt. James Alden
Colorado / 50 / Commo. Henry K. Thatcher
Fort Donelson / 1 / Lt. Thomas Pickering
Juniata / 14 / Capt. William Rogers Taylor
Mackinaw / 10 / Cmdr. John C. Beaumont
Maumee / 8 / Lt. Cmdr. Ralph Chandler
Minnesota / 46 / Commo. Joseph Lanman
Mohican / 9 / Cmdr. Daniel Ammen
Pawtuxet / 10 / Cmdr. James H. Spotts
Powhatan / 24 / Commo. James F. Schenck
Seneca / 5 / Lt. Cmdr. Montgomery Sicard
Shenandoah / 6 / Capt. Daniel B. Ridgley
Susquehanna / 18 / Commo. Sylvanus W. Godon
Ticonderoga / 14 / Capt. Charles Steedman
Tuscarora / 10 / Cmdr. James M. Frailey
Vanderbilt / 16 / Capt. Charles W. Pickering
Wabash / 44 / Capt. Melancton Smith
Yantic / 5 / Lt. Cmdr. Thomas Harris

Ships of Line No. 3
Chippewa / 6 / Lt. Cmdr. Aaron Weaver
Fort Jackson / 11 / Capt. Benjamin F. Sands
Iosco / 10 / Cmdr. John Guest
Monticello / 6 / Acting Vol. Lt. Daniel A. Campbell

APPENDIX B—Orders of Battle

Osceola / 10 / Cmdr. J. M. B. Clitz
Quaker City / 7 / Cmdr. William F. Spicer
Rhode Island / 12 / Cmdr. Stephen D. Trenchard
Santiago de Cuba / 11 / Capt. Oliver S. Glisson
Sassacus / 12 / Lt. Cmdr. John L. Davis
Tacony / 12 / Lt. Cmdr. William T. Truxton

Ships of Reserve Line

A. D. Vance / 5 / Lt. Cmdr. John H. Upshur
Aries / 7 / Acting Vol. Lt. Francis S. Wells
Alabama / 10 / Acting Vol. Lt. Frank Smith
Anemone / 4 / Acting Ens. William C. Borden
Banshee / 3 / Acting Vol. Lt. W. H. Garfield
Britannia / 6 / Acting Vol. Lt. Samuel Huse
Cherokee / 6 / Acting Vol. Lt. William E. Dennison
Emma / 8 / Acting Vol. Lt. Thomas C. Dunn
Eolus / 4 / Acting Mstr. Edward S. Keyser
Gettysburg / 7 / Lt. R. H. Lamson
Gov. Buckingham / 6 / Acting Vol. Lt. J. MacDiarmid
Howquah / 5 / Acting Vol. Lt. John W. Balch
Keystone State / 6 / Cmdr. Henry Rolando
Lillian / 2 / Acting Vol. Lt. T. A. Harris
Little Ada / 2 / Acting Mstr. Samuel P. Crafts
Malvern / 12 / Lt. Cmdr. Benjamin H. Porter
Maratanza / 6 / Lt. Cmdr. George Young
Moccasin / 3 / Acting Ens. James Brown
Montgomery / 6 / Acting Vol. Lt. Edward H. Faucon
Nansemond / 3 / Acting Mstr. James H. Porter
R. R. Cuyler / 12 / Cmdr. Charles H. B. Caldwell
Tristram Shandy / 4 / Act. Vol. Lt. Edward F. Devens
Wilderness / 4 / Acting Mstr. Henry Arey

Second Expedition Against Fort Fisher
January 13-15, 1865

Department of Virginia and North Carolina

TERRY'S PROVISIONAL CORPS
Bvt. Maj. Gen. Alfred H. Terry, commanding

XXIV Army Corps
First Division

Second Brigade
Col. Joseph C. Abbott
6th Connecticut, Col. Alfred P. Rockwell
7th Connecticut, Capt. John Thompson
Capt. William S. Marble
3rd New Hampshire, Capt. William H. Trickey
7th New Hampshire, Lt. Col. Augustis W. Rollins
16th New York Heavy Artillery Cos. A, B, C, F, G, K,
Maj. Frederick W. Prince

Second Division
Brig. Gen. Adelbert Ames

First Brigade
Bvt. Brig. Gen. N. Martin Curtis (W)
Maj. Ezra L. Walrath
3rd New York, Capt. James H. Reeve (W)
Lt. Edwin A. Behan
112th New York, Col. John F. Smith
117th New York, Lt. Col. Francis X. Meyer
142nd New York, Lt. Col. Albert M. Barney

Second Brigade
Col. Galusha Pennypacker (W)
Maj. Oliver P. Harding
47th New York, Capt. Joseph McDonald
48th New York, Lt. Col. William B. Coan (W)
Maj. Nere A. Elfwing
76th Pennsylvania, Col. John S. Littell
97th Pennsylvania, Lt. John Wainwright
203rd Pennsylvania, Col. John W. Moore (K)
Lt. Col. Jonas W. Lyman, Maj. Oliver P. Harding,
Capt. Heber B. Essington

Third Brigade
Col. Louis Bell (K)
Col. Alonzo Alden
13th Indiana, Lt. Col. Samuel M. Zent
4th New Hampshire, Capt. John H. Roberts
115th New York, Lt. Col. Nathan J. Johnson
169th New York, Col. Alonzo Alden
Lt. Col. James A. Colvin

Artillery Brigade
Capt. Richard H. Lee
16th New York Independent Battery Light Artillery

XXV Army Corps
Third Division
Brig. Gen. Charles J. Paine

Second Brigade
Col. John W. Ames
4th U. S. Colored Troops, Lt. Col. George Rogers
6th U. S. Colored Troops, Maj. Augustus S. Boernstein
30th U. S. Colored Troops, Lt. Col. Hiram A. Oakman
39th U. S. Colored Troops, Col. Ozora P. Stearns

Third Brigade
Col. Elias Wright
1st U.S. Colored Troops, Lt. Col. Giles H. Rich
5th U.S. Colored Troops, Maj. William R. Brazie
10th U.S. Colored Troops, Lt. Col. Edward H. Powell
27th U.S. Colored Troops, Col. Albert M. Blackman
37th U.S. Colored Troops, Col. Nathan Goff, Jr.

Artillery Brigade
3rd U.S., Regular Army, Battery E
Lt. John Myrick

Artillery
Bvt. Brig. Gen. Henry L. Abbot
1st Connecticut Heavy Artillery Cos. B, G, L,
Capt. William G. Pride

Engineers
15th New York, Cos. A, I (or A, B, H),
Lt. K. Samuel O'Keefe

UNITED STATES NAVY
North Atlantic Blockading Squadron
Cape Fear Task Force
Rear Adm. David D. Porter, commanding

Ship's Name / Number of Guns / Commanding Officer

Ships of Line No. 1
Brooklyn / 26 / Capt. James Alden
Canonicus (ironclad) / 2 / Lt. Cmdr. George Belknap
Huron / 5 / Lt. Cmdr. Thomas O. Selfridge
Kansas / 8 / Lt. Cmdr. Pendleton G. Watmough
Mahopac (ironclad) / 2 / Lt. Cmdr. Edward Potter
Maumee / 8 / Lt. Cmdr. Ralph Chandler
Mohican / 9 / Cmdr. Daniel Ammen
Monadnock (ironclad) / 4 / Cmdr. Enoch G. Parrott
New Ironsides (ironclad) / 20 / Cmdr. William Radford
Pawtuxet / 10 / Cmdr. James H. Spotts
Pequot / 8 / Lt. Cmdr. Daniel Braine
Pontoosuc / 12 / Lt. Cmdr. William G. Temple
Saugus (ironclad) / 2 / Cmdr. Edmund R. Colhoun
Seneca / 5 / Lt. Cmdr. Montgomery Sicard
Tacony / 12 / Lt. Cmdr. William T. Truxton
Unadilla / 6 / Lt. Cmdr. Frank M. Ramsay
Yantic / 5 / Lt. Cmdr. Thomas C. Harris

Ships of Line No. 2
Colorado / 50 / Commo. Henry K. Thatcher
Juniata / 14 / Capt. William Rogers Taylor
Mackinaw / 10 / Cmdr. John C. Beaumont
Minnesota / 46 / Commo. Joseph Lanman
Powhatan / 24 / Commo. James F. Schenck
Shenandoah / 6 / Capt. Daniel B. Ridgley
Susquehanna / 18 / Commo. Sylvanus W. Godon
Ticonderoga / 14 / Capt. Charles Steedman
Tuscarora / 10 / Cmdr. James M. Frailey
Vanderbilt / 16 / Capt. Charles W. Pickering
Wabash / 44 / Capt. Melancton Smith

Ships of Line No. 3
Chippewa / 6 / Lt. Cmdr. Aaron Weaver
Fort Jackson / 11 / Capt. Benjamin F. Sands
Iosco / 10 / Cmdr. John Guest

Maratanza / 6 / Lt. Cmdr. George Young
Montgomery / 6 / Acting Vol. Lt. Thomas C. Dunn
Monticello / 6 / Lt. Cmdr. William B. Cushing
Osceola / 10 / Cmdr. J. M. B. Clitz
Quaker City / 7 / Cmdr. William F. Spicer
R. R. Cuyler / 12 / Cmdr. Charles H. B. Caldwell
Rhode Island / 12 / Cmdr. Stephen D. Trenchard
Santiago de Cuba / 11 / Capt. Oliver S. Glisson
Sassacus / 12 / Lt. Cmdr. John L. Davis

Ships of Reserve Line
A. D. Vance / 5 / Lt. Cmdr. John H. Upshur
Alabama / 10 / Acting Vol. Lt. Amos R. Langthorne
Aries / 7 / Acting Vol. Lt. Francis S. Wells
Britannia / 6 / Acting Vol. Lt. William B. Sheldon
Cherokee / 6 / Acting Vol. Lt. William E. Dennison
Emma / 8 / Acting Vol. Lt. James M. Williams
Eolus / 4 / Acting Mstr. Edward S. Keyser
Fort Donelson / 1 / Acting Mstr. George W. Frost
Gettysburg / 7 / Lt. R. H. Lamsom
Gov. Buckingham / 6 / Acting Vol. Lt. J. MacDiarmid
Launch No. 6 / 1 / Gunner Hubert Peters
Lillian / 2 / Acting Vol. Lt. T. A. Harris
Little Ada / 2 / Acting Mstr. Samuel P. Crafts
Malvern / 12 / Lt. Cmdr. Benjamin H. Porter
Nansemond / 3 / Acting Mstr. James H. Porter
Republic / 1 / Acting Mstr. John W. Bennett
Tristram Shandy / 4 / Act. Vol. Lt. Edward F. Devens
Wilderness / 4 / Acting Mstr. Henry Arey

U.S. Army Transports
Atlantic, Blackstone, California, Champion, Charles Leary,
Commodore DuPont, De Molay, Euterpe, General Lyon,
Governor Chase, Idaho, L. C. Livingston, McClellan,
Montauk, North Point, Prometheus, Russia, Thames,
Thomas R. Scott, Tonawanda, Varuna, Weybossett

The Advance on Wilmington
February 11-22, 1865

Department of Virginia and North Carolina

WILMINGTON EXPEDITIONARY FORCE
Maj. Gen. John M. Schofield, commanding

XXIII Army Corps
Second Division

Second Brigade
Col. Orlando Moore
107th Illinois, Maj. Thomas J. Milholland
80th Indiana, Lt. Col. Alfred D. Owen
26th Kentucky, (100 men from First Brigade)
23rd Michigan, Col. Oliver L. Spaulding
111th Ohio, Lt. Issac R. Sherwood
118th Ohio, Lt. Col. Edgar Sowers

Third Division
Maj. Gen. Jacob D. Cox

First Brigade
Col. Oscar W. Sterl
12th Kentucky, Lt. Col. Laurence Rousseau
16th Kentucky, Lt. Col. John S. White
100th Ohio, Capt. Frank Rundell
104th Ohio, Lt. Col. William J. Jordan
8th Tennessee, Capt. James W. Berry

Second Brigade
Col. John S. Casement
65th Illinois, Maj. George H. Kennedy
Lt. Col. William S. Stewart
65th Indiana, Lt. Col. John W. Hammond
103rd Ohio, Capt. Henry S. Pickands
177th Ohio, Col. Arthur T. Wilcox
5th Tennessee, Lt. Col. Nathaniel Witt

Third Brigade
Col. Thomas J. Henderson
112th Illinois, Lt. Col. Emery S. Bond
63rd Indiana, Lt. Col. Daniel Morris
140th Indiana, Col. Thomas J. Brady

Artillery
Battery D, 1st Ohio Light Artillery
Lt. Cecil C. Reed

Signal Corps (detachment)
Lt. E. H. Russell

Terry's Provisional Corps
Maj. Gen. Alfred H. Terry

XXIV Army Corps
First Division

Second Brigade
Bvt. Brig. Gen. Joseph C. Abbott
6th Connecticut, Lt. Col. Daniel Klein
7th Connecticut, Lt. Col. Seager S. Atwell
3rd New Hampshire, Capt. William H. Trickey
Lt. Col. James F. Randlett
7th New Hampshire, Lt. Col. Augustus W. Rollins
16th New York Heavy Artillery
Cos. A, B, C, F, G, K, Lt. Freeman Huntington

Second Division
Bvt. Maj. Gen. Adelbert Ames

First Brigade
Col. Rufus Daggett
3rd New York, Lt. George E. Avent
112th New York, Lt. Col. Ephraim A. Ludwick
117th New York, Capt. Edward Downer
142nd New York, Lt. Col. Albert M. Barney

Second Brigade
Lt. Col. James A. Colvin
47th New York, Capt. Joseph M. McDonald
Capt. Frank A. Butts
48th New York, Maj. Nere A. Elfwing (W)
Capt. Van Rensselaer Hilliard
76th Pennsylvania, Maj. Charles Knerr
97th Pennsylvania, Maj. William H. Martin
203rd Pennsylvania, Capt. Heber B. Essington
Lt. Col. Amos W. Bachman

Third Brigade
Col. Frank Granger
13th Indiana, Lt. Col. Samuel M. Zent
9th Maine, Lt. Col. Joseph Noble
4th New Hampshire, Capt. John H. Roberts
Lt. Col. Frank Parker
115th New York, Maj. Ezra Walrath
Lt. Col. Nathan J. Johnson
169th New York, Lt. Col. James A. Colvin
Capt. Edwin R. Smith

Artillery
1st Connecticut Heavy Artillery Cos. B, G, L
Capt. William Pride
16th New York Independent Battery Light Artillery
Capt. Richard H. Lee
2nd Pennsylvania Heavy Artillery Co. A
Capt. Benjamin F. Everett

Engineers
15th New York Engineers Cos. A, I
Lt. K. Samuel O'Keefe

XXV Army Corps
Brig. Gen. Charles J. Paine

Third Division

Second Brigade
Col. John W. Ames
4th U.S. Colored Troops, Lt. Col. George Rogers
6th U.S. Colored Troops, Maj. Augustus S. Boernstein
30th U.S. Colored Troops, Lt. Colonel Hiram Oakman
39th U.S. Colored Troops, Col. Ozora P. Stearns

Third Brigade
Col. Elias Wright
1st U.S. Colored Troops, Lt. Col. Giles H. Rich
5th U.S. Colored Troops, Maj. William R. Brazie
10th U.S. Colored Troops, Lt. Col. Edward Powell
27th U.S. Colored Troops, Bvt. Brig. Gen. Albert Blackman
Lt. Col. John Donnellan
37th U.S. Colored Troops, Col. Nathan Goff, Jr.

Artillery
3rd U.S., Regular Army, Battery E
Lt. John Myrick

UNITED STATES NAVY
**Disposition of Navy Vessels Near Wilmington,
North Carolina, February 1, 1865**
Rear Adm. David D. Porter, commanding

Ship's Name / Number of Guns / Commanding Officer

Cape Fear River
Berberry / 4 / Acting Ens. Robert W. Rowntree
Chippewa / 6 / Lt. Cmdr. Aaron Weaver
Eolus / 4 / Acting Mstr. Edward S. Keyser
Gettysburg / 7 / Acting Mstr. Charles B. Dahlgren
Huron / 5 / Lt. Cmdr. Thomas O. Selfridge
Iosco / 10 / Cmdr. John Guest
Kansas / 8 / Lt. Cmdr. Pendleton G. Watmough
Launch No. 6 / 1 / Gunner Hubert Peters
Lenapee / 10 / Lt. Cmdr. Samuel Magaw
Little Ada / 2 / Acting Mstr. Samuel P. Crafts
Mackinaw / 10 / Cmdr. John C. Beaumont
Malvern / 12 / Ensign William C. Wise
Maumee / 3 / Lt. Cmdr. Ralph Chandler
Moccasin / 3 / Acting Ens. James Brown
Montauk / 2 / Lt. Cmdr. Edward Stone
Nansemond / 3 / Acting Mstr. James H. Porter
Nyack / 8 / Lt. Cmdr. L. Howard Newman
Osceola / 10 / Cmdr. J. M. B. Clitz
Pawtuxet / 10 / Cmdr. James H. Spotts
Pequot / 3 / Lt. Cmdr. Daniel Braine
Pontoosuc / 12 / Lt. Cmdr. William Temple
Republic / 1 / Acting Ens. John W. Bennett
Sassacus / 12 / Lt. Cmdr. John L. Davis
Seneca / 5 / Lt. Cmdr. Montgomery Sicard
Shawmut / 8 / Lt. Cmdr. John G. Walker
Tacony / 12 / Lt. Cmdr. William T. Truxton
Unadilla / 6 / Lt. Cmdr. Frank M. Ramsay
Wilderness / 4 / Acting Mstr. Henry Arey
Yantic / 5 / Lt. Cmdr. Thomas C. Harris

New Inlet / Fort Fisher
Aries / 7 / Acting Vol. Lt. James M. Williams
Emma / 8 / Acting Mstr. James Hamilton
Fahkee / 5 / Acting Mstr. Francis R. Webb
Fort Donelson / 1 / Acting Mstr. George W. Frost
Gov. Buckingham / 6 Acting Vol. Lt. J. MacDiarmid

Howquah / 5 / Acting Vol. Lt. John W. Balch
Keystone State / 6 / Cmdr. Henry Rolando
Montgomery / 6 / Acting Vol. Lt. Thomas C. Dunn
Vicksburg / 6 / Lt. William U. Grozier

Old Inlet / Smithville
Bat / 3 / Lt. Cmdr. John S. Barnes
Maratanza / 6 / Lt. Cmdr. George Young
Monticello / 6 / Lt. Cmdr. William B. Cushing
R. R. Cuyler / 12 / Cmdr. Charles H. B. Caldwell

**Disposition of Navy Vessels Near Wilmington,
North Carolina, February 15, 1865**
Rear Adm. David D. Porter, commanding

Ship's Name / Number of Guns / Commanding Officer

Cape Fear River
Bat / 3 / Lt. Cmdr. John S. Barnes
Berberry / 4 / Acting Ens. Robert W. Rowntree
Chippewa / 6 / Lt. Cmdr. Aaron Weaver
Emma / 8 / Acting Mstr. James Hamilton
Eolus / 4 / Acting Mstr. Edward S. Keyser
Huron / 5 / Lt. Cmdr. Thomas O. Selfridge
Kansas / 8 / Lt. Cmdr. Pendleton G. Watmough
Launch No. 1 / 1
Launch No. 6 / 1 / Acting Ens. C. S. Willcox
Lenapee / 10 / Lt. Cmdr. John S. Barnes
Little Ada / 2 / Acting Mstr. Samuel P. Crafts
Mackinaw / 10 / Cmdr. John C. Beaumont
Malvern / 12 / Ensign William C. Wise
Maratanza / 6 / Lt. Cmdr. George Young
Maumee / 3 / Lt. Cmdr. Ralph Chandler
Moccasin / 3 / Acting Ens. James Brown
Montauk / 2 / Lt. Cmdr. Edward Stone
Nansemond / 3 / Acting Mstr. James H. Porter
Nyack / 8 / Lt. Cmdr. L. Howard Newman
Osceola / 10 / Cmdr. J. B. M. Clitz
Pawtuxet / 10 / Cmdr. James H. Spotts
Pequot / 8 / Lt. Cmdr. Daniel Braine
Pontoosuc / 12 / Lt. Cmdr. William G. Temple
Republic / 1 / Acting Ens. John W. Bennett
Sassacus / 12 / Lt. Cmdr. John L. Davis
Seneca / 5 / Lt. Cmdr. Montgomery Sicard
Shawmut / 8 / Lt. Cmdr. John G. Walker
Unadilla / 6 / Lt. Cmdr. Frank M. Ramsay
Wilderness / 4 / Acting Mstr Henry Arey
Yantic / 5 / Lt. Cmdr. Thomas C. Harris

New Inlet / Fort Fisher
Aries / 7 / Acting Vol. Lt. James M. Williams
Howquah / 5 / Acting Vol. Lt. John W. Balch
Keystone State / 6 / Cmdr. Henry Rolando
Montgomery / 6 / Acting Vol. Lt. Thomas C. Dunn
Monticello / 6 / Lt. Cmdr. William B. Cushing
R. R. Cuyler / 12 / Cmdr. Charles H. B. Caldwell
Vicksburg / 6 / Acting Mstr. William Grozier

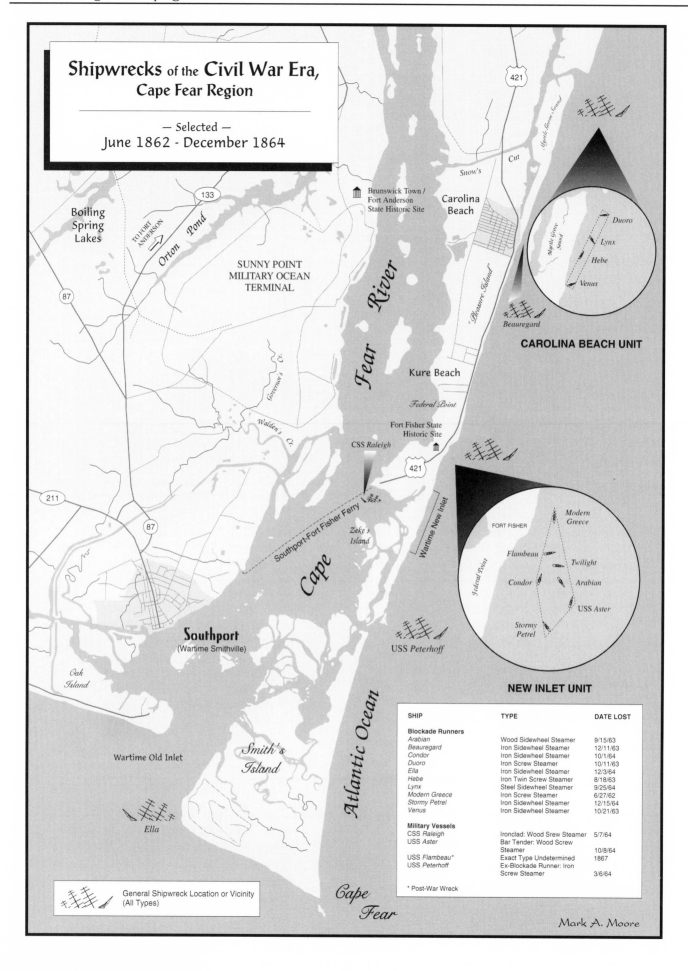

Shipwrecks of the Civil War Era, Cape Fear Region

— Selected —
June 1862 - December 1864

Boiling Spring Lakes

TO FORT ANDERSON

Orton Pond

SUNNY POINT MILITARY OCEAN TERMINAL

Brunswick Town / Fort Anderson State Historic Site

Snow's Cut

Carolina Beach

"Pleasure Island"

Fear River

Governor's Cr.

Walden's Cr.

Kure Beach

Federal Point

Fort Fisher State Historic Site

CSS Raleigh

Southport-Fort Fisher Ferry

Zeke's Island

Cape

Southport
(Wartime Smithville)

Oak Island

Wartime Old Inlet

Smith's Island

Ella

Wartime New Inlet

USS Peterhoff

Atlantic Ocean

Cape Fear

CAROLINA BEACH UNIT

Myrtle Grove Sound

Duoro
Lynx
Hebe
Venus

Beauregard

NEW INLET UNIT

FORT FISHER

Federal Point

Modern Greece
Flambeau
Twilight
Condor
Arabian
USS Aster
Stormy Petrel

General Shipwreck Location or Vicinity (All Types)

SHIP	TYPE	DATE LOST
Blockade Runners		
Arabian	Wood Sidewheel Steamer	9/15/63
Beauregard	Iron Sidewheel Steamer	12/11/63
Condor	Iron Sidewheel Steamer	10/1/64
Duoro	Iron Screw Steamer	10/11/63
Ella	Iron Sidewheel Steamer	12/3/64
Hebe	Iron Twin Screw Steamer	8/18/63
Lynx	Steel Sidewheel Steamer	9/25/64
Modern Greece	Iron Screw Steamer	6/27/62
Stormy Petrel	Iron Sidewheel Steamer	12/15/64
Venus	Iron Sidewheel Steamer	10/21/63
Military Vessels		
CSS Raleigh	Ironclad: Wood Srew Steamer	5/7/64
USS Aster	Bar Tender: Wood Screw Steamer	10/8/64
USS Flambeau*	Exact Type Undetermined	1867
USS Peterhoff	Ex-Blockade Runner: Iron Screw Steamer	3/6/64

* Post-War Wreck

Mark A. Moore

Appendix C

Civil War Era Shipwrecks of the Cape Fear Region

As identified and studied by the North Carolina Underwater Archaeology Unit

NEW INLET UNIT

A group of seven wrecks is located above the mouth of wartime New Inlet, the most active point of entry for blockade runners seeking access to the Cape Fear River. New Inlet was closed in the late nineteenth century.

Modern Greece (Blockade Runner) - Iron screw steamer. *Length*: 224 feet. *Beam*: 29 feet. *Draft*: 17 feet, three inches. Built in Stockton-on-Tess, England, 1859. Lost on June 27, 1862, with a full cargo of clothing, brandy, cutlery, weapons, and ammunition. She was run aground by Union blockaders, and the Confederates managed to save a portion of her cargo. Today, the Fort Fisher visitor center displays items salvaged from this wreck.

Arabian (Blockade Runner) - Wood sidewheel steamer. *Length*: 174 feet. *Beam*: 24 feet. Built in Ontario, Canada, 1851. Lost September 15, 1863. She was chased aground off New Inlet and subsequently broken apart during a storm. The majority of her cargo of cotton was salvaged and later sold.

Condor (Blockade Runner) - Iron sidewheel steamer. *Length*: 220 feet. *Beam*: 20 feet. Built in Glasgow, Scotland, 1864. Lost October 1, 1864. Inbound from Halifax, Nova Scotia, she ran aground off Fort Fisher with two prominent passengers on board: James B. Holcomb (Confederate Commissioner to Great Britain), and Confederate spy Rose O'Neal Greenhow. Mrs. Greenhow drowned when her lifeboat capsized in the surf. Two months after grounding the ship broke apart in the surf. The hulk was then used for target practice by the gunners of Fort Fisher. The death date on Mrs. Greenhow's tombstone reads September 30, 1864.

Stormy Petrel (Blockade Runner) - Wood sidewheel steamer. *Length*: 240 feet. *Beam*: 32 feet. Built in Scotland, 1851. Lost December 15, 1864, with a cargo of clothing and munitions of war. She was driven aground on the south breakers by Union gunboats. Federal attempts to destroy the vessel failed, but a northeast gale accomplished the task. Today, a bell salvaged from this vessel and bearing its name is on display in the Fort Fisher visitor center.

USS Aster (Union Bar Tender) - Wood screw steamer. *Length*: 122.5 feet. *Beam*: 23 feet. *Draft*: 10-12 feet. Oceangoing tug purchased at Philadelphia, Pennsylvania, and converted for blockade duty. Lost October 8, 1864. She ran aground on the eastern extremity of Carolina Shoals while chasing a blockade runner.

CSS Raleigh (Confederate Warship) - Ironclad Steamer, Richmond Class. *Length*: 150 feet. *Beam*: 32 feet. Built in Wilmington, North Carolina, 1863-1864. Lost May 7, 1864. Outfitted with four 6-inch rifles and inadequate steam engines, this vessel ran aground inside New Inlet after several hours of indecisive naval maneuvers. Unable to refloat the heavy warship, the Confederates destroyed it. This wreck remained a dangerous obstacle in the shipping channel until New Inlet was closed.

Twilight - Sank December 1865.

Flambeau - Former transport USS *Flambeau*, sank 1867. Transported troops to the Wilmington area.

CAROLINA BEACH UNIT

A group of four wrecks is located roughly midway between New Inlet and Masonboro Inlet, north of present-day Carolina Beach.

Venus (Blockade Runner) - Iron sidewheel steamer. *Length*: Uncertain. Possibly 265 feet. Date of origin uncertain. Lost October 21, 1863, with a cargo of quartermaster and commissary stores. She was chased aground by Union blockaders while en route to New Inlet.

Lynx (Blockade Runner) - Steel sidewheel steamer. *Length*: 220 feet. *Beam*: 24 feet. Built in Liverpool, England, 1864. Lost September 25, 1864, with a cargo of 600 bales of cotton and $50,000 in government gold. She was chased aground while outbound from Wilmington. The gold was removed and the vessel burned to prevent capture. Much of the ship's cotton was thrown overboard in her attempt to outrun Union blockaders.

Hebe (Blockade Runner) - Iron twin screw steamer. *Length*: 165 feet. *Beam*: 23 feet. Built in London, England, 1863. Lost August 18, 1863. Inbound from Nassau, Bahamas, she ran aground en route to New Inlet. Much of the vessel's cargo was salvaged, and the wreck was shelled by Union blockaders.

Duoro (Blockade Runner) - Iron screw steamer. Outfitted for blockade running at Liverpool, England, 1862. Lost October 11, 1863, with a cargo of cotton, tobacco, and naval stores. Outbound from New Inlet, she reversed course when spotted by Union blockaders, but was run aground and destroyed.

Individual Wrecks

Beauregard (Blockade Runner) - Iron sidewheel steamer. *Length*: 223 feet. *Beam*: 26.5 feet. *Draft*: 7 feet, 6 inches. Built in Glasgow, Scotland, 1858. Lost December 11, 1863, off present-day Carolina Beach. Inbound for New Inlet, she was boxed in by Federal blockaders before being run aground and destroyed. This wreck remains visible at low tide.

USS Peterhoff (Union Blockader) - Iron screw steamer. *Length*: 210 feet. *Beam*: 28 feet. Built before the war in Petrodvorets, on the Gulf of Finland, as a pleasure yacht for the Czar of Russia. Lost March 6, 1864. This one-time blockade runner was seized by the U.S. Navy and converted into a blockader—outfitted with deck guns from stem to stern. She was lost off Smith's Island after colliding with the USS *Monticello*. Confederate historian T. C. Davis remembered that the vessel was sunk by Confederate artillery onshore. See page 11. Two 32-pounder cannon tubes were salvaged from this wreck and are on display at Fort Fisher—one at Shepherd's Battery, and one in front of the visitor center.

Ella (Blockade Runner) - Iron sidewheel steamer. *Length*: 225 feet. *Beam*: 28 feet. Built in Dumbarton, Scotland, 1864. Lost December 3, 1864, with a cargo of luxury items and munitions of war. Inbound from Nassau, Bahamas, she ran aground at Old Inlet and was destroyed. For an account of the loss of this vessel, see page 11.

Interestingly, the remains of the USS *Louisiana*—Gen. Benjamin Butler's ill-fated "powder vessel"—have never been identified.

Not Pictured: Lockwood's Folly Unit—*Elizabeth*, *Bendigo*, and USS *Iron Age*. Others—*Phantom*, *Wild Dayrell*, *Sophia*, and *Ranger*. All are blockade runners except *Iron Age*.

The Underwater Archaeology Unit is charged with conducting and/or supervising the surveillance, protection, preservation, survey, and systematic underwater archaeological recovery of shipwrecks and other underwater archaeological sites throughout North Carolina. The unit's fascinating exhibit, *Hidden Beneath the Waves*, is open to the public at Fort Fisher. For more information contact:

Underwater Archaeology Unit
P.O. Box 58
Kure Beach, NC 28449
Phone: (910) 458-9042
Fax: (910) 458-4093

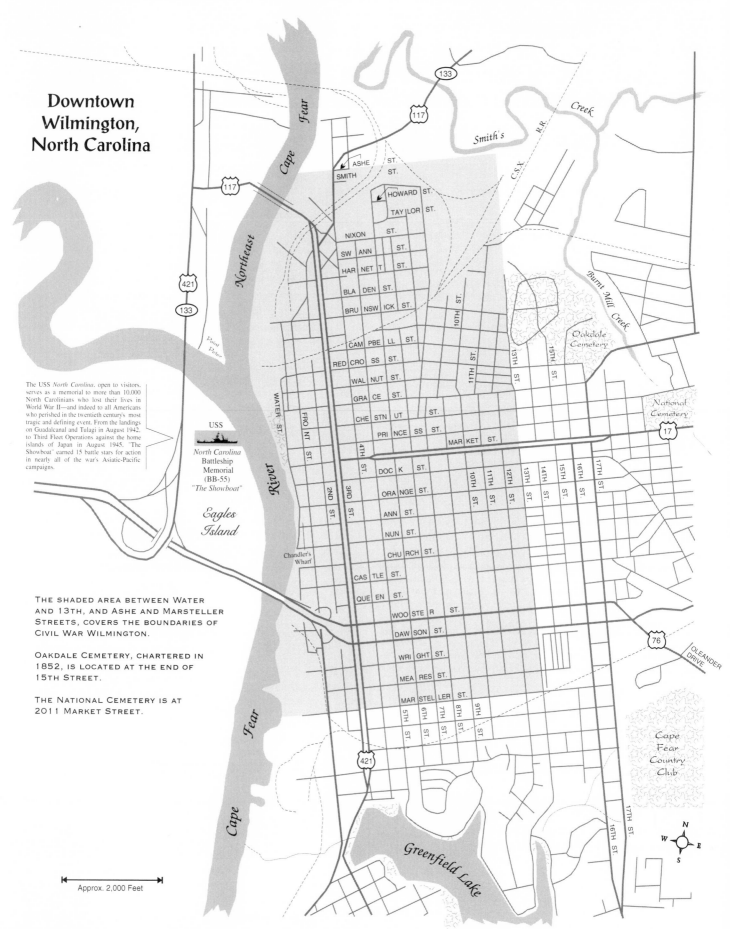

Downtown
Wilmington,
North Carolina

The USS *North Carolina*, open to visitors, serves as a memorial to more than 10,000 North Carolinians who lost their lives in World War II—and indeed to all Americans who perished in the twentieth century's most tragic and defining event. From the landings on Guadalcanal and Tulagi in August 1942, to Third Fleet Operations against the home islands of Japan in August 1945, "The Showboat" earned 15 battle stars for action in nearly all of the war's Asiatic-Pacific campaigns.

USS
North Carolina
Battleship
Memorial
(BB-55)
"The Showboat"

*Eagles
Island*

THE SHADED AREA BETWEEN WATER AND 13TH, AND ASHE AND MARSTELLER STREETS, COVERS THE BOUNDARIES OF CIVIL WAR WILMINGTON.

OAKDALE CEMETERY, CHARTERED IN 1852, IS LOCATED AT THE END OF 15TH STREET.

THE NATIONAL CEMETERY IS AT 2011 MARKET STREET.

Approx. 2,000 Feet

Mark A. Moore

Appendix D

Wartime and Other Points of Interest in Wilmington, North Carolina

Bellamy Mansion

Fifth & Market Streets. Grand home of retired physician and wealthy planter Dr. John D. Bellamy. The house served as headquarters for Northern military authorities during the Federal occupation of Wilmington. Among them were Maj. Gen. Jacob D. Cox and Brig. Gen. Joseph R. Hawley, the stern post commandant. General Hawley refused to allow Dr. Bellamy and his family to return to their home during the occupation. Today the structure houses the Bellamy Mansion Museum of History and Design Arts. *Fee.* (910) 251-3700

Beery's Shipyard

Stood on Eagles Island, opposite the Wilmington waterfront. Benjamin W. and William L. Beery's shipyard was in operation before the outbreak of hostilities, and saw additional prosperity during the war with a contract to build and repair vessels for the Confederate government.

Burgwin-Wright House

Third and Market Streets. (ca. 1770). Built in the Georgian style on the stone foundation of the old town jail. This colonial gentleman's townhouse served as headquarters for Lt. Gen. Lord Cornwallis of the British Army, upon his retreat to Wilmington following the Battle of Guilford Court House during the American Revolution. *Fee.* (910) 762-0570

Clarendon Iron Works

Stood on Queen Street, between Surry & Water Streets. This metal fabric shop was started during the war to help keep up with the Confederacy's increasing demands for industrial output. It handled machine work for both of Wilmington's major shipyards. *See map on page 135.*

City Market

Middle of Market & Front Streets. Located in the center of Wilmington's business district, the City Market peddled poultry, fish, and produce from stalls along the street. Slaves were also bought and sold here.

Cassidey's Shipyard

Foot of Church Street. James Cassidey's shipyard was in operation before the outbreak of hostilities, and saw additional prosperity during the war with a contract to build and repair vessels for the Confederate government. *See map on page 135.*

Causten House

Stood on Orange Street, between 8th & 9th Streets. Regimental headquarters of the 3rd New Hampshire Infantry during the occupation of Wilmington in 1865. The main body of the regiment camped north of Orange Street, between 9th & 10th, facing east.

Chestnut St. Presbyterian Church

710½ Chestnut Street. Established in 1858, this is the only surviving Carpenter Italianate church. It originated as a mission church for the First Presbyterian Church, and has served an African American congregation since 1867.

City Hall

Third & Princess Streets. With Thalian Hall, built for combined government and theater use, both of which continue today. At this place Mayor John Dawson, a Union sympathizer, formally surrendered Wilmington to Maj. Gen. Alfred H. Terry on February 22, 1865. *Groups by appointment. Fee.* (910) 343-3660

DeRosset House

Second and Dock Streets. Headquarters of Gen. Braxton Bragg, Confederate District of the Cape Fear. During the Federal occupation, the DeRosset family—ardent Southern sympathizers—were required to pay rent for the privilege of living in their own home. Unable to make payment, the family was forced to accept a Union boarder. The house is the present-day headquarters for the Historic Wilmington Foundation, Inc. (910) 762-2511

First Baptist Church

Fifth and Market Streets. (1859-1870). The congregation of this Early English Gothic Revival church was founded in 1808. Designed by architect Samuel Sloan, of Philadelphia, Pennsylvania.

Front Street

Wilmington Waterfront. Federal troops of Maj. Gen. Alfred H. Terry entered Wilmington around 9:30 a.m. on February 22, 1865, and marched northward up Front Street. They were led by the 3rd New Hampshire Infantry of Abbott's Brigade. Curious throngs of slaves and residents lined the streets as the Federal army poured into Wilmington.

Hart & Baily's Iron and Copper Works

Stood on South Front Street. Hart & Baily's was a metal fabric shop, and supplier of machine work to both of Wilmington's major shipyards.

Paddy's Hollow

Waterfront. Wilmington's "red light district" during the Civil War. In September 1863, three policemen were beaten and stabbed in Paddy's Hollow by a group of drunken soldiers from Texas. The blockade-running trade transformed Wilmington from a quiet port city to a crowded and bustling maritime center teeming with the dregs of society.

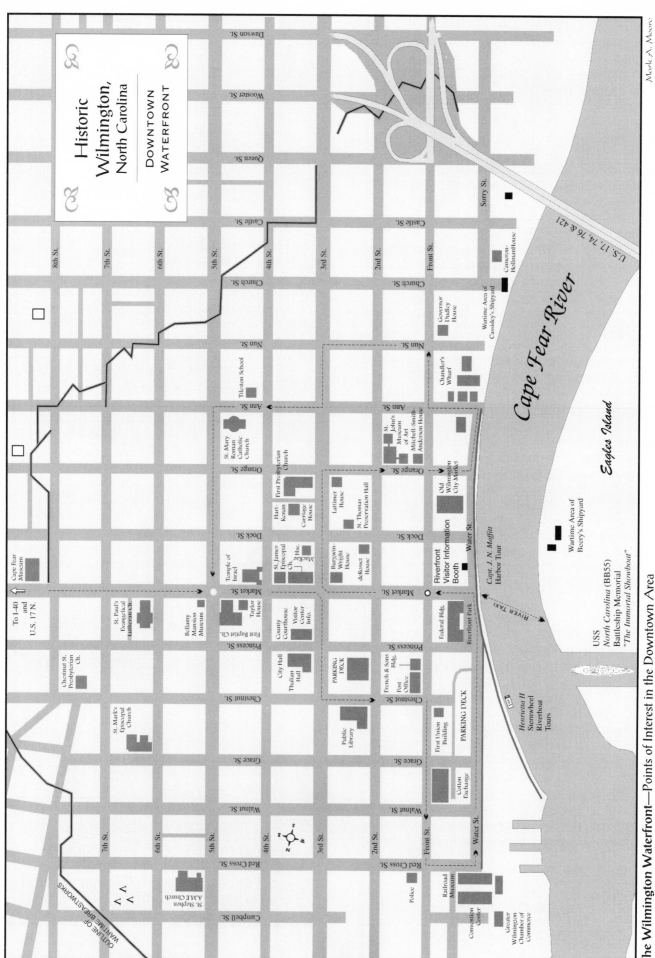

Historic Wilmington, North Carolina

DOWNTOWN WATERFRONT

Mark A. Moore

The Wilmington Waterfront—Points of Interest in the Downtown Area

Crime and prostitution were rampant, and military forces were brought in to protect the interests of the Confederate government. *See map on page 135.*

Surrender of Wilmington

Corner of Front & Market Streets. Here a mounted Federal advance was greeted by Wilmington Mayor John Dawson and others, in preparation for the surrender of the city, February 22, 1865. The official surrender occurred in City Hall at 3rd & Princess Streets.

Marine (General) Hospital

Stood on 8th Street, between Nun & Church Streets. At the former U.S. Marine Hospital, a large and substantial brick building, surgeons from the 3rd New Hampshire and others attended sick and wounded soldiers during the occupation. *See map on page 135.*

St. James Episcopal Church

Third and Market Streets. (1839-1840). Congregation established 1729. Designed by Thomas U. Walter of Philadelphia, in the Gothic Revival style. During the occupation, the Rev. Alfred A. Watson (a native of New York) was accused of allowing his congregation to avoid expressing allegiance to the Union. Wilmington's Federal post commandant, Joseph R. Hawley, reacted by closing St. James and suspending Watson's religious privileges. In the care of surgeon C. MacFarlane, this Gothic Revival church was soon converted into a general hospital for sick Union soldiers. The altar and pews were removed by a squad of United States Colored Troops, and iron bedsteads were fitted in their places. The hospital at St. James was considered sacrilege by the pro-Confederate Episcopalians of Wilmington, and the "*desecration rankled in their hearts.*" Nevertheless, surgeon MacFarlane considered it "*a model hospital—the show hospital and I was very proud of it.*" The church was returned to its congregation by Christmas 1865, and remains in use today. The St. James Graveyard (ca. 1745-1855) features many eighteenth-century tombstones.

St. Paul's Evangelical Lutheran Church

Sixth and Market Streets. (1859-1869). The congregation of this Greek Revival and Gothic Revival church was founded in 1858, to accommodate a growing German population.

Wilmington Theater (Thalian Hall)

Third and Chestnut Streets, next to City Hall. With City Hall, built for combined government and theater use, both of which continue today. The theater was a source of great entertainment for Federal soldiers, and the site of a Union rally on March 14, 1865, during the occupation of Wilmington. Here, having remained relatively quiet during the war, loyal residents reaffirmed their support for the United States. The meeting made national headlines in the north, and shocked the Southern presses. *Groups by appointment. Fee.* (910) 343-3660

St. James Episcopal Church, as it appeared in the late nineteenth century. From *Wilmington: Past, Present, and Future,* 1884.

BELOW: 1 South Third Street: St. James Church as it appears today, in a photograph taken from the opposite angle of the historic view above.

Author's Collection

APPENDIX D—Wilmington Attractions

The Wilmington Waterfront, north of the foot of Market Street, in a view taken from Eagles Island.

A large Coast Guard cutter is docked along the riverwalk.

On the left, below the Hilton Hotel, is the sternwheel cruise vessel *Henrietta II*.

Author's Collection

USS *North Carolina* Battleship Memorial (BB55)

Cape Fear River at Eagles Island, Jct. Highways 17/74/ 76/421. A moving tribute to veterans, and a memorial to the 10,000 North Carolinians who did not return from World War II. "The Showboat"—a technological marvel of its era—spent 40 months in World War II combat zones, was torpedoed off the island of Guadalcanal on September 15, 1942, and earned 15 battle stars in the major actions of the Pacific theater. *Fee.* (910) 350-1817

Cape Fear Coast Convention and Visitors Bureau

Third and Princess Streets. Visitor information center. Located in the Third County Courthouse (1892), the center features an orientation video, maps, brochures, and tourist information. (910) 341-4030 OR (800) 222-4757. Handicap Accessible.

Cape Fear Museum

814 Market Street. Established 1898. Interprets southeastern North Carolina history, from prehistory to the twentieth century. (910) 341-7413. Handicap Accessible.

Captain J. N. Maffitt Harbor Tour

Seasonal. Cruise into Wilmington's historic past aboard a Cape Fear River tour boat. *Fee.* (910) 343-1611

Chandler's Wharf

Ann and Water Streets. Specialty shops and fine dining on the Cape Fear River in historic downtown Wilmington. Five acres of nostalgic Wilmington! Free parking.

Cotton Exchange

North Front Street, 300 block. A complex of unique shops in well preserved turn-of-the-century buildings. Free parking. (910) 343-9896

Henrietta II

Sternwheeler Riverboat Cruises. Board at the Riverwalk, across from the Parking Deck, and enjoy narrated sightseeing tours, dinner, moonlight cruises, or private charters. *Fee.* (910) 343-1611 OR (800) 676-0162

Horse-drawn Carriage Tours

Water and Market Streets. Costumed drivers. Available year-round. *Fee.* (910) 251-8889

Latimer House

Third and Orange Streets. Headquarters of the Lower Cape Fear Historical Society. Built in 1852 for a prominent merchant's family, this Italianate home features original furnishings. The house, surrounded by a beautifully restored Victorian garden, recreates the opulent lifestyle of *ante-bellum* Wilmington. *Fee.* (910) 762-0492

Old Wilmington City Market

119 S. Water Street. Permanent shops and daily vendors. (910) 763-9748

Railroad Museum

Red Cross and Water Streets. The story of railroading during Wilmington's heyday—from the Wilmington & Weldon to present-day railroads. For more than a century, railroading was Wilmington's chief industry. *Fee.* (910) 763-2634

Oakdale Cemetery

520 North 15th Street (End of 15th). Chartered in 1852, this scenic 165-acre cemetery is the last resting place for many people associated with Civil War Wilmington and the defense of Fort Fisher. Among the more than twenty-two thousand burials are Maj. Gen. W. H. C. Whiting, Maj. James Reilly, Col. John J. Hedrick, Maj. Charles P. Bolles, Benjamin Beery, Rose O'Neal Greenhow, John Newland Maffitt (the famous blockade-running captain), and James Sprunt (chronicler of Cape Fear lore). Confederate dead were reinterred here beginning in 1867. Other prominent burials include George Davis (attorney general of the Confederacy), Edward B. Dudley (the first governor of North Carolina elected by popular vote), and Henry Bacon Jr. (architect of the Lincoln Memorial in Washington, D.C.). *See map on page 168.* (910) 762-5682

National Cemetery

2011 Market Street. In 1867, Union dead from Fort Fisher were reinterred on this ground, outside the city limits of Wilmington. Today, row upon row of small white markers identify the resting places of our nation's servicemen and their families, from veterans of the Civil War through World War I, World War II, Korea, and Vietnam. The caretaker's lodge houses offices for the Disabled American Veterans and the New Hanover Veterans Council. *See map on page 168.* (910) 815-4877

"Wild Rose"

"A BEARER OF DISPATCHES TO THE
CONFEDERATE GOVERNMENT.
DROWNED OFF FORT FISHER,
FROM THE STEAMER CONDOR,
WHILE ATTEMPTING TO RUN THE BLOCKADE
SEPTEMBER 30, 1864"

—From the tombstone of Rose O'Neal Greenhow

Wilmington, N.C., Oct. 1, 1864

The Late Mrs. Rose A. [O'Neal] Greenhow

"We have recorded the following letter, detailing the last rite of respect to the lady whose name is above written:

"On Saturday morning, October 1, a dispatch was received in Wilmington, by Mrs. De Prossoi, President of the Soldiers' Aid Society, stating that the body of Mrs. Greenhow had been recovered from the sea at Fort Fisher, and would be sent to town for internment. The ill-fated lady — passenger in the Steamer Condor, which got aground in attempting to run in at New Inlet — was drowned in trying to reach the shore in a small boat, which swamped the 'rips.'

"A hundred houses were open to receive the lady, but a meeting of the Soldiers' Aid Society being hastily convened, it was judged proper to have the funeral obsequies as public as possible, to which end the chapel attached to Hospital No. 4 was beautifully arranged, by order of the surgeon in charge, Dr. Micks, and here it was proposed the corpse should lie in state.

"On the arrival of the steamer Cape Fear, which was appointed to convey the remains to town, the ladies lined the wharf, closing round and receiving into their midst the lifeless form of her who had been so zealous, so devoted, and so self-sacrificing an adherent of the cause dearest to all their hearts. She was then carried to the chapel, where a guard of honor was stationed at the door.

"It was a solemn and imposing spectacle. The profusion of wax lights round the corpse; the quantity of choice flowers in crosses, garlands and bouquets, scattered over it; the silent mourners, sable-robed, at the head and foot; the tide of visitors, women and children with streaming eyes, and soldiers, with bent heads and hushed stares, standing by, paying the last tribute of respect to the departed heroine. On the bier, draped with a magnificent Confederate flag, lay the body, so unchanged as to look like a calm sleeper, while above rose the tall ebony crucifix, emblem of the faith she embraced in happier hours, and which, we humbly trust, was her consolation in passing through the dark waters of the river of death.

"She lay there until 2 o'clock of Sunday afternoon, when the body was removed to the Catholic Church of St. Thomas. Here the funeral oration was delivered by the Rev. Dr. Corcoran, which was a touching tribute to the heroism and patriotic devotion of the deceased, as well as a solemn warning on the uncertainty of all human projects and ambition, even though of the most laudable character.

"The coffin, which was as richly decorated as the resources of the town admitted and still covered with the Confederate flag,

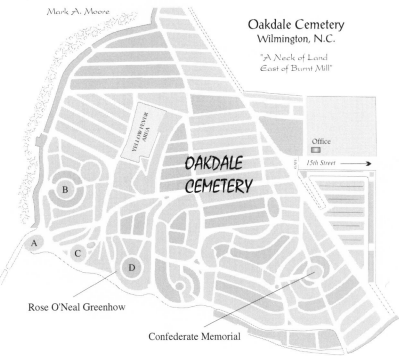

Mark A. Moore

Oakdale Cemetery
Wilmington, N.C.

"A Neck of Land
East of Burnt Mill"

YELLOW FEVER AREA

OAKDALE CEMETERY

Office

15th Street →

Rose O'Neal Greenhow

Confederate Memorial

was borne to Oakdale Cemetery followed by an immense funeral cortege. A beautiful spot on a grassy slope, overshadowed by wavering trees and in sight of a tranquil lake was chosen for her resting place. Rain fell in torrents during the day, but as the coffin was being lowered into the grave, the sun burst forth in the brightest majesty, and a rainbow of the most vivid colour spanned the horizon. Let us accept the omen not only for her, the quiet sleeper, who after many storms and a tumultuous and checkered life came to peace and rest at last, but also for our beloved country, over which we trust the rainbow of hope will ere long shine with brightest dyes.

"The pall-bearers were Colonel Tansill, chief of staff to General Whiting, Major Vanderhorst, J. M. Seixas. Esq., Dr. de Prossett, Dr. Micks and Dr. Medway.

"General Whiting and Captain C. B. Poindexter, representing the two services, were prevented from acting as pall-bearers, the former by reason of absence, the latter in consequence of illness.

"The ladies of the Wilmington Soldiers' Aid Society would have performed the last office for anyone coming to them under similar sad circumstances, but with how much greater respect and affection for her who endured imprisonment, sickness, losses of various kinds, and finally death itself, through devotion to the holy cause which was the very main spring and breath of her existence.

"At the last day, when the martyrs who have with their blood sealed their devotion to liberty shall stand together firm witnesses that truth is stronger than death, foremost among the shining throng, coequal with the Rolands and Joan d'Arcs of history will appear the Confederate heroine, Rose A. Greenhow." •

—*Wilmington newspaper clipping from the Alexander Robinson Boteler Papers, Special Collections Library, Duke University, Durham, N.C.*

Author's Collection

The Wilmington National Cemetery

The marker at left reads:

"50 U.S. Soldiers
From Fort Fisher
N.C."

Oakdale Cemetery

The plaque below
adorns the base of the
Confederate Memorial
Monument at Oakdale.

One marker at Oakdale Cemetery identifies a fallen soldier by name only (one of several such memorials at the cemetery). Lieutenant Zaccheus Ellis, a Wilmingtonian of the 1st Battalion North Carolina Heavy Artillery, had survived the Wilmington Campaign unscathed, but the young officer was not so fortunate in battling the minions of Maj. Gen. William T. Sherman in the pine barrens of North Carolina:

"Lieutenant Zaccheus Ellis,
Born in Wilmington, North Carolina,
January 15, 1839.
Killed in Defence of His Country
at the Battle of Bentonville, N.C.,
March 19, 1865.
He Sleeps in an Unknown Grave
on The Battlefield.
Son of Charles D. Ellis."

—From the stately monument marking Lieutenant Ellis' memorial at Oakdale.

"You can have no idea, Mother, of my feelings," Ellis had written a week after the fall of Wilmington, *"knowing that our old town was doomed. The shops are all closed, Government property being destroyed, huge piles of cotton and rosin being set afire, tobacco being thrown into the river. You can't imagine anything like it."*

Zaccheus Ellis died while fighting with Johnson Hagood's Brigade in the swampy wilderness below the old Goldsboro Road, on the first day of the Battle of Bentonville.

Appendix E

A Driving Tour of Points of Interest Associated with the Wilmington Campaign

Mileage is approximate and may vary according to vehicle

The first leg of the tour follows the opposite direction taken by Maj. Gen. Alfred Terry's Union troops in their advance from Sugar Loaf to Wilmington in February 1865.

— The Engagement at Forks Road and the Advance on Wilmington —

An actual avenue named "Forks Road" has never been identified. This label, however, appeared on several of Maj. Gen. Robert F. Hoke's official dispatches during his defense of the area. In traditional lore, the name for the engagement — unsupported by historical documentation—has come down through the years as the "Battle of Jumpin' Run."

♦ *From downtown Wilmington, drive south on 16th Street and merge onto 17th Street. Continue southward on 17th Street Extension, across Shipyard Blvd. The remnants of Hoke's Confederate earthworks are at the intersection of 17th Street Extension and Independence Blvd. Extension.*

A portion of Hoke's final defensive line against Terry's Union infantry was located here. These works, at the end of residential Charles Paine Drive and southeast of the main intersection, are on *private property*. No trespassing.

♦ *Follow 17th Street Extension until it ends. At the stoplight, turn right onto N.C. Highway 132 (College Road). From N.C. Highway 132, merge onto U.S. Highway 421. As you travel south on Highway 421 toward Carolina Beach, you are following—in the opposite direction—the approximate route that Terry's Union soldiers took during their advance on Wilmington. Continue on 421 and cross the bridge over Snow's Cut.*

Distance traveled from the 17th St./Independence Blvd. intersection to the Dow Road turnoff south of Snow's Cut: 10.8 miles.

FOR A MAP OF THE ENGAGEMENT ALONG THE FORKS ROAD ENTRENCHMENTS, SEE PAGE 120.

— The Engagement at Sugar Loaf —

The formidable Confederate defenses at Sugar Loaf kept Terry's Union infantry at bay until the fall of Fort Anderson—west of the Cape Fear River—forced Hoke's Division to retire toward Wilmington.

A Portion of the Forks Road Entrenchments *Author's Collection*
"About 18 February [1865], the division [Hoke's] received orders to move back to Wilmington. This we did, and occupied for a day or so a line much nearer to Wilmington—the breastworks of which can now be seen on riding from Wilmington to the beach on the Seacoast Railroad." —**Adjutant George M. Rose**, 66th North Carolina Infantry

For those willing to make the trek, Sugar Loaf Hill itself can be reached via Carolina Beach State Park (accessible from Dow Road above Carolina Beach). Sugar Loaf, on the banks of the Cape Fear River, is located in the southwest corner of the park.

♦ *Just south of Snow's Cut, turn right from Highway 421 onto Dow Road. At about three-quarters of a mile on Dow Road, at the intersection with Raleigh Street, the remnants of a portion of Hoke's earthworks can be seen in the woods north of the road. Further down, at the intersection with Hamlet Avenue, a small, battered granite monument identifies the area as Hoke's defensive position. Continue south on Dow Road to the intersection with 421 at Kure Beach.*

Distance traveled from the Dow Road turnoff to the intersection with Highway 421 at Kure Beach: 4 miles.

FOR A MAP OF THE ENGAGEMENT AT SUGAR LOAF, SEE PAGE 96.

"I remember as though it were yesterday, when the Federal fleet made its second attack on [Fort Fisher]. They were gathered all night in front of our home . . . keeping the air ablaze with their signal rockets. In the dawn of the morning the fleet resembled a city sitting on the sea." —**Myles Walton**, Masonboro resident

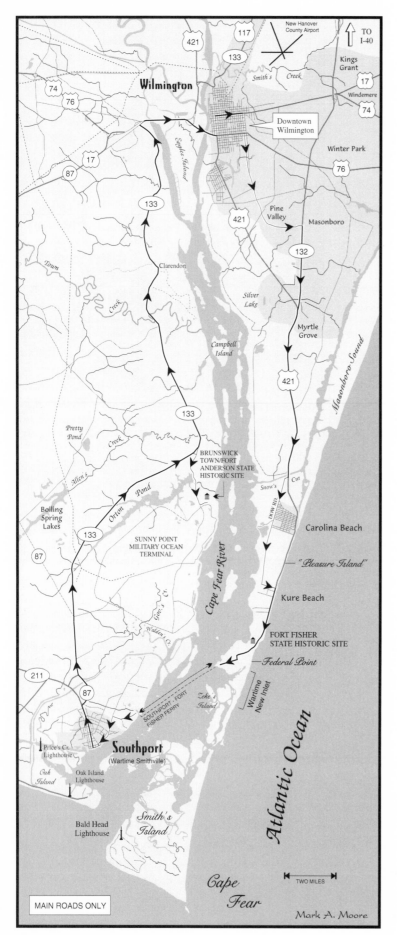

The Wilmington Tour Loop

— The Battles for Fort Fisher —

Fort Fisher State Historic Site, nestled among scenic live oak groves between the Atlantic Ocean and the Cape Fear River, is the first major stop on the Wilmington loop. The site offers exhibits, an audiovisual program, a gift shop, and guided tours of the massive remains of Fort Fisher.

♦ *At Kure Beach, turn right from Dow Road onto Highway 421, and drive southward to Fort Fisher.*

For a walking tour of Fort Fisher, with highlighted points of interest for the December 1864 and January 1865 engagements, refer to the maps on pages 34, 74, and 75. For the general vicinity of Fort Fisher, refer to the map on page 30.

Distance traveled from the Dow Rd./421 intersection to the Fort Fisher visitor center: 2 miles.

FOR MAPS OF THE DECEMBER 1864 ENGAGEMENT AT FORT FISHER, SEE PAGES 20, 22, AND 24. FOR MAPS OF THE JANUARY 1865 ENGAGEMENT AT FORT FISHER, SEE PAGES 36, 38, 40, 42, 44, 48, 57, AND 58.

— Battery Buchanan and the Fort Fisher-Southport Ferry —

Battery Buchanan is located at the tip of Federal Point, just below the ferry landing. The garrison of Fort Fisher surrendered to Federal forces here on the night of January 15, 1865.

♦ *From Fort Fisher, continue southward on Highway 421 to the ferry landing on the right.*

Also of interest in the area is the North Carolina Aquarium at Fort Fisher, located between the Civil War site and the ferry landing. Marine life exhibits highlight this fun family attraction. For the aquarium's location and contact information, refer to the map on page 30.

Distance traveled from the Fort Fisher visitor center to the ferry landing: 1.7 miles (via 421).

"There is now a terrible war of criminations and recriminating going on about the fall of Ft. Fisher, but I am sickened by it & have neither room nor interest to record it."
—**Catherine Ann Devereaux Edmondston**

To continue the tour, ride the toll ferry across the Cape Fear River to Southport.

— FERRY SCHEDULE —

Capacity is approximately 34 cars. Crossing time is approximately one-half hour. Fares and rates are applicable one way.

— Notice —
Rates and schedules are subject to change.

As a general rule, during the peak tourist hours of the summer schedule, the ferry leaves Fort Fisher every 45 minutes. The ferry's winter schedule is abbreviated, with one and one-half-hour departure intervals.

Fares and Rates:
—Pedestrian	$ .50
—Bicycle and Rider	$1.00
—Single vehicle or combination 20 feet or less in length and motorcycles (minimum fare for licensed vehicle)	$3.00
—Single vehicle or combination from 20 feet up to and including 55 feet	$6.00

Call N.C. Ferry Information at 1-800-BY-FERRY for more information.

Be sure to pick up a River Circle Tour brochure from the Fort Fisher visitor center (or elsewhere) for exact ferry departure times.

— The River Crossing —

As you depart Federal Point aboard the ferry, look to your left for a prominent view of the remnants of Battery Buchanan, located just south of the landing. As the ferryboat moves further away from shore, cross to the right-hand side of the vessel and look back toward the northeast. The earthen mounds of Fort Fisher's interior western land front will be visible in the distance.

Traveling this route takes you on essentially the same cross-channel journey that Federal steam transports took in ferrying Union troops to Smithville (now Southport) in February 1865.

— Southport, North Carolina —

The village of Southport was known as Smithville during the Civil War. Lieutenant Cmdr. William B. Cushing came ashore here in February 1865, and proclaimed himself "military governor." As you travel northward along the west side of the Cape Fear River, you are following the general direction of the Federal advance and Confederate retreat toward Wilmington.

♦ *From the ferry landing in Southport, drive .8 miles and turn left at the stop sign.*

♦ *Drive 1.2 miles and turn left onto residential Atlantic Avenue.*

♦ *Drive .1 miles on Atlantic and turn right onto Bay Street. This is the Southport waterfront.*

Colonial Fort Johnston (renamed Fort Pender during the Civil War) stood on the bluffs to the right. All that remains of the old structure is the brick officers' quarters building (now remodeled).

♦ *Continue a short distance along Bay Street and turn right onto Howe Street in downtown Southport.*

♦ *Drive 1.5 miles north and turn right onto N.C. Highway 87/133.*

Also of interest in town is the Southport Maritime Museum, which houses a collection highlighting the vast nautical history of the Lower Cape Fear. (910) 457-0003

Distance traveled from the Southport Ferry landing to the N.C. Highway 87/133 turnoff: 3.8 miles.

Fort Johnston (Pender), Southport, N.C. - Barracks
BELOW: The large rocks on the river beach are from the fort's original masonry.

Author's Collection

APPENDIX E—The Wilmington Loop

— Fort Anderson —

Due to the restricted access of Sunny Point Military Ocean Terminal, tourists cannot drive along the approximate routes of the Federal advance on Fort Anderson. Access to Brunswick Town/Fort Anderson State Historic Site—the second major stop on the Wilmington loop—must be gained through a circuitous route. Once you reach the head of Orton Pond, however, you are following the approximate route of Cox's flank march around the pond to the rear of Fort Anderson.

♦ *Drive northward on N.C. Highway 87/133. When 87 veers off to the left, continue northward on Highway 133.*

♦ *After traveling 10.7 miles from the turnoff above Southport, turn right onto Orton Road.*

♦ *Drive .2 miles and turn right onto Plantation Road. At .6 miles—traveling south on Plantation Road—Orton Pond is visible on the right.*

♦ *After driving another mile further, turn left onto St. Philips Road, and drive .3 miles to the gate at Brunswick Town/ Fort Anderson State Historic Site.*

Confederate forces west of the Cape Fear River fell back to this stronghold following the capture of Fort Fisher by Union troops in January 1865. Nestled among the foundation ruins of colonial Brunswick Town, Fort Anderson—the largest interior structure in the Cape Fear defensive network—guarded the western approaches to Wilmington.

The visitor center at this atmospheric site offers exhibits relating to both colonial and Civil War periods, an audiovisual presentation, and tours of the grounds.

For a walking tour of Brunswick Town/Fort Anderson, refer to the maps on pages 112 and 113.

Distance traveled from the 87/133 turnoff above Southport to Brunswick Town/ Fort Anderson: 12.8 miles.

For maps of the engagement at Fort Anderson, see pages 103, 104, and 106.

— Orton Plantation —

Located a short distance north of Fort Anderson is Orton Plantation, built by "King" Roger Moore in 1725. It was here, during the first attack on Fort Fisher in December 1864, that an anxious Daisy Lamb awaited news from her husband, Col. William Lamb—Fort Fisher's commanding officer. Today, Orton Plantation offers visitors a view of one of America's finest gardens. The grounds, resplendent with majestic trees, azaleas, camellias, annuals, and rare flowering plants, are open to tourists for a small fee. The plantation house itself is a private residence not open to the public.

♦ *From St. Philips Road at Brunswick Town/Fort Anderson, turn right onto Plantation Road. Drive 1.6 miles and turn right into the Orton Plantation entrance.*

— The Engagement at Town Creek —

The narrow but deep Town Creek constituted the final line of defense for Confederate troops west of the Cape Fear River. Johnson Hagood's infantry and artillery withdrew to an entrenched position above the creek following the evacuation of Fort Anderson in February 1865. After a final brief engagement here with Cox's Federals, Confederate forces retreated to Wilmington, leaving the way clear for Union troops to occupy the city.

♦ *From Orton Plantation, turn right onto Plantation Road. Drive .4 miles to the stop sign and turn right onto N.C. Highway 133. As you drive north you are following the same route as the Federal advance toward Town Creek. The road here is essentially the same as it was in 1865.*

♦ *Drive 5.2 miles from the Plantation Rd./N.C. 133 turnoff and cross Town Creek (the third creek from the turnoff). NOTE: Stopping along the roadside near Town Creek is not recommended. The shoulder is narrow and the highway is well traveled.*

♦ *A short distance north of Town Creek is the community of Clarendon. In this vicinity, to the right of the road, Cox's Federals overwhelmed a portion of Hagood's Confederates. The remainder of Hagood's troops were forced to withdraw, resulting in the loss of the Town Creek position and assuring the fall of Wilmington.*

♦ *Continue northward on Highway 133 to Leland, and turn right onto U.S. Highway 17. Cross the Brunswick and Cape Fear rivers and re-enter Wilmington.*

Distance traveled from Orton Plantation to Leland: 12.9 miles.

For maps of the engagement at Town Creek, see pages 116, 124, and 125.

— Wilmington, North Carolina —

Refer to Appendix D, page 169, for points of interest in downtown Wilmington—the "City by the Sea."

For maps of wartime Wilmington, see pages 2 and 135.

"Found the city to be a fine place. Some good buildings and plenty of shade on the sidewalks."
—**Charles Thomas Shanner**, 63rd Indiana Infantry

— Highway Historical Markers Associated with Wilmington and its Defense —

Oakdale Cemetery
Chartered 1852; Graves of Confederate leaders, officers, & soldiers. Many yellow fever victims. Six blocks North on 15th St.
U.S. 17 Business (Market Street) at 15th Street in Wilmington, New Hanover County

Wilmington & Weldon Railroad
Longest railroad in the world when completed in 1840. Length 161 ½ mi. Terminus was 4 blocks W.
U.S. 17 Business (3rd Street) at Brunswick Street in Wilmington, New Hanover County

Rose Greenhow
Confederate spy and Washington society woman. Drowned near Fort Fisher in 1864, while running Federal blockade. Grave 1mi. N.E.
U.S. 17 Business (3rd Street) at Dock Street in Wilmington, New Hanover County

Cassidey Shipyard
Confederate shipyard and outfitting station which completed the ironclad steam sloop *Raleigh* in 1863. Site is three blocks west.
U.S. 17 Business (3rd Street) at Church Street in Wilmington, New Hanover County

Beery's Shipyard
Many Confederate naval vessels, including the ironclad *North Carolina*, built here. Site lies across river on Eagles Island, ¼ mile west.
U.S. 17 Business (Market Street) between 3rd & 4th Streets in Wilmington, New Hanover County

John N. Maffitt
Captain of Confederate cruiser *Florida* and ironclad *Albemarle*. With U.S. Coast Survey, 1848-1858. Blockade-runner. Grave 14 blks. N.E.
U.S. 17 Business (3rd Street) at 15th Street in Wilmington, New Hanover County

Prisoner Exchange
Thousands of Civil War soldiers, including many held in Confederate prison at Salisbury, were exchanged here, Feb. 26-Mar. 4, 1865.
U.S. 117 at Northeast Cape Fear River bridge, New Hanover County

Topsail Battery
Confederate breastworks were constructed in this vicinity in 1862 to protect Wilmington from an attack from the north and for coastal defense.
U.S. 17 south of Hampstead, Pender County

Fall of Wilmington
Union assault on Hoke's entrenched Confederates led to the city's fall, February 22, 1865. Earthworks were nearby.
Shipyard Boulevard at 17th Street in Wilmington, New Hanover County

Fort Fisher
Built by Confederacy. Its fall, January 15, 1865, closed Wilmington, last important southern port for blockade running.
U.S. 421 at Fort Fisher, New Hanover County

W. H. C. Whiting, 1824-1865
Confederate major general and engineer. He devised the Cape Fear defense system. Wounded nearby in fall of fort. Died in Union hospital.
U.S. 421 at Fort Fisher, New Hanover County

Fort Johnston
Built 1748-64; burned by Whigs, 1775; rebuilt by U.S. government, 1794-1809. Only the officers' quarters remain.
Bay Street in Southport, Brunswick County

Fort Caswell
Named for Gov. Caswell. Begun by U.S. in 1826; seized by N.C. Troops, 1861; abandoned by Confederates, 1865. Stands five miles southeast.
N.C. 133 north of Southport, Brunswick County

Fort Caswell
Seized by N.C. militia three months before the firing on Fort Sumter, Governor Ellis ordered its return to Federal authority, three mi. E.
N.C. 133 in Yaupon Beach, Brunswick County

Fort Anderson
Large Confederate fort stands 2 mi. E. After a strong Union attack it was evacuated Feb. 18, 1865, resulting in the fall of Wilmington.
N.C. 133 at Brunswick Town/Fort Anderson, Brunswick County

Fort Anderson
Large Confederate fort stands 13 mi. S. After a strong Union attack it was evacuated Feb. 18, 1865, resulting in the fall of Wilmington
N.C. 133 in Belville, Brunswick County

"Those days of reconstruction worked a hardship on everybody . . . . One morning when I was about two miles from the city, and just before day dawned, I saw the most fearful looking object I ever beheld, coming meeting me right in the road . . . . I have never been able to guess which was the worse frightened, myself or the horse I was driving. I reckon it was the poor animal that was to be pitied the most . . . . [thereafter] the horse would keep looking and dodging as soon as he came within half a mile of the place we had met the Ku Klux [Klan]."
—**Myles Walton**, Masonboro resident

The World War II Airstrip at Fort Fisher. In this view, taken along U.S. Hwy. 421, the long path of the Fort Fisher airstrip is clearly discernible. The building in the distance, in the middle of the strip, is the Fort Fisher visitor center. From this perspective, the visitor center marks the point where the airstrip cut through the fort's land front.

World War II Observation Tower Remnants at Fort Fisher. This image, taken from the stone revetment along the beach, shows the concrete base for one of the old towers. The two mounds of earth visible behind the concrete base are unrestored traverses from Fort Fisher's land front. These unrestored mounds are located east of the highway, between 421 and the Atlantic. Just above the sand ridge where the concrete base lies, the tops of Fort Fisher's reconstructed palisades are visible. For reference, see the maps on pages 74 and 75.

Author's Collection

Appendix F

Fort Fisher and World War II

Much like the Civil War's impact in the 1860s, America's involvement in World War II brought profound social and economic changes to Wilmington, North Carolina. As the nation's home front prepared to support America's war machine, Wilmington and New Hanover County underwent a major expansion in the shipbuilding, chemical, and petroleum industries. Thousands migrated to the Wilmington area pursuing defense work—and military personnel were not far behind.

Camp Davis

In late December 1940, nearly one year before the bombing of Pearl Harbor catapulted the United States into World War II, construction began on a new military facility at the tiny village of Holly Ridge, about 30 miles northeast of Wilmington on U.S. Highway 17. Within five months, the new base—named Camp Davis—sprang to life, and its first military cadre arrived in April 1941. By August, the post was swarming with some 20,000 officers and men. Camp Davis, home to one of the U.S. Army's seven antiaircraft artillery training centers, was attached to the First Army, Fourth Corps Area.

For a brief period, Camp Davis enjoyed the distinction of having all three of the principle elements of coastal artillery under one command: antiaircraft, seacoast defense, and barrage balloon training. Davis was also unique in that its firing ranges were not located on the main reservation. Instead, the facility employed five remote training sites for antiaircraft gunnery and automatic weapons practice. These ranges were dispersed along the state's southern coast at Sears Point, New Topsail Inlet, Maple Hill, Holly Shelter, and Fort Fisher.

"Seeking isolation from interference to insure uninterrupted training," asserted Col. Adam E. Potts, *"the camp proper is located in the great Holly Shelter pocosin whose massive silence is now broken by the din of ack-ack, while the shores near Sears Landing echo the cannonade of larger calibers. Nor is this the first time that the noise of war has broken the peace of these lowlands, still haunted by the memories of Indians and pirates, slavers and Spanish marauders, Regulators and Taxmasters, Green and Cornwallis, and climaxed by the greatest naval bombardment in the world's history at Fort Fisher. Now a new chapter is written here, as men bivouac on these same trails to prepare for global service."*

As the reservation expanded, the Fort Fisher site—located 50 miles south of the main base—became the primary firing range for Camp Davis. And as Fisher's importance grew, so did its facilities.

Original specifications called for a host of features that would make the remote firing range a self contained post. These included 48 frame buildings, 316 tent frames, showers and latrines, mess halls, warehouses, radio and meteorological sta-

tions, a post exchange, photo lab, recreation hall, outdoor theater, guardhouse, infirmary, and an administration building. In addition to these facilities, the site featured a 10,000-gallon water storage tank, a motor pool, a large parade ground, and three steel observation towers along the beach.

The main highway in the area, U.S. 421, bisected the sandy ruins of the land front of historic Fort Fisher. New firing installations were erected along the beach, between the highway and the Atlantic Ocean—not unlike Fisher's oceanside batteries during the Civil War. These included, among others, batteries of 40-millimeter automatic cannons and 50-caliber machine guns. In addition, the site's utilities, living quarters, and other features sprang up west of the shore installations, between the highway and the Cape Fear River. The area surrounding the old Civil War fort was soon dotted with the trappings of a modern military facility, and expansion would continue throughout its tenure as a firing range.

At an isolated sector on Federal Point, an anti-mechanized target range was constructed in the summer of 1942. Here, antiaircraft gunners at Fort Fisher received versatility training and learned to be effective against tanks and other armored vehicles of modern warfare. Ammunition bunkers were also dug along the highway north of Battery Buchanan—the massive four-gun bastion below Fort Fisher that had commanded New Inlet during the Civil War. Buchanan's remains were damaged as a result of military construction.

The crowning addition to these improvements was the construction of a large airstrip at Fort Fisher—an endeavor that destroyed a sizable portion of the once-formidable land front of the 80-year-old bastion. In these unstable times, national defense took precedence over historic preservation. Nevertheless, most of the new trainees were aware of the area's significance, and Camp Davis' promotional literature highlighted Fisher's historic past.

By the time antiaircraft training operations ceased at Fort Fisher in 1944, the facility had grown to include an 80-seat cafeteria, a 350-bed hospital and dental clinic, and covered an area of several hundred acres. The post had become an integral site for activities associated with Camp Davis' Antiaircraft Artillery Training Center, and additional units from other ground forces also saw duty here. This important auxiliary range of Camp Davis was maintained by the Army Service Forces (ASF) through the Fourth Service Command, and the necessary complement of ASF personnel and equipment were stationed at Fisher.

Antiaircraft Training at Fort Fisher

Training at the Fort Fisher range began in October 1941. *"As of yore, when the most powerful guns of the day were blasting away at Fort Fisher,"* noted one of the camp's brochures, *"the famed Strato-gun of AA is now blasting at targets from the same ground."* Almost eight decades earlier, African American troops had served on Federal Point as part of the Union expeditionary force sent to capture Fort Fisher. With the arrival of the 54th Coast Artillery in 1941, black soldiers were once again in the area for military service—along the very sand mounds and beaches that once marked the Confederate stronghold. The 54th—the army's only black 155-millimeter antiaircraft artillery unit—brought 24 "one-five-fives" to Fort Fisher for their two-month training session. The unit also trained with other weapons, including machine guns.

That December, news of the Japanese attack on Pearl Harbor, Hawaii, shook the nation to its core. On the day following the December 7 catastrophe, with overwhelming support from Congress, President Franklin D. Roosevelt signed a declaration of war against the Empire of Japan. Three days later, Germany and Italy declared war on the United States, forcing Roosevelt to end America's official neutrality on the war then raging in Europe.

As the nation prepared for global conflict, Camp Davis bustled with activity, and training at its remote firing ranges escalated. As more emphasis was placed on antiaircraft artillery training, the barrage balloon school was transferred to a post in Tennessee.

The training schedule was vigorous—six days a week—and the air over coastal North Carolina was loud with military activity. Planes towing target sleeves on long cables roared back and forth above the beaches of Fort Fisher and Camp Davis' other firing ranges, while antiaircraft gunners below pumped streams of shells at the soaring targets.

Two towing squadrons and a base squadron were stationed at Camp Davis Army Airfield. These aircraft flew thousands of miles each week—both day and night—in missions along the coast. At night the planes gave the searchlight battalions—the "Moonlight Cavalry"—practice in picking up enemy raiders in the darkness. One such battalion attached to Camp Davis was the 225th AAA Searchlight Battalion (Semi-mobile), which trained for a short period at Burgaw (40 miles west of the main base) before departing for duty overseas.

As training intensified at Fort Fisher, many of Camp Davis' visitors ventured to the sandy post to observe the reservation's primary firing point. The year 1943 proved to be its busiest, and included a visit from a British antiaircraft battery that arrived to conduct exercises with American gunners.

The nation's war effort was in full swing, and 1943 brought a significant change in the use of its resources. The army needed more pilots, and thanks to the strong-willed efforts of female pilot Jacqueline Cochran, it now had a group of talented women to serve in national defense. The Women Airforce Service Pilots (WASPs) arrived at Camp Davis on July 24, 1943—in their first assignment beyond ferrying duty. On August 1, the WASPs were put to work piloting A-24s and A-25s, and took on the duty of towing targets for Camp Davis' antiaircraft artillery training. In addition to target duty (both day and night), the women stationed at Davis flew radar deception and tracking missions. The WASPs went on to fly missions from a number of bases across the United States.

By the time the range closed in 1944, at least 43 different antiaircraft battalions and coast artillery regiments, as well as engineer, signal corps, ordnance, and air warning units, had trained \ at Fort Fisher.

Camp and Social Life

The harsh conditions on Federal Point had not changed in the long years since the Civil War, and trainees and other personnel were forced to coexist with the ubiquitous sand and mosquitoes—the same problems faced by Fisher's original garrison. It was "*a forlorn spit of sand and scrub growth pinched between the Atlantic Ocean and the Cape Fear River,*" asserted a member of the 558th AAA Battalion, "*a quagmire of sand, sand, and more sand. It was strictly a no-nonsense place designed to put grit and fire in the bowels and brains of its trainees.*" In the summer months, however, the beach atmosphere and constant ocean breezes appealed to many of the troops at the sandy post. For some, the surroundings inspired a festive attitude. Indeed, one veteran remembered that his entire battalion—the 535th—was once reprimanded and denied weekend leave due to sloppiness and lack of discipline.

Fort Fisher lacked the elaborate recreational facilities found at Camp Davis, but by the spring of 1943 it boasted a full schedule of activities. In August, the new post theater opened with a screening of *Stormy Weather*, starring Lena Horne. There were also plays and musical variety shows, most of which were performed by the soldiers themselves. Professional performances, sponsored by the United Services Organization (USO) were an added treat, and were often joined by "home grown" talent—including the Fort Fisher Swing Band and other groups.

Many of the post's trainees were from interior regions of the United States, and had never before seen a beach—let alone tried to live near one. The adjustment was difficult, and more than a few soldiers balked at the notion of dining on fried clams and oysters. To acclimate the men to their new environment, the post offered swimming lessons, advice on how to avoid sunburn, and beach safety instructions.

Sports were also popular at Fisher, and went a long way toward boosting morale. The trainees enjoyed games of volleyball, horseshoes, and golf—but boxing was by far the most popular. Throngs of spectators gathered for the matches, held indoors or outdoors according to the season. The fervor reached its peak in January 1944, when boxing champ Joe Louis arrived for a visit.

The soldiers also enjoyed the Fort Fisher station because of its proximity to Wilmington, and recreational opportunities at nearby Carolina Beach. The war transformed Wilmington into a boomtown—its population soared and its businesses flourished. And not surprisingly, the bustle of wartime activity and throngs of military men conspired to erode existing moral restrictions. Agnes Meyer, a *Washington Post* correspondent on assignment in Wilmington in April 1943, complained that "*the state of things*" in Wilmington "*is pathetic if not indecent . . . . I would not be a worker in Wilmington if you gave me the whole city.*"

Through the years, Wilmington and its environs have been greatly affected by our nation's wars and their participants. The Civil War brought a peculiar amalgam of prosperity, hardship, and destruction to the port city, and the town faced a long, hard road through Reconstruction. And while the social climate may have suffered in Wilmington during the Second World War, that conflict served only to strengthen the city.

Camp Davis and its satellite ranges closed in October 1944—with nearly one full year of war yet to be waged in both theaters of conflict. In summarizing the post's accomplishments, the *Coast Artillery Journal* asserted that Camp Davis would *"live in every shot fired at Axis Planes; in high morale and combat efficiency . . . and forever will live in the hearts of all World War II antiaircraft artillerymen."*

Fort Fisher Under Attack?

Since the end of the war, there have been rumors of German submarine activity associated with the Wilmington area. Indeed, many U-boat operations were conducted along the east coast of the United States during World War II, and several American vessels were sunk in North Carolina waters—including a few downed by the famed German U-boat captain, Erich Topp.

Through the years, a popular story has been told regarding a U-boat attack near Kure Beach on July 15, 1943. Carlton Sprague, a platoon commander in C Battery, 558th AAA Battalion, remembered that while his unit was stationed at Fort Fisher, a German submarine surfaced under cover of darkness and lobbed five shells at the Ethyl-Dow chemical plant. This facility manufactured a key ingredient for high octane fuel. According to the story, all of the enemy shells overshot their mark and plunged into the Cape Fear River. Apparently, a news blackout followed, and over time the story has drifted into legend.

Some residents recalled that on the night of the supposed attack on the chemical plant, the shipyard in Wilmington suddenly went black. Due to the demand for new ships, however, this facility remained open day and night, and its lights were usually left burning during the city's routine air raid drills. The citizens had been warned that if these lights ever went out, it meant that a real raid was at hand—for production at the shipyard never stopped. The blackout supposedly frightened Wilmington residents, but an attack never materialized.

Carlton Sprague related another interesting anecdote more directly related to Fort Fisher. "*Some time in August of 1943,*" he recalled, "*while we were stationed at Fort Fisher, members of C Battery were on guard duty, and the patrol on the beach, not far from our gun emplacements, encountered four German military personnel from a submarine that landed on our beach and we turned them over to the S-2 for processing.*" Did members of the *Kriegsmarine* come ashore at Fort Fisher? And if so, why?

"*I was officer of the day,*" continued Sprague. "*It was my recollection that they were to sabotage the channel in the Cape Fear River, which would detain ship traffic at the Wilmington navy base. They had missed their location by just a few miles. I don't believe their final intent was to complete their assigned mission, but rather to surrender to American authorities.*" According to Sprague, this incident was one of four in which German U-boats landed saboteurs on the American mainland. The other locations included Hancock, Maine; Long Island,

New York; and the New Jersey coast.

At least one additional landing occurred on American soil near Jacksonville, Florida—four nights after a landing at Long Island, New York. The eight Germans in the Florida incident—all former residents of the United States—were supposedly caught with large supplies of cash and explosives.

While there seems to be some historical basis for the Florida landing, the North Carolina incidents are more difficult to prove. No hard evidence or official accounts have surfaced to lend authenticity to these stories. Nevertheless, the tales are interesting and thought provoking—and have not been disproved. If nothing else, they add to the long-standing mystique, traditions, and colorful maritime legends of the Lower Cape Fear.

The Fort Fisher Hermit

One of the most amusing legacies of the World War II era at Fort Fisher is the home that one of its abandoned structures provided for a man named Robert Harrill. Between 1955 and 1972, Harrill achieved cult status as a curiosity embraced by the local media, and he was visited by thousands of tourists.

Seeking a more simple life, Robert dropped out of society and took up residence in an old World War II bunker at Fort Fisher, not far from the present-day North Carolina Aquarium. Having abandoned the familiar trappings of everyday life—family and friends, the comforts of home, fresh water, and indoor plumbing—Robert explained that he hoped to write a book about dysfunctional people: *A Tyrant in Every Home*. Though obviously dysfunctional himself, there was nothing sinister about the old man, who was born in 1893. He relished his natural surroundings, enjoyed the companionship of a multitude of pets, and greeted visitors with warm philosophy.

Robert Harrill's lair became such a popular tourist attraction that he started a guest register, and logged over 17,000 visitors from season to season. As his story spread, curious locals and tourists drove down the sandy path to the old bunker, or walked three-quarters of a mile from U.S. Highway 421 to see Robert for themselves. They often left donations in an old frying pan—the same utensil in which Robert cooked his meals.

Countless newspapers ran stories about the "Fort Fisher Hermit" during his 17-year stay on Federal Point. Reporters soaked up the man's preachings about "*crooked politicians, on-the-take law enforcement, the free-loaders and the millionaires who are running this beautiful country of ours.*" It was a simpler time, when stories about the lifestyles of men like Robert Harrill did not conjure the antisocial and negative images that they would in today's world. His simple outlook on life centered on "getting back to Nature" and common sense, and crowds of tourists would gather for a dose of "hermit philosophy."

Robert's existence soon passed into the folklore of the region, and rumors and legends arose about his great wealth, and how it was buried somewhere on the wastes of lower Federal Point, and how it might still be there to this very day. Indeed, more than $1,000 in change was found in the bunker upon the man's death in 1972.

At the time of his passing, it was said that Robert had planned to file a deed for the land he claimed by "homestead rights." He never achieved the status of landowner, but 27 years after his death Robert's story and the old bunker remain prominent in popular lore, and the structure is still visited by old friends and tourists.

On their way down the old marsh trail to the bunker, visitors will pass two stone pylons (wartime observation tower remnants) painted with this simple message: "The Fort Fisher Hermit—In Loving Memory."

—For more information about the "Hermit," see Michael F. Edwards' book titled *Robert E. Harrill: The Fort Fisher Hermit*, available at many tourist attractions along the Wilmington loop.

Appendix G

Medal of Honor Recipients

For the period of December 24, 1864-February 22, 1865
—the capture of Fort Fisher and Wilmington

United States Army

Anderson, Bruce
Rank and organization: Private, Company K, 142d New York Infantry. *Place and date*: At Fort Fisher, N.C., 15 January 1865. *Entered service at*: Ephratah, N.Y. *Born*: Mexico, Oswego County, N.Y., 9 June 1845. *Date of issue*: 28 December 1914. *Citation*: Voluntarily advanced with the head of the column and cut down the palisading.

Chapin, Alaric B.
Rank and organization: Private, Company G, 142d New York Infantry. *Place and date*: At Fort Fisher, N.C., 15 January 1865. *Entered service at*: Pamelia, N.Y. *Birth*: Ogdensburg, N.Y. *Date of issue*: 28 December 1914. *Citation*: Voluntarily advanced with the head of the column and cut down the palisading.

Curtis, Newton Martin
Rank and organization: Brigadier General, U.S. Volunteers. *Place and date*: At Fort Fisher, N.C., 15 January 1865. *Entered service at*: De Peyster, N.Y. *Born*: 21 May 1835, De Peyster, N.Y. *Date of issue*: 28 November 1891. *Citation*: The first man to pass through the stockade, he personally led each assault on the traverses and was four times wounded.

Freeman, William H.
Rank and organization: Private, Company B, 169th New York Infantry. *Place and date*: At Fort Fisher, N.C., 15 January 1865. *Entered service at*: Troy, N.Y. *Birth*: Troy, N.Y. *Date of issue*: 27 May 1905. *Citation*: Volunteered to carry the brigade flag after the bearer was wounded.

Merrill, George
Rank and organization: Private, Company I, 142d New York Infantry. *Place and date*: At Fort Fisher, N.C., 15 January 1865. *Entered service at*: ———. *Birth*: Queensberry, N.Y. *Date of issue*: 28 December 1914. *Citation*: Voluntarily advanced with the head of the column and cut down the palisading.

Neahr, Zachariah C.
Rank and organization: Private, Company K, 142d New York Infantry. *Place and date*: At Fort Fisher, N.C., 16 [15] January 1865. *Entered service at*: ———. *Birth*: Canajoharie, N.Y. *Date of issue*: 11 September 1890. *Citation*: Voluntarily advanced with the head of the column and cut down the palisading.

Pennypacker, Galusha
Rank and organization: Colonel, 97th Pennsylvania Infantry. *Place and date*: At Fort Fisher, N.C., 15 January 1865. *Entered service at*: West Chester, Pa. *Born*: 1 June 1844, Valley Forge, Pa. *Date of issue*: 17 August 1891. *Citation*: Gallantly led the charge over a traverse and planted the colors of one of his regiments thereon; was severely wounded.

Wainwright, John
Rank and organization: First Lieutenant, Company F, 97th Pennsylvania Infantry. *Place and date*: At Fort Fisher, N.C., 15 January 1865. *Entered service at*: West Chester, Pa. *Born*: 13 July 1839, Syracuse, Onondaga County, N.Y. *Date of issue*: 24 June 1890. *Citation*: Gallant and meritorious conduct, where, as first lieutenant, he commanded the regiment.

Walling, William H.
Rank and organization: Captain, Company C, 142d New York Infantry. *Place and date*: At Fort Fisher, N.C., 25 December 1864. *Entered service at*: ———. *Birth*: Hartford, N.Y. *Date of issue*: 28 March 1892. *Citation*: During the bombardment of the fort by the fleet, captured and brought the flag of the fort, the flagstaff having been shot down.

United States Navy

Angling, John
Rank and organization: Cabin Boy, U.S. Navy. *Born*: 1850, Portland, Maine. *Accredited to*: Maine. G. O. No.: 59, 22 June 1865. *Citation*: Served on board the U.S.S. *Pontoosuc* during the capture of Fort Fisher and Wilmington, 24 December 1864 to 22 January [February] 1865. Carrying out his duties faithfully during this period, C. B. Angling was recommended for gallantry and skill and for his cool courage while under the fire of the enemy throughout these various actions.

Barnum, James
Rank and organization: Boatswain's Mate, U.S. Navy. *Born*: 1816 Massachusetts. *Accredited to*: Massachusetts. G. O. No.: 59, 22 June 1865. *Citation*: Barnum served on board the U.S.S. *New Ironsides* during action in several attacks on Fort Fisher, 24 and 25 December 1864; and on 13, 14, and 15 January 1865. The ship steamed in and took the lead in the ironclad division close inshore and immediately opened its starboard battery in a barrage of well-directed fire to cause several fires and explosions and dismount several guns during the first two days of fighting. Taken under fire as she steamed into position on 13 January, the *New Ironsides* fought all day and took on ammunition at night despite severe weather conditions. When the enemy came out of his bombproofs to defend the fort against the storming party, the ship's battery disabled nearly every gun on the fort facing the shore before the cease-fire orders were given by the flagship. Barnum was commended for highly meritorious conduct during this period.

Barter, Gurdon H.
Rank and organization: Landsman, U.S. Navy. *Born*: 1843, Williamsburgh, N.Y. *Accredited to*: New York. G. O. No.: 59, 22 June 1865. *Citation*: On board the U.S.S. *Minnesota* in action during the assault on Fort Fisher, 15 January 1865. Landing on the beach with the assaulting party from his ship, Barter advanced to the top of the sandhill and partly through the breach in the palisades despite enemy fire which killed and wounded many officers and men. When more than two-thirds of the men became seized with panic and retreated on the run, he remained with the party until dark, when it came safely away, bringing its wounded, its arms, and its colors.

Bass, David L.
Rank and organization: Seaman, U.S. Navy. *Born*: 1843, Ireland. *Accredited to*: New York. G. O. No.: 59, 22 June 1865. *Citation*: On board the U.S.S. *Minnesota* in action during the assault on Fort Fisher, 15 January 1865. Landing on the beach with the assaulting party from his ship, Seaman Bass advanced to the top of the sand hill and partly

through the breach in the palisades despite enemy fire which killed and wounded many officers and men. When more than two-thirds of the men became seized with panic and retreated on the run, he remained with the party until dark, when it came safely away, bringing its wounded, its arms, and its colors.

Bazaar, Philip

Rank and organization: Ordinary Seaman, U.S. Navy. *Born*: Chile, South America. *Accredited to*: Massachusetts. G. O. No.: 59, 22 June 1865. *Citation*: On board the U.S.S. *Santiago de Cuba* during the assault on Fort Fisher on 15 January 1865. As one of a boat crew detailed to one of the generals on shore, O. S. Bazaar bravely entered the fort in the assault and accompanied his party in carrying dispatches at the height of the battle. He was one of six men who entered the fort in the assault from the fleet.

Betham, Asa

Rank and organization: Coxswain, U.S. Navy. *Born*: 1838, New York, N.Y. *Accredited to*: New York. G. O. No.: 59, 22 June 1865. *Citation*: Served on board the U.S.S. *Pontoosuc* during the capture of Fort Fisher and Wilmington, 24 December 1864, to 22 January [February] 1865. Carrying out his duties faithfully during this period, Betham was recommended for gallantry and skill and for his cool courage while under the fire of the enemy throughout these various actions.

Bibber, Charles J.

Rank and organization: Gunner's Mate, U.S. Navy. *Born*: 1838, Portland, Maine. *Accredited to*: Maine. G. O. No.: 45, 31 December 1864. *Citation*: Bibber served on board the U.S.S. *Agawam*, as one of a volunteer crew of a powder boat which was exploded near Fort Fisher 23 [24] December 1864. The powder boat, towed in by the *Wilderness* to prevent detection by the enemy, cast off and slowly steamed to within 300 yards of the beach. After fuses and fires had been lit and a second anchor with short scope let go to assure the boat's tailing inshore, the crew again boarded the *Wilderness* and proceeded a distance of 12 miles from shore. Less than two hours later the explosion took place, and the following day fires were observed still burning at the forts.

Blair, Robert M.

Rank and organization: Boatswain's Mate, U.S. Navy. *Born*: 1836, Peacham, Vt. *Accredited to*: Vermont. G. O. No.: 59, 22 June 1865. *Citation*: Served on board the U.S.S. *Pontoosuc* during the capture of Fort Fisher and Wilmington, 24 December 1864 to 22 January [February] 1865. Carrying out his duties faithfully throughout this period, Blair was recommended for gallantry and skill and for his cool courage while under the fire of the enemy throughout these actions.

Bowman, Edward R.

Rank and organization: Quartermaster, U.S. Navy. *Born*: 1828, Eastport, Maine. *Accredited to*: Maine. G. O. No.: 59, 22 June 1865. *Citation*: On board the U.S.S. *Ticonderoga* during attacks on Fort Fisher 13 to 15 January 1865. Despite severe wounds sustained during the action Bowman displayed outstanding courage in the performance of duty as his ship maintained its well-placed fire upon the batteries on shore, and thereafter, as she materially lessened the power of guns on the mound which had been turned upon our assaulting columns. During this battle the flag was planted on one of the strongest fortifications possessed by the rebels.

Burton, Albert

Rank and organization: Seaman, U.S. Navy. *Born*: 1838, England.

Accredited to: New York. G. O. No.: 59, 22 June 1865. *Citation*: Served on board the U.S.S. *Wabash* in the assault on Fort Fisher, 15 January 1865. Advancing gallantly through the severe enemy fire while armed only with a revolver and cutlass which made it impossible to return the fire at that range, Burton succeeded in reaching the angle of the fort and going on, to be one of the few who entered the fort. When the rest of the body of men to his rear were forced to retreat under a devastating fire, he was forced to withdraw through lack of support, and to seek the shelter of one of the mounds near the stockade from which point he succeeded in regaining the safety of his ship.

Campbell, William

Rank and organization: Boatswain's Mate, U.S. Navy. *Born*: 1838, Indiana. *Accredited to*: Indiana. G. O. No.: 59, 22 June 1865. *Citation*: On board the U.S.S. *Ticonderoga* during attacks on Fort Fisher, 24 and 25 December 1864; and 13 to 15 January 1865. Despite heavy return fire by the enemy and the explosion of the 100-pounder Parrott rifle which killed eight men and wounded 12 more, Campbell, as captain of a gun, performed his duties with skill and courage during the first two days of battle. As his ship again took position on the line on the 13th [15th], he remained steadfast as the *Ticonderoga* maintained a well-placed fire upon the batteries on shore, and thereafter, as she materially lessened the power of guns on the mound which had been turned upon our assaulting columns. During this action the flag was planted on one of the strongest fortifications possessed by the rebels.

Conlan, Dennis

Rank and organization: Seaman, U.S. Navy. *Born*: 1838, New York N.Y. *Accredited to*: New York. G. O. No.. 45, 31 December 1864. *Citation*: Conlan served on board the U.S.S. *Agawam*, as one of a volunteer crew of a powder boat which was exploded near Fort Fisher, 23 [24] December 1864. The powder boat, towed in by the *Wilderness* to prevent detection by the enemy, cast off and slowly steamed to within 300 yards of the beach. After fuses and fires had been lit and a second anchor with short scope let go to assure the boat's tailing inshore, the crew again boarded the *Wilderness* and proceeded a distance of 12 miles from shore. Less than two hours later the explosion took place, and the following day fires were observed still burning at the forts.

Connor, Thomas

Rank and organization: Ordinary Seaman, U.S. Navy. *Born*: 1842, Ireland. *Accredited to*: Maryland. G. O. No.: 59, 22 June 1865. *Citation*: On board the U.S.S. *Minnesota*, in action during the assault on Fort Fisher, 15 January 1865. Landing on the beach with the assaulting party from his ship, Connor charged up to the palisades and, when more than two-thirds of the men became seized with panic and retreated on the run, risked his life to remain with a wounded officer. With the enemy concentrating his fire on the group, he waited until after dark before assisting in carrying the wounded man from the field.

Dees, Clement

Rank and organization: Seaman (colored), U.S. Navy. U.S.S. *Pontoosuc*. Dees, a native of the Cape Verde Islands off the west coast of Africa, was nominated for a Medal of Honor by Cmdr. William G. Temple on March 31, 1865. Dees was nominated with seven other crew members of the *Pontoosuc*—all of whom appear on this list. Though Department General Order Number 59—dated June 22, 1865—listed Dees' citation, the black sailor apparently never received his medal, and deserted the navy before it was awarded. His desertion notwithstanding, Dees was formally recognized by the United States

Navy for gallantry in action during the capture of Fort Fisher and Wilmington.

Dempster, John

Rank and organization: Coxswain, U.S. Navy. *Born*: 1839, Scotland. *Accredited to*: Pennsylvania. G. O. No.: 59, 22 June 1865. *Citation*: Dempster served on board the U.S.S. *New Ironsides* during action in several attacks on Fort Fisher, 24 and 25 December 1864; and 13, 14, and 15 January 1865. The ship steamed in and took the lead in the ironclad division close inshore and immediately opened its starboard battery in a barrage of well-directed fire to cause several fires and explosions and dismount several guns during the first two days of fighting. Taken under fire as she steamed into position on 13 January, the *New Ironsides* fought all day and took on ammunition at night despite severe weather conditions. When the enemy came out of his bombproofs to defend the fort against the storming party, the ship's battery disabled nearly every gun on the fort facing the shore before the cease-fire orders were given by the flagship.

Dunn, William

Rank and organization: Quartermaster, U.S. Navy. *Born*: Maine. *Accredited to*: Maine. G. O. No.: 59, 22 June 1865. *Citation*: On board the U.S.S. *Monadnock* in action during several attacks on Fort Fisher, 24 and 25 December 1864; and 13, 14, and 15 January 1865. With his ship anchored well inshore to insure perfect range against the severe fire of rebel guns, Dunn continued his duties when the vessel was at anchor, as her propellers were kept in motion to make her turrets bear, and the shooting away of her chain might have caused her to ground. Disdainful of shelter despite severe weather conditions, he inspired his shipmates and contributed to the success of his vessel in reducing the enemy guns to silence.

English, Thomas

Rank and organization: Signal Quartermaster, U.S. Navy. *Born*: 1819, New York, N.Y. *Accredited to*: New York. G. O. No.: 59, 22 June 1865. *Citation*: English served on board the U.S.S. *New Ironsides* during action in several attacks on Fort Fisher, 24 and 25 December 1864; and 13, 14, and 15 January 1865. The ship steamed in and took the lead in the ironclad division close inshore and immediately opened its starboard battery in a barrage of well-directed fire to cause several fires and explosions and dismount several guns during the first two days of fighting. Taken under fire as she steamed into position on 13 January, the *New Ironsides* fought all day and took on ammunition at night despite severe weather conditions. When the enemy came out of his bombproofs to defend the fort against the storming party, the ship's battery disabled nearly every gun on the fort facing the shore before the cease-fire orders were given by the flagship.

Erickson, John P.

Rank and organization: Captain of the Forecastle, U.S. Navy. *Birth*: London, England. *Accredited to*: New York. G. O. No.: 59, 22 June 1865. *Citation*: Served on board the U.S.S. *Pontoosuc* during the capture of Fort Fisher and Wilmington, 24 December 1864, to 22 February 1865. Carrying out his duties faithfully throughout this period, Erickson was so severely wounded in the assault upon Fort Fisher that he was sent to the hospital at Portsmouth, Va. Erickson was recommended for his gallantry, skill, and coolness in action while under the fire of the enemy.

Foy, Charles H.

Rank and organization: Signal Quartermaster, U.S. Navy. *Birth*: Portsmouth, N.H. *Accredited to*: New Hampshire. G. O. No.: 59, 22 June 1865. *Citation*: Served on board the U.S.S. *Rhode Island* during the

action with Fort Fisher and the Federal Point batteries, 13 to 15 January 1865. Carrying out his duties courageously during the battle, Foy continued to be outstanding by his good conduct and faithful services throughout this engagement which resulted in a heavy casualty list when an attempt was made to storm Fort Fisher.

Garvin, William

Rank and organization: Captain of the Forecastle, U.S. Navy. *Born*: 1835. *Accredited to*: Virginia. G. O. No.: 45, 31 December 1864. *Citation*: Garvin served on board the U.S.S. *Agawam*, as one of a volunteer crew of a powder boat which was exploded near Fort Fisher, 23 [24] December 1864. The powder boat, towed in by the *Wilderness* to prevent detection by the enemy, cast off and slowly steamed to within 300 yards of the beach. After fuses and fires had been lit and a second anchor with short scope let go to assure the boat's tailing inshore, the crew again boarded the *Wilderness* and proceeded a distance of 12 miles from shore. Less than two hours later the explosion took place, and the following day fires were observed still burning at the fort.

Griffiths, John

Rank and organization: Captain of the Forecastle, U.S. Navy. *Born*: 1835, Wales. *Accredited to*: Massachusetts. G. O. No.: 59, 22 June 1865. *Citation*: On board the U.S.S. *Santiago de Cuba* during the assault on Fort Fisher on 15 January 1865. As one of a boatcrew detailed to one of the generals on shore, Griffiths bravely entered the fort in the assault and accompanied his party in carrying dispatches at the height of the battle. He was one of six men who entered the fort in the assault from the fleet.

Haffee, Edmund

Rank and organization: Quarter Gunner, U.S. Navy. *Born*: 1832, Philadelphia, Pa. *Accredited to*: Pennsylvania. G. O. No.: 59, 22 June 1865. *Citation*: Haffee served on board the U.S.S. *New Ironsides* during action in several attacks on Fort Fisher, 24 and 25 December 1864; and 13, 14, and 15 January 1865. The ship steamed in and took the lead in the ironclad division close inshore, and immediately opened its starboard battery in a barrage of well-directed fire to cause several fires and explosions and dismount several guns during the first two days of fighting. Taken under fire, as she steamed into position on 13 January, the *New Ironsides* fought all day and took on ammunition at night despite severe weather conditions. When the enemy came out of his bombproofs to defend the fort against the storming party, the ship's battery disabled nearly every gun on the fort facing the shorebefore the cease-fire orders were given by the flagship.

Harcourt, Thomas

Rank and organization: Ordinary Seaman, U.S. Navy. *Born*: 1841, Boston, Mass. *Accredited to*: Massachusetts. G. O. No.: 59, 22 June 1865. *Citation*: On board the U.S.S. *Minnesota* in action during the assault on Fort Fisher, 15 January 1865. Landing on the beach with the assaulting party from his ship, Harcourt advanced to the top of the sandhill and partly through the breach in the palisades despite enemy fire which killed and wounded many officers and men. When more than two-thirds of the men become seized with panic and retreated on the run, he remained with the party until dark when it came safely away, bringing its wounded, its arms and its colors.

Hawkins, Charles

Rank and organization: Seaman, U.S. Navy. *Born*: 1834, Scotland. *Accredited to*: New Hampshire. G. O. No.. 45, 31 December 1864. *Citation*: Hawkins served on board the U.S.S. *Agawam*, as one of a volunteer crew of a powderboat which was exploded near Fort Fisher,

23 [24] December 1864. The powderboat, towed in by the *Wilderness* to prevent detection by the enemy, cast off and slowly steamed to within 300 yards of the beach. After fuses and fires had been lit and a second anchor with short scope let go to assure the boat's tailing inshore, the crew again boarded the *Wilderness* and proceeded a distance of 12 miles from shore. Less than two hours later the explosion took place, and the following day fires were observed still burning at the forts.

Hayden, Joseph B.

Rank and organization: Quartermaster, U.S. Navy. *Born*: 1834, Maryland. *Accredited to*: Maryland. G. O. No.: 59, 22 June 1865. *Citation*: On board the U.S.S. *Ticonderoga*, as quartermaster in charge of steering the ship into action, during attacks on Fort Fisher, 13 to 15 January 1865. Hayden steered the ship into position in the line of battle where she maintained a well-directed fire upon the batteries to the left of the palisades during the initial phases of the engagement. Although several of the enemy's shots fell over and around the vessel, the *Ticonderoga* fought her guns gallantly throughout three consecutive days of battle until the flag was planted on one of the strongest fortifications possessed by the rebels.

Hinnegan, William

Rank and organization: Second Class Fireman, U.S. Navy. *Born*: 1841, Ireland. *Accredited to*: New York. G. O. No.: 45, 31 December 1864. *Citation*: Hinnegan served on board the U.S.S. *Agawam*, as one of a volunteer crew of powder boat which was exploded near Fort Fisher, 23 [24] December 1864. The powder boat, towed in by the *Wilderness* to prevent detection by the enemy, cast off and slowly steamed to within 300 yards of the beach. After fuses and fires had been lit and a second anchor with short scope let go to assure the boat's tailing inshore, the crew again boarded the *Wilderness* and proceeded a distance of 12 miles from shore. Less than two hours later the explosion took place, and the following day fires were observed still burning at the forts.

Jones, Thomas

Rank and organization: Coxswain, U.S. Navy. *Born*: 1820, Baltimore, Md. *Accredited to*: Maryland. G. O. No.: 59, 22 June 1865. *Citation*: On board the U.S.S. *Ticonderoga* during attacks on Fort Fisher, 24 and 25 December 1864; and 13 to 15 January 1865. Despite heavy return fire by the enemy and the explosion of the 100-pounder Parrott rifle which killed eight men and wounded 12 more, Jones, as captain of a gun, performed his duties with skill and courage during the first two days of battle. As his ship again took position on the line on the 13th [15th], he remained steadfast as the *Ticonderoga* maintained a well-placed fire upon the batteries on shore, and thereafter, as she materially lessened the power of guns on the mound which had been turned upon our assaulting columns. During this action the flag was planted on one side of the strongest fortifications possessed by the rebels.

Kane, Thomas

Rank and organization: Captain of the Hold, U.S. Navy. *Born*: 1841 Jersey City, N.J. *Accredited to*: New Jersey. G. O. No.: 84, 3 October 1867. *Citation*: On board the U.S.S. *Nereus* during the attack on Fort Fisher, on 15 January 1865. Kane, as captain of the hold, displayed outstanding skill and courage as his ship maintained its well-directed fire against fortifications on shore despite the enemy's return fire. When a rebel steamer was discovered in the river back of the fort, the *Nereus*, with forward rifle guns trained, drove the ship off at the third fire. The gallant ship's participation contributed to the planting of the flag on one of the strongest fortifications possessed by the rebels.

Lear, Nicholas

Rank and organization. Quartermaster, U.S. Navy. *Born*: 1826, Rhode Island. *Accredited to*: Pennsylvania. G. O. No.: 59, 22 June 1865. *Citation*: Lear served on board the *U.S.S. New Ironsides* during action in several attacks on Fort Fisher, 24 and 25 December 1864; and 13, 14, and 15 January 1865. The ship steamed in and took the lead in the ironclad division close inshore and immediately opened its starboard battery in a barrage of well-directed fire to cause several fires and explosions and dismount several guns during the first two days of fighting. Taken under fire as she steamed into position on 13 January, the *New Ironsides* fought all day and took on ammunition at night despite severe weather conditions. When the enemy came out of his bombproofs to defend the fort against the storming party, the ship's battery disabled nearly every gun on the fort facing the shore before the cease-fire order was given by the flagship.

McWilliams, George W.

Rank and organization: Landsman, U.S. Navy. *Born*: 1844, Pennsylvania. *Accredited to*: Pennsylvania. G.O). No.: 59, 22 June 1865. *Citation*. Served on board the U.S.S. *Pontoosuc* during the capture of Fort Fisher and Wilmington, 24 December 1864, to 22 February 1865. Carrying out his duties faithfully throughout this period, McWilliams was so severely wounded in the assault upon Fort Fisher that he was sent to the hospital at Portsmouth, Va. McWilliams was recommended for his gallantry, skill and coolness in action while under the fire of the enemy.

Milliken, Daniel

Rank and organization: Quarter Gunner, U.S. Navy. *Born*: 1838 Maine. *Accredited to*: New York. G. O. No.: 59, 22 June 1865. *Citation* Milliken served on board the U.S.S. *New Ironsides* during action in several attacks on Fort Fisher, 24 and 25 December 1864 and 13, 14, and 15 January 1865. The ship steamed in and took the lead in the Ironclad division close inshore and immediately opened its starboard battery in a barrage of well directed fire to cause several fires and explosions and dismount several guns during the first two days of fighting. Taken under fire as she steamed into position on 13 January, the *New Ironsides* fought all day and took on ammunition at night despite severe weather conditions. When the enemy came out of his bombproofs to defend the fort against the storming party, the ship's battery disabled nearly every gun on the fort facing the shore before the cease-fire orders were given by the flagship.

Mills, Charles

Rank and organization: Seaman, U.S. Navy. *Born*: 1843, Upster, N.Y. *Accredited to*: New York. G. O. No.: 59, 22 June 1865. *Citation*: On board the U.S.S. *Minnesota*, in action during the assault on Fort Fisher, 15 January 1865. Landing on the beach with the assaulting party from his ship, Mills charged up to the palisades and, when more than two-thirds of the men became seized with panic and retreated on the run, risked his life to remain with a wounded officer. With the enemy concentrating his fire on the group, he waited until after dark before assisting the wounded man from the field.

Montgomery, Robert

Rank and organization: Captain of the Afterguard, U.S. Navy. *Born*: 1838, Ireland. *Accredited to*: Virginia. G. O. No.: 45, 21 December 1864. *Citation*: Montgomery served on board the U.S.S. *Agawam*, as one of a volunteer crew of a powder boat which was exploded near Fort Fisher, 23 [24] December 1864. The powder boat, towed in by the *Wilderness* to prevent detection by the enemy, cast off and slowly steamed to within 300 yards of the beach. After fuses and fires had been lit and a second anchor with short scope let go to assure the boat's tailing inshore, the crew again boarded the *Wilderness* and proceeded a distance of 12 miles from shore. Less than two hours later the explosion took place, and the following day fires were observed still burning at the forts.

Neil, John

Rank and organization: Quarter Gunner, U.S. Navy. *Born*: 1837, Newfoundland. *Accredited to*: Virginia. G. O. No.: 45, 31 December 1864. *Citation*: Neil served on board the U.S.S. *Agawam*, as one of a volunteer crew of a powder boat which was exploded near Fort Fisher, 23 [24] December 1864. The powder boat, towed in by the *Wilderness* to prevent detection by the enemy, cast off and slowly steamed to within 300 yards of the beach. After fuses and fires had been lit and a second anchor with short scope let go to assure the boat's tailing inshore, the crew again boarded the *Wilderness* and proceeded a distance of 12 miles from shore. Less than two hours later the explosion took place, and the following day fires were observed still burning at the forts.

Prance, George

Rank and organization: Captain of the Main Top, U.S. Navy. *Born*: 1827, France. *Accredited to*: Massachusetts. G. O. No.: 59, 22 June 1865. *Citation*: On board the U.S.S. *Ticonderoga* during attacks on Fort Fisher, 24 and 25 December 1864; and 13 to 15 January 1865. Despite heavy return fire by the enemy and the explosion of the 100-pounder Parrott rifle which killed eight men and wounded 12 more, Prance as captain of a gun, performed his duties with skill and courage during the first two days of battle. As his ship again took position on the line on the 13th [15th], he remained steadfast as the *Ticonderoga* maintained a well-placed fire upon the batteries on shore, and thereafter as she materially lessened the power of guns on the mound which had been turned upon our assaulting columns. During this action the flag was planted on one of the strongest fortifications possessed by the rebels.

Province, George

Rank and organization: Ordinary Seaman, U.S. Navy. *Born*: 1842, New York, N.Y. *Accredited to*: New York. G. O. No.: 59, 22 June 1865. *Citation*: On board the U.S.S. *Santiago de Cuba* during the assault on Fort Fisher on 15 January 1865. As one of a boat crew detailed to one of the generals on shore, Province bravely entered the fort in the assault and accompanied his party in carrying dispatches at the height of the battle. He was one of six men who entered the fort in the assault from the fleet.

Rice, Charles

Rank and organization: Coal Heaver, U.S. Navy. *Born*: 1840, Russia. *Accredited to*: Maine. G. O. No.: 45, 31 December 1864. *Citation*: On board the U.S.S. *Agawam*, as one of a volunteer crew of a powder boat which was exploded near Fort Fisher, 23 [24] December 1864. The powder boat, towed in by the *Wilderness* to prevent detection by the enemy, cast off and slowly steamed to within 300 yards of the beach. After fuses and fires had been lit and a second anchor with short scope let go to assure the boat's tailing inshore, the crew again boarded the *Wilderness* and proceeded a distance of 12 miles from shore. Less than two hours later the explosion took place, and the following day, fires were observed still burning at the fort.

Roberts, James

Rank and organization: Seaman, U.S. Navy. *Born*: 1837, England. *Accredited to*: Virginia. G. O. No.: 45, 31 December 1864. *Citation*: Roberts served on board the U.S.S. *Agawan*, as one of a volunteer

crew of a powder boat which was exploded near Fort Fisher, 23 [24] December 1864. The powder boat, towed in by the *Wilderness* to prevent detection by the enemy, cast off and slowly steamed to within 300 yards of the beach. After fuses and fires had been lit and a second anchor with short scope let go to assure the boat's tailing inshore, the crew again boarded the *Wilderness* and proceeded a distance of 12 miles from shore. Less than two hours later the explosion took place and the following day fires were observed still burning at the forts.

Savage, Auzella

Rank and organization: Ordinary Seaman, U.S. Navy. *Born*: 1846, Maine. *Accredited to*: Massachusetts. G. O. No.: 59, 22 June 1865. *Citation*: On board the U.S.S. *Santiago de Cuba* in the assault on Fort Fisher, 15 January 1865. When the landing party to which he was attached charged on the fort with a cheer, and the determination to plant the colors on the ramparts, Savage remained steadfast when more than two-thirds of the marines and sailors fell back in panic during the fight. When enemy fire shot away the flagstaff above his hand, he bravely seized the remainder of the staff and brought his colors safely off.

Shepard, Louis C.

Rank and organization: Ordinary Seaman, U.S. Navy. *Born*: 1843, Ohio. *Accredited to*: Ohio. G. O. No.: 59, 22 June 1865. *Citation*: Served as seaman on board the U.S.S. *Wabash* in the assault on Fort Fisher, 15 January 1865. Advancing gallantly through severe enemy fire while armed only with a revolver and cutlass which made it impossible to return the fire at that range, Shepard succeeded in reaching the angle of the fort and in going on, to be one of the few who entered the fort. When the rest of the body of men to his rear were forced to retreat under a devastating fire, he was forced to withdraw through lack of support and to seek the shelter of one of the mounds near the stockade from which point he succeeded in regaining the safety of his ship.

Shipman, William

Rank and organization: Coxswain, U.S. Navy. *Born*: 1831, New York, N.Y. *Accredited to*: New York. G. O. No.: 59, 22 June 1865. *Citation*: On board the U.S.S. *Ticonderoga* in the attack upon Fort Fisher on 15 January 1865. As captain of No. 2 gun, stationed near the 100-pounder Parrott rifle when it burst into fragments, killing eight men and wounding 12 more, Shipman promptly recognized the effect produced by the explosion and, despite the carnage surrounding them, and the enemy's fire, encouraged the men at their guns by exclaiming "Go ahead, boys! This is only the fortunes of war!"

Stevens, Daniel D.

Rank and organization. Quartermaster, U.S. Navy. *Born*: 1840, Sagnange, Tenn. *Accredited to*: Massachusetts. Letter 15 July 1870, Secretary of the Navy to Hon. S. Hooper. *Citation*: On board the U.S.S. *Canonicus* during attacks on Fort Fisher, on 13 January 1865. As the *Canonicus* moved into position at 700 yards from shore, the enemy troops soon obtained her range and opened with heavy artillery fire, subjecting her to several hits and near misses until late in the afternoon when the heavier ships coming into line drove them into their bombproofs. Twice during the battle, in which his ship sustained 36 hits, the flag was shot away and gallantly replaced by Stevens.

Sullivan, James

Rank and organization: Ordinary Seaman, U.S. Navy. *Born*: 1833, New York, N.Y. *Accredited to*: New York. G. O. No.: 45, 31 December 1864. *Citation*: On board the U.S.S. *Agawam* as one of a volunteer crew of a powder boat which was exploded near Fort Fisher, 2

[24] December 1864. The powder boat, towed in by the *Wilderness* to prevent detection by the enemy, cast off and slowly steamed to within 300 yards of the beach. After fuses and fires had been lit and a second anchor with short scope let go to assure the boat's tailing inshore, the crew boarded the *Wilderness* and proceeded a distance of 12 miles from shore. Less than two hours later the explosion took place, and the following day fires were observed still burning at the forts.

Summers, Robert
Rank and organization. Chief Quartermaster, U.S. Navy. *Born*: 1838, Prussia. *Accredited to*: New York. G. O. No.: 59, 22 June 1865. *Citation*: Summers served on board the U.S.S. *Ticonderoga* in the attacks on Fort Fisher, 13 to 15 January 1865. The ship took position in the line of battle and maintained a well-directed fire upon the batteries to the left of the palisades during the initial phase of the engagement. Although several of the enemy's shots fell over and around the vessel, the *Ticonderoga* fought her guns gallantly throughout three consecutive days of battle until the flag was planted on one of the strongest fortifications possessed by the rebels.

Swanson, John
Rank and organization: Seaman, U.S. Navy. *Born*: 1842, Sweden. *Accredited to*: Massachusetts. G. O. No.: 59, 22 June 1865. *Citation*: On board the U.S.S. *Santiago de Cuba* during the assault on Fort Fisher on 15 January 1865. As one of a boat crew detailed to one of the generals on shore, Swanson bravely entered the fort in the assault and accompanied his party in carrying dispatches at the height of the battle. He was one of six men who entered the fort in the assault from the fleet.

Swatton, Edward
Rank and organization: Seaman, U.S. Navy. *Born*: 1836, New York, N.Y. *Accredited to*: New York. G. O. No.: 59, 22 June 1865. *Citation*: On board the U.S.S. *Santiago de Cuba* during the assault on Fort Fisher on 15 January 1865. As one of a boat crew detailed to one of the generals on shore, Swatton bravely entered the fort in the assault and accompanied his party in carrying dispatches at the height of the battle. He was one of six men who entered the fort in the assault from the fleet.

Taylor, William G.
Rank and organization: Captain of the Forecastle, U.S. Navy. *Born*: 1831, Philadelphia, Pa. *Accredited to*: Pennsylvania. G. O. No.: 59, 22 June 1865. *Citation*: On board the U.S.S. *Ticonderoga* during attacks on Fort Fisher, 24 and 25 December 1864. As captain of a gun, Taylor performed his duties with coolness and skill as his ship took position in the line of battle and delivered its fire on the batteries on shore. Despite the depressing effect caused when an explosion of the 100-pounder Parrott rifle killed eight men and wounded 12 more, and the enemy's heavy return fire, he calmly remained at his station during the two days' operations.

Tripp, Othniel
Rank and organization: Chief Boatswain's Mate, U.S. Navy. *Born*: 1826, Maine. *Accredited to*: Maine. G. O. No.: 59, 22 June 1865. *Citation*: On board the U.S.S. *Seneca* in the assault on Fort Fisher, 15 January 1865. Despite severe enemy fire which halted an attempt by his assaulting party to enter the stockade, Tripp boldly charged through the gap in the stockade although the center of the line, being totally unprotected, fell back along the open beach and left too few in the ranks to attempt an offensive operation.

Verney, James W.
Rank and organization: Chief Quartermaster, U.S. Navy. *Born*: 1834 Maine. *Accredited to*: Maine. G. O. No.: 59, 22 June 1865. *Citation.* Served as chief quartermaster on board the U.S.S. *Pontoosuc* during the capture of Fort Fisher and Wilmington, 24 December 1864 to 22 February 1865. Carrying out his duties faithfully throughout this period, Verney was recommended for gallantry and skill and for his cool courage while under fire of the enemy throughout these various actions.

Webster, Henry S.
Rank and organization: Landsman, U.S. Navy. *Born*: 1845, Stockholm, N.Y. *Accredited to*: New York. G. O. No.: 49, 22 June 1865. *Citation*: On board the U.S.S. *Susquehanna* during the assault on Fort Fisher, 15 January 1865. When enemy fire halted the attempt by his landing party to enter the fort and more than two-thirds of the men fell back along the open beach, Webster voluntarily remained with one of his wounded officers, under fire, until aid could be obtained to bring him to the rear.

White, Joseph
Rank and organization: Captain of the Gun, U.S. Navy. *Born*: 1840, Washington, D.C. *Accredited to*: Pennsylvania. G. O. No.: 59, 22 June 1865. *Citation*: White served on board the U.S.S. *New Ironsides* during action in several attacks on Fort Fisher, 24 and 25 December 1864; and 13, 14, and 15 January 1865. The ship steamed in and took the lead in the ironclad division close inshore and immediately opened its starboard battery in a barrage of well-directed fire to cause several fires and explosions and dismount several guns during the first two days of fighting. Taken under fire as she steamed into position on 13 January, the *New Ironsides* fought all day and took on ammunition at night despite severe weather conditions. When the enemy came out of his bombproofs to defend the fort against the storming party, the ships battery disabled nearly every gun on the fort facing the shore before the cease-fire order was given by the flagship.

Wilcox, Franklin L.
Rank and organization: Ordinary Seaman, U.S. Navy. *Born*: 1831, Paris, N.Y. *Accredited to*: New York. G. O. No.: 59, 22 June 1865. *Citation*: On board the U.S.S. *Minnesota* in action during the assault on Fort Fisher, 15 January 1865. Landing on the beach with the assaulting party from his ship, Wilcox advanced to the top of the sandhill and partly through the breach in the palisades despite enemy fire which killed and wounded many officers and men. When more than two-thirds of the men became seized with panic and retreated on the run, he remained with the party until dark when it came safely away, bringing its wounded, its arms and its colors.

Williams, Anthony
Rank and organization: Sailmaker's Mate, U.S. Navy. *Born*: 1822, Plymouth, Mass. *Accredited to*: Maine. G. O. No.: 59, 22 June 1865. *Citation*: Served as sailmaker's mate on board the U.S.S. *Pontoosuc* during the capture of Fort Fisher and Wilmington, 24 December 1864 to 22 February 1865. Carrying out his duties faithfully throughout this period, Williams was recommended for gallantry and skill and for his cool courage while under the fire of the enemy throughout these various actions.

Williams, Augustus
Rank and organization: Seaman, U.S. Navy. *Born*: 1842, Norway. *Accredited to*: Massachusetts. G. O. No: 59, 22 June 1865. *Citation*: On board the U.S.S. *Santiago de Cuba* during the assault by the fleet on Fort Fisher, on 15 January 1865. When the landing party to which

he was attached charged on the fort with a cheer, and with determination to plant their colors on the ramparts, Williams remained steadfast when they reached the foot of the fort and more than two-thirds of the marines and sailors fell back in panic. Taking cover when the enemy concentrated his fire on the remainder of the group, he alone remained with his executive officer, subsequently withdrawing from the field after dark.

Willis, Richard

Rank and organization: Coxswain, U.S. Navy. *Born*: 1826, England. *Accredited to*: Pennsylvania. G. O. No.: 59, 22 June 1865. *Citation*: Willis served on board the U.S.S. *New Ironsides* during action in several attacks on Fort Fisher, 24 and 25 December 1864; and 13, 14 and 15 January 1865. The ship steamed in and took the lead in the ironclad division close inshore and immediately opened its starboard battery in a barrage of well-directed fire to cause several fires and explosions and dismount several guns during the first two days of fighting. Taken under fire as she steamed into position on 13 January, the *New Ironsides* fought all day and took on ammunition at night, despite severe weather conditions. When the enemy troops came out of their bombproofs to defend the fort against the storming party, the ship's battery disabled nearly every gun on the fort facing the shore before the cease-fire order was given by the flagship.

United States Marine Corps

Binder, Richard

Rank and organization: Sergeant, U.S. Marine Corps. *Born*: 1840, Philadelphia, Pa. *Accredited to*: Pennsylvania. *Citation*: On board the U.S.S. *Ticonderoga* during the attacks on Fort Fisher, 24 and 25 December 1864, and 13 to 15 January 1865. Despite heavy return fire by the enemy and the explosion of the 100-pounder Parrott rifle which killed eight men and wounded 12 more, Sgt. Binder, as captain of a gun, performed his duties with skill and courage during the first two days of battle. As his ship again took position on the 13th [15th], he remained steadfast as the *Ticonderoga* maintained a well-placed fire upon the batteries on shore, and thereafter, as she materially lessened the power of guns on the mound which had been turned upon our assaulting columns. During this action the flag was planted on one of the strongest fortifications possessed by the rebels.

Fry, Isaac N.

Rank and organization: Orderly Sergeant, U.S. Marine Corps. *Accredited to*: Pennsylvania. G. O. No.: 59, 22 June 1865. *Citation*: On board the U.S.S. *Ticonderoga* during attacks on Fort Fisher, 13 to 15 January 1865. As orderly sergeant of marine guard, and captain of a gun, Orderly Sgt. Fry performed his duties with skill and courage as the *Ticonderoga* maintained a well-placed fire upon the batteries to the left of the palisades during the initial phases of the three-day battle, and thereafter, as she considerably lessened the firing power of guns on the mound which had been turned upon our assaulting columns. During this action the flag was planted on one of the strongest fortifications possessed by the rebels.

Rannahan, John

Rank and organization: Corporal, U.S. Marine Corps. *Born*: 1836, County of Monahan, Ireland. *Accredited to*: Pennsylvania. G. O. No.: 59, 22 June 1865. *Citation*: On board the U.S.S. *Minnesota* in the assault on Fort Fisher, 15 January 1865. Landing on the beach with the assaulting party from his ship, Cpl. Rannahan advanced to the top of the sandhill and partly through the breach in the palisades despite enemy fire which killed or wounded many officers and men. When

more than two-thirds of the men became seized with panic and retreated on the run, he remained with the party until dark when it came safely away, bringing its wounded, its arms, and its colors.

Shivers, John

Rank and organization: Private, U.S. Marine Corps. *Born*: 1830 Canada. *Accredited to*: New Jersey. G. O. No.. 59, 22 June 1865. *Citation*: On board the U.S.S. *Minnesota*, in the assault on Fort Fisher, 15 January 1865. Landing on the beach with the assaulting party from his ship, Pvt. Shivers advanced to the top of the sandhill and partly through the breach in the palisades despite enemy fire which killed or wounded many officers and men. When more than two-thirds of the men became seized with panic and retreated on the run, he remained with the party until dark when it came safely away, bringing its wounded, its arms, and its colors.

Thompson, Henry A.

Rank and organization: Private, U.S. Marine Corps. *Born*: 1841, England. *Accredited to*: Pennsylvania. G. O. No.: 59, 22 June 1865. *Citation*: On board the U.S.S. *Minnesota* in the assault on Fort Fisher, 15 January 1865. Landing on the beach with the assaulting party from his ship, Private Thompson advanced partly through a breach in the palisades and nearer to the fort than any man from his ship despite enemy fire which killed or wounded many officers and men. When more than two-thirds of the men became seized with panic and retreated on the run, he remained with the party until dark, when it came safely away, bringing its wounded, its arms, and its colors.

Tomlin, Andrew J.

Rank and organization: Corporal, U.S. Marine Corps. *Born*: 1844, Goshen, N.J. *Accredited to*: New Jersey. G. O. No.: 59, 22 June 1865. *Citation*: As corporal of the guard on board the U.S.S. *Wabash* during the assault on Fort Fisher, on 15 January 1865. As one of 200 marines assembled to hold a line of entrenchments in the rear of the fort which the enemy threatened to attack in force following a retreat in panic by more than two-thirds of the assaulting ground forces, Cpl. Tomlin took position in line and remained until morning when relief troops arrived from the fort. When one of his comrades was struck down by enemy fire, he unhesitatingly advanced under a withering fire of musketry into an open plain close to the fort and assisted the wounded man to a place of safety.

Glossary

Abatis: defensive obstacles consisting of felled trees with sharpened branches, designed to impede the progress of an enemy assault.

Banquette: a step or platform along the inner base of an embrasure or parapet in a fort; used for soldiers to stand on while servicing their weapons.

Barbette: heavy seacoast weapons mounted "en barbette" are elevated on high carriages for firing above the parapet of a fortification.

Bastion: a fort, or a projecting or protruding portion of a fortification.

Battlement: a parapet with open spaces atop a wall used for defense.

Battery: a parapet or fortification equipped with artillery; also two or more pieces of artillery used for combined action.

Bowlines: ropes used for keeping a ship's square sails taut.

Crenel: the open spaces between the merlons of a battlement. See Battery.

Curtain: a comparatively low sand wall constructed for joining the main batteries, or bastions in a fortification or defensive work.

Cutwater: the forepart of a ship's stem (bow).

Demilune: an outwork of a fortification resembling a bastion, with a crescent or half-moon shape.

Earthwork: an embankment or mound of earth employed as a field or siege fortification, used for protection against enemy fire.

Fascine: a long bundle of sticks bound together, used to strengthen earthwork batteries or the ramparts of large fortifications. Used in the defenses of Sebastopol during the Crimean War.

Fathom: a unit of length equal to six feet used for measuring the depth of water.

Fore-and-aft: a nautical term used to describe objects (such as sails) positioned along or parallel to a line from the stem of a ship to its stern.

Fortification: the art or science of constructing military defensive works for protection against an enemy assault; [n] a military defensive work.

Gabion: a cylinder of wickerwork filled with earth, used to revet or strengthen defensive batteries or fortifications. Used in the defenses of Sebastopol during the Crimean War.

Gaff: a pole (yard) rising aft from a ship's mast to support a four-sided, fore-and-aft sail.

Gangway: either of the sides of the upper deck of a ship.

Glacis: a bank of earth having an easy slope from the top of an earthwork fortification to the open plain below.

Guy: a rope, chain, rod, or wire attached to an object as a brace or guide.

Haul: to change the course of a ship.

Hawser: a large rope used for towing, mooring, or securing a ship.

Inshore: situated near the shore of the ocean.

Kedge: [n] a small anchor; [v] to move a ship by means of a line attached to a kedge dropped at the distance and in the direction desired.

Lunette: an angled or salient defensive work with two parallel sides, open at the rear.

Merlon: solid interval between crenels of a battlement. See Traverse.

Orlop Deck: the lowermost of four or more decks above the space at the bottom of a ship's hull.

Palisade: a tall fence of strong stakes, pointed at the top, used as a defensive obstacle.

Parapet: a wall or elevation of earth employed for the protection of gun emplacements and soldiers. Though technically a specific part of a fortification, many of the Federal soldiers who attacked Fort Fisher used the term as all inclusive when describing the battle.

Pintle: the pin or bolt on which a gun carriage rotates or pivots.

Port: the left side of a ship (also known as larboard).

Rampart: a broad elevation or mound of earth raised as a fortification and capped with a parapet.

Rigging: the ropes and chains used to support and work the masts, yards, booms, and sails of a ship.

Sally Port: a gate or passage in a fortification.

Shroud: a taut rope or wire running from the top of a ship's mast (usually in pairs) to help anchor it against lateral sway.

Spanker: a fore-and-aft sail on the aftermost lower mast of a ship.

Stand: to hold a course at sea.

Starboard: the right side of a ship.

Stays: large wires used to support the masts of a ship.

Stem: the bow or forward part of a ship.

Stern: the rear or after part of a ship.

Terreplein: the top platform or horizontal surface of a rampart.

Traverse: a protective projecting wall or mound of earth in a fort or trench. Extends above the parapet between gun emplacements to protect gunners from enfilade fire.

Truck: a small, strong wheel on a swiveling gun carriage.

Selected Bibliography

NOTE: Space limitations preclude a thorough documentation of this study. The following sources encompass manuscript and published materials, both primary and secondary.

AA Barrage (Camp Davis Military News), Holly Ridge, N.C., April 10, 1943; January 1, 22, 1944

Ames, Adelbert. "The Capture of Fort Fisher." *Civil War Papers of the Commandery of the State of Massachusetts, Military Order of the Loyal Legion of the United States*, 1 (1900), pp. 271-295.

Ammen, Daniel. *A Sketch of Our Second Bombardment of Fort Fisher: A Paper Read before the District of Columbia Commandery of the Military Order of the Loyal Legion of the United States*. Washington, D.C.: Judd and Detweiler, Printers, 1887.

Angley, Wilson. *A History of Fort Johnston on the Lower Cape Fear*. Southport, N.C.: Southport Historical Society, 1996.

Bailey, Kristin S. *Fort Fisher During World War II: A Study of Fort Fisher and Camp Davis, North Carolina*. Unpublished report prepared for the North Carolina Division of Archives and History (October 1990).

Baker, Gertrude Elizabeth. "The Diary of William Lamb, August 18, 1859-May 21, 1860." Master's Thesis, College of William and Mary, Williamsburg, Virginia, 1960.

Barefoot, Daniel W. *General Robert F. Hoke: Lee's Modest Warrior*. Winston-Salem, N.C.: John F. Blair, 1996.

Barnette, Jeff. "Camp Davis," *Coast Artillery Journal*, vol. 84, no. 5 (September/October, 1941); vol. 85, no. 1 (January/February, 1942).

Barrett, John G. *The Civil War in North Carolina*. Chapel Hill, N.C.: University of North Carolina Press, 1963.

Basler, Roy P., ed. *The Collected Works of Abraham Lincoln*. Vol. 8. New Brunswick, N.J.: Rutgers University Press, 1953.

G. H. Beatty Papers. Letter of G. H. Beatty, November 14, 1861. Special Collections Library. Duke University, Durham, North Carolina.

Bentley, James R., ed. "The Civil War Memoirs of Captain Thomas Speed." *The Filson Club Historical Quarterly*, 44, no. 3 (July 1970), pp. 235-267.

Bentley, Nicolas, ed. *Russell's Despatches from the Crimea, 1854-1856. William Howard Russell, Special Correspondent*. London: Andre Deutsch, 1966.

Bragg, Braxton. Letter in "Defence and Fall of Fort Fisher," *Southern Historical Society Papers*, 10 (July 1882), pp. 346-349.

Beyer, W. F. and O. F. Keydel, eds. *Deeds of Valor: How America's Civil War Heroes Won The Medal of Honor*. Detroit, Mich.: The Perrien-Keydel Company, 1903.

—. *Acts of Bravery* (Vol. 2 of *Deeds of Valor*). Detroit, Mich.: The Perrien-Keydel Company, 1907.

Bright, Leslie S. *The Blockade Runner 'Modern Greece' and Her Cargo*. Raleigh, N.C.: Archaeology Section, North Carolina Division of Archives and History, 1977

Buell, Augustus. "The Cannoneer," Washington, D.C., *National Tribune*, 1890.

Alexander Robinson Boteler Papers. Special Collections Library, Duke University, Durham, North Carolina.

Caldwell, Charles K. *The Old Sixth Regiment: Its War Record, 1861-5*. New Haven, Connecticut: Tuttle, Morehouse & Taylor, 1875.

Joseph Canning Journal. McEachern and Williams Collection, University of North Carolina, Wilmington, N.C.

Cannon, Robert K. *Volunteers for Union and Liberty: History of the 5th Tennessee Infantry, U.S.A. 1862-1865*. Knoxville, Tenn.: Bohemian Brigade, 1995.

Carter, Solon A. "Fourteen Months' Service With Colored Troops."

Civil War Papers of the Commandery of the State of Massachusetts, Military Order of the Loyal Legion of the United States, 1 (1900), pp. 155-179.

Chisman, James A., ed. *76th Regiment Pennsylvanis Volunteer Infantry, Keystone Zouaves: The Personal Recollections 1861-1865 of Sergeant John A. Porter*. Wilmington, N.C.: Broadfoot Publishing Company, 1988.

Clark, Isaac C. "Reminiscences of an Old 63rd Indiana Soldier," *Spence's Peoples Paper*. Covington, Ind.: November 27, 1875.

Clark, James. *The Iron Hearted Regiment: Being an Account of the Battles, Marches and Gallant Deeds Performed by the 115th Regiment N.Y. Vols*. Albany, New York: J. Munsell, 1865.

Clark, Walter, ed. *Histories of the Several Regiments and Battalions from North Carolina in the Great War 1861-'65. Written by Members of the Respective Commands*. 5 vols. Goldsboro, N.C.: Nash Brothers, 1901.

Cler, Jean Joseph Gustave. *Reminiscences of an Officer of Zouaves*. Translated from the French. New York: D. Appleton and Company, 1860.

Codman, John. *An American Transport in the Crimean War*. New York, 1896.

Coggins, Jack. *Arms and Equipment of the Civil War*. Wilmington, N.C.: Broadfoot Publishing Company, 1989. (Originally published 1962).

Committee of the Regiment. *Battery D, First Ohio Veteran Volunteer Light Artillery, It's Military History, 1861-1865*. Oil City, Pa.: The Derrick Publishing Company, 1908. (Reprinted as *Battered Destinies, Story of Battery D, 1861-1865*. Pasadena, Tex.: Infotrans Press, 1996).

Congressional Medal of Honor: The Names, The Deeds. [n.a.] Forest Ranch, Cal.: Sharp and Dunnigan, 1984.

Copp, Elbridge. *Reminiscences of the War of the Rebellion, 1861-1865*. Nashua, N.H.: The Telegraph Publishing Company, 1911.

Cox, Jacob D. *The March to the Sea—Franklin, and Nashville*. New York: Charles Scribner's Sons, 1882.

Jacob D. Cox Diary. Oberlin College Archives, Oberlin, Ohio.

Crabtree, Beth G. and James W. Patton, eds. *"Journal of a Secesh Lady": The Diary of Catherine Ann Devereux Edmondston, 1860-1866*. Raleigh, N.C.: Division of Archives & History, 1979.

Curtis, Newton Martin. "The Capture of Fort Fisher." *Civil War Papers of the Commandery of the State of Massachusetts, Military Order of the Loyal Legion of the United States*, 1 (1900), 299-327.

—. "Reminiscences of the Storming and Capture of Fort Fisher. Address Before the Congressional Club of Brooklyn, October 27, 1890." *N. Martin Curtis Papers*. Ogdensburg Public Library, Ogdensburg, New York.

—. "The Capture of Fort Fisher," *N. Martin Curtis Papers*. Ogdensburg Public Library, Ogdensburg, New York.

William B. Cushing Journal. United States National Archives and Records Services. Record Group 45, Washington, D.C.

Davidson, Roger A., Jr. "'They Have Never Been Known to Falter': The First United States Colored Infantry in Virginia and North Carolina." *Civil War Regiments*, 6, no. 1, July 1998.

Davis, Jefferson. *Rise and Fall of the Confederate Government*. 2 vols. New York: D. Appleton and Company, 1881.

Davis, T. C. "Fortieth Regiment (Third Artillery)," In *Histories of the Several Regiments and Battalions from North Carolina in the Great War 1861-'65. Written by Members of the Respective Commands*. 5 vols. Edited by Walter Clark. Goldsboro, N.C.: Nash Brothers, 1901.

Davis, William C. *Jefferson Davis: The Man and His Hour*. New York: Harper Collins Publishers, 1991.

Delafield, Richard. *Report on the Art of War in Europe in 1854, 1855, and 1856.* Washington, D.C.: George W. Bowman, 1861.

William Lord DeRosset Papers. James A. Reilly remembrance. North Carolina Division of Archives and History, Raleigh, North Carolina.

Dillard, Richard. *The Civil War in Chowan County, North Carolina.* n.p., 1916.

Dowdy, Clifford and Louis H. Manarin, eds. *The Wartime Papers of R. E. Lee.* New York: Bramhall House, 1961.

Drobnich, Bill. *Memories of the 558th AAA AW Bn.* [Antiaircraft Artillery Automatic Weapons Battalion (Mobile)]. n.p., 1995.

Dyer, Frederick H. *A Compendium of the War of the Rebellion.* 2 volumes. Dayton, Ohio: Morningside Bookshop (reprint), 1979.

Earp, Charles A. "Father John B. Tabb Aboard Confederate Blockade Runners." *America's Civil War,* January 1996.

Eldredge, Daniel. *The Third New Hampshire and All About It.* Boston: E. B. Stillings and Company, 1893.

Elliott, Charles G. "The Martin-Kirkland Brigade," In *Histories of the Several Regiments and Battalions from North Carolina in the Great War 1861-'65. Written by Members of the Respective Commands.* 5 vols. Edited by Walter Clark. Goldsboro, N.C.: Nash Brothers, 1901.

Evans, Robely D. *A Sailor's Log: Recollections of Forty Years of Naval Life.* New York: D. Appleton and Company, 1901.

Evans, William McKee. *Ballots and Fence Rails: Reconstruction on the Lower Cape Fear.* Chapel Hill: University of North Carolina Press, 1967.

Fourth Service Command, Camp Davis, N.C. *Introducing Camp Davis* (wartime pamphlet).

Fonvielle, Chris E. *Last Rays of Departing Hope: The Wilmington Campaign.* Campbell, Cal.: Savas Publishing Company, 1997.

—. "'Making the Obstinate Stand': The Battle of Town Creek and the Fall of Wilmington." *Civil War Regiments,* 6, no. 1, July 1998.

—. "The Last Rays of Departing Hope: The Fall of Wilmington, Including the Campaigns Against Fort Fisher." *Blue and Gray,* 12, no. 2, December 1994.

—. "William B. Cushing, Commando at the Cape Fear." *Blue and Gray,* 14, no. 6 (Summer 1997).

Fremantle, Arthur J. L. *Three Months in the Southern States, April-June, 1863.* New York: John Bradburn, 1864.

Furnas, Adam. *Fourty-four Months at the Front, from September 1, 1861 to April 25, 1865.* Muscatine, Iowa: n.p., 1995.

Gaskill, J. W. *Footprints Through Dixie: Everyday Life of the Man Under A Musket, On the Firing Line and in the Trenches, 1862-1865.* Alliance, Ohio: Bradshaw Printing Company, 1919.

J. F. Gilmer Map Collection. Southern Historical Collection, University of North Carolina, Chapel Hill.

Gleason's Pictorial Drawing Room Companion. Boston, Mass.: July 16, 1853.

Gragg, Rod. *Confederate Goliath: The Battle of Fort Fisher.* New York: Harper Collins Publishers, 1991.

Grant, Ulysses S. *Personal Memoirs of U. S. Grant.* 2 vols. New York: Charles L. Webster & Company, 1885.

Greater Wilmington Chamber of Commerce. *What, When, Why, How in Wartime Wilmington.* Wilmington, N.C., n.d.

Guernsey, Alfred H. and Henry M. Alden. *Harper's Pictorial History of the Great Rebellion in the United States.* New York: 1866.

Hagood, Johnson. *Memoirs of the War of Secession, From the Original Manuscripts of Johnson Hagood.* Columbia, S.C.: The State Company, 1910.

—. "Captain William E. Stoney. Gen. Johnson Hagood Pays Tribute to His Memory." *Confederate Veteran.* 4, no. 11 (November 1896), p. 383.

Harper's Weekly: A Journal of Civilization. New York: February 4,

1865.

Henderson, E. Prioleau. *Autobiography of Arab.* Columbia, S.C.: R. L. Bryan Co., 1901.

Herring, Ethel and Carolee Williams. *Fort Caswell in War and Peace.* Wendell, N.C.: Broadfoot's Bookmark, 1983.

Hewlett, Crockette W. and Mona Smalley. *Between the Creeks, Revised: Masonboro Sound, 1735-1985.* Wilmington, N.C.: New Hanover Printing and Publishing Company, 1985 (Originally published 1971).

Hill, Michael, ed. *Guide to North Carolina Highway Historical Markers (Eighth Edition).* Raleigh, N.C.: North Carolina Division of Archives and History, 1990.

Historical and Pictorial Review: Antiaircraft Training Center, Camp Davis, North Carolina. Baton Rouge: The Army and Navy Publishing Company, 1941.

Hodasevich, R. A. *A Voice from Within the Walls of Sebastopol.* London: John Murray, 1856.

Lorenzo Wesley Holder Diary. Indiana Historical Society, Indianapolis, Indiana.

Honeycutt, A. L. "Fort Fisher—Malakoff of the South." Master's thesis, Duke University, 1963.

Hoy, Patrick C. "Personal Recollections of Lt. Patrick C. Hoy," Petersburg, Va.: Petersburg National Battlefield, 1903.

Hutchinson, John G. *History of the Fourth Regiment New Hampshire Volunteers: What it Was, Where it Went, What it Accomplished.* Manchester, N.H.: John B. Clarke Company, 1913.

—. *Roster of the Fourth New Hampshire Volunteers.* Manchester, N.H.: John B. Clarke Company, 1896.

Hyde, William L. *History of the One Hundred and Twelfth Regiment N.Y. Volunteers.* Fredonia, New York: William McKinstry, 1866.

Illustrated London News, January 23, 1864

Izlar, William V. *A Sketch of the War Record of the Edisto Rifles, 1861-1865.* Columbia, S.C.: The State Company, 1914.

Jackson, Harry F. and Thomas F. O'Donnell, eds. *Back Home in Oneida: Hermon Clarke and His Letters.* Syracuse, N.Y.: Syracuse University Press, 1965.

Johns, John. "Wilmington During the Blockade." *Harper's New Monthly Magazine,* 33 (1886), pp. 497-503.

Johnson, Thomas. "My War Experiences: Rebellion 1861-1864." Indiana Historical Society, Indianapolis, Indiana.

Kinglake, A. W. *The Invasion of the Crimea: It's Origin, and An Account of its Progress Down to the Death of Lord Raglan.* 9 vols., London: William Blackwood and Sons, 1888.

Lamb, William. "Fort Fisher, The Battles Fought There in 1864 and '65," *Southern Historical Society Papers,* 21 (1893), pp. 257-290.

—. "Defence and Fall of Fort Fisher," *Southern Historical Society Papers,* 10 (July 1882), pp. 350-368.

—. "The Defense of Fort Fisher," in Robert U. Johnson and Clarence C. Buel, eds., *Battles and Leaders of the Civil War,* 4, pp. 642-654. 4 vols. New York: The Century Company, 1884-1889.

—. "The Heroine of Confederate Point," *Southern Historical Society Papers,* 20 (1892), pp. 301-306.

—. "Thirty-sixth Regiment (Second Artillery)," In *Histories of the Several Regiments and Battalions from North Carolina in the Great War 1861-'65. Written by Members of the Respective Commands.* 5 vols. Edited by Walter Clark. Goldsboro, N.C.: Nash Brothers, 1901.

William Lamb Papers. E. G. Swemm Library, College of William and Mary, Williamsburg, Virginia. Diaries, January 6—December 31, 1855; January 1856 (fragments); January 1—December 31, 1861; October 24, 1864—January 14, 1865; January 15—December 30, 1865.

Lamb, Wilson G. "Seventeenth Regiment," In *Histories of the Sev-*

eral Regiments and Battalions from North Carolina in the Great War 1861-'65. Written by Members of the Respective Commands. 5 vols. Edited by Walter Clark. Goldsboro, N.C.: Nash Brothers, 1901.

Lambert, Andrew and Stephen Badsey. *The Crimean War*. Phoenix Mill, Stroud, and Gloucestershire: Alan Sutton, 1994.

Lambert, Andrew D. *The Crimean War: British Grand Strategy, 1853-56*. Manchester and New York: Manchester University Press, 1990.

Leigh, Larry, ed. *J. J. Scroggs' Diary and Letters, 1852-1865*. Thomaston, Ga.: n.p., 1996.

Leone, Paul M., ed. *Do Just as You Think Best: The Civil War Letters of William Depledge*. Jamestown, N.Y.: Fenton Historical Society, 1995.

Lewis, Paul. *Yankee Admiral: A Biography of David Dixon Porter*. New York: David McKay Company, Inc., 1968.

Little, Henry F. W. *The Seventh New Hampshire Volunteers in the War of the Rebellion*. Concord, N.H.: Ira C. Evans, 1896.

Livingston, Mary P. *A Civil War Marine at Sea: The Diary of Medal of Honor Recipient Miles M. Oviatt*. Shippensburg, Pa.: White Mane, 1998.

Longacre, Edward G., ed. *From Antietam to Fort Fisher: The Civil War Letters of Edward King Wightman, 1862-1865*. Cranbury, N.J.: Associated University Presses, 1985.

Ludwig, H. T. J. "Eighth Regiment," In *Histories of the Several Regiments and Battalions from North Carolina in the Great War 1861-'65. Written by Members of the Respective Commands*. 5 vols. Edited by Walter Clark. Goldsboro, N.C.: Nash Brothers, 1901.

Luvaas, Jay. "The Fall of Fort Fisher," *Civil War Times Illustrated*, III (August 1964).

McKoy, Elizabeth Francenia. *Early Wilmington Block by Block, from 1700 On*. Wilmington, N.C.: 1967.

McLean, Alexander Torrey, III. "The Fort Fisher and Wilmington Campaign: 1864-1865." Master's thesis, University of North Carolina, Chapel Hill, 1969.

McNeill, T. A. "Ninth Battalion (First Heavy Artillery)," In *Histories of the Several Regiments and Battalions from North Carolina in the Great War 1861-'65. Written by Members of the Respective Commands*. 5 vols. Edited by Walter Clark. Goldsboro, N.C.: Nash Brothers, 1901.

McPherson, James M. and Patricia R. McPherson. *Lamson of the Gettysburg: The Civil War Letters of Lieutenant Roswell H. Ramson, U. S. Navy*. New York: Oxford University Press, 1997.

MacFarlane, C. *Reminiscences of an Army Surgeon*. Oswego, N.Y.: Lake City Print Shop, 1912.

Maynard, Felix, ed. *Recollections of a Zouave Before Sebastopol*. Translated from the French. Philadelphia: Hayes & Zell, 1856.

Medal of Honor Recipients, 1863-1978. Washington, D.C.: United States Government Printing Office, 1979.

Mends, Bowen S. *Life of Admiral Sir William Robert Mends, G.C.B., Late Director of Transports*. London: John Murray, 1899.

Mitchell, Joseph B. *The Badge of Gallantry: Recollections of Civil War Congressional Medal of Honor Winners*. New York: The Macmillan Company, 1968.

Moore, John W. "Third Battalion (Light Artillery)," In *Histories of the Several Regiments and Battalions from North Carolina in the Great War 1861-'65. Written by Members of the Respective Commands*. 5 vols. Edited by Walter Clark. Goldsboro, N.C.: Nash Brothers, 1901.

Mowris, J. A. *A History of the One hundred and Seventeenth Regiment, N. Y. Volunteers*. Hartford, Connecticut: Case, Lockwood and Company, 1866.

New York Herald. February 16, 1865

New York Times. January 19, 1865.

New York World. February 24, 1865.

Nichols, James M. *Perry's Saints, or The Fighting Parson's Regiment in the War of the Rebellion*. Boston: D. Lothrop and Company, 1886.

Niven, John. *Salmon P. Chase*. New York and Oxford: Oxford University Press, 1995.

Nolan, Edward H. *The Illustrated History of the War Against Russia*. 2 vols. London: James S. Virtue, 1857.

Norton, Chauncey S. *"The Red Neck Ties," Or, History of the Fifteenth New York Volunteer Cavalry, Containing a Record of the Battles, Skirmishes, Marches, etc., that the Regiment Participated in, from Its Organization in August 1863, to the Time of Its Discharge in August 1865*. Ithaca, N.Y.: Journal, Book and Job Printing House, 1891.

Oakdale Cemetery Company. *A Tribute to Oakdale*. Wilmington, N.C., 1991.

Palmer, Abraham J. *The History of the Forty-Eighth Regiment New York State Volunteers in the War for the Union, 1861-1865*. Brooklyn, N.Y.: Veterans Association of the Regiment, 1885.

Pemberton, W. Baring. *Battles of the Crimean War*. London: B. T. Batsford Ltd., 1962.

Personal Reminiscences and Experiences, By Members of the One Hundred and Third Ohio Volunteer Infantry, Campaigning in the Union Army, From 1862 to 1865. [n.a.] Oberlin, Ohio: News Print Company, 1950.

Pinney, Nelson. *History of the 104th Regiment Ohio Volunteer Infantry During the War of Rebellion*. Akron, Ohio: Werner & Lohmann, 1886.

Pool, Stephen D. "Tenth Regiment (First Artillery)," In *Histories of the Several Regiments and Battalions from North Carolina in the Great War 1861-'65. Written by Members of the Respective Commands*. 5 vols. Edited by Walter Clark. Goldsboro, N.C.: Nash Brothers, 1901.

Powell, Charles S. "Wilmington's City and River Defenses: Reminiscences." *Charles Powell Papers*, Southern Historical Collection. University of North Carolina, Chapel Hill, North Carolina.

Price, Isaiah. *History of the Ninety-Seventh Regiment, Pennsylvania Volunteer Infantry During the War of the Rebellion, 1861-1865*. Philadelphia: Author for the Subscribers, 1875.

Public Relations Office, Camp Davis, N.C. *Camp Davis: A Guide Book* (wartime pamphlet).

James Ryder Randall Papers. J. R. Randall to Kate, February 26, 1864. Southern Historical Collection, University of North Carolina, Chapel Hill, North Carolina.

Tyre B. Ray Papers. Letters of Cabe L. Ray. Special Collections Library. Duke University, Durham, North Carolina.

Redkey, Edwin S., ed. "Rocked in the Cradle of Secession, by Henry M. Turner." *American Heritage*, 31 (October/November 1980), pp. 70-79.

Reid, Douglas Arthur. *Memories of the Crimean War, January 1855 to June 1856*. London: The St. Catherine Press, 1911.

Reid, Whitelaw. *After the War: A Southern Tour*. Cincinnati: Moore, Wilstach, & Baldwin, 1866.

Reilly, J. S. *Wilmington: Past, Present, & Future, Embracing Historical Sketches of its Growth and Progress from its Establishment to the Present Time, Together with Outline of North Carolina History*. Wilmington, N.C.: n.p., 1884.

Robertson, John, ed. *Michigan in the War*. Lansing: W. S. George & Company, State Printers and Binders, 1882.

Robinson, Charles M. III. *Hurricane of Fire: The Union Assault on Fort Fisher*. Annapolis, Md.: Naval Institute Press, 1998.

Rose, George M. "Sixty-sixth Regiment," In *Histories of the Several Regiments and Battalions from North Carolina in the Great War*

1861-'65. Written by Members of the Respective Commands. 5 vols. Edited by Walter Clark. Goldsboro, N.C.: Nash Brothers, 1901.

Ross, FitzGerald. *A Visit to the Cities and Camps of the Confederate States.* Edinburgh and London: Blackwood, 1865.

Russell, William Howard. *The British Expedition to the Crimea.* London: George Routledge and Sons, 1877.

—. *General Todleben's History of the Defence of Sebastopol, 1854-5: A Review.* New York: D. Van Nostrand, 1865.

Sanders, John W. "Additional Sketch Tenth Regiment (First Artillery)," In *Histories of the Several Regiments and Battalions from North Carolina in the Great War 1861-'65. Written by Members of the Respective Commands.* 5 vols. Edited by Walter Clark. Goldsboro, N.C.: Nash Brothers, 1901.

Schneller, Robert J., Jr., ed. *Under the Blue Pennant, or Notes of a Naval Staff Officer, by John W. Grattan, Acting Ensign, United States Navy.* New York: John Wiley & Sons, 1999.

Schofield, John M. *Forty-Six Years in the Army.* New York: The Century Company, 1897.

Seagrave, Pia Seija. *A Boy Lieutenant: Memoirs of Freeman S. Bowley, 30th United States Colored Troops.* Fredericksburg, Va.: Sergeant Kirkland's Museum and Historical Society, Inc., 1997. (Originally published Philadelphia: H. Altemus Company, 1906).

Selfridge, Thomas O. "The Navy at Fort Fisher," in Robert U. Johnson and Clarence C. Buel, eds., *Battles and Leaders of the Civil War*, 4, pp. 655-661. 4 vols. New York: The Century Company, 1884-1889.

Charles Thomas Shanner Diary. Indiana Historical Society, Indianapolis, Indiana.

Sherman, William T. *Memoirs.* 2 volumes. New York: Da Capo Press, 1984 (Reprint of original 1875 edition).

Simon, John Y., ed. *The Papers of Ulysses S. Grant, Volume 12: August 16-November 15, 1864.* Carbondale and Edwardsville: Southern Illinois University Press, 1984.

Slater, John E. "Farewell to Camp Davis," *Coast Artillery Journal*, vol. 84, no. 5 (September/October, 1941); vol. 87, no. 5 (September/October, 1944).

Speed, Thomas. *Union Regiments of Kentucky.* Louisville, Ky.: Courier-Journal Job Printing Company, 1897.

Sprunt, James. *Chronicles of the Cape Fear River 1660-1916.* Raleigh, N.C.: Edwards & Broughton Printing Company, 1916.

—. *Tales of the Cape Fear Blockade.* Raleigh, N.C.: Capitol Printing Company, 1902.

Stallman, David A. *A History of Camp Davis, Holly Ridge, N.C.* Hampstead, N.C.: Hampstead Services, Cedar on the Green, 1990.

Stick, David. *Bald Head: A History of Smith Island and Cape Fear.* Wendell, N.C.: Broadfoot Publishing Company, 1985.

Sumner, Merlin E. *The Diary of Cyrus B. Comstock.* Dayton, Ohio: Morningside House, Inc., 1987.

Taylor, Thomas E. *Running The Blockade: A Personal Narrative of Adventures, Risks, and Escapes During the American Civil War.* London: John Murray, 1896.

Thoburn, Lyle, ed. *My Experiences During the Civil War, by Major Thomas C. Thoburn.* Cleveland, Ohio: [n.p.], 1963.

Thompson, B. F. *History of the 112th Regiment of Illinois Volunteer Infantry in the Great War of the Rebellion 1862-1865.* Toulan, Ill.: Stark County News Office, 1885.

Thompson, Robert Means and Richard Wainwright, eds. *The Confidential Correspondence of Gustavus Vasa Fox, Assistant Secretary of the Navy 1861-1865. Vol. 2.* New York: The Naval Historical Society, 1919.

Thurstin, W. S. *History of the One Hundred and Eleventh Regiment Ohio Volunteer Infantry.* Toledo, Ohio: Vrooman, Anderson and Bateman, 1894.

The Times, London, August 7, 1854.

Trotter, William R. *Ironclads and Columbiads, The Civil War in North Carolina Volume III: The Coast.* Greensboro, N.C.: Signal Research, Inc., 1989.

Trudeau, Noah Andre. *Like Men of War: Black Troops in the Civil War 1861-1865.* Boston, New York, Toronto and London: Little, Brown and Company, 1998.

Tyler, Lyon G, ed. *Men of Mark in Virginia: Ideals of American Life. A Collection of Biographies of the Leading Men of the State.* 5 vols. Washington, D.C.: Men of Mark Publishing Company, 1906.

United States Bureau of Naval Personnel. *Medal of Honor, 1861-1949: The Navy.* Washington, D.C.: 1949.

United States Department of the Interior, National Park Service. *National Register of Historic Places Inventory—Nomination Form: Cape Fear Civil War Shipwrecks.*

United States Navy Department. *Official Records of the Union and Confederate Navies in the War of the Rebellion.* Washington, D.C.: Government Printing Office, 1900-1901.

United States War Department. *Atlas to Accompany the Official Records of the Union and Confederate Armies.* Washington, D.C.: Government Printing Office, 1891-1895.

—. *The War of the Rebellion, A Compilation of the Official Records of the Union and Confederate Armies.* Washington, D.C.: Government Printing Office, 1880-1901.

Van Arsdol, Ted. *Battalion from the Mohave: History of the 535th Anti-Aircraft Artillery Unit from 1942 to 1944.* Vancouver, Wash.: n.p., 1971.

Vance, J. W. *Report of the Adjutant General of the State of Illinois, Volume VI, Containing Reports for the Years 1861-1866.* Springfield, Ill.: H. W. Rokker, State Printer and Binder, 1886.

Catherine Vanderslice Collection. United States Army Military History Institute, Carlisle Barracks, Carlisle, Pennsylvania.

Wadelington, Charles W. *African Americans at Fort Fisher During the Civil War, 1861-1865.* Raleigh, N.C.: Historic Sites Section, Division of Archives and History, Department of Cultural Resources. n.p., January 1996.

Walkley, Stephen. *History of the Seventh Connecticut Volunteer Infantry, Hawley's Brigade, Terry's Division, Tenth Army Corps, 1861-1865.* Southington, Connecticut, 1905.

Warner, Philip. *The Crimean War: A Reappraisal.* London: Arthur Barker Limited, 1972.

Washington, Versalle F. *Eagles on Their Buttons: The Fifth Regiment of Infantry, United States Colored Troops in the American Civil War.* Ph.D. dissertation, Ohio State University, 1995.

Wayne Family Papers. Letters from and concerning Galusha Pennypacker. Clements Library, University of Michigan, Ann Arbor, Michigan.

Welles, Gideon. *Diary of Gideon Welles, Secretary of the Navy Under Lincoln and Johnson. Vol 2: April 1, 1864-December 31, 1866.* Boston and New York: Houghton Mifflin Company, 1911.

Wetzel, David. *The Crimean War: A Diplomatic History.* New York: Columbia University Press, 1985.

Robert Whitcomb Letters. Clements Library, University of Michigan, Ann Arbor, Michigan.

William Henry Chase Whiting Papers. North Carolina Division of Archives and History, Raleigh, North Carolina.

Wilkinson, John. *The Narrative of a Blockade Runner.* New York: Sheldon and Company, 1877.

Wilmington Weekly Journal, May 15, 1862

Woodworth, Steven E. *Jefferson Davis and His Generals: The Failure of Confederate Command in the West.* Lawrence: University Press of Kansas, 1990.

Index

Mark A. Moore (left) with renowned Civil War historian Edwin C. Bearss, at the Bentonville battlefield, September 1997.

About the Author

Mark A. Moore, a graduate of East Carolina University, is a Digital Information Specialist for the North Carolina Division of Archives and History in Raleigh. In addition to his Fort Fisher-Wilmington study, he is the author of *Moore's Historical Guide to the Battle of Bentonville* (Savas 1997).

Many of the author's original maps and plans are also featured in other Savas titles, including *Last Stand in the Carolinas: The Battle of Bentonville*, by Mark L. Bradley; *Last Rays of Departing Hope: The Wilmington Campaign*, by Chris E. Fonvielle; *Capital Navy: The Men, Ships, and Operations of the James River Squadron*, by John Coski; *The Peninsula Campaign: Yorktown to the Seven Days, Volume Three*, edited by William J. Miller; numerous issues of *Regiments: A Journal of the American Civil War*; and many others.

Mark A. Moore has also prepared maps for magazines and other publishing companies. He lives in Raleigh with his wife, Nancy Carter Moore, who is currently co-authoring a history of Wake County with historian Elizabeth Reid Murray.